Contemporary Islamic Business Strategies and Applications

De Gruyter Studies in Islamic Economics, Finance and Business

Edited by
Abbas Mirakhor and Idris Samawi Hamid

Volume 12

Contemporary Islamic Business Strategies and Applications

Edited by
Léo-Paul Dana, Ahmad Rafiki, Veland Ramadani
and Sutan Emir Hidayat

DE GRUYTER

ISBN 978-3-11-157537-7
E-ISBN (PDF) 978-3-11-157540-7
E-ISBN (EPUB) 978-3-11-157661-9
ISSN 2567-2533
e-ISSN 2567-2568

Library of Congress Control Number: 2025942971

Bibliographic information published by the Deutsche Nationalbibliothek
The Deutsche Nationalbibliothek lists this publication in the Deutsche Nationalbibliografie; detailed bibliographic data are available on the internet at http://dnb.dnb.de.

Cover image: nnnnae/iStock/Getty Images Plus
Typesetting: Integra Software Services Pvt. Ltd.
Printing and binding: CPI books GmbH, Leck

www.degruyterbrill.com
Questions about General Product Safety Regulation:
productsafety@degruyterbrill.com

Contents

Editors' Biographies

Léo-Paul Dana is Professorial Research Fellow at the Next Society Institute (NSI) of Kazimieras Simonavicius University (KSU), in Lithuania. He is also Professor at ICD Business School Paris, and at Dalhousie University and currently Visiting Professor at LUT School of Business and Management, Lappeenranta University of Technology. He is also associated with the Sorbonne Business School. A graduate of McGill University, he has served as Marie Curie Fellow at Princeton University and Visiting Professor at INSEAD and at Kingston University. He has published extensively in a variety of journals including *Entrepreneurship: Theory & Practice, International Business Review, International Small Business Journal, Journal of Business Research, Journal of Small Business Management, Journal of World Business, Small Business Economics, and Technological Forecasting & Social Change.*

Ahmad Rafiki is currently as an Associate Professor and the Dean of Faculty of Economics and Business and the Head of Islamic Management and Halal Industry Center at Universitas Medan Area, Indonesia. Previously he was an Assistant Professor in Department of Business Administration of University College of Bahrain. He obtained his BBA with a major of Marketing from MARA University of Technology (UiTM) and Masters in Management from International Islamic University of Malaysia (IIUM). In 2014, he completed his PhD program from Islamic Science University of Malaysia (USIM). He is holding Certified Islamic Marketer (CIMA) from the International Islamic Marketing Association (IIMA). He actively engages with other consultation centers as the co-founders and members such as Islamic Management and Education Center, TAIF Digital Institute of Islamic Finance, and the Indonesian Association of Islamic Economist. He is now appointed as Visiting Research Fellow at Universiti Malaysia Kelantan (UMK). He has also published many chapters of books and articles/papers related to the field of management, entrepreneurship, SMEs, leadership and halal industry by international publishers such as IBA-MacMillan, IGI Global, Emerald Publishing, Springer, IntechOpen, Routledge etc. He also became the editorial advisory board and reviewer in reputable publishers of Emerald and Elsevier, and has presented academic papers in various international conference/seminars in several countries. He just won as the Outstanding Reviewer of Literati Awards 2020 by Emerald Publishing.

Veland Ramadani is a Professor of Entrepreneurship and Family Business at the Faculty of Business and Economics, South-East European University, North Macedonia. His primary areas of research focus on entrepreneurship, family businesses, innovation, and sustainability. Dr. Ramadani has an extensive body of work to his name, having authored or co-authored around 150 research articles, 90 book chapters, 15 textbooks, and 33 edited books. His research contributions are notably featured in prestigious academic journals, including the *Journal of Business Research, Technological Forecasting and Social Change, Technology in Society, International Journal of Entrepreneurial Behavior & Research*, and *Review of Managerial Science*, among others. He received the Award for Excellence in 2016 for an Outstanding Paper published by Emerald Group Publishing, a testament to his outstanding contributions to the field. In addition to his research, Dr. Ramadani has been invited as a keynote speaker at numerous international conferences and as a guest lecturer at President University (Indonesia), Telkom University (Indonesia), University of Trás-os-Montes and Alto Douro (Portugal), and Universum International – UNI (Kosovo). Furthermore, his research influence is underscored by his consistent inclusion among the World's Top 2% of the most influential researchers, as determined by Elsevier and Stanford University for the last five consecutive years. Between 2017 and 2021, Dr. Ramadani served as a member of the Supervisory Board of the Development Bank of North Macedonia, where he also took on the role of Chief Operating Officer for 10 months. Dr. Ramadani has remained actively engaged in various projects, including those funded by the European Union and universities in Saudi Arabia, Kuwait, and the United Arab Emirates. Additionally, he regularly offers consultancy services to private companies.

https://doi.org/10.1515/9783111575407-203

Sutan Emir Hidayat currently serves as the Director of Sharia Ecosystem Infrastructure at the National Committee of Islamic Economy and Finance (KNEKS), the Republic of Indonesia and Associate Professor at Gunadarma University. He earned his PhD and MBA in Islamic Banking and Finance from the International Islamic University Malaysia (IIUM) and a Bachelor's degree in Agribusiness Management from the Bogor Agricultural University (IPB) University. He was once the Head of Business School (Dean) at the University College of Bahrain (UCB). Emir is an expert in Islamic economics and finance with recognized global influence. He was listed in the Islamica 500 released by IsFIN as one of the Top 50 individuals influencing the world's Islamic economy in 2015 and 2020, and continued to gain recognition by being included in the Top 500 personalities in 2016, 2017, 2018 and 2019. In addition, Emir is also listed in the 1001 Minangkabau People Directory at the world level and received an award from BSI Maslahat as a supporting figure for the Islamic economic youth movement in 2023. Emir is also a consultant for Islamic economics and finance for the World Bank Group by providing training to members of parliament and executive officials of the Bangsamoro Autonomous Region in Muslim Mindanao (BARMM) government, where the impact (outcome) of the training The BARMM government has issued the 2024–2028 Islamic Finance Development Roadmap, which is the direction for the development of Islamic economics and finance in BARMM.

List of Contributors

Aimi Fadzirul Kamarubahrin
Universiti Putra Malaysia
Malaysia

Aidin Salamzadeh
University of Tehran
Iran

Agron Hajdari
International Business College of Mitrovica
Mitrovica
Republic of Kosovo

Agus Iswanto
National Research and Innovation Agency
Indonesia

Ali Esmaeil Zadeh
University of Tabriz
Iran

Amirul Afif Muhamat
Universiti Teknologi MARA
Selangor Branch
Malaysia

Arief Wibison Lubis
Universitas Indonesia
Indonesia

Besnik Krasniqi
University of Prishtina
Republic of Kosovo

Cicilia Larasati Rembulan
Universitas Ciputra
Surabaya
Indonesia

Dewi Santri
Universitas Islam Negeri Sumatera Utara
Indonesia

Eset Qerimi
"Zejnullah Blakcori"
Mosque in Podujevo
Republic of Kosovo

Farooq Haq
Canadian University Dubai
UAE

Fitriani Tobing
Universitas Medan Area
Indonesia

Gadaf Rexhepi
South East European University
Tetovo
North Macedonia

Hasan Mukhibad
Universitas Negeri Semarang
Indonesia

Hery Syahrial
Universitas Medan Area
Indonesia

Izra Berakon
UIN Sunan Kalijaga Yogyakarta
Indonesia

Ja'far Hamzah Pulungan
Universitas Islam Negeri Sumatera Utara
Indonesia

Joko Tri Haryanto
National Research and Innovation Agency
Indonesia

Koeswinarno
National Research and Innovation Agency
Indonesia

Leo Paul Dana
Dalhousie University
Canada

Mahameru Rosy Rochmatullah
Universitas Muhammadiyah Surakarta
Indonesia

https://doi.org/10.1515/9783111575407-204

Millenia Ayu Nur 'Aini
UIN Sunan Kalijaga Yogyakarta
Indonesia

Mohamad Sayuti Md Saleh
Universiti Teknologi MARA
Kelantan Branch
Malaysia

Mohd Afzanizam Abdul Rashid
Bank Muamalat Malaysia Berhad
Malaysia

Mohamad Nizam Jaafar
Universiti Teknologi MARA
Malaysia

Mohammad Mominul Islam
Universiti Brunei Darussalam
Brunei Darussalam

Morteza Hadizadeh
University of Tehran
Iran

Muhammad Rizky Prima Sakti
University College of Bahrain
Bahrain

Muhammad Iqmal Hisham Kamaruddin
Universiti Sains Islam Malaysia
Malaysia

Muhammad Dharma Tuah Putra Nasution
Universitas Pembangunan Panca Budi
Indonesia

Naveed Yasin
Abu Dhabi School of Management
UAE

Nor Farradila Abdul Aziz
Universiti Teknologi MARA
Selangor Branch
Malaysia

Nor Nabilla Muhammad
UIN Sunan Kalijaga Yogyakarta
Indonesia

Nurul Aini Muhamed
Universiti Sains Islam Malaysia
Malaysia

Nurul Syifaa Mohd Shakil
Universiti Teknologi MARA
Selangor Branch
Malaysia

Nur'asyiqin Ramdhan
Universiti Teknologi MARA
Selangor Branch
Malaysia

Pipit Buana Sari
Universitas Pembangunan Panca Budi
Indonesia

Putri Ayu Puspieta Wardhani
UniversitasCiputra
Surabaya
Indonesia

Rafisah Mat Radzi
Universiti Sains Islam Malaysia
Malaysia

Roslina Mohd Shafi
Universiti Teknologi MARA
Selangor Branch
Malaysia

Safwan Kamal
IAIN Langsa
Langsa
Aceh
Indonesia

Sama Hosseini
University of Tehran
Iran

Seyed Morteza Mortazavi
Imam Khomeini International University Qazvin
Iran

Shahsuzan Zakaria
Universiti Teknologi MARA
Selangor Branch
Malaysia

Thuraya Saleh Al-Qarni
University College of Bahrain
Bahrain

Vjosë Latifi
International Business College of Mitrovica
Republic of Kosovo

Wan Nur Fazni Wan Mohamad Nazarie
Universiti Sains Islam Malaysia
Malaysia

Yessy Agustia Lestari
Universitas Islam Negeri Sumatera Utara
Indonesia

Yossie Rossanty
Universitas Pembangunan Panca Budi
Indonesia

Zakiyah
National Research and Innovation Agency
Indonesia)

Léo-Paul Dana, Ahmad Rafiki, Veland Ramadani, Sutan Emir Hidayat

Introduction

Contemporary Islamic Business Strategies and Applications: Concepts and Practices in Emerging Economies provides a comprehensive overview of how Islamic principles are integrated into modern business operations. This topic explores key concepts such as Shariah compliance, halal standards, Islamic finance, ethical branding, and corporate social responsibility, demonstrating how these values shape business decisions and practices in Muslim-majority and global markets. Through case studies and real-world examples, the subject emphasizes the balance between profitability and ethical responsibility, highlighting how Islamic business models respond to contemporary challenges such as globalization, sustainability, and digital transformation. The discussion also covers consumer behavior, regulatory frameworks, and the strategic role of Islamic values in fostering inclusive and socially responsible enterprises.

The aim of this book is to provide a thorough exploration of contemporary Islamic business practices, offering readers a deep understanding of how Islamic principles guide business strategies, ethics, and operations in today's global economy. It seeks to bridge the gap between traditional Islamic values and modern business practices by examining the implementation of Shariah compliance, halal standards, ethical finance, and corporate responsibility. Through case studies, theoretical insights, and practical applications, the book aims to equip students, professionals, and scholars with the knowledge necessary to navigate and succeed in the increasingly important field of Islamic business.

Furthermore, the book underscores the importance of strategic diversification as a means for Islamic organizations to not only enhance their competitiveness but also to uphold their core values of sustainability. It serves as an indispensable resource for a diverse audience, including entrepreneurs, practitioners, policymakers, academics, and students, offering actionable insights and strategies tailored to the unique challenges and opportunities within Islamic business contexts.

Chapter 1 – A Bibliometric Analysis on Donation-Based Crowdfunding Has Evolved Collaboratively Over Time. The authors explore recent trends in donation-based crowdfunding by conducting a bibliometric analysis of relevant papers from the Scopus database published between 2012 and 2022. A total of 25 papers were selected for analysis, using keywords like "donation-based" and "crowdfunding." The study utilized various tools such as Microsoft Excel for frequency analysis, VOS Viewer for data visualization, and Harzing's Publish or Perish for citation metrics. The findings highlight the growing interest in donation-based crowdfunding, with increasing literature on the topic over the past decade. The study also provides insights into research trends, top countries contributing to the field, citation patterns, authorship, and keyword analysis, underscoring the expanding role of donation-based crowdfunding in addressing financial challenges.

https://doi.org/10.1515/9783111575407-001

Chapter 2 – Islamic Branding: Navigating Principles, Identities and Challenges, in Contemporary Marketing. The authors provide a detailed exploration of Islamic branding, focusing on how brands can address the needs of Muslim consumers while adhering to Islamic principles. It identifies four key classifications of Islamic brands: true Islamic, traditional Islamic, inbound, and outbound brands. The chapter also outlines five essential dimensions for developing Islamic brand identities: modesty, purity, comfort, quality, and authenticity. Additionally, it highlights opportunities arising from cultural exchanges and the branding of Halal products, emphasizing the importance of understanding religious sensitivities in marketing. Drawing on extensive research, the chapter offers valuable insights for academics, practitioners, and policymakers in the fields of branding, marketing, and consumer behavior, enhancing their understanding of the growing significance of Islamic branding in the global market.

Chapter 3 – Halal Café: Religious Identity and the Lifestyle of the Young Generation. The authors highlight the growing café culture among young Muslims in Yogyakarta, Indonesia, where cafés serve as spaces for socializing, working, and connecting with peers. Cafés are categorized based on price and consumer base, and young people are increasingly aware of the halal status of the food and drinks they consume, reflecting their religious identity. The research underscores how cafés are not just places for consumption but also for fostering community and maintaining religious values, especially among Muslim youth.

Chapter 4 – Malaysia's Shariah-Compliant Business Ecosystem: A Blueprint for Global Ethical Economies. The authors analyze Malaysia's Shariah-compliant business ecosystem, which serves as a global model for ethical and sustainable economic practices. Anchored in Islamic principles, its growth is driven by government initiatives, robust regulation, and industry engagement. Key enablers include the Islamic Finance Masterplan, the Halal Industry Development Corporation, and targeted incentives. The chapter highlights the role of Shariah governance and infrastructure, illustrated through case studies such as Maybank Islamic, Nestlé Malaysia, and Lembaga Tabung Haji. Despite challenges like regulatory harmonization, Malaysia's commitment to innovation positions it as a leader in ethical economic development.

Chapter 5 – What matters to the probability of default? the role of Indonesia Sharia firms in normal and crisis periods. The authors investigate the Probability of Default (PD) estimator using Merton's Structural Model, incorporating both fundamental (liquidity, solvency, profitability) and macroeconomic factors (inflation, interest rates, exchange rates). Using data from the Indonesia Sharia Stock Index (ISSI) between 2016 and 2022, the study employs hierarchical regression analysis to explore these relationships. Key findings suggest that solvency ratios and inflation are critical factors influencing PD, particularly for smaller and younger firms. The research also highlights the importance of reducing debt levels and optimizing internal funds for Sharia firms to ensure financial sustainability. Robustness tests further validate these results across different firm sizes, periods, and control variables.

Chapter 6 – The Surge of Islamic Entrepreneurship: Analyzing the Strategic Motivations and Far-Reaching Impacts. The authors examine the growth and influence of Islamic entrepreneurship, emphasizing its strategic motivations and broader societal impacts. It explores how factors such as moral and socially conscious economic practices drive business owners in Islamic contexts, alongside challenges like regulatory issues and the need for a deeper understanding of Islamic principles. The research, based on a qualitative case study in Kosovo with unstructured interviews of eight entrepreneurs, reveals that Islamic entrepreneurship encourages responsibility towards state institutions and wealth management in line with religious values. Entrepreneurs are driven by both personal success and societal contributions, fostering resilience and purpose. The findings offer valuable insights for policymakers to support Islamic entrepreneurship through policies that align with its unique principles, aiming to improve economic and social outcomes.

Chapter 7 – Faith-Driven Enterprise: Navigating Modern Markets with Islamic Values in Contemporary Entrepreneurship. The authors investigate the integration of Islamic values into contemporary entrepreneurship, focusing on how faith-driven businesses balance modern market demands with core religious principles. Through case studies of Al Baik (Saudi Arabia), Osmanli Oud (Turkey), My Salah Mat (UK), and J. (Pakistan), the chapter examines how Islamic values shape business practices in various industries, including fast food, fragrance, educational technology, and more. It highlights how principles such as social responsibility, ethical transparency, and cultural authenticity contribute to competitive advantage and foster brand loyalty. The findings offer valuable insights for scholars, policymakers, and practitioners interested in the intersection of faith and commerce in a globalized world.

Chapter 8 – Islamic Business Ecosystems: UAE's Innovation Incentives and Iran's Knowledge-driven Approach. The authors explore how governance frameworks, grounded in Islamic principles, shape business environments by influencing strategic incentives, policy directives, and alignment with national priorities. The study compares the economic impacts of Islamic business models in the UAE and Iran, two countries with distinct governance structures. In the UAE, governance fosters innovation, global integration, and economic diversification by supporting sectors like technology, tourism, and trade, aligning with national priorities. In contrast, Iran's governance emphasizes self-reliance and knowledge-based development, guiding businesses toward science-driven sectors and reducing dependency on external resources. Through this comparative analysis, the work highlights the crucial role of government in shaping business ecosystems, promoting sustainable development, and aligning business practices with national values.

Chapter 9 – Performance Banking Baselines Under Maqashid Sharia. The authors review the Maqashid Sharia as a framework for managing business in Islamic banking. It introduces the scope of Islamic banking, the religious rationale behind establishing Islamic banks, and evaluates their performance using the Maqashid Sharia index (MSI). The chapter outlines key stakeholders, governance structures, asset management, and performance measures in Islamic banking, with a focus on a study of 12 Islamic banks in Indonesia. The results show that the average MSI score is only 31.64%, indicating that Islamic banks are not fully aligned with Maqashid Sharia principles. The analysis points to intense competition between conventional and Islamic banks, leading to Islamic banking practices resembling conventional banking, and highlights the need for better managerial adherence to Sharia principles. The chapter concludes that MSI is a valid tool for assessing Sharia bank performance and recommends that Islamic banking authorities adopt it for performance measurement. Further research is suggested to refine MSI and apply it in non-Islamic countries.

Chapter 10 – Examining Self-Congruity among Muslim Consumers: The Intersection of Islamic Beliefs and Beauty brand Attributes. Indonesia's growing demand for halal and Islamic-oriented beauty products reflects a shift toward more values-driven consumer behavior. While halal certification remains important, this study reveals that Islamic branding in beauty extends to elements like Muslim representation, ethical practices, and social media narratives. Using a mixed-method approach with 112 Muslim emerging adults, findings show that self-religiosity significantly influences preferences, but consumers also scrutinize labels and practices to ensure alignment with their Islamic identity. The study highlights the importance of integrating both religious and practical brand attributes, offering insights for marketers and future research

Chapter 11 – The Critical Success Factors and Challenges of Women-Run and Owned Businesses in Contemporary Saudi Arabia: A Perspective on Islam and Modernity. The authors explore the role of women-run and women-owned businesses in contemporary Saudi Arabia, focusing on their contribution to the country's modernization under Vision 2030. Through a qualitative thematic analysis of interviews with ten Saudi women entrepreneurs, the study identifies critical success factors and challenges they face in the business landscape. Key findings indicate that family and personal networks, strong government support for women in business, and the importance of Shariah law play pivotal roles in shaping their entrepreneurial journeys. However, women entrepreneurs also face significant challenges, including socio-cultural norms, limited opportunities, and legal complexities tied to Sharia law and broader commercial legal frameworks. The study highlights that these entrepreneurs understand the importance of acquiring knowledge of Sharia law to navigate the business environment effectively. The findings are essential for both women entrepreneurs and policymakers aiming to empower women in business and support the goals of Vision 2030 by fostering an environment conducive to their success.

Chapter 12 – Determinants of Enterprise Risk Management (ERM) Adoption Amongst the Shariah-Compliant Construction Companies in Malaysia. The authors investigate the factors influencing the adoption of Enterprise Risk Management (ERM) among Shariah-compliant publicly listed construction companies in Malaysia from 2007 to 2016—a period marked by major infrastructure projects like the East Coast Rail Link (ECRL) and the Klang Valley Mass Rapid Transit (KVMRT). Using logistic regression analysis, the study finds that company size, financial leverage, foreign auditor reputation, and profitability significantly impact ERM adoption. Conversely, stock price volatility and board independence are not statistically significant. These findings offer valuable insights for regulators to craft policies that encourage ERM implementation, thereby promoting transparency, strong governance, and sustainable growth in the Shariah-compliant construction sector.

Chapter 13 – The Role of Artificial Intelligence in Developing Halal Cosmetic. The authors explore the transformative role of Artificial Intelligence (AI) in the development of cosmetic products, particularly in enhancing product safety, quality, and compliance with halal standards. Using a qualitative descriptive method and content analysis based on secondary data from academic literature and relevant online sources, the research highlights AI's contributions to optimizing cosmetic formulations, identifying halal ingredients, and addressing challenges in the halal cosmetics industry. AI enables precise ingredient analysis through sensor technology, ensuring products meet safety and validity requirements. Furthermore, AI supports innovative research and marketing strategies, strengthening the global competitiveness of halal cosmetic brands.

Chapter 14 – The Strategic Aspects of the Resource-based View (RBV) of Halal Certification for Halal Marketing. The authors discuss halal certification as both a tangible and intangible strategic asset, aligning with the Resource-Based View (RBV) and Knowledge-Based View (KBV) to achieve Halal Competitive Advantage (HCA). By meeting VRIN criteria—valuable, rare, inimitable, and non-substitutable—halal certification provides not only a market edge but also a spiritual dimension grounded in Islamic Shariah. The chapter emphasizes that integrating Islamic principles with RBV and KBV allows firms to develop marketing strategies rooted in religious authenticity. Ultimately, it argues for using Islamic teachings from the Qur'an and Sunnah as a theoretical foundation for transforming halal certification into a spiritually meaningful and economically valuable resource.

Contemporary Islamic business represents a harmonious integration of faith-based values with modern commercial practices. Rooted in Shariah principles, it emphasizes ethical conduct, social justice, and mutual benefit over pure profit maximization. By prioritizing fairness, transparency, and community welfare, Islamic business offers a sustainable and morally grounded alternative to conventional business models. As the global demand for ethical and responsible business grows, Islamic business practices are increasingly seen as relevant, adaptable, and forward-looking, not just for Muslim communities but for anyone seeking values-driven commerce.

Future research in contemporary Islamic business could explore the integration of Islamic principles with emerging technologies, such as blockchain, artificial intelligence, and fintech, to develop innovative yet Shariah-compliant business solutions. Comparative studies between Islamic and conventional business models may provide valuable insights into their relative effectiveness in promoting ethical behavior, sustainability, and stakeholder satisfaction. Additionally, researchers can investigate how Islamic values influence consumer behavior, particularly in areas like Halal branding, marketing, and perceptions of Shariah compliance.

Another promising area involves examining Islamic corporate governance and leadership frameworks, including the impact of prophetic or value-based leadership styles on organizational performance. The alignment of Islamic business practices with global environmental, social, and governance (ESG) goals also warrants further study, particularly in the context of Maqasid al-Shariah and sustainable development. Moreover, research can focus on regulatory and legal challenges faced by Islamic businesses, especially startups operating in secular or non-Muslim-majority jurisdictions.

Finally, the role of Islamic social finance in corporate social responsibility initiatives remains an important topic, offering potential models for poverty alleviation and ethical wealth distribution through business activities. Collectively, these avenues can contribute to a deeper understanding and more effective implementation of Islamic business principles in the modern world.

Aimi Fadzirul Kamarubahrin, Nurul Aini Muhamed, Wan Nur Fazni Wan Mohamad Nazarie, Rafisah Mat Radzi, Muhammad Iqmal Hisham Kamaruddin

Chapter 1 A Bibliometric Analysis on Donation-based Crowdfunding has Evolved Collaboratively Over Time

Abstract: In recent years, the study of donation-based crowdfunding has been remodelling and reconfiguration to address financial challenges. The purpose of this study is to demonstrate current donation-based crowdfunding trends using the bibliometric analysis approach. The papers on donation-based crowdfunding that were pulled from the Scopus database between 2012 and 2022 underwent a thorough evaluation. The study has gathered 25 papers for further analysis based on the keywords "donation-based" and "crowdfunding." Several programmes have been utilised, such as Microsoft Excel for the frequency analysis, VOS viewer for data visualisation, and Harzing's Publish or Perish for citation metrics and analysis. The study's findings were reported using a variety of criteria, including language, topic matter, research trends by year of publication, top nations, citation analysis, authorship analysis, and keyword analysis. Based on findings, from 2012 to 2022 the literature on donation-based crowdfunding has grown at an increasing rate.

Keywords: Bibliometrics, Donation-based, Crowdfunding, Scopus database

1.1 Introduction

The term "crowdfunding" refers to an open solicitation for gathering funds, especially online, in exchange for rewards or equity to support the future development of an idea or project (Lu et al., 2022; Leonelli et al., 2020). Meanwhile, it also was defined as a novel method of financing ideas, businesses, or projects that involves obtaining numerous modest amounts of finance from numerous individual funders, generally through internet platforms (Cicchiello et al., 2020). According to Wang et al. (2022), crowdfund-

Acknowledgement: This research was funded by the Ministry of Higher Education (MOHE) under the Fundamental Research Grant Scheme (NRGS) USIM/FRGS/FEM/KPT/51121. Faculty of Economics and Muamalat, Universiti Sains Islam Malaysia.

https://doi.org/10.1515/9783111575407-002

ing is defined as "an open call, conducted primarily online, for the allocation of financial resources in exchange for future products, rewards, voting rights, or donations". Crowdfunding has become a more popular and successful way to raise money for the arts, video games, and even certain technological goods in recent years. Crowdfunding is the "practise of soliciting financial contributions from a large number of people notably from the online community" (Mitra et al., 2021).

Crowdfunding is a significant tool for funding both for-profit and non-profit activities (Teichmann et al., 2022). Crowdfunding is a newer digitally non-banking financing tool that has been created primarily for start-up businesses with little financial strength, few resources, and/or ineligibility for bank loans, as well as for non-profit organisations (Ahn, 2022). Meanwhile, non-profit organisations look for donations that serve a broader cause—prosocial campaigns—individuals or businesses typically turn to crowdfunding to finance initiatives including research ideas or innovative, creative, artistic products and services (Masrizal et al., 2022). The entity looking for money (founder of project) posts the project together with all of its supporting information on a website called the crowdfunding platform (CFP). Thus, the CFP serves as a bridge between those seeking money and contributors (also called lenders, funders).

Innovation has been cited as a benefit of crowdsourcing (St John et al., 2022). A special form of crowdsourcing called crowdfunding is aimed at raising money for a project (Li et al., 2020). The former's objective is to amass the required sum of smart money to fund their project (Al-Qershi et al., 2022). Scholars and practitioners alike have been interested in crowdfunding as it has risen dramatically and is now a significant source of funding, raising tens of billions of dollars annually (Li et al., 2020; Hossain & Oparaocha, 2017; Short et al., 2016). Crowdfunding has a global market value of $8.54 billion in 2020, and by 2023, it is anticipated to reach $11.98 billion (Learnbonds.com, 2020). A funder may be a basic donor (a donation made without expecting any financial or non-financial gain), a lender getting non-financial benefits (reward-based crowdfunding), a lender (loan-based crowdfunding), or an investor (equity-based crowdfunding), depending on the kind of crowdfunding (Chen et al., 2022).

Donation-based crowdsourcing, incentive-based crowdfunding, lending-based crowdfunding, and equity-based crowdfunding are the four primary categories of crowdfunding models (Cicchiello & Kazemikhasragh, 2022). Crowdfunding that is based on donations is typically done for philanthropic or social objectives (Muhamed et al., 2023). The investors' primary incentive is altruism, and they give money without anticipating anything in return (Liu et al., 2018). The majority of creative and inventive projects in the fields of technology, design, music, gaming, and the arts are funded through reward-based crowdfunding. As the name suggests, non-monetary rewards are presented to donors who made financial contributions to the initiative. Before entering the market, reward models are frequently employed as a type of pre-selling (Shneor & Munim, 2019). A viable alternative to traditional loans is lending-based crowdfunding, which can be done in the form of peer-to-peer lending for consumers or peer-to-business lending for businesses.

In this form of crowdsourcing, funders (lenders) lend money to individuals or businesses (borrowers) in exchange for a set interest rate (Kgoroeagira et al., 2019). Equity-based crowdfunding allows investors to become shareholders in the financed company by acquiring a small equity stake. Investors will receive a portion of the company's potential profits and risks in exchange for their contributions (Estrin et al., 2018). Equity-based crowdfunding has emerged as a new player in entrepreneurial finance during the past ten years (Block et al., 2018), giving young, innovative businesses the opportunity to acquire money by issuing securities in an easy and affordable manner. Practitioners, politicians, and scholars have all paid greater attention as a result of the crowdfunding industry's explosive rise (Bruton et al., 2015).

Although crowdfunding has grown in popularity among project owners looking to collect money; yet, because of the environment's openness and flexibility requirements, it also presents a significant risk for fraudulent activities. According to Cummings et al. (2015), scammers never offer well-written project proposals, avoid having a social media presence, and are less likely to engage in prior CF activities. They also suggest numerous rewards for backers in the form of pledge categories. Furthermore, as donation-based crowdfunding platforms are ineligible for use in commercial fundraising, they could be utilised to enable money-laundering activities (Stack et al., 2017). The process of transforming cash or property obtained through illicit activity is known as money laundering.

Donation-based crowding, in contrast to other forms, is founded on intrinsic motivation and the ideas of generosity and almsgiving without requesting rewards (Kamaruddin et al., 2023; Allah Pitchay et al., 2021). Three groups are usually involved in any type of crowdfunding: platforms; donors/funders; and beneficiaries. Platforms will operate as the go-betweens for the money transfers from funders to recipients. The recipients have no responsibility to repay the funders because return is not a deciding factor in their involvement or contribution. Crowdfunding that is based on donations is important because it enables members of underserved and bank-inaccessible groups to get funding and use it for their needs. The beneficiaries of the platforms for crowdsourcing can benefit from the sustainability of the services.

By analysing the most commonly used keywords in donation-based articles, it is possible to ascertain whether the most popular topics have been previously sufficiently investigated and whether there are any opportunities to learn about new subjects that are pertinent for additional research. The frequency with which the keywords appear in the texts can be used to gauge the significance of a particular issue (de Oliveira et al., 2019).

There are several systematic studies of donation-based research in the literature, but they were limited to certain types of crowdfunding. Earlier researchers like Thottoli and Hou et al. (2022) restricted their research to SLR and systematic reviews by looking into crowdsourcing. Meanwhile, a quantitative study on the characteristics that influence involvement in crowdfunding was conducted by Rodriguez-Ricardo et al. (2018). According to Macari and Chun (2021), academics looking into crowdfunding need to pay it more attention. Thus, these literature reviews still have a limited ability to evaluate vast amounts of different literature (Thottoli, 2022). However, as Table 1.1 illustrates, only a small number of studies have emphasised research trends, determined the most pertinent subject or keywords, the global network of collaboration, and identified discrepancies in the literature.

Table 1.1: Past articles on crowdfunding systematic literature review – related studies.

Author & Year	Title	Remarks
Thottoli (2022)	The starring role of crowdfunding in GCC: A structured literature review	Role of CF
Hou et al. (2022)	Success factors of medical crowdfunding campaigns: Systematic review	Success factors CF
Baber & Ivanovici (2022)	Fifteen years of crowdfunding – a bibliometric analysis	Crowdfunding
Ribeiro et al. (2022)	Does microfinance foster the development of its clients? A bibliometric analysis and systematic literature review	Microfinance
Gil-Gomez et al. (2021)	Crowdfunding: A bibliometric analysis	Crowdfunding
Martínez-Climent et al. (2018)	Financial return crowdfunding: Literature review and bibliometric analysis	Financial return

Source: Authors.

However, a bibliometric analysis is not used in any literature reviews on donation-based crowdfunding to assess the state of the art. In order to address these issues, bibliometric measurement is used to evaluate the publication activity on donation-based crowdfunding and identify knowledge gaps that may support the empirical demand and uniqueness of the study. Furthermore, since research trends typically contribute to the important field of microfinance, future study areas can be predicted. As a result, this paper provides bibliometric study of donation-based crowdfunding by concentrating on three key research questions (RQs): RQ1: How has research on donation-based crowdfunding changed and been disseminated over time? What are the main areas of discussion in research on donation-based crowdfunding? and how did they work together?

Bibliometric analysis is increasingly used to show the trends in the studies (Gil-Gomez et al., 2021; Ahmi & Mohd Nasir, 2019). Numerous crowdfunding systematic review studies have been out in the past (see Table 1.1). The earlier studies made significant contributions. Nevertheless, new arrangements involving these findings are being brought about by other fundamental advances in the global context. The review study of the success elements of medical crowdfunding projects was also presented by Hou et al. in 2022. They determined the dynamics of change in the companies with the highest levels of productivity, the citation system, and publication activity. Additionally, they released information on research area trends, data on publication rates in both domestic and international journals, and an evaluation of international crowdfunding collaboration, particularly in the wake of the Covid-19 outbreak.

Researchers have to ascertain how these changes are mirrored in academia and investigate the situation of donation-based crowdfunding research in current scholarly debates, considering the growing significance of crowdfunding studies. For instance, is the acknowledged importance of the theoretical Goldilocks' debate (Cuervo-Cazurra, 2012) concerning emerging economies' specificities explored in the donation-based crowdfunding research? In order to close this gap, we will look at how the literature on donation-based crowdfunding has changed in emerging and developing nations while taking into account shifts in these nations' relative positions in the world economy.

The aim of this paper is to outline the field's development and point out its trends, obstacles, and fresh approaches. We use bibliometric and content analysis to do this. The bibliometric approach, which involves the aggregation of large amounts of bibliographic data, makes the study less susceptible to judgment bias and the idiosyncrasies of the reviewers reflected in qualitative reviews (Elango, 2019; Zupic & Čater, 2015; Vogel & Güttel, 2013). Using the Bibliometrix package in the R and VOSviewer programme, together with the content analysis approach, we want to determine the study clusters, how they evolved, and the trends for future research.

The structure of the paper is as follows. We outline the approach and data extraction procedure in the following section. Following that, a summary of the most significant journals, papers, organisations, and writers is provided based on the findings of the bibliometric analysis. We also take notice of the research clusters that have been identified, the field's historical development, and the literature's conceptual framework. Subsequently, we employ bibliographic approaches in conjunction with content analysis of the most referenced publications to define four study areas. Lastly, drawing from the above findings, we outline future research directions for the study of donation-based crowdfunding.

1.2 Methodology

1.2.1 Methods for Content Analysis and Bibliometrics

Different approaches exist for both qualitative and quantitative literature reviews. Examples include systematic literature reviews, meta-analyses, bibliometric analyses, and content analyses (Apriliyanti & Alon, 2017; Gaur & Kumar, 2018; Maditati, Munim, Schramm, & Kummer, 2018; Zupic & Čater, 2015). To investigate our research topics, this study combines the content analysis method with bibliometric analysis techniques (bibliographic coupling, citation and historiographic citation analysis, keyword co-occurrence, and conceptual theme mapping).

The methodologies of bibliometric analysis are grounded in a quantitative methodology intended to locate, characterise, and assess published research. Using transparent, reproducible search and review processes increases the reliability of the results and reduces the subjective bias of the literature reviews (Garfield, 1979; Maditati et al., 2018; Zupic & Čater, 2015). The content analysis is useful for summarizing the trends in the literature, identifying "hot spots" and "blind spots" and obtaining a more comprehensive understanding of the articles reviewed (Gaur & Kumar, 2018; Sassmannshausen & Volkmann, 2018). To put it another way, data analysis makes it possible to identify the most developed (hot spots) and less developed (blind spots) themes in the literature, which, when paired with other bibliometric techniques, indicate directions for future research. According to Gaur and Kumar (2018), the potential of content analysis lies in its combination with other methods.

We used VOSviewer version 1.6.12 and the R programme Bibliometrix for data processing and visualisation. The most pertinent studies, authors, journals, and organisations in the topic are first examined by a performance citation analysis. Next, we use bibliographic coupling to explain the development and intellectual framework of the literature. Bibliographic coupling analyses the similarity between two documents using the number of references shared by them (Elango, 2019; Sanchez-Famoso, Maseda, Iturralde, Danes, & Aparicio, 2020; Zupic & Čater, 2015). We employ association normalisation and the Bibliometrix R louvain clustering algorithm for bibliographic coupling. The R packages ggraph, graphlayouts, and Kamada-Kawai layout are used for visualisation. To reveal the chronological evolution of the most relevant citations, historiographic direct citation analysis is carried out using Bibliometrix R (Aria & Cuccurullo, 2017; Zupic & Čater, 2015).

This study explores the thematic structure of the field through an analysis of the co-occurrence of the authors' keyword using VOSviewer software (Donthu, Kumar, Ranaweera, Sigala, & Sureka, 2021; Emich, Kumar, Lu, Norder, & Pandey, 2020). We also use Bibliometrix R-package to create a conceptual thematic map, illustrating how the research streams are positioned in terms of centrality and density (Aria & Cuccurullo, 2017; Zupic & Čater, 2015). Finally, we conduct a content analysis to increase the understanding of the intellectual and conceptual structures that emerged using the previous techniques (Gaur & Kumar, 2018), identify the literature's theoretical lenses and trends, and suggest avenues for future research (Alon, Anderson, Munim, & Ho, 2018).

1.2.2 Procedure for Extracting Data

This review is based on a compilation of bibliographic information from the database of Scopus. The two main bibliographic databases are Clarivate Analytics' Web of Science (WoS) and Scopus (Aria & Cuccurullo, 2017). Scopus offers a wider coverage than the WoS database. More than 20,000 peer-reviewed journals are included by Scopus, including those released by Inderscience, Elsevier, Emerald, Taylor & Francis, Springer, and

Informs. Web of Science includes only ISI indexed journals, and is limited to 12,000 journals (Fahimnia, Sarkis, & Davarzani, 2015; Yong-Hak, 2013).

Therefore, Scopus is more suitable for mapping smaller research areas that would be insufficiently covered by other databases (Zupic & Čater, 2015), which is the case for the literature about donation-based crowdfunding. In addition, a number of articles concerning donation-based crowdfunding appear in regional publications. There are more indexed journals from developing nations in the Scopus database. For instance, there are 1954 journals from develop countries indexed in Scopus and only 434 in Web of Science (Elsevier, 2020; Web of Science Group, 2020). This study adopted a two-stage data extraction approach, following Alon et al. (2018), Apriliyanti and Alon (2017), and Fetscherin, Voss, and Gugler (2010). Table 1.2 details the procedure for searching and extracting data in detail.

The study took into account the following elements of the literature on donation-based crowdfunding. The research trends and document languages throughout time were seen in publications related to the creation and spread of donation-based crowdfunding. The major contributions in donation-based crowdfunding study revealed the top contributing countries to publications, the most potent organisations, the most well-liked source titles, the citation analysis, and the authorship analysis. With regard to its global reach and cooperation, this study sought to gain a deeper knowledge of trends in donation-based crowdfunding research. Academics will need to screen the current data before making recommendations for upcoming research projects in the field of donation-based crowdfunding.

The review used the most recent Preferred Reporting Items for Systematic Reviews and Meta-Analyses (PRISMA) criteria to conduct systematic reviews of studies (Zakaria et al., 2021). The procedures for locating sources for the review of donation-based crowdsourcing are shown in Figure 1.1, along with data analysis approaches. The data repository for document extraction and searching was decided upon as the Scopus index. In addition to providing thorough coverage of resources for disciplines other than the physical sciences and medicine, Scopus produces accurate citation search results (Hallinger & Kovaevi, 2019). Data from the Scopus database as of April 20, 2022, are used in this study. "Donation-based" and "crowdfunding" were used as search terms to find relevant papers related to this research since they are commonly used in the article's title, abstract, and keyword list. We did not pay attention to the titles of the publications even when the article itself covers a topic related to the research field and the study's goal, as many databases did not have the keywords donation-based crowdfunding in their titles. The phrases "donation-based" and "crowdfunding" were located using the Scopus search engine. Afterwards, Scopus subject filters were used. The search was limited to published journals and publications from 2012 to 2022 in the Scopus database. The search engine can therefore locate the oldest studies that have recently been published in the literature (within the previous ten years of their publication).

To exclude irrelevant articles, the study's scope and coverage were determined based on the search field, time range, source type, and document type. Following this search, 27 documents were discovered. Further exclusions were determined based on subject relevancy after going over each item on the list's abstract. The final database included 27 documents on donation-based crowdfunding after the documents were filtered.

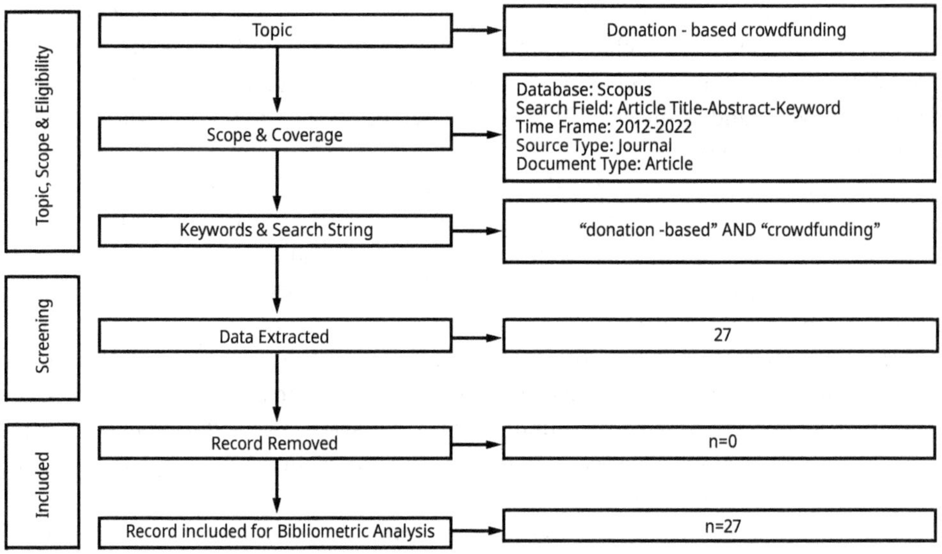

Figure 1.1: The search strategy flow diagram.

To obtain the knowledge required to respond to the RQs, the data was analysed using a variety of techniques. Using the tool to analyse search results, certain conclusions were directly sourced from Scopus. Additional results were manually input or exported into an additional Excel file. As part of the data sets, the data was exported in Comma-Separated Values (CSV) and Research Information Systems (RIS) formats. Information like percentages and cumulative percentages were reviewed in the file created for all of the findings. The researcher computed the citation metrics and some other frequencies using Harzing's Publish or Perish software. Also, the bibliometric networks were displayed using the VOSviewer because it provides a free tool for creating and viewing the networks (Ahmi & Mohd Nasir, 2019). The resulting observations on the patterns in the finance literature will be improved and enlarged as a result of this work.

1.3 Results and Discussion

Using information from the Scopus database, the research design concentrated on analysing the bibliometric properties of documents, including languages, subject areas, and research trends according to the year of publication, as well as the most significant nations, organisations, and journals in donation-based crowdfunding. Most of the results are shown as percentages and frequencies, and the co-occurrence of author keywords, citations based on countries, authorship, and co-citations are mapped using VOSviewer.

Results showed 27 out of the 28 papers on donation-based crowdfunding research are in English. Due to English being the accepted academic language, papers that were published in English would often have a better chance of being found by academics and researchers of the social science community.

Table 1.2: The number of donation-based crowdfunding area research publications by year.

Year	TP	NCP	TC	C/P	C/CP	*h*	*g*
2012	-	-	-	-	-	-	-
2013	-	-	-	-	-	-	-
2014	-	-	-	-	-	-	-
2015	-	-	-	-	-	-	-
2016	2		7	3.50	1.17	2	2
2017	1		3	3.00	0.60	1	1
2018	4		44	11.00	11.00	3	4
2019	7		56	8.00	18.67	4	7
2020	5		51	10.20	25.50	3	5
2021	7		26	3.71	26.00	2	5
2022	1		-	-	-	-	-

The following variables are included in the notes: TC is the total number of citations; h is the h-index; g is the g-index; C/P is the average citations per publication; and NCP is the number of cited publications.

The number of articles on donation-based crowdfunding from 2012 to 2022 is shown in Table 1.2. In the ten years, two years experienced a noticeable increase in publications. The years were 2019 and 2021, and 7 documents were released in each of those years. The highest productivity, with a total of 27 papers, was found in 2019 and 2021, while the lowest production, with a total of 1 document for each year given, was discovered in 2017 and 2022. In general, more publications were published between 2019 and 2021, showing the growing need for research on donation-based crowdfunding and its enormous potential for progress. However, as shown in Figure 1.2 from 2019 to 2022, the number of citations for works on donation-based crowdfunding gradually decreased.

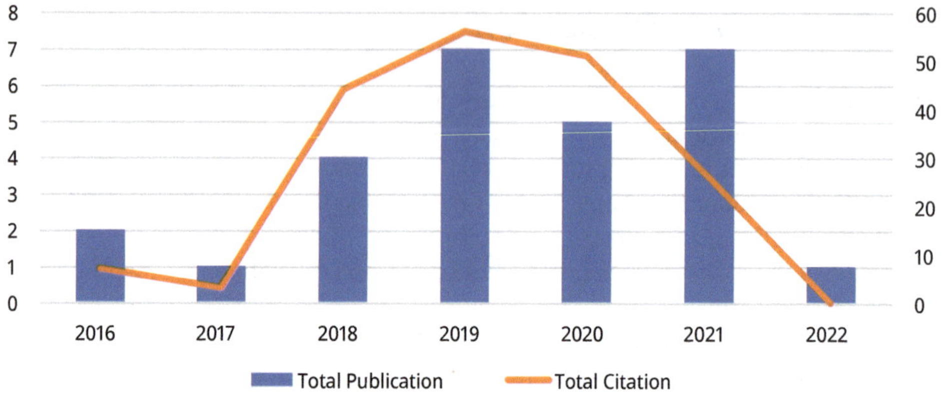

Figure 1.2: Total publications and citations by year.

For documents published in 2019, there were the most citations (56), while there were none for those published in 2022. (0 citations per publication). In terms of productivity, 2017 has writers with the greatest h-index (4). Hirsch (2005) also suggested the h-index, which estimates the importance, significance, and high effect of all researchers' combined research efforts. Most bibliographic databases, such Scopus and Web of Science, now incorporate the h-index, a widely used metric for evaluating scientific performance (Van Eck & Waltman, 2017).

The second research question in this study is concerned with determining the major subject areas based on co-occurrence analysis, top keywords, and subject categories. In order to respond to RQ2, we looked at the citation networks of 27 publications based on (a) the subject area in which a document was published and (b) a co-occurrence analysis of the main keywords. An efficient content analysis technique to map the degree of correlation between keywords in the literature is keyword co-occurrence analysis (Shmagun et al., 2020). Following this, the materials were categorised based on their subject areas, as indicated in Table 1.3.

Table 1.3: Subject area.

Subject Area	Total Publications (TP)	Percentage (%)
Business, management and accounting	9	33.3
Computer science	9	33.3
Economics, econometrics and finance	6	22.2
Engineering	6	22.2
Social sciences	4	14.8
Arts and humanities	2	7.4
Decision sciences	2	7.4
Psychology	2	7.4

Table 1.3 (continued)

Subject Area	Total Publications (TP)	Percentage (%)
Energy	1	3.7
Environmental science	1	3.7
Mathematics	1	3.7
Medicine	1	3.7
Multidisciplinary	1	3.7
Physics and astronomy	1	3.7

Overall, the distribution showed that research on donation-based crowdfunding has advanced in a number of subject areas. According to the information provided, the majority of the papers analysed are found in publications related to business, management, and accounting (33.3%), computer science (33.3%), economics, econometrics, and finance (22.2%), engineering (22.2%), and social sciences (14.8%).

In order to respond to RQ2, the study concentrated on finding the terms that academics in donation-based crowdfunding research use the most. In Table 1.4, the important terms from the 27 crowdfunding studies based on donations have been compiled. The term "donation-based crowdfunding" was found to be the one that was used the least frequently in the literature on this topic. Crowdfunding is the second most frequently used keyword. This conclusion makes sense given that researchers, academicians, and practitioners in the field of financial management rarely study the micro financial topic. Digital platforms were among the other frequently used keywords.

The bibliometric networks were visualised and the authors' keywords were mapped using the VOSviewer programme, which can be downloaded at https://www.vosviewer.com. The links between the terms were illustrated by the text size, circle size, thickness of the connecting line, and colour. When two keywords appear in the same article, it is known as a "keyword co-occurrence," and it indicates that the two concepts are connected (Baker et al., 2020).

Table 1.4: Top keywords.

Author Keywords	Total Publications	Percentage (%)
Donation-based crowdfunding	11	40.7
Crowdfunding	10	37.0
Digital platforms	4	14.8

Figure 1.3 displays the author's keyword network visualisation, which reveals that every keyword appeared at least three times. As a result, three of the 92 total keywords met these specifications. The overall co-occurrence strength correlations with other phrases were computed for each of the three keywords (Van Eck & Waltman, 2008, 2017; Waltman & Van Eck, 2010). After that, these terms were divided into two clusters,

with the size of the nodes representing the terms' frequency. Meanwhile, the different colours of the nodes indicated the different clusters to which they belonged.

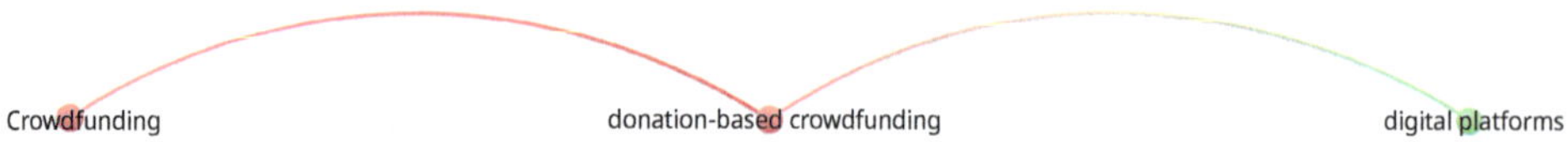

Figure 1.3: Author keywords' network visualization map with at least 4 occurrences.

In order to eliminate inter-cluster similarities and cluster natural network divisions based on similarity, cluster analysis employs a range of techniques (Bazm & Seyyed Mehdi Kalantar, 2016). This group of keywords belonged to a certain cluster and were taken from the publication's title, abstract, and author's keywords (Van Eck & Waltman, 2017). The parameter selected for this study was 10 in order to establish the fundamental cluster of a subject area for every tenth publication (Nadzar et al., 2017). The first cluster (in red) is centred on "donation-based crowdfunding" and "crowdfunding," with the latter being the greatest node size. The number of publications that contained the phrase determined the cluster's size. Furthermore, the number of clusters to which the terms were assigned represented the "total link strength," or the total of all connections to other nodes (Van Eck & Waltman, 2017; Shmagun et al., 2020). The node for "donation-based crowdfunding" was closest to the node for "crowdfunding," and their proximity suggested that these two terms have a close relationship and a significant connection (Nadzar et al., 2017; Van Eck & Waltman, 2017). Digital platforms were found in Cluster 2 (green colour), which connected to Cluster 1 in some way. In addition, keyword analysis offered valuable insight into the level of significance or appeal of a certain topic within a given study subject.

To address research question RQ3, this study did this by analysing (a) the top contributors to publications by country, (b) the citations analysis, and (c) the authorship analysis to look at the features of scientific collaborations on donation-based crowdfunding research. The top countries listed in Table 1.5 are those whose authors contributed to crowdfunding publications that received donations. China (4 publications), Japan (3 publications), and the United States (2 publications) were in the lead. National linkages revealed that authors from Jordan and Jordania, as well as authors from Spain, the UK, Argentina, and the Netherlands, contributed to one publication. Donation-based crowdsourced research seems to have a big influence across a wide range of regions.

Table 1.5: Top countries contributed to the publications.

Country	TP	NCP	TC	C/P	C/CP	*h*	*g*
United States	6	14	60	19.00	8.44	5	8
China	5	33	45	12.83	9.63	5	8
Spain	5	7	22	4.00	4.00	1	4

The following variables are included in the notes: TC is the total number of citations; h is the h-index; g is the g-index; C/P is the average citations per publication; and NCP is the number of cited publications.

Figure 1.4 displayed the network visualisation map of country-specific scholarly citations. The visualisation map showed three clusters based on the co-occurrence of countries, covering all countries that are referenced in four or more publications, based on the linkages made by the authors. China-related countries need to fulfil this prerequisite.

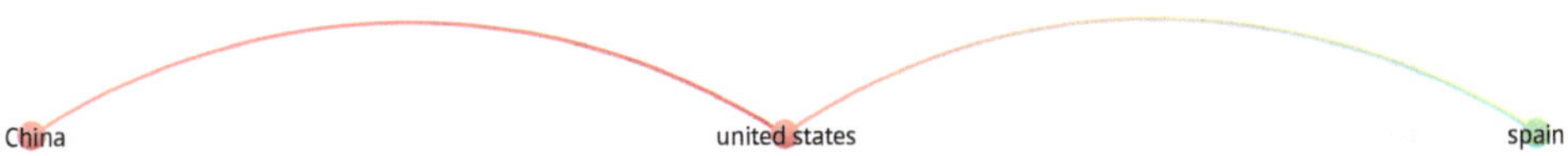

Figure 1.4: Network Visualization Map of the Citation based on Different Countries.
Note: Minimum number of documents of an countries = 5; Minimum number of citations of an countries =0.

The number of publications linked to a country is indicated by the size of its node. United States and China are the two nations in the first cluster (red). Spain is the only nation in the second cluster (green).

Citation analysis is a tool for systematically evaluating the significance and calibre of research publications because it is simple to perform (Aristodemou & Tietze, 2018; Hou et al., 2018). The papers' citation metrics, as reported in Table 1.6, were taken from the Scopus database. In the ten years from 2012 to 2022, 27 papers received a total of 187 citations, averaging 6.93 citations per piece and 5.2 citations annually.

Table 1.6: Citations metrics.

Metrics	Data
Publication years	2012 – 2022
Citation years	10
Papers	27
Citations	187
Citations/year	31.17
Citations/paper	6.93
Papers/author	1.00
h-index	9
g-index	13

Co-citation analysis essentially creates similarity metrics between texts, authors, or journals using co-citation counts. Therefore, it is more likely that the two writers' content is related if they are cited together more frequently (Zupic & Ater, 2015; Hallinger, 2019). The concept of author co-citation can be better understood by looking at Figure 1.5, which includes two publications by Kamal et al. (2022) and Torres et al.

adopted (2020). Both were displayed in the references from the two additional studies, van der Voort et al. (2017) and Fu et al. (2021). So, the two articles were referred to as "cited papers", and the other three publications, which are connected to the two cited documents, were referred to as "citing documents". The links show a relationship to indicate the similarities among documents (Hallinger, 2019).

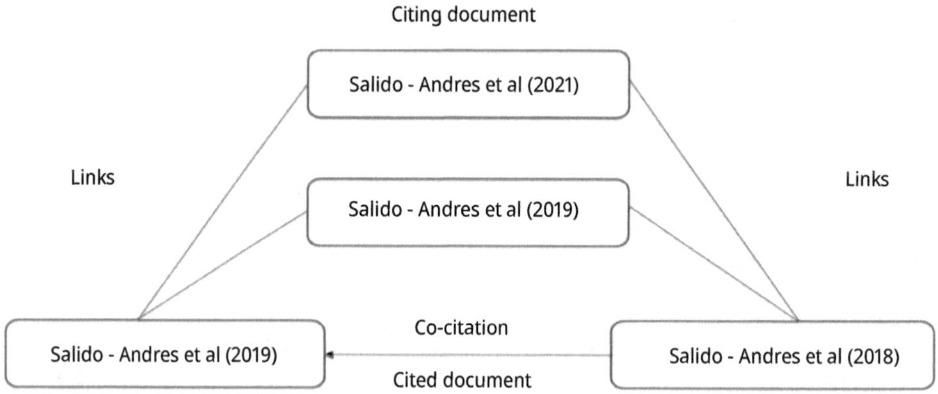

Figure 1.5: Example of co-citation and links.

A total of 27 papers on donation-based crowdfunding have had contributions from 51 authors. Table 1.7 displays the number of authors for each document. Of the 27 papers considered in this analysis, five had a single author, while the other 27 had multiple authors. The majority of the papers on crowdfunding with a donation-based model had two co-authors (25.9%), followed by three (18.5%) and four (29.6%).

Table 1.7: Number of author(s) per document.

Author Count	Total Publications	Percentage (%)
1	5	18.5
2	7	25.9
3	5	18.5
4	8	29.6

When two or more authors work together to write a paper, co-authorship maps are used, and these collaboration patterns show the structure of scientific networks (Zupic & Ater, 2015). A minimum of four papers are required for the co-authorship network map shown in Figure 1.6. As a result, 51 authors out of a total of 4 satisfied the criteria for the analysis. Be aware that one cluster in various colours was included in the author co-authorship map.

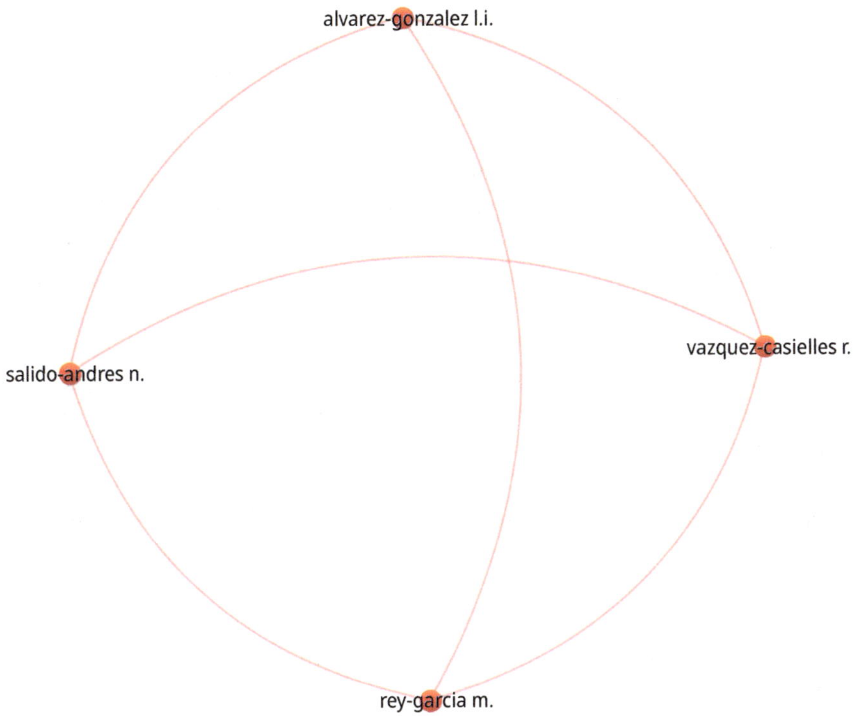

Figure 1.6: Network visualization map of the co-authorship.
Note: Unit of analysis = Authors; Counting method: Full counting; Minimum number of documents of an author = 4; Minimum number of citations of an author = 0.

According to Figure 1.6, Cluster 1 is represented by the colour red. The patterns change depending on the text size, circle size, and line thickness. The patterns of connecting lines show how strongly the authors are connected (Wahid et al., 2020). Among the visible co-authors, Salido-Andres, Vazquez-Casielles, Alvarez-Gonzalez, and Salido-Andres comprised the largest node, signifying him as the most prolific author with the greatest number of collaborations and publications.

1.4 Conclusion

Bibliometric analysis was used to examine articles related to crowdfunding that relied on donations between 2012 and 2022. Also, the bibliometric properties of 27 publications were obtained using the Scopus database. English was discovered to be the most widely used language in response to the RQ1, based on the publication trend in donation-based crowdfunding. The findings show that the number of journals produced on this subject has increased slowly and is not widely disseminated. However, between 2019 and 2022, the total number of article citations annually declined. The goal of the second research question is to identify the main subjects covered in this analysis. It was determined that, with 33.3% of replies, the primary topic areas were accounting, management, and business. "Donation-based crowdfunding" accounted for 40.7% of all terms regularly cited in donation-based crowdfunding research, making it the most commonly used term among academics conducting this type of research. Since many of these earlier studies discuss challenges and misunderstandings in understanding donation-based in crowdfunding, the co-occurrence network of keywords revealed that the focus of research trends in donation-based crowdfunding has shifted from management investigation to business methods to develop scientific reasoning abilities about reactions in donation-based crowdfunding.

In the meantime, the analysis revealed the key contributors in response to Research Question 3 by (a) identifying the top contributors to publications by nation, (b) analysing citations, and (c) identifying the authors in donation-based crowdfunding research and elucidating the nature of their collaboration. Utilising the features of scientific collaboration on donation-based crowdfunding research, the VOSviewer software was able to trace the network of citations and co-authorships in this study. Using Harzing's Publish or Perish software, the citation metrics showed that 27 articles received 187 citations during a ten-year period (2012–2022), averaging 31.17 citations annually and 6.93 citations per piece. The following is a summary of the result on RQ3: (1) The hub of the donation-based crowdfunding network, which worked with numerous nations including China, Spain, Indonesia, India, France, Iran, Korea, and Malaysia, was the United States. Transferable information and technology are generated through scientific collaboration across nations, and this is crucial for the advancement of education, particularly for donation-based crowdfunding of new viewing.

A study's limitations ought to be made explicit in order to recognise the high calibre and added value of the research. First, the keywords chosen for article titles and the Scopus database were the only sources of information used in this study. This study did not use any of the other extensive databases, including Google Scholar, Web of Science, Dimensions, Lens, and PubMed articles addressing donation-based crowdfunding. Second, because the notions of donation-based crowdfunding cover a larger domain, we only looked at a sample of the pertinent literature and employed a restricted set of search phrases. If not, the time frame covered was set. Thirdly, no other techniques have been used to triangulate the co-authorship network mapping. Lastly, self-citations and intrinsic, unclear justifications for mentioning a certain text are also provided by citation analysis flaws. It may be advised that the following be investigated further in the future: To triangulate the results, (1) use additional analysis and counting techniques like fractional counting and bibliographic coupling; (2) repeat the study using additional databases, such as Web of Science, to display a greater representation of publications; and (3) investigate further research and help close any knowledge gaps that may arise in the development of donation-based crowdfunding. This will facilitate the achievement of various topic study aims amongst donation-based crowdfunding stakeholders worldwide. Notwithstanding these drawbacks, the study offers some fascinating new perspectives on the state of donation-based crowdfunding research and publishing practices today. Furthermore, every indicator seeks to advance research in this field, which may yield additional insights into how crowdfunding research that is donation-based will change in the future while supporting the creation of technology that helps businesses manage their finances and evaluates the importance of these insights in the growth of entrepreneurial ventures.

Abbreviations

VOS	Virtual Operating System
CF	Crowdfunding
CFP	Crowdfunding Platform
SLR	Systematic Literature Review
RQ	Research Question
GCC	Gulf Cooperation Council
PRISMA	Preferred Reporting Items for Systematic Reviews and Meta-Analyses
TP	Total Number of Publications
NCP	Number of Cited Publications
TC	Total Citations
C/P	Average Citations Per Publication
C/CP	Average Citations Per Cited Publication
RIS	Research Information Systems
CSV	Comma-Separated Values

References

Ahmi, A., & Mohd Nasir, M.H. (2019). Examining the trend of the research on extensible business reporting language (XBRL): A bibliometric review. *International Journal of Innovation, Creativity and Change, 5*(2), 1145–1167.

Ahn, S. (2022). To buy or to back? Backers' motivations for fashion crowdfunding projects, *Journal of Fashion Marketing and Management*, Vol. ahead-of-print No. ahead-of-print. https://doi.org/10.1108/JFMM-01-2022-0013.

Allah Pitchay, A., Aboue Eliz, N.M., Ganesan, Y., Mydin, A.-A., Ratnasari, R.T. & Mohd Thas Thaker, M.A. (2022). Self-determination theory and individuals' intention to participate in donation crowdfunding, *International Journal of Islamic and Middle Eastern Finance and Management, 15*(3), 506–526. https://doi.org/10.1108/IMEFM-08-2020-0424

Al-Qershi, O.M., Kwon, J., Zhao, S. & Li, Z. (2022). Predicting crowdfunding success with visuals and speech in video ads and text ads, *European Journal of Marketing, 56*(6), 1610–1649. https://doi.org/10.1108/EJM-01-2020-0029.

Baber, H., & Ivanovici, M.F. (2022). Fifteen years of crowdfunding – a bibliometric analysis, *Technology Analysis and Strategic Management*, DOI: 10.1080/09537325.2022.2089548.

Block, J.H., Colombo, M.G., Cumming, D.J. & Vismara, S. (2018). New players in entrepreneurial finance and why they are there, *Small Business Economics, 50*(2), 239–250.

Bruton, G., Khavul, S., Siegel, D. & Wright, M. (2015). New financial alternatives in seeding entrepreneurship: microfinance, crowdfunding, and peer-to-peer innovations, *Entrepreneurship Theory and Practice, 39*(1), 9–26.

Chen, Y., Zhou, S., Jin, W. & Chen, S. (2022). Investigating the determinants of medical crowdfunding performance: a signaling theory perspective, *Internet Research*, Vol. ahead-of-print No. ahead-of-print. https://doi.org/10.1108/INTR-09-2021-0652.

Cicchiello, A.F.F. & Kazemikhasragh, A. (2022). Tackling gender bias in equity crowdfunding: an exploratory study of investment behaviour of Latin American investors, *European Business Review, 34*(3), 370–395. https://doi.org/10.1108/EBR-08-2021-018.

Cicchiello, A.F., Pietronudo, M.C., Leone, D. and Caporuscio, A. (2021). Entrepreneurial dynamics and investor-oriented approaches for regulating the equity-based crowdfunding, *Journal of Entrepreneurship and Public Policy, 10*(2), 235–260.

Cumming, D.J., Leboeuf, G. & Schwienbacher, A. (2015). Crowdfunding models: Keep-it-all vs all-or nothing, *Financial Management, 49*(2), 331–360.

de Oliveira, O.J., da Silva, F.F., Juliani, F., Barbosa, L.C.F.M., & Nunhes, T.V. (2019). Bibliometric method for mapping the state-of-the-art and identifying research gaps and trends in literature: An essential instrument to support the development of scientific projects. In *Scientometrics Recent Advances* (Issue tourism, p. 13). IntechOpen. https://www.intechopen.com/books/advanced-biometric-technologies/liveness-detection-in-biometrics.

Estrin, S., Gozman, D. & Khavul, S. (2018). The evolution and adoption of equity crowdfunding: Entrepreneur and investor entry into a new market, *Small Business Economics, 51*(2), 425–439.

Gil-Gomez, H., Oltra-Badenes, R., Guerola-Navarro, V. & Saldana, P.Z. (2021). Crowdfunding: A bibliometric analysis. *International Entrepreneurship and Management Journal.* https://doi.org/10.1007/s11365-021-00784-0.

Hallinger, P., & Kovacevic, J. (2019). A bibliometric review of research on educational administration: Science mapping the literature, 1960 to 2018, *Review of Educational Research, 89*(3), 335–369.

Hossain, M. & Oparaocha, G.O. (2017). Crowdfunding: motives, definitions, typology and ethical challenges, *Entrepreneurship Research Journal, 7*(2), doi: 10.1515/erj-2015-0045.

Hou, X., Wu, T., Chen, Z., & Zhou, L. (2022). Success factors of medical crowdfunding campaigns: Systematic review, *Journal of Medical Internet Research, 24*(3), e30189. doi: 10.2196/30189.

Kamaruddin, M.I.H., Muhamed, N.A., Radzi, R.M., Nazarie, W.N.F.W.M., & Kamarubahrin. (2023). Financial management practices in Islamic donation-based crowdfunding (DCF) platforms in Malaysia. *Future Business Journal, 9*, 32. https://doi.org/10.1186/s43093-023-00210-7.

Kgoroeagira, R., Burke, A. & Van Stel, A. (2019). Small business online loan crowdfunding: Who gets funded andwhat determines the rate of interest?, *Small Business Economics, 52*(1), 67–87.

Learnbonds.com (2020), *Global Crowdfunding Transaction Value to Top $12bn by 2023: Outsourcing Portal – Outsourcing Industry Portal*, Outsourcing Portal, 16 March, available at: http://www. outsourcingportal.eu/en/global-crowdfunding-transaction-value-to-top-12bn-by-2023 (accessed 28 July 2022).

Leonelli, S., Pietro, F.D. & Masciarelli, F. (2020). Narcissism, Machiavellianism and Psychopathy: How Do Displayed Entrepreneurs' Personality Dark Traits Influence Crowdfunding Success? Caputo, A. & Pellegrini, M.M. (Ed.) *The Entrepreneurial Behaviour: Unveiling the cognitive and emotional aspect of entrepreneurship (Entrepreneurial Behaviour Series)*, Emerald Publishing Limited, Bingley, pp. 41–65. https://doi.org/10.1108/978-1-78973-507-920201007.

Li, Y.-M., Liou, J.-H. & Li, Y.-W. (2020). A social recommendation approach for reward-based crowdfunding campaigns, *Information and Management, 57*(7), 103246, doi: 10.1016/j.im.2019.103246.

Liu, L., Suh, A. & Wgner, C. (2018). Empathy or perceived credibility? An empirical study on individual donation behavior in charitable crowdfunding, *Internet Research, 28*(3), 623–651.

Lu, B., Xu, T. & Wang, Z. (2022). Signaling innovativeness in crowdfunding entrepreneurial narratives: the moderating roles of entrepreneurial passion and social endorsement, *Internet Research*, Vol. ahead-of-print No. ahead-of-print. https://doi.org/10.1108/INTR-03-2021-0155.

Macari, A. & Chun, G.G. (2021). Perceived violations of reward delivery obligations in reward-based crowdfunding: an integrated theoretical framework, *New England Journal of Entrepreneurship, 24*(1), 43–59. https://doi.org/10.1108/NEJE-08-2019-0035.

Masrizal., Sukmana, R., Trianto, B. & Zaimsyah, A.M. (2022). Determinant factor of crowdfunders' behavior in using crowdfunding waqf model in Indonesia: two competing models, *Journal of Islamic Marketing*, Vol. ahead-of-print No. ahead-of-print. https://doi.org/10.1108/JIMA-08-2021-0246.

Martínez-Climent, C., Zorio-Grima, A., & Ribeiro-Soriano, D. (2018). Financial return crowdfunding: Literature review and bibliometric analysis, *International Entrepreneurship and Management Journal; New York, 14*(3), 527–553. DOI:10.1007/s11365-018-0511-x.

Mitra, P., Kickul, J.R. & Robb, C. (2021). Helper Networks and Crowdfunding: Mobilizing Social Entrepreneurship, Wasieleski, D.M. & Weber, J. (Ed.) *Social Entrepreneurship (Business and Society 360, Vol. 5)*, Emerald Publishing Limited, Bingley, pp. 233–251. https://doi.org/10.1108/S2514-175920220000005011.

Muhamed, N.A., Kamaruddin, M.I.H., Nazarie, W.N.F.W.M., Kamarubahrin, A.F., Radzi, R.M. (2023). *Shariah Governance Framework for Islamic Donation-Based Crowdfunding Platforms in Malaysia*. In: Rafiki, A., Dana, LP., Nasution, M.D.T.P. (eds) Open Innovation in Small Business. Contributions to Environmental Sciences & Innovative Business Technology. Springer, Singapore. https://doi.org/10.1007/978-981-99-5142-0_18.

Ribeiro, J.P.C., Duarte, F. & Gama, A.P.M. (2022). Does microfinance foster the development of its clients? A bibliometric analysis and systematic literature review. *Financial Innovation, 8*(34), 1–35. https://doi.org/10.1186/s40854-022-00340-x.

Rodriguez-Ricardo, Y., Sicilia, M. & López, M. (2018). What drives crowdfunding participation? The influence of personal and social traits, Spanish Journal of Marketing – ESIC, 22(2), 163–182. https://doi.org/10.1108/SJME-03-2018-004.

Shneor, R. & Munim, Z.H. (2019). Reward crowdfunding contribution as planned behaviour: An extended framework, *Journal of Business Research, 103*, 56–70.

Short, J.C., Ketchen, D.J., McKenny, A.F., Allison, T.H. & Ireland, R.D. (2016). Research on crowdfunding: reviewing the (very recent) past and celebrating the present, *Entrepreneurship Theory and Practice, 41*(2), 149–160, doi: 10.1111/etap.12270.

Stack, P., Feller, J., O'Reilly, P., Gleasure, R., Li, S. & Cristoforo, J., (2017). *Managing risk in business centric crowdfunding platforms*. In Proceedings of the 13th International Symposium on Open Collaboration (pp. 1–4).

St John, J., St John, K. & Han, B. (2022). Entrepreneurial crowdfunding backer motivations: a latent Dirichlet allocation approach, *European Journal of Innovation Management, 25*(6), 223–241. https://doi.org/10.1108/EJIM-05-2021-0248

Teichmann, F., Boticiu, S.R. & Sergi, B.S. (2022). Compliance risks for crowdfunding. A neglected aspect of money laundering, terrorist financing and fraud, *Journal of Financial Crime*, Vol. ahead-of-print No. ahead-of-print. https://doi.org/10.1108/JFC-05-2022-0116.

Thottoli, M.M. (2022). The starring role of crowdfunding in GCC: A structured literature review, *Asian Journal of Economics and Banking*, Vol. ahead-of-print No. ahead-of-print. https://doi.org/10.1108/AJEB-02-2022-0022.

Zakaria, R., Ahmi, A., Ahmad, A. H., & Othman, Z. (2021). Worldwide melatonin research: A bibliometric analysis of the published literature between 2015 and 2019. *Chronobiology International, 38*(1), 27–37.

Muhammad Dharma Tuah Putra Nasution, Yossie Rossanty,
Pipit Buana Sari

Chapter 2 Islamic Branding: Navigating Principles, Identities and Challenges, in Contemporary Marketing

Abstract: Islamic branding serves as a cornerstone in contemporary marketing, addressing the diverse needs of Muslim consumers while upholding Islamic principles. This chapter offers a comprehensive examination of Islamic brands, exploring their classifications, dimensions, challenges, and opportunities within the realm of branding and marketing. It delineates four primary classifications: true Islamic, traditional Islamic, inbound, and outbound brands. Additionally, it delves into the intricacies of developing Islamic brand identities, focusing on five key dimensions: modesty, purity, comfort, quality, and authenticity. Moreover, the chapter discusses the emerging opportunities stemming from cultural exchanges and the branding of Halal products. Drawing on extensive research, it provides nuanced insights into effectively engaging with Muslim consumers and navigating religious sensitivities. This chapter serves as a valuable resource for academics, practitioners, and policymakers involved in branding, marketing, and consumer behavior research, enriching their understanding of the dynamic landscape of Islamic branding.

Keywords: Islamic branding; Muslim consumers; halal products; branding types; religion

2.1 Introduction

The realm of Islamic branding is a multifaceted domain that holds significant importance for businesses aiming to cater to the needs of Muslim consumers while respecting cultural sensitivities and aligning with Islamic values.

Islamic branding goes beyond mere product offerings; it encapsulates a fusion of cultural, religious, and ethical considerations that shape consumers' perceptions and purchasing decisions. Research indicates that factors such as religiosity, brand trust, and adherence to Islamic principles significantly influence consumers' attitudes towards halal products (Elseidi, 2018). However, the definition of what constitutes Halal goes beyond product quality and cost-efficiency; it encompasses adherence to Islamic guidelines and values (Wilson & Liu, 2010). This highlights the complexity of Islamic branding, where authenticity and alignment with Islamic principles are paramount.

Moreover, the influence of self-expressive values on Islamic brand loyalty underscores the emotional connection that consumers have with Islamic brands (Aji & Musli-

https://doi.org/10.1515/9783111575407-003

chah, 2022). Understanding the universal appeal of Halal products and the acceptance of such products in non-Muslim countries is crucial for businesses seeking to expand their market reach (Wilkins et al., 2019). Islamic branding extends beyond products to services like Islamic banking, where factors like brand familiarity and profit-sharing rates impact consumers' investment decisions (Hati et al., 2021).

In a globalized world, where Muslim consumers wield significant purchasing power, the dynamics of Muslim consumers' behavior towards Halal products are essential for businesses to comprehend (Al–Kwifi et al., 2019). The interplay between religiosity and branding in influencing consumers' decision-making processes emphasizes the need for businesses to align their branding strategies with Islamic values (Razzaque & Chaudhry, 2013). The development of Islamic brand personality models underscores the importance of creating unique brand experiences that resonate with Muslim consumers (Zaki et al., 2021; Ahmed et al., 2019).

As businesses navigate the complexities of Islamic branding, it is imperative to consider the multidimensional nature of religiosity and its impact on consumers' attitudes and purchasing behavior (Aruan & Wirdania, 2020). The role of Islamic marketing in shaping consumers' perceptions and driving consumption of Halal products underscores the strategic significance of aligning branding efforts with religious awareness (Musa et al., 2022). By exploring the nuances of Islamic branding and its implications for consumer behavior, businesses can forge stronger connections with Muslim consumers and establish a robust global brand presence.

This chapter delves into the intricate world of Islamic branding, encompassing various dimensions, classifications, challenges, and opportunities within the branding and marketing sphere. By shedding light on the dynamic and ever-evolving landscape of Islamic branding, this chapter aims to offer valuable insights for academics, practitioners, and policymakers engaged in branding, marketing, and consumer behavior research and practice.

2.2 Research Methodology

In our research methodology, we employed content analysis to investigate Islamic branding. Content analysis, as an objective research method, entails systematically identifying, classifying, and analyzing data from various sources. We assembled a corpus of relevant data, including academic articles, reports, and marketing materials. Subsequently, we systematically examined the content to identify key themes, trends, and patterns. Employing a coding scheme, we classified the data, and both statistical and qualitative methods were applied to analyze the results. The methodology adhered to principles of rigor, objectivity, and transparency, following established guidelines for systematic literature reviews in management research.

This study has collected data from Scopus, a widely used database for research across various fields. Scopus is particularly favored for its extensive coverage in the field of Business and Management. Research indicates that Scopus covers a higher percentage of journals compared to Web of Science (WoS) in this domain (Mongeon & Paul-Hus, 2015). The authors conducted searches on the Scopus database using specific titles such as "Islamic branding," "Islamic brand," "Halal brand," and "Islamic Marketing" to identify relevant articles for this study. The analysis is focused solely on the business and management discipline, particularly emphasizing Islamic branding (Table 2.1).

Table 2.1: Search syntax on Scopus database.

Data Source	Search syntax
Search syntax on Scopus database	TITLE ("Islamic branding" OR "Islamic brand" OR "Halal brand" OR "Islamic Marketing") AND PUBYEAR > 2008 AND PUBYEAR < 2024 AND (LIMIT-TO (SUBJAREA, "BUSI"))

Source: Author's compilation.

The articles included in the analysis span from 2009 to 2023 (see Fig.2.1 and 2.2). Among the analyzed documents, journal articles are the most prevalent, comprising 63 of the total. Additionally, there are 15 book chapters, 11 reviews, 5 books, and 2 conference reviews included in this analysis. All articles were published exclusively in English. Furthermore, the review or search query was conducted based on a total of 101 retrieved articles. The search process commenced by scanning for the specified keywords within various parts of the documents, such as the title. A comprehensive examination was conducted on the selected 101 articles.

2.3 Result and Discussion

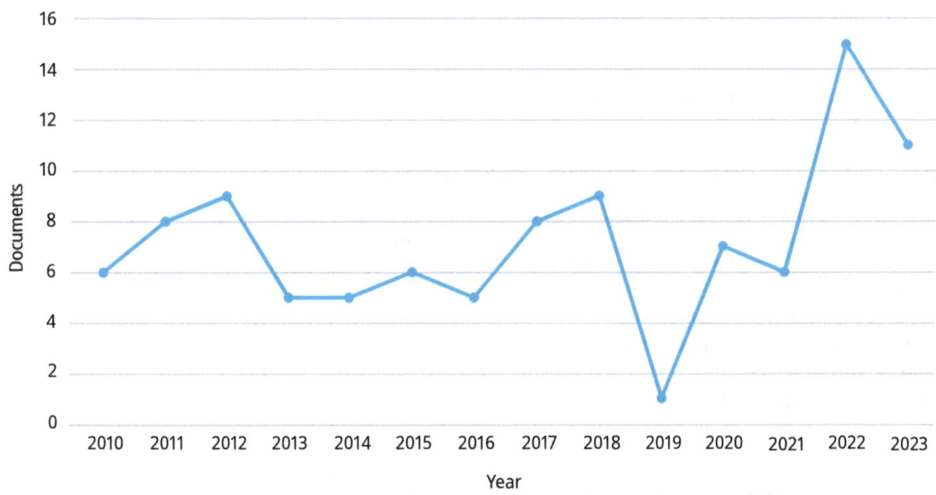

Figure 2.1: Document by year.

Table 2.2: Summary of results.

Criteria	Number
Articles	101
Journals/Book series	27
Authors	172
Institutions	102
Country	29

Table 2.2 provides a comprehensive summary of the results obtained from the analysis. It reveals that there are a total of 101 articles included in the dataset. Among these articles, 27 belong to journals or book series. A diverse group of 172 authors contributed to these articles. Furthermore, the research originates from 102 different institutions across various regions. The dataset encompasses contributions from 29 different countries or territories.

Figure 2.2: Document per year by source.

Table 2.3: Distribution of Documents Across Journals/Book Series.

Source	Document Count
Journal of Islamic Marketing	47
Contributions to Management Science	3
International Journal of Business and Society	3
Marketing Theory	3
Springer Proceedings in Business and Economics	3
Others (two documents below)	42
Total	101

Table 2.3 presents the breakdown of documents across various journals and book series. The preeminent contributor is the Journal of Islamic Marketing, with a substantial count of 47 documents. Additionally, there are 3 documents each from Contributions to Management Science, International Journal of Business and Society, Marketing Theory, and Springer Proceedings in Business and Economics. The remaining 42 documents are categorized as "Others," denoting various publications beyond the aforementioned sources. In total, this analysis encompasses 101 documents.

Table 2.4: Key Author Distribution of Documents.

Key Author	Document Count
Alserhan, B.A.	7
Ali, A.	6
Wilson, J.A.	4
Jafari, A.	3
Jumani, Z.A.	3
Sandikci, O.	3
Sherwani, M.	3
Sukhabot, S.	3
Bhutto, M.Y.	2
Khan, M.A.	2
Ramadani, V	2
Rice, G.	2
El-Bassiouny, N.	2
Others	59
Total	101

Table 2.4 presents an overview of how documents are distributed among key authors. Alserhan leads the list with 7 documents attributed to them, closely followed by Ali, who authored 6 documents. Wilson comes in third with 4 documents, while Jafari, Jumani, Sandikci, Sherwani, and Sukhabot share the fourth position, each contributing 3 documents. Additionally, there's a diverse group labeled as "Others," responsible for a substantial portion of the total documents, amounting to 59. In total, this analysis covers 101 documents

Table 2.5: Country/Territory Distribution of Documents.

Country/Territory	Document Count
Malaysia	22
Indonesia	16
United Kingdom	14
Turkey	8
United States	8

Table 2.5 (continued)

Country/Territory	Document Count
Pakistan	7
United Arab Emirates	6
China	5
Egypt	5
Bangladesh	4
Others	6
Total	101

Table 2.5 illustrates the distribution of documents across different countries and territories. Malaysia takes the lead with 22 documents, followed by Indonesia with 16 documents. The United Kingdom and Turkey are closely behind, each contributing 14 and 8 documents, respectively. The United States and Pakistan share the fourth position with 8 and 7 documents, respectively. The United Arab Emirates, China, Egypt, and Bangladesh each have 6, 5, 5, and 4 documents attributed to them, respectively. Additionally, there are 6 documents categorized under "Others." In total, this analysis encompasses 101 documents from various countries and territories.

Table 2.6: Affiliation Document Distribution.

Affiliation	Document Count
International Islamic University Malaysia	6
University of Greenwich	6
Bilkent Üniversitesi	5
Universiti Teknologi MARA	4
United Arab Emirates University	4
Universiti Sains Malaysia	3
Universiti Kebangsaan Malaysia	3
Prince of Songkla University	3
University of International Business and Economics	3
Xi'an Jiaotong University	3
Others	61
Total	101

Table 2.6 presents the distribution of documents across different affiliations. At the forefront are the International Islamic University Malaysia and the University of Greenwich, both contributing 6 documents each. Following closely is Bilkent Üniversitesi with 5 documents associated with its affiliation. Universiti Teknologi MARA and United Arab Emirates University each have 4 documents credited to their affiliations. Several other affiliations, such as Universiti Sains Malaysia, Universiti Kebangsaan Malaysia,

Prince of Songkla University, University of International Business and Economics, and Xi'an Jiaotong University, are also notable contributors, each contributing 3 documents. Additionally, a substantial number of documents, totaling 61, fall under the "Others" category. Overall, this analysis encompasses 101 documents distributed across various affiliations.

2.3.1 Key Principles of Islamic Branding

Islamic branding is guided by key principles that resonate with Muslim consumers while upholding Islamic values. Firstly, Islamic branding involves being compliant with Shariah principles, ensuring products and services are in line with Islamic teachings (Bukhari & Isa, 2019). This authenticity is crucial for Muslim consumers who seek products that align with their religious beliefs. Secondly, Islamic branding emphasizes emotional connections and values, aiming to create a deep bond with consumers beyond just a transactional relationship (Wilson & Liu, 2011). This emotional resonance is vital in engaging Muslim consumers who prioritize sincerity and integrity in brand interactions. Thirdly, Islamic branding involves portraying religious values in brand messaging, appealing to Muslim consumers' sense of identity and values (Harun et al., 2023). By aligning with Islamic principles, brands can establish a strong emotional attachment with Muslim consumers who seek products that reflect their beliefs. Overall, Islamic branding focuses on authenticity, emotional connection, and alignment with Islamic values to effectively resonate with Muslim consumers and uphold their religious principles. For a brief overview of these key principles, refer to Table 2.7.

Table 2.7: Key principles of Islamic Branding.

Key principles	Description	Key Sources
Compliance with Shariah Principles	Islamic branding involves strict adherence to Shariah principles, ensuring that products and services align with Islamic teachings. This authenticity is crucial for Muslim consumers seeking religiously compliant products.	Bukhari & Isa (2019)
Emotional Connections and Values	Islamic branding emphasizes emotional connections, aiming to create deep bonds with consumers beyond transactions. Muslim consumers prioritize sincerity and integrity, making emotional resonance vital.	Wilson & Liu (2011)
Portrayal of Religious Values	Islamic branding entails portraying religious values in brand messaging, appealing to Muslim consumers' sense of identity and values. Brands align with Islamic principles to establish emotional attachment.	Harun et al. (2023)

Islamic branding and traditional branding differ significantly in several aspects, as highlighted in the Table 2.8. Firstly, Islamic branding places a strong emphasis on adherence to Sharia principles, ensuring that products and services align with Islamic teachings, particularly in terms of being Halal certified (Bukhari & Isa, 2019). Conversely, traditional branding does not inherently incorporate religious considerations into its core identity.

Moreover, Islamic branding often involves products originating from Islamic countries, with a focus on providing Halal products for Muslim consumers (Alserhan et al., 2016). In contrast, traditional branding may not prioritize the country of origin, and products may not necessarily be produced in Islamic countries.

Compliance with Islamic principles is another key aspect of Islamic branding, with products and services strictly adhering to Halal certification and other Islamic standards (Temporal, 2011). Traditional branding, on the other hand, may focus more on compliance with general industry standards, with less emphasis on religious considerations.

In terms of brand compliance, Islamic branding places a high importance on ensuring that brands fully comply with Islamic principles, while traditional branding may have varying levels of compliance with industry standards, with religious considerations potentially not being prioritized (Sukhabot & Jumani, 2021).

The consideration of the country of origin is also different between Islamic branding and traditional branding. Islamic brands often originate from Muslim-majority or minority countries, whereas traditional brands are not specifically tied to any particular country of origin (Jumani & Sukhabot, 2020).

Customer focus is another aspect where Islamic branding differs, with a strong customer-centric approach aimed at meeting the specific needs and preferences of Muslim consumers (Singkheeprapha et al., 2021). Traditional branding, however, may have varying levels of customer focus.

Finally, Islamic branding has a deep connection to cultural and religious values, aiming to resonate with Muslim consumers by reflecting their beliefs and values (Aji & Muslichah, 2022). In contrast, traditional branding may have a limited connection to cultural and religious values. In essence, Islamic branding goes beyond traditional branding by incorporating religious principles, focusing on specific customer segments, and deeply connecting with cultural and religious values to resonate with Muslim consumers effectively. In short, the details are laid out in Table 2.8:

Table 2.8: Comparative Analysis of Islamic Branding and Traditional Branding Characteristics.

Aspect	Islamic Branding	Traditional Branding	Key sources
Core Principles	Adherence to Sharia principles	No religious considerations embedded in core identity	Bukhari & Isa (2019)
Product Origin	Halal products from Islamic countries	May not necessarily be produced in Islamic countries	Alserhan et al. (2016)

Table 2.8 (continued)

Aspect	Islamic Branding	Traditional Branding	Key sources
Compliance with Islamic principles	Products and services comply with Islamic principles, including Halal certification	Compliance with general industry standards, religious considerations may not be a priority	Temporal (2011)
Emphasis on Brand Compliance	High importance placed on brand compliance with Islamic principles	Compliance with industry standards may vary, religious considerations may not be prioritized	Sukhabot & Jumani (2021)
Consideration of Country of Origin	Originating from Muslim-majority or minority countries	Not specifically tied to country of origin	Jumani & Sukhabot (2020)
Customer Focus	Customer-centric approach	Customer focus may vary	Singkheeprapha et al. (2021)
Connection to Cultural and Religious Values	Deep connection to cultural and religious values	Limited connection to cultural and religious values	Aji & Muslichah (2022)

Islamic branding has demonstrated success across various sectors, exemplified by brands spanning from food and fashion to finance and entertainment. Brands such as Mecca Cola, Muslim Up, and Qibla Cola in the beverage industry, Mecca Burger in fast food, and Ummah Foods in chocolate products have resonated well with Islamic consumers (Boubekeur, 2016). Additionally, companies like Da'wah Wear offering Islamic men's fashion, Razanne Barbie dolls, and Islamic rap for children by Yusuf Islam have effectively tapped into the Muslim consumer market (Karoui & Khemakhem, 2019). Islamic branding extends to services like Islamic banking, where services are uniquely based on religious principles (Junaidi et al., 2021). The success of Islamic branding lies in establishing a psychological and emotional connection with Muslim consumers, understanding their values, behaviors, and religiosity to develop brands that align with their preferences (Bukhari & Isa, 2019). By incorporating Islamic principles, such as halal practices and adherence to Islamic beliefs, brands can foster loyalty among Muslim consumers, leading to successful Islamic branding strategies. Table 2.9 illustrates the success of Islamic branding across various sectors:

Table 2.9: Islamic Branding Across Various Sectors.

Sector	Examples	Sources
Beverage	Mecca Cola, Muslim Up, Qibla Cola	Boubekeur (2016)
Fast Food	Mecca Burger	
Chocolate	Ummah Foods	
Fashion	Da'wah Wear	Karoui & Khemakhem (2019)
Toys	Razanne Barbie dolls	
Entertainment	Islamic rap for children by Yusuf Islam	
Finance	Islamic banking services	Junaidi et al. (2021)

2.3.2 The Classification of Islamic Brands

Islamic brands constitute a unique subset within the broader branding landscape, characterized by their adherence to Islamic principles and values. The classification of Islamic brands is crucial for marketers and businesses aiming to effectively target Muslim consumers and engage with this specific market segment. Scholars have proposed various classifications for Islamic brands, each with its distinguishing features and criteria.

One prominent classification of Islamic brands is outlined by Alserhan (2010a), who categorizes them into four main groups: True Islamic Brands, Traditional Islamic Brands, Inbound Islamic Brands, and Outbound Islamic Brands. True Islamic Brands are those produced in Islamic countries and specifically target Muslim consumers. These brands are deeply rooted in Islamic culture and values, catering to the religious and cultural needs of Muslim consumers. Traditional Islamic Brands, however, also originate from Islamic countries but are not exclusively targeted at Muslims. These brands may have a broader appeal beyond the Muslim market while still reflecting Islamic heritage and traditions.Inbound Islamic Brands refer to brands originating from Islamic countries but not necessarily targeting Muslim consumers. These brands may have a more universal appeal or cater to diverse customer segments, irrespective of religious affiliations. Conversely, Outbound Islamic Brands originate from non-Islamic countries and may not primarily focus on targeting Muslim consumers. These brands may incorporate Islamic elements or values in their products or marketing strategies to appeal to Muslim consumers or tap into the growing demand for Islamic-inspired products globally. Table 2.10 depicts the classification of Islamic brands.

Table 2.10: Classification of Islamic Brands.

Classification	Description	Sources
True Islamic Brands	Produced in Islamic countries and exclusively targeting Muslim consumers, these brands are deeply rooted in Islamic culture and values.	Alserhan (2010a)
Traditional Islamic Brands	Originating from Islamic countries, these brands have a broader appeal beyond the Muslim market while still reflecting Islamic heritage.	
Inbound Islamic Brands	Brands originating from non-Islamic countries but targeting Muslim consumers may adapt Islamic elements to cater to this market segment	
Outbound Islamic Brands	Brands produced in Islamic countries but targeting non-Muslim consumers may incorporate universal values while retaining their Islamic identity	

Islamic brands can also be classified based on their geographical origin and target customer segments (Alharbi et al., 2021). Brands rooted in Islamic countries may have a distinct advantage in understanding the cultural nuances and preferences of Muslim consumers, enabling them to create products and marketing campaigns that resonate with their target audience (Alserhan, 2010a). Conversely, brands from non-Islamic countries may need to adapt their strategies to effectively engage with Muslim consumers and build trust within this market segment (Azam, 2016).

Key factors that distinguish Islamic brands from one another include adherence to Islamic principles, specificity in target audience, and cultural resonance. Islamic brands incorporate cultural values into their branding through various strategies to effectively connect with their target audience, build brand loyalty, and align with cultural values important to Muslim consumers. One key strategy is "cultural sensitivity," which involves being mindful of cultural nuances and variations within the global Muslim community when designing marketing campaigns (Wilson & Liu, 2011). Table 2.11 presents different facets of Islamic branding.

Table 2.11: Various Aspects of Islamic Branding.

Aspect	Description	Sources
Geographical origin and target customer segments	Islamic brands can be categorized based on their geographical origin and target customer segments, with brands from Islamic countries having unique advantages in understanding cultural nuances.	Alharbi et al., (2021); Alserhan (2010a)
Cultural sensitivity	Islamic brands incorporate cultural sensitivity into their branding strategies, considering cultural nuances and variations within the global Muslim community.	Wilson & Liu (2011)
Emotional connection	Establishing an emotional connection with Muslim consumers is vital for Islamic brands, enhancing brand loyalty and resonance in the modest fashion industry.	Wilson & Liu (2011); Zainudin et al. (2019)
Expression of brand values	Expressing brand values effectively and aligning with cultural norms are essential for success in Islamic markets, contributing to brand loyalty among Muslim consumers.	Zaki et al. (2021)
Integration of Islamic values	Integration of Islamic values from sources such as the Qur'an, the practices of Prophet Muhammad, and the 99 names of Allah is crucial for Islamic branding success.	Temporal (2011)
Modest fashion market trends	Brands prioritizing modesty in their branding efforts have observed significant shifts in the market landscape, driven by global trends and consumer preferences.	Jamal & Sharifuddin (2015)
Inclusivity and diversity	Recognition of modest fashion as a significant trend underscores the importance of inclusivity and diversity in the fashion industry, necessitating adaptation by brands.	O'Cass et al., (2013); Hassan & Ara (2021)

Additionally, emotional connection plays a significant role in establishing a bond with the target audience by triggering emotions and adding charisma to the brand, enhancing brand loyalty among Muslim consumers in the modest fashion industry ((Wilson & Liu, 2011)). Clearly expressing the brand mission and spending time perfecting the ultimate message can help Islamic brands communicate their values effectively (Zaki et al., 2021). Moreover, incorporating "sophistication" into the brand personality contributes to creating brand loyalty among Muslim consumers in the modest fashion sector (Zainudin et al., 2019).

Some Islamic brands that prioritize modesty in their branding have experienced a notable shift in the market landscape, particularly with the emergence of established fashion houses like Dolce & Gabbana venturing into this realm (Jamal & Sharifuddin, 2015). Brands such as Burberry, Mango, Tommy Hilfiger, and DKNY have recognized the significance of catering to Muslim consumers by entering the modest fashion market (Jamal & Sharifuddin, 2015). Moreover, companies like All Saints, Reebok, and Asos have expressed interest in engaging with the modest fashion market, often releasing collections tailored for Ramadan or Eid and collaborating with Muslim influencers for marketing purposes (Zaki et al., 2021).

This strategic adaptation in branding reflects a broader trend within the fashion industry toward inclusivity and diversity, acknowledging the importance of the Muslim consumer segment and their preferences for modest attire (O'Cass et al., 2013). Integrating Islamic values into brand building is a multifaceted process that draws from various sources such as the Qur'an, the practices of Prophet Muhammad, and the 99 names of Allah (Temporal, 2011). Such integration necessitates a nuanced understanding of the cultural and religious sensitivities of the Muslim consumer segment.

Furthermore, the global recognition of modest fashion as a significant trend has led to the acknowledgment of Islamic clothing as one of the fastest-growing industries worldwide (Hassan & Ara, 2021). This growth underscores the imperative for brands to adapt and cater to the needs of Muslim consumers seeking modest yet fashionable clothing options. Through prioritizing modesty in their branding efforts, these brands not only tap into a burgeoning market segment but also demonstrate a commitment to embracing cultural diversity and inclusivity in the fashion industry.

2.3.3 The Dimensions Involved in Islamic Branding

Islamic branding is a multifaceted concept that encompasses various dimensions crucial in shaping brand identity and positioning within the Islamic market. Cultural and religious creolization factors, as highlighted by Mirvaisi and Kaffashpoor (2023), play a significant role in influencing how brands are perceived by Muslim consumers. This involves blending cultural elements with Islamic principles to create a brand image that resonates with the target audience's values and beliefs.

Islamic religiosity, as studied by Eid and El-Gohary (2015), is another essential dimension in Islamic branding. Understanding the level of religiosity among Muslim consumers is vital for brands to tailor their marketing strategies effectively. Brands that align with Islamic values and principles can establish a deeper connection with consumers, leading to increased brand loyalty and trust.

Spiritual brand attributes, as discussed by Hamid et al. (2019), contribute to creating a brand aura that reflects sacredness and reverence in Islamic branding. By incorporating spiritual elements into branding strategies, companies can appeal to the emotional and psychological aspects of Muslim consumers, thereby influencing their purchasing behavior.

Emotional aspects, as researched by Wilson and Liu (2011), are also crucial in Islamic branding. Brands that evoke positive emotions such as trust, respect, and admiration can build stronger relationships with Muslim consumers. Moreover, adherence to Islamic principles such as Halal, as emphasized by Wilson and Liu (2010), is essential for brands operating in the Islamic market to ensure compliance with religious guidelines regarding permissible products and services.

Alignment with Islamic teachings, as explored by Ismail et al. (2022), is a key dimension in Islamic branding. Brands that embody Islamic values in their brand personality can differentiate themselves in the market and appeal to Muslim consumers seeking products and services that align with their beliefs.

The embodiment of Islamic values in brand personality, as studied by Zaki et al. (2021), is crucial for establishing a strong brand identity in the Islamic market. By integrating Islamic values into brand personality models, companies can enhance their appeal to Muslim consumers and foster long-term brand loyalty.

Islamic branding extends beyond mere compliance with Islamic guidelines; it involves creating a holistic brand experience that reflects the values and beliefs of the target audience. Wahyuni & Fitriani (2017) emphasize the importance of creating a brand aura that exudes sacredness and reverence, leading to enhanced brand loyalty among Muslim consumers.

Influencing consumer behavior, as highlighted by Singkheeprapha et al. (2021), is a key outcome of effective Islamic branding strategies. By understanding the cultural, religious, and psychological dimensions that influence consumer behavior, brands can tailor their marketing efforts to resonate with the target audience and drive purchase decisions.

The integration of Islamic teachings and principles into brand personality models, as researched by Ahmed et al. (2019), is essential for developing a brand identity that aligns with Islamic values. By aligning brand characteristics with Islamic teachings, brands can establish a meaningful connection with Muslim consumers, fostering trust and loyalty.

Halal branding is a fundamental aspect of Islamic marketing, emphasizing the importance of Halal compliance in products and services. Zainudin et al. (2019) propose Halal brand personality models that focus on dimensions such as purity, safety, righteousness, excitement, and sophistication. Ensuring Halal compliance and authenticity is crucial for building trust and credibility among Muslim consumers, who prioritize Halal products in their purchasing decisions.

In conclusion, Islamic branding encompasses a wide range of dimensions that collectively contribute to shaping brand identity and positioning in the Islamic market. By integrating cultural, religious, and psychological aspects into branding strategies, companies can create a brand experience that resonates with Muslim consumers, leading to increased brand loyalty, trust, and market acceptance. Table 2.12 showcases different dimensions of Islamic branding.

Table 2.12: Various dimensions of Islamic Branding.

Dimension	Description	Sources
Cultural and Religious Creolization Factors	Islamic branding incorporates cultural and religious creolization factors, reflecting the fusion of Islamic and local cultural elements, contributing to brand identity and positioning.	Mirvaisi & Kaffashpoor (2023)
Islamic Religiosity	The level of Islamic religiosity influences consumer behavior and brand perception, emphasizing alignment with Islamic principles and teachings.	Eid & El-Gohary (2015)
Spiritual Brand Attributes	Islamic brands often embody spiritual dimensions, resonating with the spiritual needs and beliefs of Muslim consumers.	Hamid et al. (2019)
Emotional Aspects	Emotional connections play a significant role in Islamic branding, fostering brand loyalty and influencing consumer behavior.	Wilson & Liu (2011)
Adherence to Islamic Principles	Brands aligning with Islamic principles, such as Halal, demonstrate authenticity and credibility, crucial for gaining trust among Muslim consumers.	Wilson & Liu, (2010); Zainudin et al. (2019)
Alignment with Islamic Teachings	Incorporating Islamic teachings into brand personality models strengthens the connection with Muslim consumers, promoting brand loyalty and trust.	Ismail et al. (2022)
Embodiment of Islamic Values	Brand personality reflects Islamic values, resonating with Muslim consumers and fostering brand loyalty.	Zaki et al.(2021)
Brand Religiosity Aura	The presence of a brand religiosity aura influences brand loyalty in Islamic banking, emphasizing the significance of sacred elements in brand perception.	Wahyuni & Fitriani (2017)
Integration of Islamic Teachings into Brand Personality	Islamic brands integrate Islamic teachings and principles into brand personality models, aligning brand characteristics with religious values to establish trust and connection with Muslim consumers.	Ahmed et al. (2019)
Halal Brand Personality Models	Halal branding emphasizes dimensions such as purity, safety, righteousness, excitement, and sophistication, contributing to the development of Halal brand personality models that promote trust and credibility among Muslim consumers.	Zainudin et al. (2019)

The five dimensions of the Islamic apparel brand personality model serve as a framework for guiding the development of such a brand identity. Modesty, for instance, is a key dimension that emphasizes the significance of covering the body in a modest and respectful manner in Islamic teachings (Al-Qur'an 24:31). Brands seeking to incorporate this value can do so by offering clothing that covers the body appropriately, such as long sleeves and loose-fitting garments, while avoiding revealing clothing that contradicts the concept of modesty. Table 2.13 highlights the dimensions of the Islamic apparel brand personality model.

Table 2.13: Dimensions of the Islamic Apparel Brand Personality Model.

Dimension	Description
Modesty	Emphasizing covering the body in a modest and respectful manner, in alignment with Islamic teachings (Al-Qur'an 24:31). Brands offer appropriate clothing such as long sleeves and loose-fitting garments
Purity	Highlights the importance of cleanliness and hygiene in Islam (Al-Qur'an 9:108). Brands use high-quality, clean materials adhering to Islamic standards.
Comfort	The significance of comfort and ease in clothing for Muslim consumers aligns with the Islamic principle of ease in worship (Al-Qur'an 2:185). Brands prioritize soft and breathable materials to ensure maximum comfort for their customers.
Quality	Stressing the offering of high-quality products reflects Islam's encouragement of excellence in all aspects of life (Hadith, Sahih Muslim). Brands ensure premium materials and meticulous craftsmanship
Authenticity	Emphasizing originality and uniqueness reflects Islam's values of honesty and integrity (Al-Qur'an 4:135). Brands create authentic designs, establishing genuine and trustworthy brand identities

Purity, another dimension in the Islamic apparel brand personality model, underscores the importance of cleanliness and hygiene in Islam (Al-Qur'an 9:108). Brands can integrate this value into their identity by using high-quality materials that are clean and free from impurities, ensuring that their products adhere to Islamic standards of purity.

Comfort is a dimension that highlights the significance of comfort and ease in clothing for Muslim consumers. This aligns with the Islamic principle of ease and convenience in matters of worship (Al-Qur'an 2:185). Brands can embody this value by using soft and breathable materials, as well as designing clothing that is comfortable to wear throughout the day.

Quality is a fundamental dimension that emphasizes the importance of offering high-quality products to consumers. In Islam, excellence and quality are encouraged in all aspects of life (Hadith, Sahih Muslim). Brands can reflect this value by using premium materials, ensuring meticulous craftsmanship, and delivering products that are durable and long-lasting.

Authenticity, the final dimension of the Islamic apparel brand personality model, stresses the significance of originality and uniqueness in branding. Islam values honesty and integrity in all dealings (Al-Qur'an 4:135), and brands can embody this value by creating authentic designs that are not imitations of other brands, thus establishing a genuine and trustworthy brand identity. By integrating these dimensions into their brand identity, companies can create an Islam-compliant brand that resonates with Muslim consumers, meets their religious and cultural needs, and fosters a sense of connection and authenticity within the Muslim community.

2.3.4 Islamic Brand Identity: Exemplary Cases

Islamic brands that successfully integrate the dimensions of the Islamic apparel brand personality model into their brand identity have effectively resonated with Muslim consumers while meeting their religious and cultural needs. Brands such as Hijab House, Aab, Haute Hijab, Mimpi, and Mahira have each emphasized different aspects like modesty, purity, quality, authenticity, comfort, and uniqueness to appeal to their target audience (Garg & Joshi, 2018).

By strategically employing high-quality materials, distinctive designs, comfortable fabrics, and modest clothing options, these brands align with Islamic principles governing permissibility in various industries, including fashion (Karoui & Khemakhem, 2019). Their emphasis on authenticity, comfort, and modesty has not only catered to the religious and cultural preferences of Muslim consumers but also distinguished them in the market (Alserhan, 2010a).

The integration of Islamic values and principles into branding is vital for establishing a strong connection with the target audience. Through ensuring that their products adhere to Islamic guidelines and values, these brands foster trust and loyalty among Muslim consumers (Alharbi et al., 2021). Furthermore, their focus on purity, modesty, and authenticity in their offerings enhances their positioning in the market (Ismail et al., 2022).

The Islamic apparel brand personality model serves as a framework for these brands to evaluate and enhance their brand personality, enabling them to differentiate themselves effectively and appeal to their target market (Kaur et al., 2021). Recognizing the importance of Shariah compliance and Halal concepts in developing Islamic brands, these companies meet the specific requirements of Muslim consumers and establish a solid presence in the market (Aksoy & Abdulfatai, 2019).

In conclusion, by prioritizing authenticity, quality, comfort, modesty, and uniqueness, these brands create a robust brand identity that resonates with their target audience and sets them apart in the competitive market.

2.3.5 Challenges and Opportunities in Islamic Branding

Islamic branding presents both challenges and opportunities for businesses operating in this realm. One of the key challenges faced by businesses is navigating the complex landscape of emotions and halal requirements associated with Islamic branding (Wilson & Liu, 2011). Ensuring that products or services meet the expectations of Muslim consumers in terms of halal compliance and cultural sensitivity can be demanding. Additionally, the need to integrate Islamic principles into branding strategies while maintaining authenticity poses a challenge (Bukhari & Isa, 2019). Businesses must also consider the role of religiosity as a moderating factor in consumer behavior towards halal products (Lada et al., 2009).

On the other hand, there are significant opportunities for businesses in the realm of Islamic brands. Islamic branding provides a unique opportunity for businesses to cater to the growing market of Muslim consumers who seek products and services aligned with their religious beliefs (Alharbi et al., 2021). By aligning with Islamic values and principles, businesses can build trust and credibility within the Muslim community, which can translate into long-term customer relationships (Al-Nashmi & Almamary, 2017). Moreover, Islamic branding has become a significant area of interest for businesses globally, providing a lucrative market segment to explore (Wilson & Liu, 2011). The distinction between Islamic branding and Islamic marketing has become more pronounced due to increasing attention from academia and businesses (Ambarwati, 2023). Developing a well-defined Islamic branding strategy that resonates with the target audience can result in a competitive advantage and increased market share (Singkheeprapha et al., 2021).

Furthermore, businesses can leverage Islamic branding to appeal to a broader audience beyond Muslim consumers. Research indicates that non-Muslim residents in countries like Thailand also show interest in Islamic brands that adhere to Sharia principles (Sukhabot & Jumani, 2021). This indicates that Islamic branding has the potential to transcend cultural and religious boundaries, providing businesses with the opportunity to reach diverse consumer segments. Moreover, the concept of Islamic branding as a form of good deed can enhance a business's reputation and performance, showcasing ethical business practices (Alserhan, 2010b; Alharbi et al., 2021).

In conclusion, while there are challenges in meeting the expectations of Muslim consumers and ensuring halal compliance, businesses in the realm of Islamic brands have the opportunity to build strong relationships with consumers, tap into a growing market segment, and differentiate themselves through ethical and culturally sensitive branding strategies.

2.4 Conclusion

Islamic branding transcends mere marketing strategy; it embodies a profound connection to religious principles, cultural values, and consumer beliefs. Throughout this exploration, we have delved into the essence of Islamic branding, its classifications, dimensions, challenges, and opportunities.

At its core, Islamic branding entails aligning products and services with Islamic principles while authentically resonating with Muslim consumers. This requires not only ensuring compliance with Shariah guidelines but also cultivating a brand personality characterized by trustworthiness, authenticity, and adherence to Islamic values. By understanding the cultural nuances and religious sensitivities of the Muslim market, brands can establish a deeper connection with consumers, fostering loyalty and trust.

The classification of Islamic brands offers valuable insights for marketers, guiding them in tailoring strategies to meet the specific needs and preferences of Muslim consumers. By categorizing Islamic brands based on factors such as origin, target audience, and adherence to Islamic principles, marketers can navigate the complexities of the Islamic market more effectively.

Moreover, the dimensions of Islamic branding, ranging from cultural and religious creolization factors to emotional aspects and spiritual brand attributes, contribute to shaping brand identity and positioning in the Muslim market. By integrating these dimensions effectively, brands can establish themselves as authentic, trustworthy, and appealing to Muslim consumers, thereby enhancing their brand equity and market presence.

However, Islamic branding also poses challenges, including navigating emotions, ensuring halal compliance, and addressing awareness gaps, particularly in Western countries. Yet, these challenges are accompanied by significant opportunities for cultural exchange, value creation, and market growth, both within Islamic societies and beyond.

In navigating the complexities of Islamic branding, businesses must remain sensitive to religious principles, consumer perceptions, and market dynamics. By embracing these challenges and leveraging the opportunities inherent in Islamic branding, businesses can forge strong connections with diverse consumer segments while upholding Islamic principles, thereby maximizing value and fostering long-term success in the Islamic market.

References

Ahmed, M., Ali, S., Jan, M., & Hassan, A. (2019). Development of Islamic banks' brand personality (IBBP) model: A conceptual study in Malaysia. *Journal of Islamic Marketing, 11*(3), 621–642. https://doi.org/10.1108/jima-11-2018-0210

Aji, H., & Muslichah, I. (2022). Is halal universal? The impact of self-expressive value on halal brand personality, brand tribalism, and loyalty: Case of Islamic hospitals. *Journal of Islamic Marketing, 14*(4), 1146–1165. https://doi.org/10.1108/jima-10-2021-0327

Aksoy, H., & Abdulfatai, O. (2019). Exploring the impact of religiousness and culture on luxury fashion goods purchasing intention. *Journal of Islamic Marketing, 10*(3), 768–789. https://doi.org/10.1108/jima-01-2018-0022

Alharbi, R., Yahya, S., & Kassim, S. (2021). Impact of religiosity and branding on SMEs performance: Does financial literacy play a role? *Journal of Islamic Marketing, 13*(12), 2717–2741. https://doi.org/10.1108/jima-08-2019-0162

Al-Kwifi, O., Farha, A., & Ahmed, Z. (2019). Dynamics of Muslim consumers' behavior toward halal products. *International Journal of Emerging Markets, 14*(4), 689–708. https://doi.org/10.1108/ijoem-11-2017-0486

Al-Nashmi, M., & Almamary, A. (2017). The relationship between Islamic marketing ethics and brand credibility. *Journal of Islamic Marketing, 8*(2), 261–288. https://doi.org/10.1108/jima-03-2015-0024

Alserhan, B. A. (2010a). Islamic branding: A conceptualization of related terms. *Journal of Brand Management, 18*, 34–49. https://doi.org/10.1057/bm.2010.18

Alserhan, B. A. (2010b). On Islamic branding: Brands as good deeds. *Journal of Islamic Marketing, 1*(2), 101–106. https://doi.org/10.1108/17590831011055842

Alserhan, B. A., Althawadi, O., & Wood, B. P. (2016). Theories of Islamic marketing. *International Journal of Islamic Marketing and Branding, 1*(4), 297. https://doi.org/10.1504/ijimb.2016.081322

Ambarwati, R. (2023). Experiential marketing and Islamic branding: A new perspective on college decision in Islamic higher education. *Journal of Islamic Marketing, 15*(3), 745–776. https://doi.org/10.1108/jima-08-2022-0207

Aruan, D., & Wirdania, I. (2020). You are what you wear: Examining the multidimensionality of religiosity and its influence on attitudes and intention to buy Muslim fashion clothing. *Journal of Fashion Marketing and Management, 24*(1), 121–136. https://doi.org/10.1108/jfmm-04-2019-0069

Azam, A. (2016). An empirical study on non-Muslim's packaged halal food manufacturers. *Journal of Islamic Marketing, 7*(4), 441–460. https://doi.org/10.1108/jima-12-2014-0084

Boubekeur, A. (2016). Islamic business and Muslim entrepreneurs networks in Europe: Performing transnational modernity and overcoming marginalization. *Contemporary Islam, 10*(3), 421–432. https://doi.org/10.1007/s11562-016-0358-2

Bukhari, S., & Isa, S. (2019). Islamic branding: Insights from a conceptual perspective. *Journal of Islamic Marketing, 11*(6), 1743–1760. https://doi.org/10.1108/jima-02-2018-0035

Eid, R., & El-Gohary, H. (2015). The role of Islamic religiosity on the relationship between perceived value and tourist satisfaction. *Tourism Management, 46*, 477–488. https://doi.org/10.1016/j.tourman.2014.08.003

Elseidi, R. (2018). Determinants of halal purchasing intentions: Evidences from UK. *Journal of Islamic Marketing, 9*(1), 167–190. https://doi.org/10.1108/jima-02-2016-0013

Garg, P., & Joshi, R. (2018). Purchase intention of "halal" brands in India: The mediating effect of attitude. *Journal of Islamic Marketing, 9*(3), 683–694. https://doi.org/10.1108/jima-11-2017-0125

Hamid, S., Jusoh, W., & Maulan, S. (2019). Measuring the spiritual brand attribute of Islamic banks. *Journal of Business Management and Accounting, 9*(2), 51–70. https://doi.org/10.32890/jbma2019.9.2.4

Harun, M., Bakry, N., Rahman, K., Amos, F., & Johari, M. (2023). Semiotic and cultural analysis on local product brand name. *International Journal of Academic Research in Business and Social Sciences, 13*(1). https://doi.org/10.6007/ijarbss/v13-i1/15884

Hassan, S., & Ara, H. (2021). Thematic analysis of hijab fashion from Muslim clothing retailers perspective. *Journal of Islamic Marketing, 13*(11), 2462–2479. https://doi.org/10.1108/jima-03-2020-0066

Hati, S., Putri, N., Daryanti, S., Wibowo, S., Safira, A., & Setyowardhani, H. (2021). Brand familiarity vs profit-sharing rate: Which has a stronger impact on Muslim customers' intention to invest in an Islamic bank? *Journal of Islamic Marketing, 13*(8), 1703–1727. https://doi.org/10.1108/jima-08-2020-0247

Ismail, M., Harun, T., Ismail, S., Aziz, A., & Ibrahim, M. (2022). Definition of Islamic brand: A study from Islamic conjunction and its findings. *International Journal of Academic Research in Business and Social Sciences, 12*(8). https://doi.org/10.6007/ijarbss/v12-i8/14731

Jamal, A., & Sharifuddin, J. (2015). Perceived value and perceived usefulness of halal labeling: The role of religion and culture. *Journal of Business Research, 68*(5), 933–941. https://doi.org/10.1016/j.jbusres.2014.09.020

Jumani, Z., & Muhamad, N. (2022). Development and validation of key antecedents of religious brand attitude: A cross-cultural quantitative analysis using Smart PLS. *Journal of Islamic Marketing, 14*(11), 2771–2797. https://doi.org/10.1108/jima-06-2022-0177

Jumani, Z., & Sukhabot, S. (2020). Identifying the important attitude of Islamic brands and its effect on buying behavioural intentions among Malaysian Muslims. *Journal of Islamic Marketing, 12*(2), 408–426. https://doi.org/10.1108/jima-09-2019-0196

Junaidi, J., Wicaksono, R., & Hamka, H. (2021). The consumers' commitment and materialism on Islamic banking: The role of religiosity. *Journal of Islamic Marketing, 13*(8), 1786–1806. https://doi.org/10.1108/jima-12-2020-0378

Karoui, S., & Khemakhem, R. (2019). Factors affecting the Islamic purchasing behavior – A qualitative study. *Journal of Islamic Marketing, 10*(4), 1104–1127. https://doi.org/10.1108/jima-12-2017-0145

Kaur, N., Wahab, N., & Zulkifli, N. (2021). Designing, developing and evaluating a sustainable Shariah-compliant e-commerce fashion prototype. *International Journal of Business and Society, 22*(3), 1211–1225. https://doi.org/10.33736/ijbs.4296.2021

Lada, S., Tanakinjal, G., & Amin, H. (2009). Predicting intention to choose halal products using theory of reasoned action. *International Journal of Islamic and Middle Eastern Finance and Management, 2*(1), 66–76. https://doi.org/10.1108/17538390910946276

Mirvaisi, M., & Kaffashpoor, A. (2023). Culture and religion creolisation impact on digital advertisement of Muslim users of Instagram. *HTS Teologiese Studies / Theological Studies, 79*(3). https://doi.org/10.4102/hts.v79i1.8054

Mongeon, P., & Paul-Hus, A. (2015). The journal coverage of Web of Science and Scopus: A comparative analysis. *Scientometrics, 106*(1), 213–228. https://doi.org/10.1007/s11192-015-1765-5.

Musa, A., Baharuddin, F., Noh, S., Idris, A., & Selamat, S. (2022). Islamic marketing, electronic word of mouth (eWOM) and religious awareness roles in consuming halal food: A conceptual paper. *International Journal of Academic Research in Business and Social Sciences, 12*(12). https://doi.org/10.6007/ijarbss/v12-i12/16038

O'Cass, A., Lee, W., & Siahtiri, V. (2013). Can Islam and status consumption live together in the house of fashion clothing? *Journal of Fashion Marketing and Management, 17*(4), 440–459. https://doi.org/10.1108/jfmm-03-2013-0023

Razzaque, M., & Chaudhry, S. (2013). Religiosity and Muslim consumers' decision-making process in a non-Muslim society. *Journal of Islamic Marketing, 4*(2), 198–217. https://doi.org/10.1108/17590831311329313

Singkheeprapha, P., Jumani, Z., & Sukhabot, S. (2021). Is Islamic brand attitudes influence Thai Muslims' buying behavioral intentions: A quantitative analysis using Smart-PLS. *Journal of Islamic Marketing, 13*(11), 2403–2420. https://doi.org/10.1108/jima-08-2020-0252

Sukhabot, S., & Jumani, Z. (2021). Islamic brands attitudes and its consumption behavior among non-Muslim residents of Thailand. *Journal of Islamic Marketing, 14*(1), 196–214. https://doi.org/10.1108/jima-05-2021-0155

Temporal, P. (2011). Islamic branding and marketing: Creating a global Islamic business. John Wiley & Sons.

Wahyuni, S., & Fitriani, N. (2017). Brand religiosity aura and brand loyalty in Indonesia Islamic banking. *Journal of Islamic Marketing, 8*(3), 361–372. https://doi.org/10.1108/jima-06-2015-0044

Wilkins, S., Butt, M., Shams, F., & Pérez, A. (2019). The acceptance of halal food in non-Muslim countries. *Journal of Islamic Marketing, 10*(4), 1308–1331. https://doi.org/10.1108/jima-11-2017-0132

Wilson, J., & Liu, J. (2010). Shaping the halal into a brand? *Journal of Islamic Marketing, 1*(2), 107–123. https://doi.org/10.1108/17590831011055851

Wilson, J., & Liu, J. (2011). The challenges of Islamic branding: Navigating emotions and halal. *Journal of Islamic Marketing, 2*(1), 28–42. https://doi.org/10.1108/17590831111115222

Zainudin, M., Hasan, F. H., & Othman, A. K. (2019). Halal brand personality and brand loyalty among millennial modest fashion consumers in Malaysia. *Journal of Islamic Marketing, 11*(6), 1277–1293. https://doi.org/10.1108/jima-10-2018-0187

Zaki, R., Din, A., & Elseidi, R. (2021). Islamic apparel brand personality model. *Journal of Islamic Marketing, 14*(2), 484–503. https://doi.org/10.1108/jima-07-2020-0203

Zakiyah, Joko Tri Haryanto, Agus Iswanto, and Koeswinarno

Chapter 3
Halal Café: Religious Identity and the Lifestyle of the Young Generation

Abstract: "Café culture" is a rising phenomenon among the young generation, especially of the Y and Z ages category. Those young age groups are going to café not only to "drink coffee" but also to hang out with their friends as it is the fact that café now not only play as a place for consuming coffee but a place for social interaction, even as a place to work for certain people. Furthermore, those young people are mostly Muslims, therefore halal and haram doctrine about food and beverages become a concern and identity for them. This research was conducted in Yogyakarta Indonesia, where many cafés are growing rapidly. The data were collected through interviews, observations, and by distributing online questionnaires to Young Muslim generations. This article describes the trend of cafés in the city, the relationship between café culture and the lifestyle of young people, the awareness of young people about halal cafés, and the relationship between religious identity and café culture. The findings of this study show that the café provides "space" for this young generation, like connectedness and its communal nature. The café in Yogyakarta can be categorized into two classifications based on the price and consumers; *firstly*, according to the price, the café can be divided into premium, middle, and non-premium café. Secondly, café based on the consumers consist of two types; community café that is usually related to certain groups or organizations like Teras Dakwah café, and café that were initially founded by a closed community and then developed for the wider consumers such as *Silol* café and *Basa-basi* café. This study also found that the teaching of halal can be an identity of youth that unites them amid various other religious identities. Furthermore, consumers are also aware of the halal status of the product sold by a café, as they will ensure whether a café is halal or not.

Keywords: Café Halal, religious identity, youth generation, Yogyakarta

3.1 Introduction

The Indonesian young Muslim generation has been recognized to be increasingly "religious" in the recent era. They are connected to digital technology and enjoy their free time or holidays by having fun and visiting tourist destinations. The first indication regarding the increasing religiousness of this group is the increasing number of waves of "hijrah" committed by young people, the growing development of religious study groups initiated by young *ustadz* (Muslim clerics), and target participants also from among young people. For example, recitations led by *ustadz* Hanan Attaki, *Ustadz* Adi

https://doi.org/10.1515/9783111575407-004

Hidayat, and *Ustadz* Salim A Fillah (Sulistiyawan, 2020). These three names are well-known *ustadz* who are most liked by millennials and the youth age groups. According to the IDN Research Institute (2019), the millennial group is divided into two categories: junior millennials, born between 1991–1998, and senior millennials, born between 1983–1990. According to Bappenas, as quoted by the IDN Research Institute (2019), there are 63 million millennials, and it is estimated that this group of people will become the majority of the population in Indonesia, and will be the determining group in 2020–2035 when the demographic bonus occurs (IDN Research Institute, 2019).

The wave of *hijrah* (emigration) among youth has also demanded a "halal thing", such as halal products, whether food, drink, or other products such as fashion, banking, medicines, and cosmetics. Even, the halal industry has increasingly become a trend in several countries, including Indonesia, in recent years. The annual report issued by Mastercard Crescent Rating (2018) states that halal food and drinks are an important aspect for millennial generation travelers. Besides main facilities such as halal lodging/hotels, it is important to provide facilities for praying and ablution, Ramadan services, recreational and privacy services (Mastercard Crescent Rating, 2018). Besides, young people in several big cities in Indonesia show a penchant for socializing and interacting with friends as well as hanging out in restaurants or cafes. This is in line with the proliferation of several cafes in big cities in this country. For instance, in 2016 coffee shops in Indonesia reached more than 10,000 outlets, and it is predicted that this business will continue to grow in the coming years. The revenue from this business between 2013–2018 is estimated to increase from 3.4 billion US dollars to 4.16 billion US dollars (Merdeka.com, 2016).

The growth of cafes in Indonesia is predicted to continually increase, as stated by James Boy, the General Manager of Reed Panorama Exhibition. In addition, Indonesia will be the largest market for the cafe business because this country has a large population and at the same time the middle-class communities continue to grow with their increasing incomes too. Thus, it will encourage the consumption of coffee or tea in cafes (Merdeka.com, 2016). Apart from that, Indonesia is also a coffee-producing country with various varieties originating from numerous regions, among which the famous ones are Gayo coffee, Sidikalang coffee, Besemah coffee, Aceh coffee, coffee from Lampung, Toraja, and Java (Basoni, 2018; A. Hidayatullah & Monicasef, 2019). In 2017, the Central Statistics Agency released statistical data mentioning that the area of coffee plantations throughout Indonesia reached 1,251,703 hectares consisting of smallholder plantations, large plantations, and large state plantations spread across various provinces (BPS, 2018). Among the provinces that produce large amounts of coffee, South Sumatra produces 120,904 tons of coffee, and Lampung produces 115,524 tons of coffee (BPS, 2018).

Enjoying coffee now is no longer just about brewing coffee using a simple method such as pouring instant coffee or ground coffee with hot water, but has shifted from just drinking at home to a traditional coffee shop or a modern coffee shop known as a cafe like Starbucks, Coffee Bean and Tea Leaf, Excellso and startup coffee shops like Foree Coffee, Kedai Kopi Tuku, and Kopi Kenangan (KumparanFOOD, 2018; Zuhriyah, 2019).

Furthermore, visiting this cafe has become part of a "trend and lifestyle" for several groups, including youths, who go to this place not only to enjoy the drinks but also the atmosphere. In addition, it is known that some people go to cafes not only to drink or eat but also to meet colleagues and work (KumparanFOOD, 2018).

The young generation has great potential to become cafe consumers. This youth category amounts to 63.82 million people or the equivalent of a quarter of the total population of Indonesia (A. Hidayatullah & Monicasef, 2019). IDN Research Institute (2019) mentioned that the millennial group uses their income for entertainment amounting to 8% of their total income. The entertainment here includes eating at restaurants, going to the cinema, buying entertainment tickets, and clubbing (IDN Research Institute, 2019). The large number of millennials and how they use their income can indicate that the potential trend for coffee consumption among the younger generation will also be large. Apart from that, data released by the International Coffee Organization (ICO) in 2015 shows that the growth of coffee drinkers in Indonesia was 8%, this figure is greater than the growth of coffee drinkers in the world which is at 6% (A. Hidayatullah & Monicasef, 2019). The International Coffee Organization (ICO) released data that depicted in 2015, that the growth of coffee drinkers in Indonesia was 8%, this figure is greater than the growth of coffee drinkers in the world which is at 6% (A. Hidayatullah & Monicasef, 2019). Hence, this business will continue to progress and develop.

The large potential number of young consumers demands the provision of complementary cafe facilities that suit the needs of young people, such as a comfortable place for meetings, an Instagrammable place, fast WiFi connection facilities, and a good atmosphere for hanging out with friends. In addition, cafes should pay attention to the provision of halal food and beverage products. This is because the majority of youth in this country are Muslims, and the need for halal food and beverage products for Muslim consumers is part of their religion. A study conducted by Khalek states that food is an important aspect for devout religious followers, and the choice of food and beverage products for religious consumers will be greatly influenced by their religious teachings (Khalek, 2014, 2015). Similarly, Syed Ismail and Ibrahim (2015) mentioned that consumer attitudes and behavior are generally influenced by their religion. Religion is an important factor when deciding to buy food and developing the food habits of a person and society (Khalek et al., 2015). In Islam, the rules for eating halal products are stated in the Qur'an and hadiths. For instance, verse Al Maidah 87–88 mentions about halal food.

The consumption of halal food and drinks is an important part of Islamic teachings and plays a significant role in the religious identity of young Muslims. Choosing halal food products is also considered a way of life for them. According to a study conducted by Chester in 2017, religion is a cultural dimension that shapes group identity through religious practices, including food practices like selecting halal food for Muslims (Chester, 2017). Therefore, cafe managers who provide halal food and drinks should refer to existing regulations, such as Law Number 33 of 2014 concerning Halal Product Guarantees (UU-JPH Number 33/2014). Article 4 of UU-JPH Number 33/2014 states that products entering, circulating, and being traded in Indonesian territory must be certified as halal.

The issue of the halal café and its relationship with the young Muslim lifestyle has not been discussed by previous scholars. Therefore, this article will then discuss these aspects; the trend of cafés in the city, the relationship between café culture and the lifestyle of young people, the awareness of young people about halal cafés, and the relationship between religious identity and café culture. On the other hand, the existing studies concerned much on other elements, for example, the Islamic law on halal products and Islamic teaching on halal consumption (Ali, 2016; Nashirudin, 2016; Qardhawi, 1993; Salahudin et al., 2017).

The next study is more related to the empirical practices of production and consumption of halal foods. Some of those studies were conducted in the context of Indonesia (Astogini et al., 2011; Karim, 2013; Nasution & Rossanty, 2016; Sutrisno, 2010; Vristiyana, 2019), Southeast Asia (Fischer, 2016; Mohamad et al., 2015; Nik Muhammad et al., 2009; Noordin et al., 2009; Othman et al., 2016), as well as the world (Kurth & Glasbergen, 2017; Lever & Miele, 2012; Yakin, 2016). Furthermore, there have been several studies on the policy and regulation of halal foods in Indonesia (Afroniyati, 2014; Faidah, 2017; Hosen, 2012). These policy studies focus more on the political-economic analysis of halal guarantees and certification.

Research related to religious identity and halal products is usually related to the context of Muslims living in a non-Muslim "majority" environment. For example, studies on Muslim identity related to halal products in the Netherlands (Kurth & Glasbergen, 2017), and in Japan (Yakin, 2016). Another study analyzed the variables of halal products, pop culture, and identity negotiation, such as in the study of halal issues in Korean culinary delights which have become popular culture in Indonesia (Nadhifah et al., 2019). This study mentioned that Korean food became famous in Indonesia after the K-Pop wave was widely consumed in Indonesia. Facing the fact that the majority of Indonesians are Muslims, Korean culinary entrepreneurs have begun to modify Korean food ingredients to halal standards, which are then promoted through various types of media, including social media platforms such as Instagram, and Vlog. Moreover, this study described that they articulate their ideology as a cosmopolitan Muslim.

The previous research on Korean cuisine encourages further studies on how young people are aware of and practice a "halal lifestyle" in their daily lives and its relationship with their identity. The study can asses of young people's awareness of halal products (Khalek, 2014, 2015), because these young people are entering a different era and need other measures to practice a halal lifestyle. Studies on halal issues among young people can be done on other units of analysis, for instance, foreign food franchise outlets (Hartahati & Rahmawaty, 2016).

It is important to study the current phenomena of the "café lifestyle" which is popular among millennials and Z young people. In addition, how young people embrace a halal lifestyle and its relations with their identity needs to be examined. This is because young people will become a large "market" for halal products. Therefore, the article will explore this theme that differs from the previous research. This study will look more deeply at these aspects; it focuses on young people as a large potential market for halal products which is rarely seen by previous studies. The next concerns the consumption lifestyle that is popular among young people, which still receives little attention in studies of halal products and lifestyles in Indonesia. Furthermore, it will analyze the issue of halal products, young people, and their religious identities.

3.1.1 Religious Identity

Everyone has an identity, even multiple identities. This identity acts as a differentiator between a person and other people, but also as a follower of other people so that they become one group that will ultimately differentiate themselves from other groups. Therefore, some identities are personal, and some identities are social. This personal identity differentiates one person from another because of the uniqueness they have, such as physical characteristics, talents, and achievements. Meanwhile, social identity is more complex than that, because it becomes differentiation due to social groupings, whether because of race, ethnicity, religion, or profession (Mushodiq, 2017).

Religious identity is a clear differentiation of one's beliefs, faith, and religious practices, setting them apart from others. It is a powerful way of demonstrating one's belonging to a specific religious community, through the use of symbolic expressions. In Islam, for instance, identity can be seen from the use of Arabic words, written symbols in the Arabic script, Muslim clothing, and particular behaviors that align with the Sharia law. For Muslims, these symbols are essential to confirm their identity and show their commitment to the faith.

Strengthening one's identity is closely tied to the impact of communication technology. In the digital era, the use of increasingly sophisticated modes of communication has led to the widespread dissemination of information across society. McLuhan posits that this has facilitated social change, including the rapid and massive transformation of social identities (S. Hidayatullah et al., 2018). Consequently, the "syariah" way of life has been transformed into a new lifestyle known as the "syar'i" lifestyle. This lifestyle is characterized by the enhancement of physical identity that promotes "Islamic" symbols. Additionally, the consumption patterns of this lifestyle are also marked by a "halal" model.

Halal products are a significant aspect of Islamic identity as Muslims are obligated to consume only halal food and drinks. This concept is based on religious teachings originating from the Koran and Al-Hadith. The word "Halal" means things that are permissible and can be done because they are free or not bound by provisions that prohibit them (*haram*). Following these provisions will protect Muslims from harm in this world and the hereafter (Darojatun, 2018). Therefore, Muslims must be aware of these halal-haram provisions. However, many Muslims are unaware of whether what they consume is halal or contains prohibited elements. For this reason, halal guarantee institutions such as the MUI (Majlis Ulama Indonesia/ Indonesian Ulama Council) play a vital role in ensuring that Muslim consumers are protected (Syafrida, 2016).

The young generation of Muslims has a strong inclination towards everything that is perceived as "Islamic" or "syar'i". As a result, Muslim awareness regarding "Islamic" products and services has been increasing, as they are considered safer, halal, and free from usury. These products have become part of their lifestyle and are even viewed as a necessity (Darojatun, 2018). However, this group of young Muslims is still drawn towards the millennial lifestyle, which has been shaped by technological and social advancements. Social spaces such as cafes have become a characteristic of this lifestyle that young people find irresistible. Despite this, young Muslims also place great importance on their Islamic identity. This identity is not just a symbolic attribute but is also viewed as a form of obedience to Islamic principles. This can be seen from the increasing number of cafes that promote themselves as halal cafes.

3.2 Research Method

This article was written based on research that used mixed methods, namely; qualitative, and quantitative approaches. In this sense, qualitative research is a method used to gather descriptive data, which involves producing systematic, factual, and accurate descriptions of observed phenomena. The research was conducted in Yogyakarta Indonesia, a popular destination city for young people. This city is known for its dynamic youth culture and the development of cafes, making it a pioneer and model reference. To gather data for this research, field research was conducted through observations made in the city.

Field data collection was conducted between February and March 2020, using observational and interview techniques to gather information from relevant parties. Observations were made to gain direct insight into phenomena, trends, cafe development models, and the behavior of both customers and cafe owners. Interviews were conducted to explore the experiences and perspectives of both cafe business owners and young customers, with regards to their awareness of halal products.

The quantitative method was used to gather data regarding the perception of cafe business owners, young groups of cafe customers, as well as their awareness of halal products. To collect the data, researchers distributed questionnaires to the café consumers using Google Forms. A sample of this data was selected using a convenience purposive sampling method, and 257 people participated in completing the Google Form. All the collected data were analyzed using quantitative descriptive analysis.

3.3 Social and Religious Conditions in Yogyakarta

The people of Yogyakarta are a part of the Javanese cultural area, and Yogyakarta is considered the center of Javanese culture along with the city of Surakarta. This is because both cities are the continuation of the Islamic kingdoms of Demak and Mataram. In Surakarta, there is the Surakarta Kasunanan, while in Yogyakarta, there is the Ngayogyakarta Hadiningrat Sultanate. Yogyakarta is privileged due to its history of struggle, as Sri Sultan is the king or sultan in Yogyakarta and also the head of the Yogyakarta Special Region government at the governor level. Javanese culture's historical, cultural, and living traditions are not only preserved but also invite Yogyakarta Special Region to become a cultural tourism destination for tourists both from within and outside the country.

The Yogyakarta Special Region is made up of four districts and one city: Kulonprogo Regency, Bantul Regency, Gunungkidul Regency, Sleman Regency, and Yogyakarta City. According to BPS projections for DI Yogyakarta Province (2020), the population of DI Yogyakarta is 3,842,932 people, consisting of 1,901,735 men and 1,941,197 women. Yogyakarta City has the highest population density, with 13,290 residents per kilometer (BPS DIY, 2020).

Based on the statistics data, the religious adherents in Yogyakarta can be seen in the following Table 3.1;

Table 3.1: The Number of Religious Adherents in Yogyakarta Province in 2019.

District/Town	Islam	Christian	Catholics	Hindu	Buddha	Confucian
1. Kulon Progo	447,007	5,852	18,280	18	636	-
2. Bantul	945,441	12,365	13,583	2,618	200	4
3. Gunungkidul	738,325	13,067	10,988	5,428	403	4
4. Sleman	961,383	31,481	69,414	5,334	696	62
5. Yogyakarta	343,824	26,255	38,731	2,240	1,412	25
DI Yogyakarta	3,435,980	89,020	150,996	15,638	3,347	95

Source: (BPS DIY, 2020).

The data in Table 3.1 reveals that the majority of the population in Yogyakarta follows Islam. This has an impact on their daily traditions and lifestyle, particularly in terms of what they consume. Islam has certain guidelines about halal consumption that Muslims need to adhere to, which also leads to a higher demand for halal products in the area.

Yogyakarta is commonly referred to as a student city due to the large number of educational institutions, particularly at the tertiary level. The presence of numerous universities, course institutions, and other educational institutions in Yogyakarta attracts many pupils and students from various regions in Indonesia. Tables 3.2 and 3.3 are some data highlighting the number of universities and students in Yogyakarta.

Table 3.2: Number of State and Private Universities in Yogyakarta in 2019.

No	District / Town	State University	Private University	Numbers
1.	Kulon Progo	–	1	1
2.	Bantul	1	24	25
3.	Gunungkidul	–	1	1
4.	Sleman	3	32	35
5.	Yogyakarta	–	48	48
	DI Yogyakarta	**4**	**106**	**110**

Source: (BPS DIY, 2020).

Table 3.3: Number of Students at Satet and Private University in Yogyakarta in 2019.

No	District / Town	Students of State University	Students of Private University	Numbers
1.	Kulon Progo	–	597	597
2.	Bantul	5,555	69,370	74,925
3.	Gunungkidul	–	956	956
4.	Sleman	94,268	111,025	205,293
5.	Yogyakarta	–	86,295	86,295
	DI Yogyakarta	**99,823**	**268,243**	**368,066**

Source: BPS DI Yogyakarta, 2020.

According to the data presented in Tables 3.2 and 3.3, young millennials constitute a significant proportion of students in Yogyakarta's tertiary institutions. The majority of these students are concentrated in the buffer districts of Yogyakarta City, such as Sleman Regency and Bantul Regency. This concentration of young millennials is one of the key factors contributing to the growth and development of cafes in these two regions, as compared to Kulon Progo and Gunungkidul districts.

Several campus areas in Yogyakarta are mostly populated by students. The largest public campus in Yogyakarta and one of the leading ones in Indonesia is Gajah Mada University (UGM), which is located in one of these areas. UIN Sunan Kalijaga is also a large and prominent religious (Islamic) campus located in this area. Additionally, there are other campuses including Yogyakarta State University (UNY), Indonesian Islamic University (UII), Muhammadiyah University Yogyakarta (UMY), Duta Wacana Christian University (UKDW), Atma Jaya University, and Sanata Dharma University. In addition, there are other tertiary institutions in the form of institutes and polytechnics in Yogyakarta.

The majority of UGM's students are living in the Depok area of Sleman Regency, particularly along the route leading to Kaliurang. Similarly, UII also has a significant student base in the same area. As a result, cafes around West Sleman are rapidly developing to cater to the economic status of students from UGM and UII, who tend to belong to a more affluent class. On the other hand, UIN's student base is situated in the southeastern part of Sleman Regency, bordering Bantul. In this region, students are more economically challenged, and cafes that cater to the more economical "Blandongan" class are thriving.

3.4 The Development of Cafes in Yogyakarta: Trends and Typology

The rise of coffee shops in Yogyakarta is closely linked to the growth of the coffee industry in Indonesia. The coffee industry in Indonesia is divided into four waves, which corresponds with the entry of international coffee brands into the country. Some of these brands include Dunkin, Exelso, Coffee Bean, Starbucks, J.C.O Donuts & Coffee, Coffee Toffee, First Crack, Tanamera, Tuku, Kopi Kenangan, and Janji Jiwa. However, these international coffee shops have not been able to dominate the local markets in each region of Indonesia, including Yogyakarta. Instead, local coffee shops that sell ready-to-drink (RTD) coffee are the ones that dominate the local market in Yogyakarta (Toffin & Majalah MIX, 2019).

In the 1980s, the first wave of coffee shops began to appear in Indonesia. These shops still faced competition from traditional coffee shops that served ready-to-drink coffee. However, some modern coffee shops like Dunkin (1985), Olala (1990), and Excelso (1991) also opened up. Although Dunkin' is better known for selling donuts, Olala and Excelso were two coffee shops that gained popularity during this time. During this period, people mostly drank coffee prepared from instant coffee sachets produced by four national brands namely Kapal Api (1927), ABC Coffee (1985), Nescafe (1971), and Torabika (1977).

The second wave of the coffee industry began in 2001, which was the start of the third millennium. During this wave, coffee consumption evolved from being a functional need to an emotional need. This means that people started to drink coffee not just for its caffeine content, but also for the pleasure of drinking it. People began to associate drinking coffee at certain coffee shops, like Starbucks or Coffee Bean, with a sense of prestige. This second wave was led by many international brands, such as Coffee Bean in 2001 and Starbucks in 2002. This wave also saw the emergence of coffee shop trademarks from Chinese descendants, such as Kopi Tiam. At this time, local coffee shops were not yet visible, although they were starting to appear in several areas.

The third wave of the coffee industry in Indonesia started in 2013. During this wave, people began to realize the immense size of the coffee market in the country. Other industrial outlets like McDonald's with McCafé shops and Lippo Group with Maxx Coffee joined the coffee business. Local coffee shops also started to emerge during this wave. Nowadays, coffee shops are not just places to drink coffee but have become popular hangouts as well.

The market for coffee shops has been expanding since 2016 and is now entering its fourth wave. This new era is characterized by the emergence of many new brands, each with its unique presentation and taste. At the same time, a growing number of coffee lovers are beginning to emerge. Some popular coffee shops that have emerged during this wave include Janji Jiwa Café and Kopi Kenangan Café, which have become favorites among young people. At the local level, many coffee shops have also appeared, catering to people's needs as a place to socialize, work, or conduct business. This fourth wave is also marked by innovation in coffee flavor variants that are mixed with milk, as well as new and easier purchasing methods. Additionally, marketing strategies that rely on the Internet have become increasingly prevalent. Coffee shops are also starting to redesign their spaces to be more appealing to younger generations, particularly high school and college students.

Throughout these four waves, at least seven types of coffee shops have developed (Toffin & Majalah MIX, 2019). Firstly, there are American coffee shop chains, like Starbucks, Coffee Bean, McCafe, and Costa Caffe. Secondly, there are Italian coffee shop chains, such as Sagafredo and Illy Coffee. Thirdly, there is a network of local coffee shops that have permanent locations, like Upnormal, and regional coffee shops such as Legend Café in Yogyakarta. Fourthly, there are coffee shops that have limited and larger spaces that provide takeaway services, like Janji Jiwa and Kopi Kenangan. Fifthly, the "premium" coffee shops that offer high-quality coffee, such as Tanamera, Ombe, and Common Ground coffee shops. Sixthly, the independent coffee shops that only have one location, like the Klinik Coffee in Yogyakarta. Lastly, the bakery and pastry shops that also offer coffee menus, such as Dunkin' Donuts, Harvest, and Jco.

In Yogyakarta, the growth of local cafes has been consistent with the national coffee shop industry trend. Coffee shops have been on the rise since the second and third waves of coffee shop development and reached their peak during the fourth wave. According to data from the Yogyakarta Coffee Shop Association, in 2016 there were approximately 600 coffee shops. And then, in 2017, the number of coffee shops in Yogyakarta soared to around 1200 (Bernas.id, 2018; D.H, 2016).

In the year 2000, local "student class" cafes began to emerge in Yogyakarta, outside of well-known brands like Starbucks or Exelso. These cafes were referred to as "kedai kopi/coffee shops" at the time. One of the first cafes was the "belandongan" cafe, founded by Nashiruddin (also known as Badrun). It was located in the southern part of the Wahid Hasyim Islamic Boarding School in Gaten, Condong Catur, Sleman Yogyakarta (Faizi, 2018). Initially, most of the visitors were IAIN/UIN students, but over time, the cafe started attracting visitors from other campuses and even general visitors. In 2005, the cafe moved to the Sorowajan area, which is now home to around seven different cafes (Arizona, 2013). These cafes are always busy with visitors who come to enjoy the coffee and other dishes served here.

After the Blandongan cafe became successful, other cafes started to emerge, such as Nusantara Cafe, Mato, and Basabasi. With the rise of wireless internet networks, cafes started to provide WiFi or hot spot areas to attract customers. Recently, some cafe owners have transformed their cafes into event venues for activities like "watching together" of certain event, live music performances, or discussions (Faizi, 2018). Basabasi Cafe has gained popularity for hosting many discussion events and has now expanded to seven branches in the Yogyakarta area. All of the cafes are located near campuses, including Sorowajan, Kotagede, Nologaten, Kragilan, Condong Catur, Yogyakarta Muhamamdiyah University (UMY), and Akademi Pemerintahan Masyarakat Desa (APMD). The cafe's tagline is "tempat kongkow & bercerita/a place to hang out & tell stories."

Basabasi Cafe was established in 2017 by Edy Mulyono, a literacy activist and owner of a publishing house named Diva Press (Khab, 2017; Kumparan.com, 2020). Before creating Basabasi, Edy was a regular customer of Blandongan Cafe and engaged in various discussions and literacy activities with the owner. However, he felt the need to have his place for more comfort and freedom, leading to the creation of Basabasi Café" (interview with Edy Mulyanto, owner of Basabasi cafe, 8 July 2020). Due to Edy's background in publishing and writing, the cafe often organizes literacy activities and is adorned with wall decorations featuring quotes from famous writers. Additionally, the cafe boasts a collection of books that customers can read on the spot.

In addition to cafes that are part of the Basabasi group and other similar groups in the Sorowajan and campus areas, numerous cafes in Yogyakarta are popular among young people, including school students and college students. These cafes are often used as a place to meet, complete assignments, or enjoy culinary delights. Examples include Legend and Silol cafes, which are located in the heart of Yogyakarta City. While some events, such as live music performances, are held in these cafes in the evenings, they are not commonly used as venues for open discussions. Unlike the Basabasi cafes, which are frequented by visitors from specific campuses, cafes like Legend and Silol attract a more diverse crowd, including travelers to the city. In addition to larger cafes that can accommodate many visitors, there are also smaller cafes designed for coffee, snacks, and work that can accommodate only a few people.

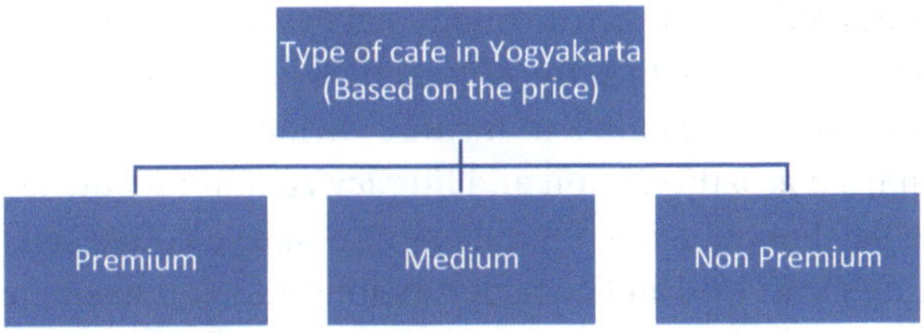

Figure 3.1: Café Typology in Yogyakarta.

Cafes in Yogyakarta can be classified into two main categories: a price and consumer-based category, and a community-based category. The former can be further divided into three subcategories: premium, medium, and non-premium. A premium cafe has high prices and tends to attract customers from the middle to upper economic classes. These types of cafes are generally well-known brands with an international presence, such as Starbucks, Excelso, and Coffee Bean. The consumers are usually young people from the middle to upper economic groups, often studying at campuses or faculties with high education costs. However, university students tend to avoid these cafes as they are usually located in shopping centers. The price of a cup of coffee at a premium cafe is typically around IDR 30,000 to 60,000.

The second type of café is known as the medium type. These cafes offer prices that are cheaper than premium cafes but not too cheap. Typically, these cafes have a local network and offer a more sophisticated ambiance with an Instagram-worthy atmosphere, enticing visitors to not only drink coffee but also enjoy the café's overall vibe. Additionally, these cafes often host live music events at night to attract more visitors. They provide free Wi-Fi, meeting rooms, and VIP rooms. The price of a cup of coffee in this type of café is typically around IDR 10,000 to 20,000. Examples of this type of café include Legend and Silol located in the center of Yogyakarta City, but there are also many other cafés with limited space that can fit into this second category.

The third type of café is usually located near campuses and attracts customers from the lower middle economic group. Examples of these cafes are Basabasi Cafe, Blandongan, and Gading café, which offers a cup of coffee for IDR 5,000 to 10,000. Despite being cheaper, the cafes still provide Wi-Fi facilities like the first and second types. Meanwhile, some of the cafes do not provide Wi-Fi, but instead provide electricity connections for customers to use their gadgets while enjoying the cafe's offerings. The owners of this type of cafe have revealed that it is popular among young people, especially school students and college students because it fits their budget.

From a community perspective, cafes can be divided into two types. The first type has a limited community and is usually opened by community activists, like the Teras Dakwah cafe. This type of cafe heavily relies on the existence and activities of the community. As long as the community exists and stays active, the cafe will continue to thrive. Prices in this type of cafe are usually medium or non-premium, and sometimes even more affordable. Additionally, such cafes usually participate in activities or events organized by the community. Meanwhile, the second type is a cafe that originates from a specific community but then expands to include various communities. For instance, the Basabasi cafe started as a discussion and literacy community owned by Edi. It began as an online media channel named Basabasi, and later a coffee shop emerged to support the community's activities and book discussions. Another example of a cafe that started as a community-based initiative is the Silol Cafe. It originated from the Harley motorbike community and developed to be a café. Moreover, the cafe also has a shop for accessories and tools related to large motorbikes (interview with F, 9 July 2020).

3.5 *Ngafe* as the Gen Z and Y Lifestyle

During the initial discussion on the development of cafes in Yogyakarta, it was noted that there are three types of cafes including premium, medium, and non-premium café. In addition, there is also a café associated with a limited community, open to everyone, and cafes that are open but cater to certain communities. From the researcher's observations, it was found that most of the café visitors were young people, particularly students. According to Toffin's research, the rise in coffee consumption in Indonesia can be partially attributed to the high consumption of coffee among young people or coffee beginners, specifically those belonging to generations Z (10–24 years) and Y (25–39 years).

Our distributed questionnaires have also revealed a similar trend in the data we collected. Out of the 257 respondents who participated in the survey, the vast majority were born between 1995 and 2010, with 101 respondents falling within this range. This means that those born in 1995 would be 25 years old in 2020, while those born in 2000 would be 20 years old. Typically, individuals within the age range of 20 to 25 are college students, which places them within the Y and Z generations. Therefore, it can be said that the Y and Z generations are the primary consumers of cafes and coffee shops, particularly in Yogyakarta. Additionally, Yogyakarta is a Student City, which means that this area is home to a large population of young people. Based on observations made by researchers in several cafes, it is evident that the majority of visitors are young individuals belonging to the Y and Z generations. For the details of this data see Figure 3.2.

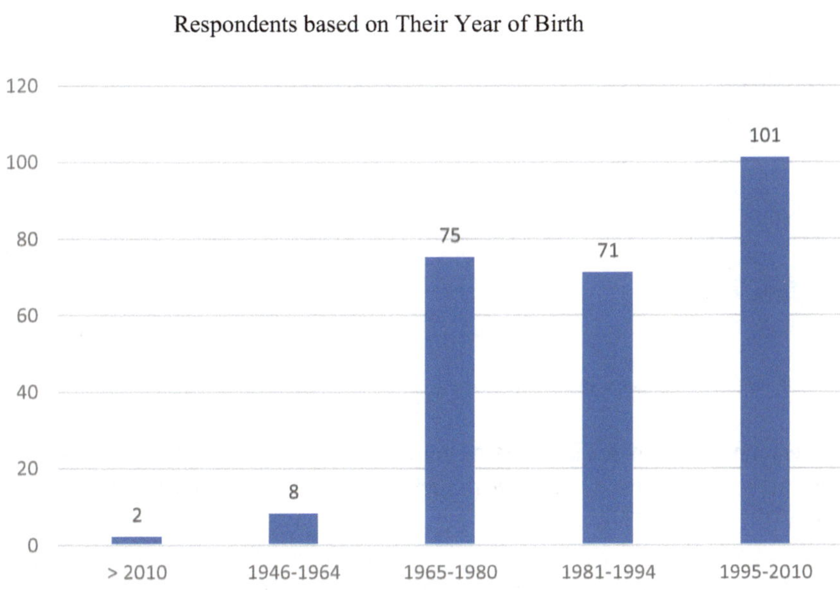

Figure 3.2: Respondents based on Their Year of Birth.

One of the defining characteristics of Generations Z and Y is their interconnectedness. They use communication technology to satisfy their culinary preferences, which include coffee (Toffin & Majalah MIX, 2019). However, it's not just about ordering coffee; it's also about their need to connect with others. This is evident in their desire to hang out and chat in coffee shops without any particular agenda, as observed by researchers.

The young generation is known for its strong sense of community and desire for social interaction. They prefer to live in an environment where they can connect with others and support each other. Hence, this communal nature is a defining characteristic of this generation (Faisal, 2017, p. 51). They often gather in cafes, which serve as a space for them to meet, interact, and discuss various topics. Whether it's school work, office work, or just casual conversations, cafes provide a comfortable setting for this generation to come together. Based on the online survey, it was found that on average, 171 out of 212 respondents visit a cafe once a week. This means that once a week they take the time to go to a cafe to interact with their friends or community. Meanwhile, 38 respondents said that they visit a café 2–3 times a week, and 3 respondents mentioned that they visit a café 4–7 times a week (see Figure 3.3).

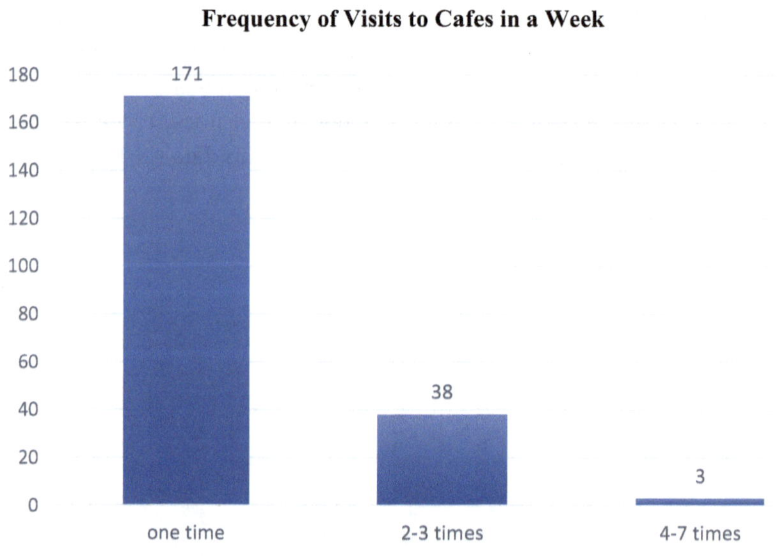

Figure 3.3: Frequency of Visits to Cafes in a Week.

Cafes have become a part of the lifestyle of young people, especially the Gen Z and Y generations. Cafes are often used as a place to socialize with friends, have meetings, chat, and engage in discussions. They are also a popular spot for building and maintaining relationships. Cafes are rarely visited solely for relaxation purposes. This indicates that cafes are closely linked to the social relationships of young people. Despite the cost factor, young people visit cafes to meet up with their friends, work on assignments together, have conversations, or even enjoy the amenities offered by cafes (Farhani et al., 2017).

3.6 Café, Young People, and Their Awareness of Halal Product

With the increasing number of cafes in Indonesia, particularly in Yogyakarta, the demand for cafe visits by young people from Gen Z and Y is growing at a rapid pace. As most of them are Muslims, the question of the halal issue of the products offered in a cafe arises. This is particularly interesting to see the growing halal awareness among young people amid the café lifestyle trend.

Based on the data we gathered through the online survey; it was found that almost all (99% of the 257) respondents knew about the teachings of halal and haram in Islam. Furthermore, 83% of them were aware of the halal product regulations in Indonesia. However, only 48% of them have actively participated in activities related to halal products. Nevertheless, it is evident that these young individuals have basic knowledge regarding the halal and haram laws of food and drink products in Islam, as proven by their efforts to find out or ensure the halal of such products using various methods. It has been observed that young people are making efforts to ensure the halal status of products through various means. One common way to do so is by checking for halal labels or certification in cafes and looking for Islamic symbols such as Muslim clothing, Islamic/Arabic calligraphy, and waiters wearing hijab/headscarf. Additionally, they scrutinize the composition of the food and drinks served. The details of this information can be seen in Figure 3.4 and Table 3.4.

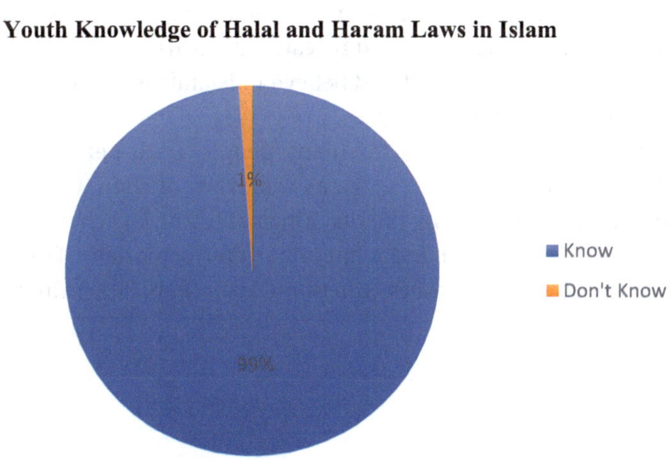

Figure 3.4: Youth Knowledge of Halal and Haram Laws in Islam.

Table 3.4: Ways to Ensure Halal Products Among Youngsters.

How to Ensure the Halalness of Food and Beverage in a Cafe	Number of respondents' answers
Check the composition of the food and drinks served	61
Finding recommendations from friends	35
Find out or check the existence of a halal label or certification in the cafe	97
Cafe waitress showing Islamic symbols (Muslim clothing, Islamic/Arabic calligraphy)	64
Total	257

Many young people may not be concerned about the issue of halal products in a particular cafe. Several interviews and FGDs conducted with young people, both students at school and college, indicate that they don't pay attention to the halal label when they visit a cafe. They assume that Yogyakarta, being a Muslim-majority area, offers only halal products, especially in international and national chain cafes that already have complete halal labels and certification. One young person stated that Starbucks, which is part of an international chain, immediately displays their halal label on their website.

3.7 Cafes and Young People's Religious Identity

According to Khalek (2015), religion has a significant impact on consumer behavior and attitudes towards food and drinks. Religious teachings and individual interpretations of religion influence the decision to purchase certain products. Islamic teachings, for example, dictate rules for consuming halal products as mentioned in the Koran and Sunnah. This is reflected in the information provided by cafes to ensure the halalness of their products. Young people who are aware of and believe in Islamic teachings will consider these teachings when making food choices.

Religion is an essential marker of identity for many people, both personally and communally. For Muslims, halal products serve as a marker of their Islamic identity. Halal food and drinks are required by the teachings of Islam, which differentiate between what is halal (permissible) and what is haram (forbidden). These teachings are derived from the Koran and hadith (Kurth & Glasbergen, 2017; Yakin, 2016).

Table 3.5: Respondents' Affiliations (Identities) and Religious Organizations.

Participating/members of the religious organization	Total Respondents
HMI (Himpunan Mahasiswa Islam)	9
IMM (Ikatan Mahasiswa Muhammadiyah)	1
IPM (Ikatan Pelajar Muhammadiyah)	1
IPNU/IPPNU	2
Jamaah Tabligh	2
Keluarga Mahasiswa Nahdlatul Ulama (KMNU)	1
Kesatuan Aksi Mahasiswa Muslim Indonesia (Kammi)	3
Lembaga Dakwah Kampus (LDK)	12
Muhammadiyah	19
NU (Nahdlatul Ulama)	80
NW (Nahdlatul Wathan)	4
PMII (Pergerakan Mahasiswa Islam Indonesia)	4
Rohis	6
Not a member of any organization	112
Total	256

Religious identities are not singular but can be composed of two or more identities depending on the understanding and ideology of the community or person. Nevertheless, there is still an identity that can unite them all, such as the Koran, which serves as the "identity" of all Muslims despite the different interpretations that may give rise to varying thoughts, activities, and identities. Additionally, the teachings about halal food and drinks are also an identity for almost all Muslims

Table 3.5 presents various religious affiliations and activities that respondents participate in, which shape their respective identities. While some don't identify themselves with any particular organization, most identify with one religious group. However, the majority of these respondents always try to determine the halal status of a product, as shown in Figure 3.4 and Table 3.4. This indicates that they still prioritize their religious identity despite enjoying cafe culture. This is consistent with the findings of research on the food preferences of Muslim youth in Korea. According to their study, Indonesian Muslims not only consume Korean food and embrace the Korean wave but also express their cosmopolitan Muslim ideology. This suggests that there is still an ongoing process of identity negotiation among youth in cafe culture as part of contemporary culinary trends (Nadhifah et al., 2019).

It is important to note that not all young people are concerned about the halal status of a product. There are at least two reasons for this. The first reason is that they believe the context of a region provides guarantees for the halal status of food or drink.

If a region is primarily Muslim, then the food and drink products produced there are assumed to be halal. As a result, they do not bother checking whether a food/drink product is halal or haram (Interview with a group of students in Yogyakarta, July 14, 2020).

The first factor relates to the second factor in that there is a lack of awareness about what is halal. This issue is mainly due to the absence of proper halal education for young people, especially those who are heavily involved in cafe culture. The halal status of a product must be not only determined by whether it is being sold in Muslim-majority or minority areas but also by the responsibility of the industry or entrepreneurs to ensure that their products are halal and that this guarantee is visible to consumers. This is especially significant in the current global industrial world where regional boundaries are irrelevant, and businesses can operate and expand anywhere. While the halal status of products in cafes with a local network in Yogyakarta may be apparent, it may not be the case for cafes with a global network. As a result, consumers need to have knowledge and make efforts to find out about the halal status of the products they consume.

3.8 Concluding Remarks

This article provides an overview of the different types of cafes in Indonesia, with a focus on Yogyakarta as the research location. The study reveals that there are at least three types of cafes in Yogyakarta based on their prices and target consumers: "premium," "medium," and "non-premium." From a community perspective, cafes can be categorized into two types. The first type is a café that caters to a specific community, usually established by community activists. Examples of such cafes include Teras Dakwah. The second type is a cafe that originates from a specific community but expands to welcome various communities, like Basabasi Café.

This article highlights cafes as a lifestyle for the younger generations of Gen Y and Z. Cafes provide a sense of community and connectedness, which is highly valued by this demographic. As a result, cafes have the potential to attract young Muslim consumers. However, it is important to note that halal products are a must for these individuals as it is an integral part of their identity. Educating this generation about halal can bring them together and create a sense of unity amongst different religious identities. However, not all young Muslims ensure halal products in every café they visit. This is influenced by two factors: the views of the majority and minority of Muslims, and the lack of education regarding halal product guarantees

References

Afroniyati, L. (2014). Analisis Ekonomi Politik Sertifikasi Halal Oleh Majelis Ulama Indonesia. *JKAP: Jurnal Kebijakan & Administrasi Publik, 18*(1), 37–52. https://doi.org/https://doi.org/10.22146/jkap.6870

Ali, M. (2016). Konsep Makanan Halal dalam Tinjauan Syariah dan Tanggung Jawab Produk Atas Produsen Industri Halal. *AHKAM : Jurnal Ilmu Syariah, 16*(2), 291–306. https://doi.org/10.15408/ajis.v16i2.4459

Arizona, N. (2013). *Revolusi Kopi Yogyakarta*. Minumkopi.Com. https://www.minumkopi.com/revolusi-kopi-yogyakarta/

Astogini, D., Wahyudin, & Wulandari, S. Z. (2011). Aspek Religiusitas dalam Keputusan Pembelian Produk Halal. *Jeba, 13*(1), 1–8.

Basoni, S. (2018). *Terus Berevolusi, Kopi Jadi Tren dan Bisnis Menjanjikan di Indonesia*. Detikfood. https://food.detik.com/cooking-event/d-4265319/terus-berevolusi-kopi-jadi-tren-dan-bisnis-menjanjikan-di-indonesia

Bernas.id. (2018). *Bisnis Warung Kopi di Yogyakarta Cukup Menjanjikan*. https://www.bernas.id/63451-bisnis-warung-kopi-di-yogyakarta-cukup-menjanjikan.html

BPS. (2018). *Statistik Kopi Indonesia 2017*. BPS-Statistic Indonesia.

BPS DIY. (2020). *Daerah Istimewa Yogyakarta dalam Angka 2020*. BPS Daerah Istimewa Yogyakarta.

Chester, A. C. (2017). *Foodie Culture, Muslim Identity, and the Rise of Halal through Media* (p. 63 p.). OhioLINK Electronic Theses and Dissertations Center.

Darojatun, R. (2018). Tren Produk Halal, Gaya Hidup Syar'i Dan Kesalehan Simbolik: Studi Tentang Muslim Kelas Menengah. *WARDAH, 19*(2), 135–157. https://doi.org/https://doi.org/10.19109/wardah.v19i2.2816

D.H, A. (2016). *Potensi Ekonomi 800 Kedai Kopi di Yogya Capai Rp350,4 Miliar*. Tirto.Id. https://www.krjogja.com/ekonomi/bisnis/prospek-bisnis-kedai-kopi-2020-masih-menjanjikan/

Faidah, M. (2017). Sertifikasi Halal di Indonesia: Dari Civil Society menuju Relasi Kuasa Antara Negara dan Agama. *Islamica: Jurnal Studi Keislaman, 11*(2), 449–476. https://doi.org/https://doi.org/10.15642/islamica.2017.11.2.449-476

Faisal, M. (2017). *Generasi Phi: Memahami Milenial Pengubah Indonesia* (Republika, Ed.).

Faizi, M. (2018). *Silsilah Warung Kopi di Jogja Dimulai dari Badrun Blandongan*. Mojok.Co. https://mojok.co/fai/esai/silsilah-warung-kopi-di-jogja-dimulai-dari-badrun-blandongan/

Farhani, H., Susetyowaty, S., & Triratnawati, A. (2017). Intensi remaja pergi ke kafe susu di Sleman DIY. *Berita Kedokteran Masyarakat, 33*(2), 85. https://doi.org/10.22146/bkm.7960

Fischer, J. (2016). Manufacturing halal in Malaysia. *Contemporary Islam, 10*(1), 35–52. https://doi.org/10.1007/s11562-015-0323-5

Hartahati, M. A., & Rahmawaty, P. (2016). Pengaruh Sikap, Norma Subjektif, dan Persepsi Kontrol Perilaku terhadap Perilaku Konsumsi Mahasiswa Muslim pada Outlet Franchise Asing di Yogyakarta yang Dikaitkan dengan Label Halal (Studi pada mahasiswa muslim Fakultas Ekonomi Universitas Negeri Yogyaka. *Jurnal Manajemen Bisnis Indonesia, 5*(1), 20–31.

Hidayatullah, A., & Monicasef. (2019). *Kedai Kopi, Bisnis Masa Kini, Menjanjikan di Masa Depan*. Yoursay.Suara.Com. https://yoursay.suara.com/lifestyle/2019/10/25/065000/kedai-kopi-bisnis-masa-kini-menjanjikan-di-masa-depan

Hidayatullah, S., Waris, A., & Devianti, R. C. (2018). Perilaku Generasi Milenial dalam Menggunakan Aplikasi Go-Food. *JURNAL MANAJEMEN DAN KEWIRAUSAHAAN, 6*(2). https://doi.org/10.26905/jmdk.v6i2.2560

Hosen, N. (2012). Hilal and Halal: How to manage islamic pluralism in Indonesia? *Asian Journal of Comparative Law, 7*(1), 1–18. https://doi.org/10.1515/1932-0205.1418

IDN Research Institute. (2019). *Indonesia Millennial Report 2019*.

Karim, M. A. (2013). *Perilaku Komunitas Muslim Perkotaan Dalam Mengonsumsi Produk Halal*. Puslitbang Kehidupan Keagamaan, Badan Litbang dan Diklat.

Khab, J. (2017). *Menikmati Kopi Basabasi*. Kompasiana. https://www.kompasiana.com/junaidi_khab/5a1954225169953c0f7220e2/menikmati-kopi-basbasi

Khalek, A. A. (2014). Young Consumers' Attitude towards Halal Food Outlets and JAKIM's Halal Certification in Malaysia. *Procedia – Social and Behavioral Sciences*, *121*(September 2012), 26–34. https://doi.org/10.1016/j.sbspro.2014.01.1105

Khalek, A. A. (2015). A Study on the Factors Influencing Young Muslims' Behavioral Intention in Consuming Halal Food in Malaysia. *Jurnal Syariah*, *23*(1), 79–102.

Khalek, A. A., Syed Ismail, S. H., & Mohamad Ibrahim, H. (2015). A Study on The Factors Influencing Young Muslims' Behavioral Intention in Consuming Halal Food in Malaysia. *Jurnal Syariah*, *23*(1), 79–102. https://doi.org/10.22452/js.vol23no1.4

Kumparan.com. (2020). *Edi Mulyono, Bos Penerbitan yang Memulai Bisnis dengan Modal Rp 0*. Kumparan.Com. https://kumparan.com/profil-orang-sukses/edi-mulyono-bos-penerbitan-yang-memulai-bisnis-dengan-modal-rp-0-1tgc19QPMy6

KumparanFOOD. (2018). *Fenomena 'Demam' Coffee Shop di Indonesia*. https://kumparan.com/kumparanfood/fenomena-mewabahnya-demam-coffee-shop-di-indonesia

Kurth, L., & Glasbergen, P. (2017). Serving a heterogeneous Muslim identity? Private governance arrangements of halal food in the Netherlands. *Agriculture and Human Values*, *34*(1), 103–118. https://doi.org/10.1007/s10460-016-9698-z

Lever, J., & Miele, M. (2012). The growth of halal meat markets in Europe: An exploration of the supply side theory of religion. *Journal of Rural Studies*, *28*(4), 528–537. https://doi.org/10.1016/j.jrurstud.2012.06.004

Mastercard Crescent Rating. (2018). *Global Muslim Travel Index 2018*.

Merdeka.com. (2016). *Menjamurnya Bisnis Cafe di Tanah Air*. Merdeka.Com. https://www.merdeka.com/uang/menjamurnya-bisnis-cafe-di-tanah-air.html

Mohamad, A. A., Baharuddin, A. S., & Ruskam, A. (2015). Halal industry in Singapore: a case study of nutraceutical products. *Sains Humanika*, *4*(2), 35–40.

Mushodiq, M. A. (2017). Teori Identitas dalam Pluralisme Agama dan Identitas (Fenomena Pluralisme dan Toleransi Beragama Desa Jrahi, Gunungwungkal, Pati, Jawa Tengah). *Fikri: Jurnal Kajian Agama, Sosial, Dan Budaya*, *2*(2), 379–406. https://doi.org/https://doi.org/10.25217/jf.v2i2.145

Nadhifah, N., Eka, S., & Tusita, A. (2019). Halal Korean Food and Glocalization. *ICEL Proceeding*. https://doi.org/10.4108/eai.23-3-2019.2284943

Nashirudin, M. (2016). Fikih), Pandangan Majlis Tafsir Al-Qur'an (MTA) tentang Makanan Halal dan Haram (Kajian Usul. *Al-Manahij*, *X*(2), 235–252.

Nasution, M. D. T. P., & Rossanty, Y. (2016). Hubungan antara Religiusitas dan Pengambilan Keputusan Membeli Panganan Halal dimoderasi oleh Persepsi Konsumen atas risiko. *Jurnal Ilmiah Research Sains*, *2*(2), 7–13.

Nik Muhammad, N. M., Isa, F. M., & Kifli, B. C. (2009). Positioning Malaysia as Halal-Hub: Integration Role of Supply Chain Strategy and Halal Assurance System. *Asian Social Science*, *5*(7), 44–52. https://doi.org/10.5539/ass.v5n7p44

Noordin, N. et al. (2009). Value chain of Halal certification system: A case of the Malaysia Halal Industry. *Proceedings of the European and Mediterranean Conference on Information Systems, EMCIS 2009*, *2009*(2008), 1–14.

Othman, B., Shaarani, S. M., & Bahron, A. (2016). The potential of ASEAN in halal certification implementation: A review. *Pertanika Journal of Social Sciences and Humanities*, *24*(1), 1–24.

Qardhawi, Y. (1993). *Halal dan Haram dalam Pandangan Islam*. PT. Bina Ilmu.

Salahudin, A. et al. (2017). Issues in Halal Meat Product and Authentication Technology from Islamic Perspectives. *International Journal of Academic Research in Business and Social Sciences*, *7*(12), 1305–1315. https://doi.org/10.6007/ijarbss/v7-i12/3768

Sulistiyawan, L. (2020). *Fenomena Hijrah Dan Islam Populer Di Kalangan Anak Muda (Studi Pada Komunitas Cah Hijrah Kota Semarang)*. UIN Walisongo Semarang.

Sutrisno, R. (2010). Perilaku Konsumen Muslim : Persepsi Religiusitas Dan Persepsi Atribut Produk Minuman Berlabel Halal Di Kalangan Mahasiswa Muslim Di Bandung Muslim Consumer Behavior : the Religiosity Perceptions and the Perceptions of Product Attributes Toward the Loyalty. *Sigma-Mu*, *5*(2), 18–36.

Syafrida, S. (2016). Sertifikat Halal Pada Produk Makanan Dan Minuman Memberi Perlindungan Dan Kepastian Hukum Hak-Hak Konsumen Muslim. *ADIL: Jurnal Hukum*, *7*(2), 159–174. https://doi.org/10.33476/ajl.v7i2.353

Toffin, & Majalah MIX. (2019). *2020 Brewing in Indonesia: Insights for Successful Coffee Shop Business*. MIX Marketing & Communication, Toffin.

Vristiyana, V. M. (2019). Pengaruh Religiusitas Dan Pengetahuan Produk Halal Terhadap Penilaian Produk Halal Dan Minat Pembelian Produk Halal. *Pengaruh Religiusitas Dan Pengetahuan Produk Halal Terhadap Penilaian Produk Halal Dan Minat Pembelian Produk Halal*, 85–100.

Yakin, A. U. (2016). Halal Food , Identity , and Authority in Japan. *Asia Leadership Fellow Program*, *May*, 1–6.

Zuhriyah, D. A. (2019). *Startup Kopi Menjamur, Persaingan Bisnis Kafe di Indonesia Memanas*. Bisnis. Com. https://ekonomi.bisnis.com/read/20190807/12/1133701/startup-kopi-menjamur-persaingan-bisnis-kafe-di-indonesia-memanas

Shahsuzan Zakaria, Amirul Afif Muhamat, Nor Farradila Abdul Aziz, Mohd Afzanizam Abdul Rashid, Mohamad Sayuti Md Saleh

Chapter 4
Malaysia's Shariah-Compliant Business Ecosystem: A Blueprint for Global Ethical Economies

Abstract: This chapter examines Malaysia's Shariah-compliant business ecosystem as a global benchmark for ethical and sustainable economic practices. Grounded in Islamic principles, the ecosystem is propelled by strong government initiatives, regulatory frameworks, and active industry collaboration. Key institutional enablers such as the Islamic Finance Masterplan and the Halal Industry Development Corporation support its development. Through case studies including Maybank Islamic, Nestlé Malaysia, and Lembaga Tabung Haji, the chapter emphasizes the importance of Shariah governance and infrastructure. Despite regulatory harmonization challenges, Malaysia's dedication to innovation cements its position as a leader in ethical economic development.

Keywords: Shariah-compliant ecosystem; Ethical economic development; Islamic finance; Halal industry; Malaysia

4.1 Introduction

The global economy is progressively embracing ethical and sustainable business practices, with Shariah-compliant business ecosystems emerging as a key model for accomplishing these objectives. Shariah-compliant businesses follow Islamic values that value fairness, transparency, and social responsibility. These principles forbid immoral practices such as interest (riba), excessive uncertainty (gharar), and investments in prohibited (haram) businesses, while encouraging profit-sharing (mudarabah) and risk-sharing (musharakah) models. Malaysia, with its well-established Islamic finance and halal businesses, has emerged as a global leader in this field.

Malaysia's success in building a Shariah-compliant business ecosystem is rooted in its proactive government policies, robust regulatory frameworks, and strong industry collaboration. The country has become a hub for Islamic finance, halal products, and ethical business practices, attracting investors and businesses from around the world. This chapter explores the key components of Malaysia's ecosystem, highlighting its strengths, challenges, and prospects. By examining Malaysia's experience, this chapter aims to provide insights into how other countries can develop similar ecosystems. The importance of Shariah-compliant business ecosystems extends beyond Muslim-major-

https://doi.org/10.1515/9783111575407-005

ity countries. As global consumers and investors increasingly prioritize ethical and sustainable practices, Shariah-compliant models offer a viable alternative to conventional business systems. Malaysia's ecosystem serves as a case study for integrating Islamic principles into modern business practices, demonstrating the potential for Shariah compliance to drive economic growth and social development.

This chapter is structured to provide a comprehensive analysis of Malaysia's Shariah-compliant business ecosystem. It begins with an overview of the concept, followed by a discussion of government policies, regulatory frameworks, and industry collaboration. The chapter also examines challenges, case studies, and prospects, concluding with reflections on Malaysia's global leadership in this field.

4.2 Overview of Shariah-Compliant Business Ecosystems

A Shariah-compliant business ecosystem refers to a network of interconnected entities that include financial institutions, businesses, regulatory bodies, and consumers, operating in alignment with Islamic principles. These principles, derived from the Quran, Sunnah, and Islamic jurisprudence (fiqh), emphasize ethical conduct, social justice, and economic equity. At its core, Shariah compliance prohibits practices such as interest (riba), excessive uncertainty (gharar), and investments in prohibited (haram) industries like alcohol, gambling, and pork production. Instead, it promotes profit-sharing (mudarabah), risk-sharing (musharakah), and asset-backed financing (murabahah), ensuring that business activities are ethical, transparent, and socially responsible.

Malaysia‘s Shariah-compliant ecosystem stands out for its seamless integration of Islamic banking, halal businesses, and technology. Unlike other Islamic finance hubs such as Saudi Arabia and the UAE, Malaysia has a dual financial system that caters to both Islamic and conventional industries. This duality fosters innovation and adaptability, allowing Malaysia to cater to diverse consumers and investors. For instance, Malaysia's Islamic banking sector accounts for over 30% of the country's total banking assets, making it one of the most developed in the world (Bank Negara Malaysia, 2021). This success is underpinned by a strong regulatory framework and government support, which have enabled Malaysia to create a robust and resilient ecosystem. The halal industry is a cornerstone of Malaysia's Shariah-compliant ecosystem. As a global leader in halal certification, Malaysia has established internationally recognized standards through the Department of Islamic Development Malaysia (JAKIM). These standards ensure that halal products, ranging from food and cosmetics to pharmaceuticals, meet stringent Shariah requirements. Malaysia's halal exports have grown significantly in recent years, reaching RM40 billion in 2022, driven by strong government support and industry collaboration (Halal Industry Development Corporation, 2022). This growth highlights the interconnectedness of Malaysia's ecosystem, where halal certification acts as a gateway to global markets.

Table 4.1: Investment of the Halal Industry in Malaysia.

Items	Units	IMP3			2021	2022	2015–2020	2020–2021	2021–2022
		2015	2020	2015–2020			CAGR	Annual Growth	
Total Investment	RM billion	8.9	16.1	75.8	16.3	16.6	12.6%	1.3%	1.7%
Domestic Investment	RM billion	3.2	6.5	29.9	6.6	6.7	15.2%	1.8%	1.2%
Foreign Investment	RM billion	5.7	9.6	45.9	9.7	9.9	11.1%	1.0%	2.1%
Employment	persons	9,251	18,841	86,513	19,238	17,186	15.3%	2.1%	−10.7%

Source: Halal Development Centre (HDC).

The investment performance of the Halal industry in Malaysia has demonstrated consistent growth from 2015 to 2022 (*see* Table 4.1). In 2015, the total investment in this industry stood at RM8.9 billion, and by 2022, it increased to RM16.6 billion, reflecting a Compound Annual Growth Rate (CAGR) of 12.6%. Foreign Direct Investment (FDI) played a significant role in driving this growth, rising from RM5.7 billion in 2015 to RM9.9 billion in 2022. Domestic investment also showed robust growth, increasing from RM3.2 billion to RM6.7 billion over the same period. Additionally, employment in the Halal industry expanded, with the number of workers rising from 9,251 in 2015 to 19,238 in 2022. This growth has been driven by several key factors. Firstly, the increasing global demand for Halal food and beverage products has attracted more investment in this sector. Secondly, the development of the Islamic digital economy through bilateral partnerships has opened new investment opportunities. Thirdly, international exhibitions such as the Malaysia International Halal Showcase (MIHAS) have successfully attracted both local and international investors to invest in various Halal sectors. Furthermore, the growing demand for Shariah-compliant financial and investment products has also contributed to the industry's growth. Overall, the Halal industry in Malaysia continues to show promising performance, with investments and employment steadily growing. The combination of domestic and foreign investments, coupled with government initiatives and global demand, has positioned Malaysia as a leading global Halal hub. This growth is expected to continue in the future, further solidifying Malaysia's position as a global leader in the Halal industry.

Technology has played a transformative role in shaping Malaysia's Shariah-compliant ecosystem. The rise of fintech has led to the development of innovative products such as Islamic digital banking, blockchain-based sukuk, and halal supply chain solutions. These advancements have enhanced the accessibility and efficiency of Shariah-compliant businesses, attracting a new generation of tech-savvy consumers and investors. A notable example is Malaysia's issuance of the world's first green sukuk in 2017, which raised RM250 million to fund solar energy projects (Securities Commission Malaysia, 2020). This innovative project set a standard for other nations and illustrated how Islamic financing can be used to solve global issues by fusing environmental sustainability with Shariah compliance. In Malaysia, the fusion of technology, halal sectors, and Islamic financing has produced a robust and dynamic ecosystem. For instance, Maybank Islamic and other Islamic financial institutions have embraced digitalization to provide Shariah-compliant products like mobile banking apps and Islamic credit cards. Similar to this, businesses such as Nestlé Malaysia have incorporated Shariah principles into their supply chains to guarantee that their goods are ethically sourced and halal certified. These instances show how Malaysia's ecosystem supports creativity while upholding Islamic values.

Malaysia's ecosystem benefits from robust government policies and regulatory frameworks. Institutions such as Bank Negara Malaysia (BNM) and the Securities Commission Malaysia (SC) provide monitoring and guidance to ensure that Shariah principles are followed throughout industries. The Shariah Governance Framework (SGF), introduced by BNM in 2010, requires Islamic financial institutions to form Shariah committees, conduct regular audits, and maintain transparency in their operations. This structure has helped to create trust and confidence in Malaysia's Islamic finance sector. In addition to regulatory assistance, Malaysia's ecosystem benefits from industry engagement. Partnerships among Islamic financial institutions, halal enterprises, and technology suppliers have fueled innovation and growth. For example, the Labuan International Business and Financial Centre (IBFC) functions as an Islamic finance hub, creating an atmosphere conducive to the growth of Shariah-compliant firms. Similarly, the Halal Development Corporation (HDC) works with both local and international partners to promote Malaysia's halal business abroad. Despite its achievements, Malaysia's Shariah-compliant ecosystem confronts obstacles such as inconsistent Shariah interpretations and global rivalry from other Islamic finance hubs. However, these challenges also present opportunities for growth and innovation. By addressing these issues, Malaysia can further strengthen its ecosystem and maintain its position as a global leader.

In summary, Malaysia's Shariah-compliant business ecosystem is a model of integration and innovation. By combining Islamic finance, halal industries, and technology, Malaysia has created a dynamic and resilient ecosystem that aligns with Islamic principles and meets the needs of modern businesses. This ecosystem serves as a blueprint for other countries seeking to develop Shariah-compliant business models, demonstrating the potential of ethical and sustainable business practices to drive economic growth and social development.

4.3 Government Policies and Institutional Support

The Malaysian government has played a pivotal role in developing a Shariah-compliant business ecosystem through aggressive legislation, institutional support, and strategic initiatives. Malaysia has established itself as a global leader in Islamic finance and halal sectors by providing an environment conducive to the growth of Shariah-compliant firms. This section delves into the key policies and institutions that have built Malaysia's ecosystem, emphasizing their influence on economic growth and global competitiveness.

4.3.1 Islamic Finance Masterplan: A Roadmap for Growth

One of the most significant initiatives is the Islamic Finance Masterplan, introduced by Bank Negara Malaysia (BNM) in 2021. This master plan outlines a comprehensive strategy to strengthen Malaysia's position as a global Islamic finance hub, focusing on areas such as digitalization, sustainability, and talent development. The master plan emphasizes the importance of innovation in Islamic financial products and services, aiming to make Malaysia a center for Shariah-compliant fintech solutions (Bank Negara Malaysia, 2021). A key focus of the master plan is cross-border collaboration. Malaysia has actively engaged with international partners to promote the harmonization of Shariah standards and facilitate cross-border Islamic finance transactions. For example, Malaysia has signed a memorandum of understanding (MoUs) with countries such as Saudi Arabia, the UAE, and Indonesia to enhance cooperation in Islamic finance (Islamic Financial Services Board, 2019). These efforts have strengthened Malaysia's global presence and reinforced its reputation as a leader in Shariah-compliant finance.

The master plan also prioritizes sustainability, aligning Islamic finance with global environmental, social, and governance (ESG) goals. Malaysia's issuance of the world's first green sukuk in 2017 is a testament to this commitment. The green sukuk, which raised RM250 million to fund solar energy projects, demonstrated the potential of Islamic finance to address global challenges such as climate change (Securities Commission Malaysia, 2020). This initiative has set a precedent for other countries and highlighted Malaysia's innovative approach to Shariah-compliant finance.

4.3.2 Halal Industry Development Corporation: Driving Global Halal Leadership

Another critical institution is the Halal Industry Development Corporation (HDC), which promotes Malaysia's halal industry globally. The HDC provides halal certification, training, and market access for businesses, ensuring compliance with Shariah principles. Malaysia's halal certification, issued by the Department of Islamic Development Malaysia (JAKIM), is recognized as one of the most stringent and credible in the world (Halal Industry Development Corporation, 2022).

The HDC's Halal Park initiative exemplifies Malaysia's dedication to developing the halal business. Halal Parks are specialized industrial zones that provide cutting-edge infrastructure for halal manufacturing, attracting both domestic and foreign businesses. For example, Penang's Halal Park has become a halal food production hub, hosting enterprises like Nestlé Malaysia and QL Resources (Halal Industry Development Corporation, 2022). These parks not only support the growth of the halal industry but also create jobs and stimulate economic development in rural areas. Malaysia's halal exports have grown significantly in recent years, reaching RM40 billion in 2022, driven by strong government support and industry collaboration (Halal Industry Development

Corporation, 2022). The HDC has also launched initiatives to promote halal tourism, halal logistics, and halal pharmaceuticals, diversifying the halal ecosystem and creating new opportunities for businesses. By leveraging its expertise in halal certification and industry development, Malaysia has become a global leader in the halal industry, setting an example for other countries.

4.3.3 Tax Incentives and Funding Programs: Encouraging Shariah-Compliant Businesses

The Malaysian government provides tax breaks and funding opportunities to help Shariahcompliant businesses grow. For example, the *Islamic Fund and Wealth Management Blueprint* offers financial support to startups and small businesses in Islamic finance. The goal is to make Malaysia a top destination for Islamic wealth management, attracting wealthy individuals and big investors (Securities Commission Malaysia, 2020). The government also gives tax exemptions on Islamic financial products like *sukuk* (Islamic bonds) and *takaful* (Islamic insurance), making Malaysia more appealing for Shariah-friendly investments. Special tax incentives for green *sukuk* (used for eco-friendly projects) encourage businesses to invest in sustainability (Bank Negara Malaysia, 2021). These policies have facilitated the growth of Islamic finance while also aiding global environmental initiatives. Malaysia also offers venture capital funds, like as MAVCAP, which invest in Shariah-compliant firms, particularly in fintech (MAVCAP, 2021). These initiatives foster a robust startup ecosystem, ensuring Malaysia's position as a global leader in Islamic finance.

4.3.4 Infrastructure Development: Building a Conducive Environment

Infrastructure development has been another priority for the Malaysian government. The Labuan International Business and Financial Centre (IBFC) serves as a hub for Islamic finance, offering a conducive environment for Shariah-compliant businesses to thrive. The IBFC provides a range of services, including Islamic banking, takaful, and wealth management, attracting investors from around the world (Labuan IBFC, 2021). The IBFC's strategic location and business-friendly policies have made it a preferred destination for Islamic finance transactions. For example, the IBFC has facilitated the issuance of US$8.5 billion in sukuk, making it one of the largest sukuk markets in the world (Labuan IBFC, 2021). The center also offers tax exemptions and regulatory flexibility, making it an attractive option for international investors. In addition to the IBFC, the government has invested in digital infrastructure to support the growth of Shariah-compliant fintech. The Malaysia Digital Economy Corporation (MDEC) has launched initiatives to promote digital banking, blockchain, and artificial intelligence in the Islamic finance sector (MDEC, 2021). These efforts have enhanced the accessibility and efficiency of Shariah-compliant financial services, attracting a new generation of tech-savvy consumers.

In a nutshell, the Malaysian government's proactive policies and institutional support have been critical drivers of the country's Shariah-compliant economic environment. Malaysia has developed an environment conducive to the growth of Shariah-compliant enterprises through efforts such as the Islamic Finance Masterplan, the Halal Industry Development Corporation, and the Labuan IBFC. Tax breaks, funding schemes, and infrastructure development have bolstered the ecosystem, establishing Malaysia as a global leader in Islamic finance and halal sectors. These initiatives highlight the significance of government involvement in establishing a successful Shariah-compliant ecosystem. Malaysia has achieved commercial success by connecting economic aims with Islamic ideals, while also contributing to the larger goal of encouraging ethical and sustainable business practices. As other countries seek to develop their own Shariah-compliant ecosystems, Malaysia's experience offers valuable lessons and insights.

4.4 Regulatory Frameworks and Shariah Governance

A robust regulatory structure is required to ensure Shariah conformity in corporate activities. In Malaysia, prominent regulatory authorities such as Bank Negara Malaysia (BNM) and the Securities Commission Malaysia (SC) supervise Shariah compliance in the financial sector. The Shariah Advisory Council (SAC), founded by BNM, advises on Shariah-related issues and ensures that financial goods and services adhere to Islamic laws. The SAC's decisions are enforceable on all Islamic financial institutions in Malaysia, promoting consistency and transparency (Bank Negara Malaysia, 2021). The Shariah Governance structure (SGF), created by the BNM in 2010, is a key component of Malaysia's regulatory structure. The SGF requires Islamic financial institutions to establish Shariah committees, conduct regular audits, and maintain transparency in their activities. This framework has been instrumental in building trust and confidence in Malaysia's Islamic finance sector. For example, the SGF requires Islamic banks to disclose their Shariah compliance status in annual reports, assuring consumers and investors (Securities Commission Malaysia, 2020). Standardization of Shariah practices is another critical aspect of Malaysia's regulatory framework. The country has adopted international standards such as those set by the Accounting and Auditing Organization for Islamic Financial Institutions (AAOIFI) to ensure consistency and harmonization across jurisdictions. These standards cover areas such as financial reporting, auditing, and ethical governance, providing a comprehensive framework for Shariah compliance (AAOIFI, 2019). By adopting these standards, Malaysia has strengthened its position as a global leader in Islamic finance.

Beyond regulations, Malaysia has also set up dedicated organizations to strengthen Shariah governance. One key player is the International Shariah Research Academy for Islamic Finance (ISRA), which focuses on research and training in Islamic finance. By tackling complex Shariah questions and helping create new financial products, ISRA has played a big role in shaping Malaysia's thriving Islamic finance sector (ISRA, 2021). All these efforts provide strong regulations, clear Shariah oversight, and specialized institutions that have made Malaysia a global leader in Islamic finance. By prioritizing fairness, transparency, and trust, the country has built a system that works. Many other nations now look to Malaysia as a model for developing their Shariah-compliant business ecosystems.

4.5 Industry Collaboration and Innovation

Collaboration between different sectors has been a driving force behind Malaysia's Shariah-compliant business ecosystem. For instance, partnerships between Islamic financial institutions and fintech companies have led to the development of innovative products such as Islamic digital banking and blockchain-based sukuk. These innovations have enhanced accessibility and efficiency in the Islamic finance sector, attracting a new generation of consumers and investors. For example, Malaysia's first Islamic digital bank, AEON Bank, was launched in 2022, offering Shariah-compliant financial services through a fully digital platform (Bank Negara Malaysia, 2022). In his study, Muhammad Ridhwan (2024) interviewed practitioners and experts in the Islamic financial sector. The findings led to the creation of the best model for Shariah-compliant digital banking, which considers the affordability and accessibility of the service to underserved customers, combines the elements of Islamic social finance and wealth creation, and more. As a result, it is feasible to construct an Islamic digital banking model for financial inclusion based on Maqasid al-Shariah (Figure 4.1).

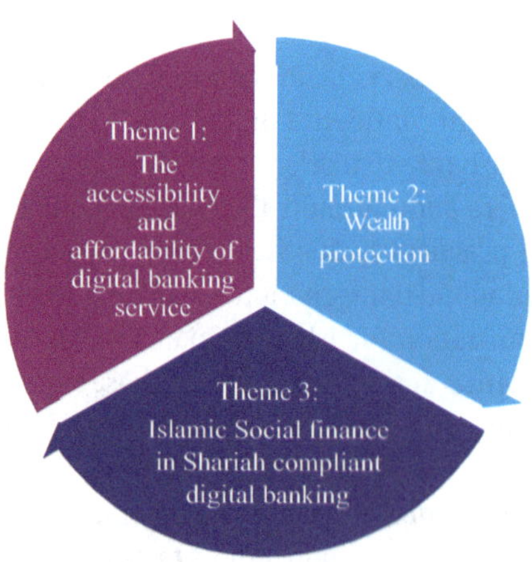

Figure 4.1: Shariah Compliant Digital Banking Model.

The halal industry has also benefited from collaboration. Companies like Nestlé Malaysia have integrated Shariah principles into their supply chain management, ensuring that their products are halal-certified and ethically sourced. Nestlé's collaboration with local halal certification bodies and suppliers has strengthened its brand reputation and expanded its market share in Muslim-majority countries (Nestlé Malaysia, 2021). Similarly, SMEs in the halal sector have leveraged government support and industry partnerships to expand their market reach. Innovation is a key theme in Malaysia's ecosystem. In 2017, the government released the world's first green sukuk, which combined Shariah compliance and environmental sustainability. This revolutionary project has established a precedent for other countries and proved Islamic finance's ability to address global concerns. Tadau Energy launched a green sukuk to fund RM250 million for solar energy projects, underscoring Islamic finance's role in encouraging sustainable development. Another example of innovation is the application of blockchain technology to Islamic finance. Malaysia's Finterra platform leverages blockchain to support Shariah-compliant crowdfunding, allowing SMEs to raise cash in a transparent and efficient manner. This innovation has created new chances for small firms and investors, hence enhancing Malaysia's ecosystem (Finterra, 2021).

In conclusion, industry collaboration and innovation have been key drivers of Malaysia's Shariah-compliant business ecosystem. By fostering partnerships and embracing new technologies, Malaysia has created a dynamic and resilient ecosystem that aligns with Islamic principles and meets the needs of modern businesses. This collaborative approach serves as a model for other countries seeking to develop Shariah-compliant business ecosystems.

4.6 Challenges in Building a Shariah-Compliant Ecosystem

Despite its achievements, Malaysia faces three key challenges in growing its Shariah-compliant business sector. First, differing interpretations of Islamic law across countries create confusion - what's approved in Malaysia may be rejected elsewhere, complicating international business (Dusuki & Abdullah, 2014). Second, many local businesses and consumers still don't fully understand Shariah-compliant practices, missing opportunities like halal certification's benefits (Halal Industry Development Corporation, 2022). Third, competition is intensifying as wealthy Gulf nations invest heavily in their Islamic finance hubs. These challenges require smart solutions. Standardizing Shariah interpretations internationally could ease cross-border transactions. More education campaigns could boost awareness among Malaysian businesses. And to stay ahead of global competitors, Malaysia must leverage its existing strengths while fostering innovation.

While these obstacles are significant, they're not insurmountable. Addressing them systematically can help Malaysia maintain its leadership in Islamic finance. The country's proven ability to adapt suggests it's well-positioned to turn these challenges into opportunities for further growth.

4.7 Case Studies: Success Stories from Malaysia

Case Study 1: Maybank Islamic – Pioneering Shariah-Compliant Financial Innovation

Maybank Islamic, the Islamic banking arm of Malayan Banking Berhad, stands as a testament to Malaysia's leadership in Shariah-compliant finance. As one of the largest Islamic banks in the world, Maybank Islamic has been at the forefront of developing innovative financial products that align with Shariah principles while meeting the needs of modern consumers. For example, the bank's Ikhwan Credit Card-i offers cash-back rewards and financing facilities without violating the prohibition of riba (interest). Instead, the card operates on a tawarruq (commodity murabahah) model, which complies with Shariah principles by using tangible assets as the basis for transactions (Maybank Islamic, 2021).

Maybank Islamic's success is deeply rooted in Malaysia's robust regulatory framework and supportive ecosystem. The bank benefits from the Shariah Governance Framework (SGF), which ensures that its products and operations are regularly audited for compliance. Additionally, Maybank Islamic collaborates with fintech companies to enhance its digital offerings, such as mobile banking apps and blockchain-based payment systems. This integration of technology and Shariah compliance has positioned Maybank Islamic as a global leader in Islamic finance, demonstrating how Malaysia's ecosystem fosters innovation while adhering to Islamic principles. The case of Maybank Islamic highlights the importance of industry collaboration and regulatory support in building a successful Shariah-compliant business ecosystem. By leveraging Malaysia's strong institutional framework and embracing technological advancements, Maybank Islamic has not only achieved commercial success but also contributed to the broader goal of promoting ethical finance.

Case Study 2: Nestlé Malaysia – Integrating Shariah Compliance into Global Supply Chains

Nestlé Malaysia provides a compelling example of how multinational corporations can integrate Shariah compliance into their operations while maintaining global competitiveness. As one of the largest halal-certified food and beverage producers in Malaysia, Nestlé has embedded Shariah principles into its supply chain management, ensuring that all its products meet stringent halal standards. For instance, Nestlé Malaysia works closely with the Department of Islamic Development Malaysia (JAKIM) to obtain halal certification for its products, which includes rigorous audits of raw materials, production processes, and packaging (Nestlé Malaysia, 2021).

Nestlé's commitment to Shariah compliance has not only strengthened its brand reputation but also expanded its market share in Muslim-majority countries. The company's halal-certified products account for over 90% of its sales in Malaysia, demonstrating the commercial viability of Shariah-compliant practices (Halal Industry Development Corporation, 2022). Moreover, Nestlé Malaysia has collaborated with local SMEs to source halal-certified ingredients, fostering economic growth and inclusivity within Malaysia's ecosystem. This case study underscores the role of government support and industry collaboration in promoting Shariah compliance. By aligning its operations with Malaysia's halal standards and leveraging the country's institutional infrastructure, Nestlé Malaysia has become a model for other multinational corporations seeking to integrate Shariah principles into their business models.

Case Study 3: Lembaga Tabung Haji – Balancing Financial and Social Objectives

Lembaga Tabung Haji, Malaysia's pilgrimage fund board, exemplifies how Shariah-compliant businesses can achieve both financial sustainability and social impact. Established in 1963, Tabung Haji manages savings for Muslims planning to perform Hajj, while also investing in Shariah-compliant ventures such as real estate, agriculture, and Islamic finance. The organization's investment portfolio is carefully curated to ensure compliance with Shariah principles, avoiding industries such as alcohol, gambling, and conventional banking (Lembaga Tabung Haji, 2021).

One of Tabung Haji's most notable achievements is its ability to generate consistent returns for its depositors while fulfilling its social mission. For example, the organization's investments in palm oil plantations and halal logistics have not only provided financial returns but also created jobs and supported rural development. Additionally, Tabung Haji has embraced digitalization by launching a mobile app that allows depositors to manage their savings and track their Hajj funds in real-time, enhancing transparency and accessibility. The success of Lembaga Tabung Haji highlights the importance of ethical governance and social responsibility in Shariah-compliant business ecosystems. By balancing financial objectives with social impact, Tabung Haji has become a trusted institution that embodies the principles of Islamic finance. Its operations also demonstrate how Malaysia's ecosystem supports the development of businesses that prioritize both profitability and ethical values.

Figure 4.2 shows a remarkable increase in Tabung Haji Zakat Payment, with amounts of RM44 million in 2012, RM47 million in 2013, RM53 million in 2014, RM59 million in 2015, and RM60 million in 2016. The trend has risen, and the value will continue to rise in tandem with an increase in the number of depositors and savings, as well as the performance of investments and other businesses.

In conclusion, these case studies highlight the key elements of Malaysia's Shariah-compliant business ecosystem: government support, regulatory frameworks, industry collaboration, and innovation. Maybank Islamic's performance highlights how a robust regulatory framework combined with technological enhancements may encourage innovation in Islamic finance. Nestlé Malaysia's integration of Shariah compliance

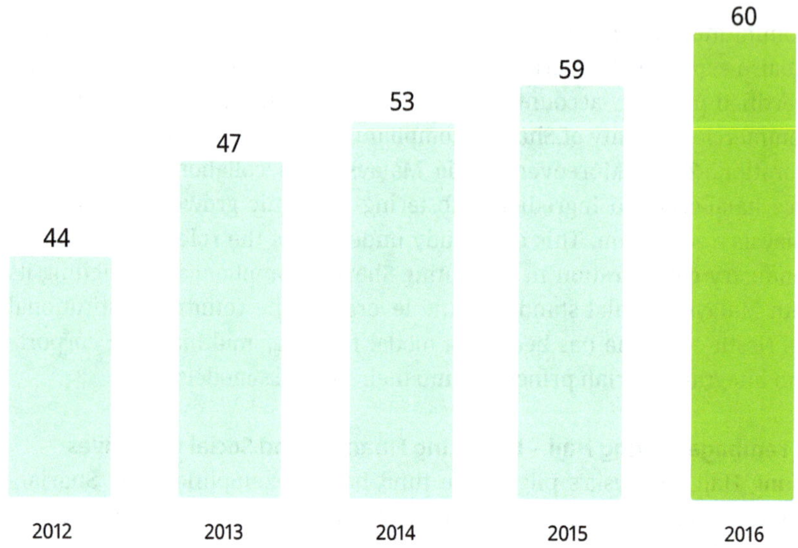

Figure 4.2: Tabung Haji Zakat payment (2012–2016).
Source: Tabung Haji (www.tabunghaji.gov.my).

into its supply chain highlights the importance of government-backed halal certification and industry partnerships. Finally, Lembaga Tabung Haji's balance of financial and social goals emphasizes the importance of ethical governance in fostering trust and sustainability. These case studies demonstrate how Malaysia's ecosystem has created a conducive climate for Shariah-compliant enterprises to flourish. They also emphasize the ecosystem's interconnection, with government policies, regulatory frameworks, and industry partnerships all working together to support ethical and sustainable business practices. Examining these success stories provides useful insights into the variables that have helped Malaysia become a global leader in Shariah-compliant business ecosystems.

4.8 Future Prospects and Global Implications

Malaysia's Shariah-compliant business ecosystem offers great potential for future expansion. The country's Vision 2025 for Islamic Finance seeks to strengthen its position as a global leader. Digitalization, sustainability, and international collaboration are among the key areas of concentration. For example, Malaysia intends to extend its green sukuk market and encourage the use of blockchain technology in Islamic finance (Bank Negara Malaysia, 2021). Malaysia's ecosystem also has global implications. By sharing its expertise and best practices, Malaysia can help other countries develop their own Shariah-compliant ecosystems. For instance, Malaysia's experience in halal certification and Islamic finance can serve as a blueprint for countries in Southeast Asia and beyond (Halal Industry Development Corporation, 2022). Technological advancements, such as AI and blockchain, will play a crucial role in shaping the future of Islamic finance and halal industries.

4.9 Conclusion

Malaysia's Shariah-compliant corporate landscape exemplifies worldwide leadership. Malaysia has established a successful ecosystem that aligns with Islamic beliefs while also addressing contemporary concerns through aggressive government policies, strong regulatory frameworks, and industry engagement. While obstacles persist, Malaysia's commitment to innovation and sustainability ensures that its ecosystem continues to thrive and inspire other countries.

References

Bank Negara Malaysia. (2021). *Islamic Finance Masterplan 2021–2025*. Retrieved from www.bnm.gov.my

Securities Commission Malaysia. (2020). *Shariah Governance Framework for Islamic Financial Institutions*. Retrieved from www.sc.com.my

Halal Industry Development Corporation. (2022). *Malaysia Halal Industry Report*. Retrieved from www.hdcglobal.com

Labuan IBFC. (2021). Annual Report 2021. Retrieved from www.labuanibfc.com

Islamic Financial Services Board. (2019). Islamic Finance and Global Financial Stability. Retrieved from www.ifsb.org

MAVCAP. (2021). Annual Report 2021. Retrieved from www.mavcap.com

Malaysia Digital Economy Corporation. (2021). Digital Investment Report 2021. Retrieved from www.mdec.com.my

Maybank Islamic. (2021). Annual Report 2021. Retrieved from www.maybankislamic.com

Muhammad Ridhwan Ab. Aziz. (2024). Islamic Digital Banking Framework in Malaysia: A Practitioners' Perspective. *International Journal of Islamic Economics and Finance Research*, *7*(1 July), 28–41.

Nestlé Malaysia. (2021). Sustainability Report 2021. Retrieved from www.nestle.com.my

Lembaga Tabung Haji. (2021). Annual Report 2021. Retrieved from www.tabunghaji.gov.my

Dusuki, A. W., & Abdullah, N. I. (2014). *Fundamentals of Shariah in Islamic Finance*. ISRA.

Islamic Financial Services Board. (2019). *Islamic Finance and Global Financial Stability*. Retrieved from www.ifsb.org

Laldin, M. A., & Furqani, H. (2013). *Innovation and Creativity in Islamic Finance*. Journal of Islamic Economics, Banking, and Finance.

World Bank. (2020). *Global Islamic Finance Report*. Retrieved from www.worldbank.org

Nor Nabilla Muhammad, Izra Berakon, Millenia Ayu Nur 'Aini, Safwan Kamal

Chapter 5 What Matters to the Probability of Default? The Role of Indonesia Sharia Firms in Normal and Crisis Periods

Abstract: This research aims to investigate the estimator for the Probability of Default (PD) which was measured by Merton's Structural Model formula by incorporating the fundamental (liquidity, solvability, and profitability ratios) and macroeconomic determinants (inflation, interest rates, and exchange rates). The data were taken from the Indonesia Sharia Stock Index (ISSI) from 2016 to 2022 and analyzed by using hierarchical regression analysis at several stages of the research model supported by STATA 17. Interestingly, both fundamental and macroeconomic estimators are pivotal factors in determining companies' PD, especially in solvability ratio and inflation. In addition, the robustness tests were conducted to gain comprehensive results by adding control variables separately, splitting samples based on firm-specific context (small-big firm's size), and testing with diverse year conditions. The results show that the debt ratio of small size and young age companies affects the PD. Investment managers should focus on the company's solvability ratio and inflation levels to overcome the PD. Moreover, the research focuses on estimating the factors both internal and external that can influence Sharia firm's probability of default in normal and crisis periods. Sharia firms need to reduce the usage of debt level and optimize the use of internal company funds to create sustainable financial performance.

Keywords: Probability of Default, Fundamental, Macroeconomics, Merton Structural Model, and Sustainable financial performance

5.1 Introduction

The development of the health crisis, which was caused by the COVID-19 pandemic, had an impact on economic activities both nationally and globally. Based on data from the Central Statistics Agency (BPS), Indonesia experienced a contraction of economic growth in 2020 by 2.07 percent. As a result of this, the Indonesian economy in 2020 experienced deflation because economic development in Indonesia had an unstable movement due to COVID-19. The COVID-19 pandemic greatly affected the Indonesian economy from the beginning of the second quarter of 2020. This was due to the regulation of Large-Scale Social Restrictions (PSBB) which caused a lockdown throughout

https://doi.org/10.1515/9783111575407-006

the country. This regulation causes an increase in the decline in the economy in formal and non-formal companies. The decline in the economy led to the emergence of termination of employment and caused many companies to decide to go out of business or go bankrupt.

Weakening economic activity in a country can signal an impending economic recession. The economic recession causes a decrease in the company's high level of investment which can further reduce capital and profits. This condition causes companies that are in debt to experience a company's probability of default (Saleh and Sudiyatno, 2013). When the country's economic conditions are sluggish, investment realization may also experience a decline. However, the Ministry of PPN/Bappenas (2023) recorded data on the realization of domestic investment in the third quarter of 2023 reaching IDR 374.4 trillion, increasing 21.6% to the third quarter of 2022, which was IDR 307.8 trillion.

Default is a condition where companies are unable to repay debts including interest or principal on their loans to investors (Malasari et al., 2020). The probability of default is an opportunity that shows a situation in which the company is unable to repay the debt which includes interest and principal on the loan to investors (Carvalho et al., 2020). Default also causes an economic downturn (Frijters & Antić, 2016; Yang & Hu, 2024). Defaults occur because the company cannot repay loans to investors on time. The company's inability to repay credit loans will have a broad impact on companies and corporate investors which can lead to a financial default (Ahmed et al., 2023). The default can be divided into two types, among others default for the issuing company and default for debt instruments. The default of the issuing company is a condition in which the issuing company fails to pay the bonds it has issued. Meanwhile, the default for debt instruments is a debt instrument that is declared to be in default during the issuance period of the debt securities (Pefindo, 2022).

The default assessment uses the Merton Structural Model which was coined by Robert C. Merton (1974). This model is based on a valuation consisting of the company's total assets, equity, and liabilities. In this assumption, a company that has an asset value less than the company's debt value will be considered a default (Kliestik et al., 2015). One component that explains the loss of default is the fundamental component (Cui & Kaas, 2020). Fundamental analysis involves assessing the company's performance in terms of the company's effectiveness and efficiency in achieving the objectives listed in the financial statements (Witkowska et al., 2021; Zhao et al., 2023). Defaults that occur in one company may have an impact on other companies because of factors that influence it, such as macroeconomics (Pasricha et al., 2021). Macroeconomics describes the problems that will be faced by the economy of a country. Therefore, macroeconomics is very helpful in predicting future investment conditions (Dibiasi & Sarferaz, 2023; Glas & Heinisch, 2023). An investor needs to pay attention to several macroeconomic variables to predict future investment conditions (Ballinari et al., 2022).

Previous studies such as Khan et al. (2021) suggest that Return on Assets (ROA) has an insignificant effect on default, so the results obtained are different from what is expected. However, according to the research of Vuković et al. (2020) financial indicators such as return on equity, return on asset, solvency, working capital turnover, and stocks/current assets can predict the possibility of a company's bankruptcy. The research results are in line with Dwiarti et al. (2021) research which proves that ROA can predict the probability of bankruptcy of non-banking financial sector companies in Indonesia. Companies with high debt ratios are considered to have higher business risks which could further lead to default (Yadav et al., 2022). This research is inversely proportional to the research conducted by Dirman (2020) which obtained the results that the debt ratio did not affect the company's Financial Distress. In addition, the study also obtained the results that the Current Ratio variable did not affect the company's financial distress condition. The results of this study are inversely proportional to the research of Boubaker et al. (2020) who obtained the current ratio results that can be used to predict the financial distress of a company.

Carvalho et al. (2020) suggest that there is a negative relationship between basic interest rates on the probability of default. Different research by López-Penabad et al. (2022) that interest rates have a positive effect on the probability of default. Low interest rates can reduce the probability of default. Then the research conducted by Kholisoh & Dwiarti (2020) regarding inflation could affect the company's financial distress level. In contrast, the research of Dewianawati & Setiawan (2022) found that inflation was not significant to the company's financial distress. Furthermore, research on the exchange rate has been carried out by Narayan (2022) who obtained the results that during crisis period, exchange rates may strengthen or weaken. Meanwhile, according to research by Kholisoh & Dwiarti (2020), the high and low exchange rates do not affect the company's level of financial distress.

The results of previous studies regarding the influence of fundamental and macroeconomic factors on the level of probability of default show inconsistencies in research results so a research gap appears. Therefore, researchers are interested in re-examining the influence of fundamental and macroeconomic factors on the level of probability of a company's default. Furthermore, most previous researchers examined the probability of default in financial companies, so researchers were very interested in adopting the influence of the probability of default in non-financial Sharia companies.

The main purpose of this study is to examine and analyze the effect of fundamental and macroeconomic factors on the probability of default of Sharia firms listed on ISSI. In addition, this research contributes to the literature related to factors that can influence a company's probability of default where researchers adopt internal and external economic factors in normal conditions and financial crises. Apart from that, researchers involve Sharia firms as research objects to look at the potential for payment failure to ensure that Sharia firms have passed financial and business screening which allows them to suppress and minimize the possibility of default. However, it needs to be reviewed so that it can become one of the concerns that must be well understood by company managers to face difficult economic or financial situations.

5.2 Literatur Review and Hypothesis Development

The probability of default (PD) is an opportunity that shows the company's inability to pay debts, including interest and principal on investors' loans. According to the default theory, a default occurs when the value of a company's future assets is lower than the value of its future debt. The estimation of the probability of default in this study uses the Merton structural model. The indicator in this model is the market value which consists of the company's total assets, equity, and debt (Bui et al., 2023). Profitable companies prefer internal funding because it can minimize the level of use of company debt and the higher external funding, the higher the default of the company (Foila et al., 2019; Luo & Luo, 2021; Melianti & Kontesa, 2022). External funding sources are used if internal funding is not able to meet the company's funding needs (Bui et al., 2023). Furthermore, according to the trade-off theory, interest payments can reduce taxable income. Debt benefits the company because of interest and dividend payments. Debt benefits the company because interest payments are calculated as expenses and reduce taxable income, so the tax results paid by the company are reduced (Kholbadalov, 2012; Sánchez-Ballesta & Yagüe, 2023).

The current Ratio (CR) is a ratio to measure the ability of the company's current assets to pay off its short-term obligations (Orlando & Pelosi, 2020). The higher CR indicates that there are a lot of idle funds that reduce the company's profitability. The better of Current Ratio, the higher the level of guarantee for the company's liquidity payments (Kholisoh & Dwiarti, 2020). That way, investors will be interested in investing their capital in the company concerned to increase the company's assets (Kurniani, 2021). The increasing of assets can minimize the occurrence of loan defaults by the company. This description is under previous research conducted by Ogachi et al. (2020) and Septine Mayliza et al. (2020) which explains that CR affects financial distress and probability of bankruptcy. Based on the explanation of the theory above and the results of previous research, the proposed hypothesis is:

Hypothesis 1 = Current Ratio (CR) has a negative effect on the probability of default.

The DER ratio aims to estimate the level of the company's capital sources financed by debt (Koh et al., 2014). According to the DER theory, the higher the DER value, the higher the interest expense and the higher the risk of the company's default (Orlando & Pelosi, 2020). The company has a low debt service capacity if it has difficulty generating cash flow due to weak earnings productivity (Uddin et al., 2020). Leverage ratios have an important role in identifying the risk of default (Sariev & Germano, 2019). If the fixed costs charged are relatively high, the company's profit will decrease which will have an impact on the company's failure to pay debts. Research conducted by Malasari et al. (2020) proves that DER has a positive effect on the possibility of default of non-financial companies in Indonesia. The higher the DER level, the higher the default probability value. Following the balance theory which has the assumption that the larger the company, the more debt financing. Based on the above theory and previous research, the hypotheses proposed by the author in this study are:

Hypothesis 2 = Debt to Equity Ratio (DER) has a positive effect on the probability of default.

Return on Assets (ROA) is a ratio to measure the level of effectiveness of the company in using its assets to generate company profits (Rahman, 2017; Trejo-Pech et al., 2023). The high ROA of the company indicates that the company is more effective in obtaining profits with its assets. Thus, it will attract investors to invest their funds in the company concerned (Suhadak et al., 2019). This causes an increase in the company's capital so the probability of the company's bankruptcy becomes small (Paletta & Alimehmeti, 2022). In line, previous studies such as research conducted by Sariev & Germano (2019) stated that ROA has a negative effect on the bankruptcy of a bank or company. While Shahriar et al. (2023) state that there is a positive influence between ROA and bankruptcy. Based on the explanation of the theory above and previous research, the proposed hypothesis is:

Hypothesis 3 = Return on Assets (ROA) has a significant negative effect on the probability of default.

Inflation is an increase in commodity prices in general and continuously in an economy and at a certain period. Inflation pushes up production costs which ultimately leads to an increase in commodity prices in various industrial sectors (Abaidoo & Agyapong, 2022). If the company does not have sufficient funds for additional production costs, the company will likely carry out a debt policy that will be repaid at a predetermined time (Arhinful & Radmehr, 2023). Countries often default on their debts and experience high of inflation or poor macroeconomic performance (Sunder-Plassmann, 2020). According to Merton's theory, a company whose debt value is above the value of its assets will be considered a default (Hull et al., 2004). In line with that, research Mulyana & Ulpah

(2020) proves that an increase in inflation has an impact on an increase in the probability of default. Based on the explanation of the theory above and previous research, the proposed hypothesis is:

Hypothesis 4 = Inflation has a significant positive effect on the probability of default.

Interest rates are a measure of a macroeconomic activity that can affect the dynamics of financial flows, inflation, company investment, and currency movements (Le & Nguyen, 2023). The interest rate can be defined as the price charged by the borrower for the loaned asset (Egbunike & Okerekeoti, 2018; Mishkin, 2014). The increase in high interest rates is a negative signal for companies that finance in the form of debt. The company will have difficulty paying debt installments to creditors. This means that the company experienced a decrease in equity (Kholisoh & Dwiarti, 2020; Subramaniam & Masron, 2022). If the company's equity is unable to pay debts with high interest rates, the company has a probability of default (Munangi, 2020). In line with this theory, previous studies such as the research of Laurin & Martynenko (2009) and Santoso et al. (2018) prove that interest rates have a significant positive effect on non-performing financing. Based on the explanation of the theory above and previous research, the hypotheses that can be proposed are:

Hypothesis 5 = Interest rates have a significant positive effect on the probability of default.

The exchange rate is the price of the currency of a country measured in the price of the foreign currency to which it is attached (Mankiw, 2016). Companies that use the exchange rate are companies that carry out export and import activities of manufactured goods. The depreciation of the rupiah value causes the price of imported goods to become more expensive, and export goods to become cheaper, and this is problematic for companies that carry out international activities (Asonuma, 2016). The decrease in profit causes the company to have financial difficulties in financing its production of raw materials and triggers the occurrence of the company's probability of default. This theory follows research conducted by Mulyana & Ulpah (2020) that the depreciation of the exchange rate has the potential to experience default. Based on the explanation of the theory above and previous research, the hypotheses that can be proposed are:

Hypothesis 6 = Exchange rate has a significant negative effect on the probability of default.

The conceptual framework is presented in Figure 5.1.

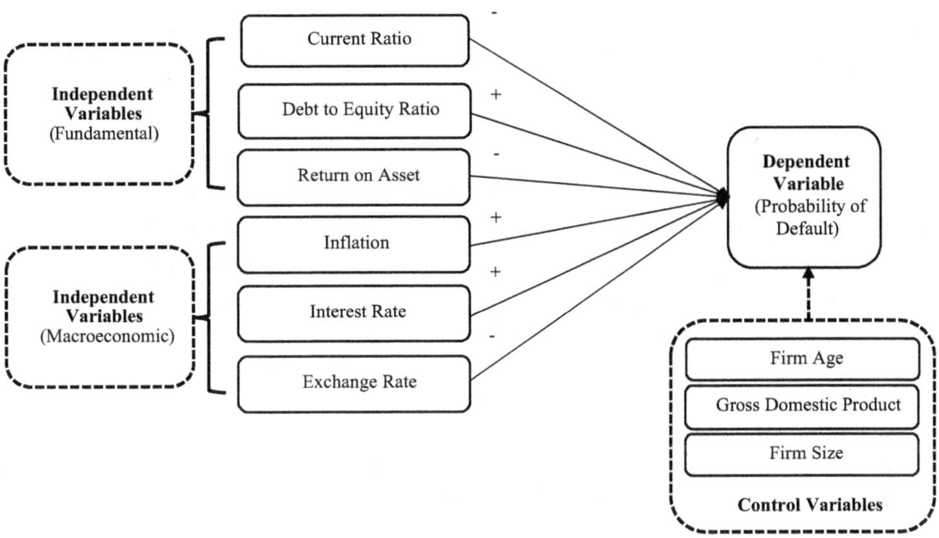

Figure 5.1: Conceptual Framework.

5.3 Methodology

The type of research used in this research is quantitative research by using the OLS (Ordinary Least Square) random effect model to see the relationship between independent and dependent variables. The researchers used the probability of default (PD) to measure the company's bankruptcy. Then, the independent variables company's fundamentals are proxied by the liquidity, solvability, and profitability ratios (variables and measurements are described in Table 5.1). Whereas macroeconomics measured inflation, interest rates, and exchange rates. The data were taken from non-financial companies listed in the Indonesia Sharia Stock Index (ISSI) from 2016 to 2022 and analyzed by using hierarchical regression analysis at several stages of the research model and analyzed using stepwise hierarchical regression analysis in the research model supported STATA 17. Furthermore, the research sample was determined using the purposive sampling technique by screening non-financial sector companies that have been listed on the Indonesian Sharia Stock Index for the 2016–2022 period. The population of data was 233 companies. The sample selection was carried out using the purposive sampling technique and obtained 21 companies.

The researchers conducted several testing methods, such as conducting descriptive statistical tests to provide an overview of the subject or research variable being studied. We also perform collinearity tests to prove the relationship between variables. More-

Table 5.1: Variables and Measurements.

Variables	Measurements	Sources
Probability of Default (PD)	*DD (Distance to Default)* = $\frac{\ln\left(\frac{A}{D}\right) + [\mu_A - 0.5\,\sigma^2_A]T}{\sigma_A\sqrt{T}}$ *PD (Probability of Default)* = *N(-DD)*	(Afik et al., 2016; Mushafiq et al., 2022; Omar & Prasanna, 2021)
Current Ratio (CR)	(Total Assets) / (Total Debt)	(Koh et al., 2014)
Debt to Equity Ratio (DER)	(Total Debt) / (Total Equity)	(Koh et al., 2014)
Return on Asset (ROA)	(Net Income) / (Total Assets)	(Koh et al., 2014)
Inflation (INF)	An increase in general commodity prices continuously in an economy and over a certain period.	Central Statistics Agency (BPS)
Interest Rate (IR)	The rate of payment on a loan	BI-7 Day Reverse Repo Rate (BI7DRR)
Exchange Rate (ER)	The price of the currency of a country which is measured in the price of the foreign currency	Central Statistics Agency (BPS)

over, the researcher conducted a panel data regression test by using Random Effect Model (REM) to examine the effect of fundamental factors and macroeconomic variables on the probability of company default by using the panel data regression method. To produce robust and consistent results, the researchers conducted a robustness test by conducting several stages of testing into 6 models (adding control variables separately in Models 4, 5, and 6). Moreover, the authors also conducted split samples by age (young and old) and size (small and big) to get the best model suitable in different contexts. And last, we carried out year conditions 2016 to 2022 and 2020 to 2022. Thus, the researcher formulated the research model as follows:

$$\textit{Probability of Default}_{i,t} = \alpha + \beta_1\,\textit{Current Ratio}_{i,t} + \beta_2\,\textit{Debt to Equity Ratio}_{i,t} + \beta_3\,\textit{Return on Asset}_{i,t} + \beta_4\,\textit{Inflation} + \beta_5\,\textit{Interest Rate} + \beta_6\,\textit{Exchange Rate} + e_{i,t}$$

5.4 Results and Discussions

5.4.1 Results

Table 5.2 is a statistic descriptive which includes the number of observations, mean, minimum, and maximum. The number of observations in the study was 147 samples. The result shows that the mean of Probability of Default (PD) is 0.4252. Meanwhile, CR shows that the mean value of the CR variable is 1.5127. The mean value of DER is 1.2169, which further shows that the average company has a good DER level, it because the company sample is Sharia firms that have fulfilled the financial screening the company's debt level should not exceed 45%. The average value of the ROA variable is 0.1248. Moreover, 2021 is the year with the lowest inflation at 0.0156. While the highest value of 0.0551 occurred in 2022. The minimum interest rate occurred in 2021, which was 0.0352 percent. Meanwhile, the highest interest rate occurred in 2019 at 0.0563 percent. The minimum exchange rate occurred in 2016 of 13,436 while the maximum exchange rate occurred in 2022 of 15,371. The mean firm age in this sample was 47. And the mean value of the GDP variable is 0.0289. The minimum GDP value of -0.0310 occurred in 2020. While the maximum GDP occurred in 2022 was 0.0531. Then the mean value of the size variable is 30.2256. The correlation value of the research data is < 90%, thus, there is no linear correlation between all variables or multicollinearity problems in the researcher's models (See Table 5.3).

Table 5.2: Statistic Descriptive.

Variables	Obs	Mean	Std.dev	Min	Max
PD	147	0.4252	0.2102	0.0239	0.8006
CR	147	1.5127	0.7394	0.2900	3.8770
DER	147	1.2169	0.7209	0.0000	3.7882
ROA	147	0.1248	0.3383	-0.1000	2.5900
INF	147	0.0307	0.0118	0.0168	0.0551
BI Rate	147	0.0461	0.0069	0.0352	0.0563
ER	147	14164	606.9331	13436	15371
Age	147	47	18	3	106
GDP	147	0.0289	0.0256	-0.0310	0.0531
Size	147	30.2256	1.9689	15.4108	33.2557

Note: PoD: Probability of Default; CR: Current Ratio; DER: Debt to Equity Ratio; ROA: Return on Asset; INF: Inflation; BI Rate: BI-7 Day Reverse Repo Rate; ER: Exchange Rate; Age: Firm Age; GDP: Gross Domestic Product; Size: Firm Size.

The researchers carried out the regression analysis through 6 models. Model 1 is a model of the fundamental factor variables of PD. Then Model 2 is the result of regression analysis of the macroeconomic factor variables on PD. Model 3 is the result of the fundamental and macroeconomic factor variables on PD. While Model 4 is the result of the fundamental, macroeconomic factor, and control 1 (Age) on PD. Model 5 is the result of the fundamental, macroeconomic factor, and control 1 and 2 (Age and GDP) on PD. And the last, Model 6 is the result of the fundamental, macroeconomic factor, and control 1, 2, and 3 (Age, GDP, and Size) on PD.

The main model in this research is represented by model 3 (See Table 5.4). The result shows that CR does not affect the firm's probability of default, so hypothesis 1 of this study is rejected. These results are consistent when tested in every model. Meanwhile, the DER variable has a negative effect on the firm's probability of default. The higher the DER value of a company, the lower the probability that the company will experience

Table 5.3: Correlation Test Results.

Variables	PD	CR	DER	ROA	INF	IR	ER	AGE	GDP	SIZE
Probability of Default (PD)	1.0000									
Current Ratio (CR)	-0.3213	1.0000								
Debt to Equity Ratio (DER)	0.2578	-0.2372	1.0000							
Return on Asset (ROA)	0.2828	-0.0539	-0.0235	1.0000						
Inflation (INF)	0.0128	0.2369	0.1444	0.0407	1.0000					
Interest Rate (IR)	0,0349	-0.1140	-0.1561	-0.0428	-0.0093	1.0000				
Exchange Rate (ER)	-0.0434	0.1722	0.2296	0.0587	0.5335	-0.4397	1.0000			
Age (AGE)	0.0159	-0.1450	0.0021	0.5767	0.0167	-0.0714	0.0891	1.0000		
Gross Domestic Product (GDP)	0.0247	0.1457	0.0478	0.0452	0.6988	0.2441	0.1948	-0.0148	1.0000	
Size (SIZE)	0.0151	-0.2155	-0.0569	-0.1265	-0.2168	0.0483	-0.1488	-0.0232	-0.1142	1.0000

default. This is not appropriate with the hypothesis testing that was previously proposed that DER has a positive relationship to the firm probability of default, thus hypothesis 2 is rejected. Furthermore, the ROA variable proved to not affect the firm's probability of default, consistent with every model.

The macroeconomic variable, such as inflation, has a positive effect on the firm's probability of default. The higher the inflation rate of a country, the higher the company's probability of default. Consistent in every model of data research, thus hypothesis 4 is accepted. Furthermore, the results of this study indicate that there is no relationship between interest rates and firm probability of default. So hypothesis 5 research is rejected. The strength of the exchange rate in a country also has no relationship with the firm's probability of default. Thus, the hypothesis 6 is rejected.

Table 5.4: Result Models 2016 to 2019.

	(1)	(2)	(3)	(4)	(5)	(6)
CR	0.00221 (0.43)		-0.000404 (-0.08)	-0.000281 (-0.05)	-0.000333 (-0.06)	0.000358 (0.07)
DER	-0.0261*** (-4.84)		-0.0223*** (-4.04)	-0.0217*** (-3.89)	-0.0217*** (-3.87)	-0.0210*** (-3.72)
ROA	-0.00366 (-0.30)		-0.00245 (-0.22)	-0.00160 (-0.14)	-0.00188 (-0.16)	-0.00330 (-0.29)
INF		0.827*** (3.79)	0.918*** (4.04)	0.811*** (3.31)	0.754* (2.40)	0.682* (2.09)
IR		0.198 (0.56)	-0.00885 (-0.02)	-0.179 (-0.47)	-0.203 (-0.52)	-0.191 (-0.49)
LOG_ER		-0.748*** (-4.77)	-0.609*** (-3.93)	-0.415 (-1.90)	-0.413 (-1.88)	-0.407 (-1.84)
Age				-0.00213 (-1.27)	-0.00209 (-1.24)	-0.00221 (-1.29)
GDP					0.0360 (0.29)	0.0421 (0.34)
Size						-0.00130 (-0.75)
_cons	0.454*** (10.44)	3.498*** (5.32)	2.952*** (4.56)	2.262** (2.65)	2.250** (2.63)	2.273** (2.64)
Obs.	147	147	147	147	147	147
N Firm	21	21	21	21	21	21
Chi-square	23.95	36.35	56.14	56.52	56.12	57.38
Adj. R-square						

t statistics in parentheses
$^{*}p < 0.05$, $^{**}p < 0.01$, $^{***}p < 0.001$

5.4.1.1 Robustness Test

The following regression model shows the research results in Table 5.4 for 2016 to 2019 (normal period) and Table 5.5 for 2020 to 2022 (crisis period). Table 5.4 shows that DER has a negative impact on the probability of default consistent in every model. Moreover, inflation is statistically positive and significant on the probability of default. Inflation causes the purchasing power of consumers to decline which in turn can distort consumer consumption decisions. The possibility of default on the company can result in a temporary decrease in productivity (Sunder-Plassmann, 2020). However, the inflation shock caused a decrease in stock and bond prices (Lou et al., 2019). Systematically, the company's cash flow was severely disrupted due to rising selling prices and reduced demand for products in the market. Thus, there is a decrease in the company's profitability. When products on the market experience delays to convert into sales and profits. This condition makes the company potentially experience a probability of default because it is unable to pay off its short-term and long-term obligations.

The fundamental factor variable measured by CR and ROA did not affect on probability of default and the macroeconomic variable measured by interest rate and exchange rate statistically didn't have an impact on the probability of default. Surprisingly, the research results of the robustness test show that the debt ratio of small-size companies affects the probability of default in every model (See Table 5.6). This is in line with the results Cathcart et al. (2020) that financial leverage has a greater impact on the possibility of default in SMEs than in large companies. So do young-age (new established) companies (See Table 5.8). However, the model demonstrates a lack of robustness when applied to big-size and old-age (long established) companies (See Tables 5.7 & 5.9).

Table 5.5: Result Models 2020 to 2022.

	(1)	(2)	(3)	(4)	(5)
CR	0.00410		0.00757	0.00754	0.00877
	(0.80)		(1.25)	(1.21)	(1.36)
DER	0.0165*		0.0205**	0.0208**	0.0216**
	(2.39)		(2.62)	(2.58)	(2.66)
ROA	-0.0116		-0.0102	-0.0103	-0.0113
	(-1.18)		(-1.01)	(-0.99)	(-1.09)
INF		0.0962	-0.216	-0.251	-0.320
		(0.63)	(-1.08)	(-1.10)	(-1.27)
IR		0.377	0.657	0.752	0.751
		(0.42)	(0.74)	(0.79)	(0.79)
Age				0.000743	0.000768
				(0.34)	(0.35)
Size					-0.00114
					(-0.65)

Table 5.5 (continued)

	(1)	(2)	(3)	(4)	(5)
_cons	0.385***	0.395***	0.354***	0.314*	0.346*
	(9.10)	(7.01)	(6.33)	(2.43)	(2.46)
Obs.	63	63	63	63	63
N Firm	21	21	21	21	21
Chi-square	7.922	0.654	9.250	8.950	9.432
Adj. R-square					

t statistics in parentheses
*$p < 0.05$, **$p < 0.01$, ***$p < 0.001$

Table 5.6: Small Size Results Models 2016 to 2022.

	(1)	(2)	(3)	(4)	(5)	(6)
CR	-0.00415		-0.00378	-0.00448	-0.00565	-0.00450
	(-0.64)		(-0.56)	(-0.54)	(-0.65)	(-0.51)
DER	-0.0568***		-0.0527***	-0.0522***	-0.0527***	-0.0517***
	(-7.64)		(-7.10)	(-5.67)	(-5.64)	(-5.48)
ROA	-0.00394		-0.00267	-0.000688	-0.00186	-0.00374
	(-0.40)		(-0.29)	(-0.06)	(-0.16)	(-0.32)
INF		0.626	0.624*	0.530	0.352	0.224
		(1.60)	(2.26)	(1.50)	(0.75)	(0.46)
IR		0.102	-0.592	-0.725	-0.832	-0.782
		(0.16)	(-1.30)	(-1.23)	(-1.34)	(-1.25)
LOG_ER		-0.894**	-0.696***	-0.554	-0.536	-0.552
		(-3.19)	(-3.61)	(-1.89)	(-1.80)	(-1.85)
Age				-0.00168	-0.00164	-0.00163
				(-0.95)	(-0.92)	(-0.91)
GDP					0.116	0.128
					(0.58)	(0.64)
Size						-0.00193
						(-0.91)
_cons	0.491***	4.097***	3.381***	2.882*	2.815*	2.936*
	(6.75)	(3.49)	(4.20)	(2.47)	(2.38)	(2.46)
Obs.	61	61	61	61	61	61
N Firm	12	12	12	12	12	12
Chi-square	59.21	14.48	82.68	54.30	53.61	54.04
Adj. R-square						

t statistics in parentheses
*$p < 0.05$, **$p < 0.01$, ***$p < 0.001$

Table 5.7: Big Size Results Models 2016 to 2022.

	(1)	(2)	(3)	(4)	(5)	(6)
CR	0.00249		-0.00398	-0.00376	-0.00363	-0.00450
	(0.34)		(-0.45)	(-0.41)	(-0.40)	(-0.52)
DER	-0.00529		-0.00102	0.000021	0.000243	-0.00544
	(-0.71)		(-0.11)	(0.00)	(0.03)	(-0.58)
ROA	-0.0202		-0.00620	0.00137	0.00167	0.0137
	(-0.36)		(-0.10)	(0.02)	(0.03)	(0.22)
INF		0.799**	0.891*	0.739	0.664	0.851
		(2.85)	(2.18)	(1.73)	(1.18)	(1.59)
IR		0.360	0.302	0.0916	0.0665	0.176
		(0.82)	(0.53)	(0.15)	(0.11)	(0.30)
LOG_ER		-0.544**	-0.527*	-0.296	-0.293	-0.577
		(-2.67)	(-1.98)	(-0.93)	(-0.91)	(-1.72)
Age				-0.00271	-0.00269	-0.00408*
				(-1.41)	(-1.39)	(-2.02)
GDP					0.0430	0.0436
					(0.22)	(0.23)
Size						0.0556*
						(2.18)
_cons	0.398***	2.610**	2.548*	1.724	1.710	1.206
	(8.53)	(3.06)	(2.29)	(1.36)	(1.33)	(0.97)
Obs.	86	86	86	86	86	86
N Firm	13	13	13	13	13	13
Chi-square	0.709	16.23	10.40	12.12	11.95	18.16
Adj. R-square						

t statistics in parentheses

$^{*}p < 0.05$, $^{**}p < 0.01$, $^{***}p < 0.001$

Table 5.8: New Established Results Models 2016 to 2022.

	(1)	(2)	(3)	(4)	(5)	(6)
CR	-0.00281		-0.00150	-0.000707	-0.000904	-0.00167
	(-0.51)		(-0.29)	(-0.15)	(-0.19)	(-0.32)
DER	-0.0437***		-0.0385***	-0.0371***	-0.0369***	-0.0361***
	(-6.70)		(-6.01)	(-6.15)	(-6.07)	(-5.52)
ROA	0.0999*		0.0885	0.0983*	0.0991*	0.126
	(2.15)		(1.93)	(2.29)	(2.29)	(1.68)
INF		0.818*	0.728**	0.381	0.267	0.281
		(2.47)	(2.62)	(1.32)	(0.74)	(0.74)
IR		0.313	-0.0991	-0.666	-0.713	-0.722
		(0.58)	(-0.24)	(-1.51)	(-1.57)	(-1.53)

Table 5.8 (continued)

	(1)	(2)	(3)	(4)	(5)	(6)
LOG_ER		-0.907***	-0.675***	-0.0677	-0.0656	-0.0578
		(-3.88)	(-3.78)	(-0.25)	(-0.24)	(-0.21)
Age				-0.00682**	-0.00673**	-0.00674**
				(-2.77)	(-2.71)	(-2.83)
GDP					0.0717	0.0694
					(0.52)	(0.48)
Size						0.00119
						(0.45)
_cons	0.485***	4.159***	3.259***	1.022	1.013	0.945
	(10.63)	(4.26)	(4.38)	(0.96)	(0.94)	(0.87)
Obs.	75	75	75	75	75	75
N Firm	12	12	12	12	12	12
Chi-square	56.19	23.11	93.40	114.7	113.5	101.8
Adj. R-square						

t statistics in parentheses

$^{*}p < 0.05$, $^{**}p < 0.01$, $^{***}p < 0.001$

Table 5.9: Long Established Results Models 2016 to 2022.

	(1)	(2)	(3)	(4)	(5)	(6)
CR	0.0105		0.0135	0.0133	0.0132	0.00573
	(1.20)		(1.21)	(1.14)	(1.12)	(0.31)
DER	-0.000728		0.00650	0.00682	0.00688	0.00856
	(-0.09)		(0.75)	(0.75)	(0.75)	(0.59)
ROA	-0.0138		-0.0109	-0.0104	-0.0101	-0.00511
	(-1.10)		(-0.95)	(-0.86)	(-0.82)	(-0.26)
INF		0.860**	0.571	0.546	0.601	0.980
		(2.96)	(1.52)	(1.30)	(1.17)	(1.21)
IR		0.0535	0.193	0.151	0.174	0.469
		(0.12)	(0.39)	(0.27)	(0.30)	(0.54)
LOG_ER		-0.632**	-0.657**	-0.610	-0.618	-1.030*
		(-2.89)	(-2.84)	(-1.75)	(-1.75)	(-2.35)
Age				-0.000544	-0.000524	0.00382
				(-0.19)	(-0.19)	(1.71)
GDP					-0.0313	-0.0434
					(-0.18)	(-0.16)
Size						0.00209
						(0.31)
_cons	0.404***	3.009**	3.091**	2.931*	2.963*	4.330*
	(6.09)	(3.28)	(3.20)	(2.21)	(2.21)	(2.44)

Table 5.9 (continued)

	(1)	(2)	(3)	(4)	(5)	(6)
Obs.	72	72	72	72	72	72
N Firm	11	11	11	11	11	11
Chi-square	2.875	14.19	16.02	14.45	14.19	8.205
Adj. R-square						

t statistics in parentheses

$^{*}p < 0.05$, $^{**}p < 0.01$, $^{***}p < 0.001$

5.4.2 Discussions

The current Ratio (CR) is a ratio to measure the ability of the company's current assets to pay off its short-term obligations (Koh et al., 2014). The high and low CR of the company will not affect the probability of the company's default. This is due to the difference in the timeframe in the estimation. The current ratio is a ratio that measures the company's liquidity in the short term, while the probability of default is a long-term company debt forecast model (Malasari et al., 2020). The results of this study are in accordance with the results of research conducted by Featherstone et al. (2017) that CR information does not explain the default of risks well. The current Ratio and probability of default are two different things in terms of the measurement period of the company. CR is an indicator of a company's short-term liquidity. The probability of bankruptcy is a measurement model of company bankruptcy that has a long period of time. In contrast, Septine Mayliza et al. (2020) obtained the results of research on current ratios that affect the probability of bankruptcy.

DER is a proxy for solvency ratio to estimate the value of debt with the total equity owned by the company. By using DER, the company will know the extent to which a company's source of funding is financed by the company's external capital (debt). A high DER value indicates the company has a lot of debt, and the total composition of debt is greater than the total equity. When the debt is increasing, the interest and principal expenses that must be paid by the company will also increase. If the fixed costs charged have increased, it will have an impact on the decline in company profits and will affect the company's inability to repay debt. The company's inability to pay the debt will lead the company to experience the probability of default (Luo & Luo, 2021).

The difficulty of obtaining additional funds in the form of debt does not rule out the possibility that the company will face the risk of bankruptcy. The results are in accordance with the research of Malasari et al. (2020) which obtained DER results have a positive influence on the potential for non-financial default in Indonesia. According to the Trade Off Theory (TOT), the use of high debt is usually carried out by large companies. Because large companies require large funding needs, and external funding in the form of debt is one way to meet these funding needs. The results of this study are also in line with the pecking order (POT) theory. According to the pecking order theory, companies using external funds (external financing) prefer bonds (debt securities) rather than issuing new shares. The reason is because the cost of issuing bonds is lower than the cost of issuing new shares. Companies that carry out external funding indicate that the company's internal sources of funds are no longer able to meet the company's funding needs. So, the company must carry out a policy of issuing bonds and issuing new shares.

These results are different from the proposed hypothesis. DER has a negative effect on the probability of default, meaning that the higher the DER, the lower the company's probability of default in a normal period. This factor is caused by the company's profitability. A high DER reflects the high use of debt by the company as a source of company capital. The use of high debt can not only increase the risk of corporate default. However, increasing the use of debt in a reasonable manner causes an increase in the company's profitability. Companies that need external funding as additional funds will issue debt securities (bonds) which are then invested in investors. Interested investors will make these investments and invest their funds in the issuing company to obtain bond profits. Investment in these bonds will cause the company to get additional funds for its production activities. Thus, it will reduce the risk of financial distress (Ogachi et al., 2020). In the research of Abdelaziz et al. (2020) increasing company profitability helps companies to reduce interest and principal loan payments for companies. In this way, the probability of the company's probability of default is reduced.

During crisis periods, DER has a positive influence on default. These results are consistent on each test model. Most companies will experience a large negative impact due to crisis conditions which will cause profitability to fall. Thus, companies encourage the use of large debts to fund the business. Thus, the higher the company's DER level in the recession period, the higher the company's probability of default (Arellano, 2004; Luo & Luo, 2021).

ROA is more suitable to be applied in research related to the rate of return on investment by investors. Investors that have to invest in the company's external funding should ignore signals about the company's profitability. This theory is in line with the results research of Widyanty et al. (2019) that ROA can't predict bank bankruptcy. The ability of assets to generate profits has no effect on the risk of the company's financial difficulties. ROA has no effect on the company's probability of default because the use of ROA is considered less precise in predicting debt, both short-term and long-term. ROA is more appropriate to be used in the calculation of the assessment of the effectiveness of investment management.

Inflation is one of the macroeconomic variables that may affect the probability of default. An increase in inflation that occurs in a country will cause production costs and losses in productive activities (Kholisoh & Dwiarti, 2020). The use of high debt will cause the company's risk of failure to repay debt which includes interest and principal. The results of this study are in accordance with research Hur et al. (2018); Parrado-Martínez et al. (2019); Mulyana & Ulpah (2020) state that inflation has a significant impact on the probability of default. When there is an increase in inflation, it will increase the risk of the company's probability of default. The company will default on a certain period. However, inflation has no influence on default during a crisis.

Interest is the cost of installments which is often expressed as a percentage of the loan amount. Interest rates cannot be used as a variable that can affect the probability of a company's default. Interest rates whose fluctuating rates are not too high or low will not affect the company in making funding decisions in the form of debt. Interest rates are less relevant for predicting loan default (Saha et al., 2023).

The exchange rate is the price of the currency of a country measured in the price of the foreign currency to which it is attached (Mankiw, 2016). The exchange rate of a country does not always strengthen or weaken. Companies that use the exchange rate are companies that carry out domestic transaction activities such as export and import activities of production goods (Casas et al., 2023). The depreciation of the rupiah against the dollar is the cause of the increase in foreign demand for domestic products, commodities or services. The weakening of the rupiah, domestic commodity prices become cheaper than those purchased abroad. Depreciation causes export goods to become cheaper. During depreciation, the price of imported commodities will become more expensive. Thus, the policy of increasing exports is relevant to carried out in times of depreciation (Kholisoh & Dwiarti, 2020). An increase in exports will cause higher profits and generate additional funds as a source of company funds. The more funds obtained, the less debt used by the company. So that it does not affect the probability of default of the company. The results of this study are in accordance with research by Kholisoh & Dwiarti (2020) which found that the exchange rate variable was unable to predict the occurrence of financial distress in property and real estate companies.

5.5 Conclusions and Recommendations

5.5.1 Conclusions

This study examines the effect of fundamental and macroeconomic factors on the probability of default in companies listed on the Indonesian Sharia Stock Index for the 2016–2022 period using the Merton Structural Model. Based on the results of empirical data, the research conducted concludes that the Current Ratio (CR) does not affect the probability of default of the company. This is because there is a discrepancy in the measurement of the duration of the two variables. The current ratio is an indicator of short-term liquidity, while the probability of default is a model for forecasting long-term defaults. The Debt to Equity Ratio (DER) variable has a negative effect on the company's probability of default in a normal period. Meanwhile, the DER has a positive impact on the probability of default when analyzed in crisis period. An increase in DER causes a decrease in the company's probability of default due to the company's profitability. The Return on

Assets (ROA) variable does not affect the company's probability of default. The company has sufficient capital to bear the risk, management can manage the company's expenses efficiently, and ROA is not appropriate to use in forecasting company debt.

Meanwhile, the macroeconomic variables show that the inflation variable has a positive effect on the company's probability of default because an increase in inflation causes the rise of raw material and operational costs. The interest rate variable is proven to not affect the company's probability of default. This is because the Indonesian state interest rate is still at a stable level or the fluctuation level is not too high so that it does not affect companies in taking debt policies. The exchange rate shows that the results do not affect the company's probability of default. Depreciation that occurred in Indonesia, led to an increase in export activities of goods and services which caused the company to experience an increase in profit. Thus, less debt is used and does not affect the company's probability of default.

Furthermore, the robustness test results show that there is no difference before and after the addition of control variables. In addition, the researcher also conducted a split sample regression analysis. Finally, the firms that are newly established and have large sizes have a negative impact on PD. Companies must pay attention to indicators of DER and inflation to maintain the sustainability of the company. DER is one indicator that has a significant effect on the probability of default of the company. The level of capital originating from debt, if not used and estimated correctly, will cause the company to have a high chance of experiencing corporate default. Moreover, the external side of the company shows that the influential variable is inflation. So companies also need to pay attention to the high and low levels of inflation in a country.

5.5.2 Implications and Recommendations

The findings in this study are very relevant to policymakers for formulating credit risk management policies and estimates of the company's probability of default. The policymakers should collaborate with the government to continue to control inflation so that it is in line with the set target range. In addition, policymakers are expected to pay attention to the determination of inflation at a certain period in response to global economic flows and maintain domestic economic growth. This is because inflation and interest rates have a causal relationship that can influence each other. In line with research, inflation can trigger an increase in interest rates as a form of monetary operations carried out by Bank Indonesia.

Reflecting on the financial ratio for screening Sharia shares that take into account the company's debt ratio to achieve company financial stabilization. The creation of debt regulations by Bank Indonesia is urgently needed to regulate the level of use of debt or the structure of conventional (non-Sharia) corporate models. Regulations regarding the standard use of corporate debt can be signs and limits for companies to increase leverage through debt. So that the balance in the company's capital structure can be more stable and measurable.

Managers must consider the company's DER level and inflation to mitigate the probability of default. Companies need to reduce the level of debt usage and optimize the use of company internal funds. Thus, the company's finances are not getting more difficult and can minimize the possibility of a company default in the face of an economic situation that is still at a high level of uncertainty. Furthermore, creditors and prospective creditors in determining investment in bond purchases must estimate the company's DER and inflation conditions to anticipate the company's default risk which has an impact on investment losses. In addition, creditors must be careful in assessing the company's credit risk before placing their capital in the issuing company.

5.6 Limitations and Futures Agenda

This study only focuses on the probability of default by Sharia firms, thus further research is expected to consider companies that are not only included in the sharia category but also all companies listed on the Indonesia Stock Exchange. In addition, further researchers are expected to be able to conduct a comparative test on whether there is a difference in the probability of default between Sharia and non-Sharia firms. Further research can use other variables that can measurement of company obligations. Big samples and long periods of time are also needed in further research.

References

Abaidoo, R., & Agyapong, E. K. (2022). Commodity prices, inflation and inflation uncertainty among emerging economies. *Journal of Economic and Administrative Sciences*. https://doi.org/10.1108/jeas-10-2021-0203

Abdelaziz, H., Rim, B., & Helmi, H. (2020). The Interactional Relationships Between Credit Risk, Liquidity Risk and Bank Profitability in MENA Region. *Global Business Review*, *23*(3). https://doi.org/https://doi.org/10.1177/0972150919879304

Afik, Z., Arad, O., & Galil, K. (2016). Using Merton model for default prediction: An empirical assessment of selected alternatives. *Journal of Empirical Finance*, *35*, 43–67. https://doi.org/10.1016/j.jempfin.2015.09.004

Ahmed, F., Nizam, K., & Ahsan, N. (2023). Credit Risk Management and Default Risk: Empirical Evidence from United Kingdom. *Journal of Business Education and Management*, *3*(2), 95–110.

Arellano, C. (2004). Default Risk, the Real Exchange Rate and Income Fluctuations in Emerging Economies. In *University of Minnesota Federal*.

Arhinful, R., & Radmehr, M. (2023). The effect of financial leverage on financial performance: evidence from non-financial institutions listed on the Tokyo stock market. *Journal of Capital Markets Studies*, *7*(1), 53–71. https://doi.org/10.1108/jcms-10-2022-0038

Asonuma, T. (2016). Sovereign Defaults, External Debt, and Real Exchange Rate Dynamics. In *IMF Working Papers* (Vol. 16, Issue 37). https://doi.org/10.5089/9781475597738.001

Ballinari, D., Audrino, F., & Sigrist, F. (2022). When does attention matter? The effect of investor attention on stock market volatility around news releases. *International Review of Financial Analysis*, *82*(February), 102185. https://doi.org/10.1016/j.irfa.2022.102185

Boubaker, S., Cellier, A., Manita, R., & Saeed, A. (2020). Does corporate social responsibility reduce financial distress risk? *Economic Modelling*, *91*(April), 835–851. https://doi.org/10.1016/j.econmod.2020.05.012

Bui, T. N., Nguyen, X. H., & Pham, K. T. (2023). The Effect of Capital Structure on Firm Value: A Study of Companies Listed on the Vietnamese Stock Market. *International Journal of Financial Studies*, *11*(3). https://doi.org/10.3390/ijfs11030100

Carvalho, J., Orrillo, J., & da Silva, F. R. G. (2020). Probability of default in collateralized credit operations for small business. *North American Journal of Economics and Finance*, *52*(January 2019), 101129. https://doi.org/10.1016/j.najef.2019.101129

Casas, C., Meleshchuk, S., & Timmer, Y. (2023). *The Dominant Currency Financing Channel of External Adjustment*.

Cathcart, L., Dufour, A., Rossi, L., & Varotto, S. (2020). The differential impact of leverage on the default risk of small and large firms. *Journal of Corporate Finance*, *60*. https://doi.org/https://doi.org/10.1016/j.jcorpfin.2019.101541

Cui, W., & Kaas, L. (2020). Default Cycles. *Journal of Monetary Economics*.

Dewianawati, D., & Setiawan, E. (2022). The effect of inflation, financial performance, and profit management on financial distress on property, real estate, and building construction companies listed on the Indonesia stock exchange. *Enrichment: Journal of Management*, *12*(5). https://doi.org/10.31258/ijeba.7.1.83-106

Dibiasi, A., & Sarferaz, S. (2023). Measuring macroeconomic uncertainty: A cross-country analysis. *European Economic Review*, *153*(January 2022), 104383. https://doi.org/10.1016/j.euroecorev.2023.104383

Dirman, A. (2020). Financial Distress: the Impacts of Profitability, Liquidity, Leverage, Firm Size, and Free Cash Flow. *International Journal of Business, Economics and Law*, *22*(1), 1.

Dwiarti, R., Hazmi, S., Santosa, A., & Rahman, Z. (2021). Does Bankruptcy Matter in Non-Banking Financial Sector Companies?: Evidence from Indonesia. *Journal of Asian Finance, Economics and Business*, *8*(3), 441–449. https://doi.org/10.13106/jafeb.2021.vol8.no3.0441

Egbunike, C. F., & Okerekeoti, C. U. (2018). Macroeconomic factors, firm characteristics and financial performance: A study of selected quoted manufacturing firms in Nigeria. *Asian Journal of Accounting Research*, *3*(2), 142–168. https://doi.org/10.1108/AJAR-09-2018-0029

Featherstone, A. M., Wilson, C. A., & Zollinger, L. M. (2017). Factors affecting risk-rating migration. *Agricultural Finance Review*, *77*(1), 181–195. https://doi.org/10.1108/AFR-05-2016-0044

Foila, M. F., Hj. Sulastri, Yuliani, & Hanafi, A. (2019). The Effect of External Financing Needs and Suistainable Growth on Firm Value in Manufacturing Companies Registered on Indonesia Stock Exchange. *Modern Economics*, *16*(1), 86–93. https://doi.org/10.31521/modecon.v16(2019)-13

Frijters, P., & Antić, N. (2016). Can collapsing business networks explain economic downturns? *Economic Modelling*, *54*, 289–308. https://doi.org/http://dx.doi.org/10.1016/j.econmod.2015.12.021

Glas, A., & Heinisch, K. (2023). Conditional macroeconomic survey forecasts: Revisions and errors. *Journal of International Money and Finance*, *138*(October 2022), 102927. https://doi.org/10.1016/j.jimonfin.2023.102927

Hull, J., Nelken, I., & White, A. (2004). Merton's Model, Credit Risk, and Volatility Skews. In *University of Toronto*. http://webs.ucm.es/info/biomol2/Tema 01.pdf%0Ahttp://dx.doi.org/10.1016/j.addr.2009.04.004

Hur, S., Kondo, I. O., & Perri, F. (2018). Real Interest Rates, Inflation, and Default. *Staff Report*. https://doi.org/https://doi.org/10.21034/sr.574

Khan, A. Z. S., Khalid, W., & Shah, N. H. (2021). Impact of Bank Profitability on Default Risk: Empirical Evidence from Pakistan. *Journal of Quantitative Methods (JQM)*, *5*(2). https://www.academia.edu/download/99429269/234.pdf

Kholbadalov, U. (2012). The relationship of corporate tax avoidance, cost of debt and institutional ownership: evidence from Malaysia. *Atlantic Review of Economics*, *2*(5), 38–68.

Kholisoh, S. N., & Dwiarti, R. (2020). The Analysis of Fundamental Variables and Macro Economic Variables in Predicting Financial Distress. *Management Analysis Journal*, *9*(1), 81–90. https://doi.org/https://doi.org/10.15294/maj.v9i1.36395

Kliestik, T., Misankova, M., & Kocisova, K. (2015). Calculation of Distance to Default. *Procedia Economics and Finance*, *23*(October 2014), 238–243. https://doi.org/10.1016/s2212-5671(15)00481-5

Koh, A., Ang, S.-K., Brigham, E. F., & Ehrhardt, M. C. (2014). *Financial Management : Theory and Practice* (An Asia ed). Singapore :Cengage Learning. https://www.worldcat.org/title/financial-management-theory-and-practice/oclc/865526681

Kurniani, N. T. (2021). The effect of liquidity ratio, activity ratio, and profitability ratio on accounting profit with firm size as a mediation. *Journal of Economics and Business Letters*, *1*(3), 18–26. https://doi.org/10.55942/jebl.v1i3.122

Laurin, M., & Martynenko, O. (2009). The Influence of Macroeconomic Factors on the Probability of Default. In *Lund University – School of Economics and Management*.

Le, H., & Nguyen, P. (2023). Monetary policy in practice: do central banks respond to movements in exchange rate and credit growth? *Journal of Economic Studies*. https://doi.org/10.1108/JES-05-2023-0258

López-Penabad, M. C., Iglesias-Casal, A., & Silva Neto, J. F. (2022). Effects of a negative interest rate policy in bank profitability and risk taking: Evidence from European banks. *Research in International Business and Finance*, *60*(October 2020). https://doi.org/10.1016/j.ribaf.2021.101597

Lou, J., Wong, T. W., Fung, K. W. T., & Shaende, J. J. N. (2019). Stock and bond joint pricing, consumption surplus, and inflation news. *Research in International Business and Finance*. https://doi.org/https://doi.org/10.1016/j.ribaf.2021.101426

Luo, X., & Luo, M. (2021). Analysis on financing structure and default probability of listed companies. *2nd International Conference on New Energy Technology and Industrial Development (NETID 2021)*, *292*(E3S Web Conf.), 4. https://doi.org/https://doi.org/10.1051/e3sconf/202129202032

Malasari, D., Adam, M., Yuliani, & Hanafi, A. (2020). Financial ratios and probability of default by using the KMV-merton method in the non-financial sector listed on the Indonesia stock exchange. *Finance: Theory and Practice*, *24*(1), 6–13. https://doi.org/10.26794/2587-5671-2020-24-1-6-13

Mankiw, N. G. (2016). Principles of Economics. *Cengage Learning*.

Melianti, & Kontesa, M. (2022). Financial Flexibility and Business Risk Effect on Capital Structure: Insight from Indonesian Energy Listed Companies. *Tanjungpura International Conference On Management, Economics And Accounting (TiCMEA)*, *1*, 318–326.

Merton, R. . (1974). On the Pricing of Corporate Debt: The Risk Structure of Interest Rates. *The Journal of Finance of Finance*, *29*, 449–470. https://doi.org/https://doi.org/10.1111/j.1540-6261.1974.tb03058.x

Ministry of PPN/Bappenas. (2023). Perkembangan Ekonomi Indonesia dan Dunia Triwulan III Tahun 2023. In *Ministry of PPN/Bappenas* (Vol. 7, Issue 3 November 2023). https://medium.com/@arifwicaksanaa/pengertian-use-case-a7e576e1b6bf

Mishkin, F. S. (2014). *The Economics of Money, Banking, and Financial Markets* (Eleventh E, Issue September). Pearson.

Mulyana, P. N. A., & Ulpah, M. (2020). The Effects of Macroeconomics on Probability of Default for the Micro Business Segment. *Proceedings of the International Conference on Business and Management Research (ICBMR 2020)*, *160*, 116–122. https://doi.org/10.2991/aebmr.k.201222.017

Munangi, E. (2020). The Impact Of Credit Risk On Financial Performance Of South African Banks. In *University of South Africa* (Issue February).

Mushafiq, M., Sami, S. A., Sohail, M. K., & Sindhu, M. I. (2022). Merton-type default risk and financial performance: the dynamic panel moderation of firm size. *Journal of Economic and Administrative Sciences*. https://doi.org/10.1108/jeas-09-2021-0181

Narayan, P. K. (2022). Understanding exchange rate shocks during COVID-19. *Finance Research Letters*, *45*(December 2020), 102181. https://doi.org/10.1016/j.frl.2021.102181

Ogachi, D., Ndege, R., Gaturu, P., & Zoltan, Z. (2020). Corporate Bankruptcy Prediction Model, a SpecialFocus on Listed Companies in KenyaCorporate Bankruptcy Prediction Model, a SpecialFocus on Listed Companies in Kenya. *Journal of Risk and Financial Management*, *13*(47). https://doi.org/http://dx.doi.org/10.3390/jrfm13030047

Omar, A., & Prasanna, P. K. (2021). Asymmetric effects of noise in Merton default risk model: Evidence from emerging Asia. *Pacific Basin Finance Journal*, *65*(December 2020), 101497. https://doi.org/10.1016/j.pacfin.2021.101497

Orlando, G., & Pelosi, R. (2020). Non-Performing Loans for Italian Companies:When Time Matters. An Empirical Research onEstimating Probability to Default and LossGiven Default. *International Journal of Financial Studies*, *8*(68), 1–22. https://doi.org/http://dx.doi.org/10.3390/ijfs8040068

Paletta, A., & Alimehmeti, G. (2022). The efficiency of the Italian preventive agreement: a legal, economic and organizational perspective. *International Journal of Law and Management*, *64*(1), 80–109. https://doi.org/10.1108/IJLMA-01-2021-0028

Parrado-Martínez, P., Gómez-Fernández-Aguado, P., & Partal-Ureña, A. (2019). Factors influencing the European bank's probability of default: An application of Symbol methodology. *Journal of International Financial Markets, Institutions and Money*. https://doi.org/https://doi.org/10.1016/j.intfin.2019.04.003

Pasricha, P., Lu, X., & Zhu, S.-P. (2021). A note on the calculation of default probabilities in "Structural credit risk modeling with Hawkes jump–diffusion processes". *Journal of Computational and Applied Mathematic*. https://doi.org/https://doi.org/10.1016/j.cam.2020.113037

Pefindo. (2022). The Default Study of Corporate and Corporate Debt Securities Rated by Pefindo. In *Pefindo Credit Rating Agency*.

Rahman, A. A. A. A. (2017). The Relationship between Solvency Ratios and Profitability Ratios: Analytical Study in Food Industrial Companies listed in Amman Bursa. *International Journal of Economics and Financial Issues*, *7*(2), 86–93. http:www.econjournals.com

Saha, A., Eam, L. H., & Yeok, S. G. (2023). Housing loan default in Malaysia: an analytical insight and policy implications. *International Journal of Housing Markets and Analysis*, *16*(2), 273–291. https://doi.org/https://doi.org/10.1108/IJHMA-01-2022-0002

Sánchez-Ballesta, J. P., & Yagüe, J. (2023). Tax avoidance and the cost of debt for SMEs: Evidence from Spain. *Journal of Contemporary Accounting & Economics*, *19*(2), 100362. https://doi.org/https://doi.org/10.1016/j.jcae.2023.100362

Santoso, W., Trinugroho, I., & Risfandy, T. (2018). What Determine Loan Rate and Default Status in Financial Technology Online Direct Lending? Evidence from Indonesia. *Otoritas Jasa Keuangan*. https://doi.org/10.1080/1540496X.2019.1605595

Sariev, E., & Germano, G. (2019). Bayesian regularized artificial neural networks forthe estimation of the probability of default. *Quantitative Finance*, *20*(2), 311–328. https://doi.org/https://www.tandfonline.com/action/showCitFormats?doi=10.1080/14697688.2019.1633014

Septine Mayliza, C., Haymans Manurung, A., & Hutahayan, B. (2020). Analysis of The Effect of Financial Ratios to Probability Default of Indonesia's Coal Mining Company Analysis of The Effect of Financial Ratios to Probability Default of Indonesia's Coal Mining Company Celly Septine Mayliza et al. *Journal of Applied Finance & Banking*, *10*(5), 1792–6599. https://www.researchgate.net/publication/342047943

Shahriar, A., Mehzabin, S., Ahmed, Z., Döngül, E. S., & Azad, M. A. K. (2023). Bank stability, performance and efficiency: an experience from West Asian countries. *IIM Ranchi Journal of Management Studies*, *2*(1), 31–47. https://doi.org/10.1108/irjms-02-2022-0017

Subramaniam, Y., & Masron, T. A. (2022). Does excessive degrees of financial depth push hyper-inflation? *Asian Journal of Economics and Banking*, *6*(3), 286–307. https://doi.org/10.1108/ajeb-03-2022-0026

Suhadak, Kurniaty, Handayani, S. R., & Rahayu, S. M. (2019). Stock return and financial performance as moderation variable in influence of good corporate governance towards corporate value. *Asian Journal of Accounting Research*, *4*(1), 18–34. https://doi.org/10.1108/AJAR-07-2018-0021

Sunder-Plassmann, L. (2020). Inflation, default and sovereign debt: The role of denomination and ownership. *Journal of International Economics*. https://doi.org/https://doi.org/10.1016/j.jinteco.2020.103393

Trejo-Pech, C. J. O., DeLong, K. L., & Johansson, R. (2023). How does the financial performance of sugar-using firms compare to other agribusinesses? An accounting and economic profit rates analysis. *Agricultural Finance Review*, *83*(3), 453–477. https://doi.org/10.1108/AFR-08-2022-0103

Uddin, M. H., Kabir, S. H., Hossain, M. S., Wahab, N. S. A., & Liu, J. (2020). Which firms do prefer Islamic debt? An analysis and evidence from global sukuk and bonds issuing firms. *Emerging Markets Review*. https://doi.org/https://doi.org/10.1016/j.ememar.2020.100712

Vuković, B., Milutinović, S., Milićević, N., & Jakšić, D. (2020). Corporate Bankruptcy Prediction: Evidence from Wholesale Companies in the Western European Countries. *Journal of Economics*, *05*, 477–498.

Widyanty, W., Oktasari, D. P., & Ekonomi, F. (2019). Financial Ratio Analysis as a Prediction Tool of Bankruptcy on Banking Companies Listed in Indonesia Stock Exchange. *European Journal of Business and Management*, *120*(Icmeb 2019), 180–184. https://doi.org/10.7176/ejbm/11-15-05

Witkowska, D., Kompa, K., & Staszak, M. (2021). Indicators for the efficient portfolio construction. The case of Poland. *Procedia Computer Science*, *192*(2021), 2022–2031. https://doi.org/10.1016/j.procs.2021.08.208

Yadav, I. S., Pahi, D., & Gangakhedkar, R. (2022). The nexus between firm size, growth and profitability: new panel data evidence from Asia–Pacific markets. *European Journal of Management and Business Economics*, *31*(1), 115–140. https://doi.org/10.1108/EJMBE-03-2021-0077

Yang, X., & Hu, Y. (2024). Default risk and stock returns: From a perspective of measurement errors. *International Review of Economics & Finance*. https://doi.org/10.1016/j.iref.2024.02.026

Zhao, C., Yuan, X., Long, J., Jin, L., & Guan, B. (2023). Financial indicators analysis using machine learning: Evidence from Chinese stock market. *Finance Research Letters*, *58*(PD), 104590. https://doi.org/10.1016/j.frl.2023.104590

Vjosë Latifi, Agron Hajdari, Gadaf Rexhepi, Besnik Krasniqi,
Eset Qerimi

Chapter 6
The Surge of Islamic Entrepreneurship: Analyzing the Strategic Motivations and Far-Reaching Impacts

Abstract: This chapter explores the growth and impact of Islamic entrepreneurship, focusing on its strategic motivations and broader implications. It highlights factors driving business owners in Islamic contexts, such as moral and socially conscious economic practices, alongside challenges like regulatory complexities and the need for deeper understanding of Islamic principles. Islamic entrepreneurship, propelled by increased awareness and financial advancements, offers opportunities for businesses to align with Islamic values while fostering local economic growth. The study employed a qualitative case study approach in Kosovo, involving unstructured interviews with eight entrepreneurs across various sectors. Findings indicate that Islamic entrepreneurship encourages responsibility towards state institutions and promotes wealth management in accordance with religious principles. Entrepreneurs are motivated by both personal success and societal contribution, fostering resilience and purpose in their endeavors. This chapter provides insights for policymakers on supporting Islamic entrepreneurship through tailored policies that accommodate its unique principles and needs, aiming to enhance economic and social outcomes in Islamic entrepreneurial ventures.

Keywords: Surge, Islam, Islamic Entrepreneurship, Motivations, Impact

6.1 Introduction

Throughout history, religion has been integral to all aspects of life worldwide, and although worship practices and ethical views differ by region, religion fosters common and harmonious functions among people (Barman, 2022). Religion's importance varies greatly depending on one's own beliefs and cultural background. According to (Dik, Daniels, & Alayan, 2024) religion significantly shapes how individuals perceive the world, creating numerous opportunities to integrate faith with work. For many, it holds great personal and societal worth and serves as a basis for moral behavior, communal involvement, and spiritual fulfillment. Religion is viewed as a crucial factor that forms the foundational institutional infrastructure of a society (Qayyum, Anjum, & Sabir, 2020) and this is because of the impact that extends beyond

https://doi.org/10.1515/9783111575407-007

the spiritual domain, affecting various aspects of social and economic life. In recent years, the relationship between religion and economic considerations has increasingly garnered significant attention (Jones, Hymer, Roccapriore, & Smith, 2024; Bhutta, Li, Chaudhry, & Akhter, 2023; Güneş, 2022; Sandikci, 2021; Buren, Syed, & Mir, 2020; Yixing, 2019). Furthermore, entrepreneurship and religion are crucial components of the economic context that are also central to the academia (Zelekha, Avnimelech, & Sharabi, 2014; Kumara, Sahoo, Lim, & Dana, 2022; Smith, Conger, McMullen, & Neubert, 2019; Smith, McMullen, & Cardon, 2021). In exploring the economic context of entrepreneurship, it's essential to consider how religion intersects with various cultural and institutional influences (Henley, 2017) and understanding these dynamics reveals how religious beliefs can influence or limit entrepreneurial activity. To understand the effect of religion, specifically Islam, on entrepreneurship, we will analyze Islamic Entrepreneurship.

Islam is a prominent world religion that offers guidance on spiritual and ethical living, and Islamic entrepreneurship incorporates these concepts into business, emphasizing ethical practices and social responsibility. To advance scientific development in the Muslim world, it is essential to foster a scientific mindset rooted in an Islamic worldview, encourage collaboration among Muslim countries, integrate scientific issues into national agendas, and raise public awareness about the importance of science (Sadri, 2010). This chapter aims to explore and evaluate the strategic motivations and challenges behind the rise of Islamic entrepreneurship in Kosovo. Kosovo is an independent state in Southeast Europe with a population of 1.8 million, faces high unemployment, leading its GDP to be predominantly focused on the service sector (Latifi, Ramadani, & Rexhepi, 2022). This research departs from traditional evaluations of Islamic entrepreneurship by focusing on the long-term effects and strategic motivations of a small sample of eight entrepreneurs. The study examines how faith affects entrepreneurship strategy and results through in-depth qualitative interviews. Our method is to provide a deeper comprehension of the relationship between entrepreneurial activities and religious values, shedding light on how these dynamics influence company choices and have wider effects. This thoughtful analysis offers insightful viewpoints on how Islamic principles promote social responsibility and business success. This, in turn, paves the way for a more comprehensive and nuanced understanding of how Islamic entrepreneurship fosters individual growth and enhances societal impact.

The organization of this chapter is as follows: Section 2 provides a general literature review on Islamic entrepreneurship. Section 3 details the methodology employed in the study, while Section 4 presents the findings and discussion. The concluding section offers insights into the conclusions, implications, and directions for future research.

6.2 Literature Review

6.2.1 Understanding Islamic Entrepreneurship

Islamic entrepreneurship is an area of business management study that examines how culture and religion, particularly Islam, influence business relationships in a dynamic global environment, though research on religion's role in entrepreneurship and management remains limited (Gümüsay, 2015; Ramadani, Dana, Ratten, & Tahiri, 2015). However, Islamic entrepreneurship is deemed a critical topic in business solutions due to the complex and dynamic nature of the business environment, where religion and culture play a crucial role in the success of SMEs (Khalique, Ramayah, Hina, & Shaari, 2020). Islamic entrepreneurship, as depicted in Figure 6.1, integrates moral and spiritual principles with economic activities, striving to balance economic goals with social responsibility while adhering to Islamic values.

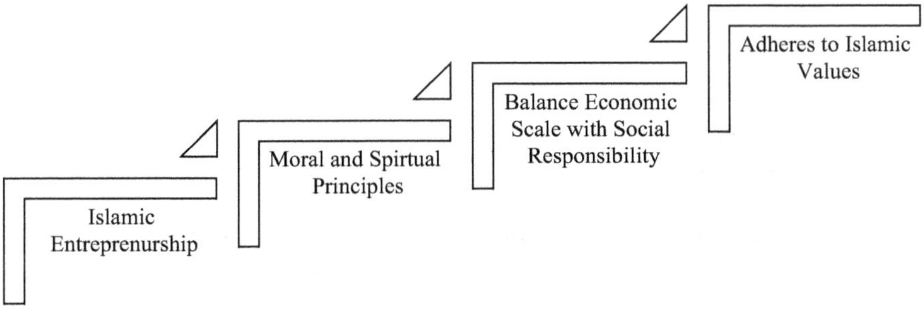

Figure 6.1: Concept of Islamic entrepreneurship.

Islam is a comprehensive way of life encompassing spiritual beliefs, ethical practices, and social responsibilities. However, religion does not inherently endorse or forbid entrepreneurship (Dana, 2010). The emergence and expansion of Islam in the early seventh century CE, akin to the development of other major religions, involved significant entrepreneurial innovation, with Muhammad demonstrating exceptional social, political, economic, and military skills to secure conversions, establish a state, and control key commercial routes; this ingenuity continued as Islamic norms and institutions evolved by creatively adapting pre-Islamic systems, including the development of Islamic contract law, which provided a uniform legal framework across the vast Islamic world, facilitating entrepreneurship by offering diverse contractual templates to support varying business needs (Landes, Mokyr, & Baumol, 2010). Islamic entrepreneurship emphasizes conducting business ethically and responsibly to benefit the Islamic community, focusing on producing halal goods and services, safeguarding consumer rights, and promoting ethical practices, while striving to generate profits in alignment with Islamic values and teachings (Ahamed & Ahammed, 2023). For more, Islamic entrepreneurship refers to business practices that adhere to Sharia, which, although primarily derived from Islamic religious texts like the Quran and Hadith, is not limited to businesses conducted by Muslims but rather encompasses a broad range of public and private life aspects, including beliefs, religious rituals, family functioning, entrepreneurial activities, crimes, and warfare (Mebroui & Mosbah, 2020). The Figure 6.2 depicts how Islamic entrepreneurship is structured, illustrating that entrepreneurial behaviors and enterprise actions and strategies are guided by Sharia guidelines, ensuring alignment with Islamic legal and ethical principles.

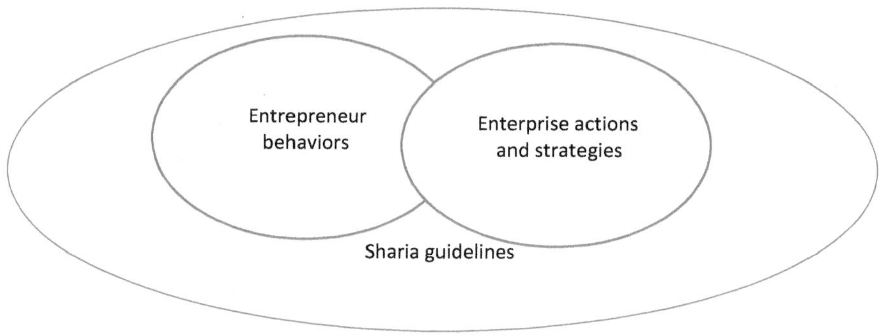

Figure 6.2: The Islamic entrepreneurship approach.
Source: (Mebroui & Mosbah, 2020).

Entrepreneurship, in general, focuses on profit-driven business activities without specific religious constraints while Islamic Entrepreneurship integrates moral values from Sharia emphasizing ethical practices, and adherence to Islamic values. According to (Kayed & Hassan, 2010) Islam accepts the Western view of entrepreneurship as an economic activity but insists that such activities must be grounded in ethical and moral principles and be socially acceptable, viewing the profit motive as legitimate and moral provided it is free from interest (Riba), greed, speculation, and exploitation, and not treated as the ultimate goal; thus, material gain should be pursued to please Allah through lawful and righteous means, integrating a religious dimension into the economic aspect of entrepreneurship, where Muslim entrepreneurs who meet their economic needs, serve their communities, and fulfill religious duties will achieve success. So, while both aim for business success, Islamic entrepreneurship uniquely aligns economic activities with religious and ethical guidelines. Table 6.1 contrasts Islamic and Western entrepreneurship, outlining their differences in motivation, financial practices, and regulatory adherence.

Also, an important issue are principles of Islamic entrepreneurship, and to illustrate them, the following outlines the divisions of ethics, ethical behaviors, and exemplary traits. According to (Vargas-Hernández, Noruzi, & Sariolghalam, 2010) Islam integrates business and religion as a unified way of life, with its own entrepreneurial culture and principles derived from the Quran and Hadith, requiring that a person prioritize being

Table 6.1: Entrepreneurial activities.

Islamic Entrepreneurship	Western Entrepreneurship
Motivated by the needs of society and desire to satisfy religious obligations	Often motivated chiefly by individual utility (wealth) maximization
Engage in productive ventures involving the creation of real goods and services	Often secular in nature
	Altruistic goals are often secondary
Financed through interest-free profit-loss sharing	Debt and equity financing
Speculation and excessive risk talking is prohibited	Speculations and risk-talking permitted.
Shari'ah-compliant	

Source: (Hassan & Hippler, 2014).

a Muslim before an entrepreneur, focusing on fulfilling religious duties and seeking God's blessings rather than merely pursuing profit; therefore to be more concise below will be detailed presented the divisions of ethics, ethical behaviors, and exemplary traits of Muslim entrepreneurship.

- *Ethics* of Muslim entrepreneurship:
  - *Avoid Laziness:* Entrepreneurship demands diligent effort.
  - *Confront Fear:* Embrace risk-taking as essential.
  - *Seek Legitimate Ventures:* Ensure business activities are lawful.
  - *Avoid Forbidden Income:* Steer clear of prohibited sources of wealth.
  - *Express Gratitude:* Show appreciation for what is gained.
  - *Promote Growth:* Focus on expanding capital and profit.
  - *Diversify Ventures:* Explore various business opportunities.
  - *Refrain from Greed:* Avoid excessive desire for wealth.
- The *ethical behavior* of Muslim entrepreneurship:
  - *Avoid Malicious Behavior:* Refrain from harmful actions.
  - *Prevent Squandering:* Manage resources wisely.
  - *Avoid Stinginess:* Be generous in dealings.
  - *Pay Alms (Zakat):* Fulfill charitable obligations.
  - *Be Trustworthy:* Maintain honesty and integrity.
  - *Pray Consistently:* Uphold regular prayer practices.
  - *Practice Tawakkal:* Rely on God while taking responsible actions.
  - *Exercise Patience*: Demonstrate resilience and forbearance.
  - *Cultivate Qana'ah:* Embrace contentment with what one has.
- *Exemplary traits* of good Muslim entrepreneurs in Islam:
  - *Prioritize Higher Callings:* Place business secondary to responding to more pressing religious duties.
  - *Avoid Self-Interest:* Refrain from using influence for personal gain.
  - *Be Cautious with Wealth:* Remain wary of accumulating excessive wealth.
  - *Exhibit Leadership Qualities:* Demonstrate strong leadership across all areas.
  - *Adopt a Moderate Lifestyle:* Practice moderation in all aspects of life.

In conclusion, Islamic entrepreneurship offers a unique strategy that carefully combines Islamic moral and spiritual precepts with commercial endeavors. It differs from traditional models in that it prioritizes not just profit but also the welfare of society, moral behavior, and religious observance. By fostering a business environment that closely aligns with both Islamic values and the broader needs of the community, this holistic framework aims to strike a balance between economic objectives and spiritual and social responsibilities. The result is a comprehensive model that harmonizes profitability with moral and spiritual integrity.

6.2.2 Strategic Motivations Behind Islamic Entrepreneurship

Motivation in entrepreneurship originates from both *internal sources*, such as personal ambition and the emotional rewards of starting a business, and *external sources*, including societal admiration and financial gains, with entrepreneurs often driven by a need for achievement and influenced by role models or previous experiences, which can lead to habitual entrepreneurial behavior despite past failures and the pursuit of internal satisfaction (Carsrud, Brännback, Elfving, & Brandt, 2017). The driving forces behind general and Islamic entrepreneurship are similar in that they both seek to achieve financial and personal success by seizing opportunities to add value and spur economic growth. However, Islamic entrepreneurship also takes into account the pursuit of religious principles and spiritual fulfillment. The Prophet Muhammad exemplified Islamic entrepreneurship by both teaching and practicing entrepreneurial principles, serving as a role model for operating businesses in alignment with religious values, and his successful entrepreneurial model, reflected in contemporary Muslim entrepreneurs, highlights the foundational traits of Tabligh (spreading faith), Amanah (trustworthiness), Siddiq (honesty), and Fathanah (wisdom) as essential components of effective and ethical business practices (Rafiki, Hidayat, & Pananjung, 2023) and these foundational traits according to (Lisnawati & Ahman, 2019) are believed to influence entrepreneurial characteristics from an Islamic perspective. Muslim entrepreneurs' motivations vary and include factors such as passion for their work, a desire for impact or autonomy, independence, and community service involvement, though their familiarity with these opportunities differs among individuals (Ahamed & Ahammed, 2023). Motivations for Islamic entrepreneurs are largely similar regardless of gender; however, women, who play a significant role in Islamic entrepreneurship, are particularly driven by personal ambition, contributing to family income, and achieving self-satisfaction, as highlighted by research of (Mahmood, Khalid, Sohail, & Babak, 2012). According to (Grine, Fares, & Meguellati, 2015) spirituality is a major motivator for ambition and work performance, with results showing it as the most crucial factor in their business success and overall entrepreneurial achievements.

In conclusion, Islamic entrepreneurship is driven by a complex interplay of religious observance, familial responsibilities, and personal ambition. Entrepreneurs aim to strike a balance between their personal aspirations and ethical and social obligations, aligning their business endeavors with Islamic values in order to foster both greater societal well-being and personal fulfillment.

6.2.3 Challenges and Opportunities in Islamic Entrepreneurship

Religious limitations significantly contribute to the differences in entrepreneurial outcomes between Western and Islamic economies, with Islamic laws restricting activities like gambling and usury to eliminate immoral and unjust practices, thereby enhancing the social value of the economy (Hassan & Hippler, 2014). Muslim entrepreneurs face threats such as intense market competition and difficulties in preserving integrity while adhering to Islamic values (Rahman, 2023). Muslim entrepreneurs encounter significant challenges in securing financing due to Sharia-compliant restrictions, yet Sharia venture capital offers a viable alternative for aligning business development with Islamic principles; however, its relatively low uptake is attributed to a lack of awareness about its procedures and benefits (Fathonih, Anggadwita, & Ibraimi, 2019). Additionally, according to (Ahamed & Ahammed, 2023) Muslim entrepreneurs face challenges such as limited funding, difficulties in networking, cultural biases, and the need to align religious values with business practices. Islamic business owners have to strike a balance between fierce market rivalry and the difficulty of upholding morality and Islamic principles and this calls for the development of Sharia-compliant strategies that can be adjusted to a changing business climate.

Islam emphasizes engaging in business activities that benefit society and adheres to Qur'anic and Shari'ah laws, with restrictions on Muslim entrepreneurs designed to prevent harm to society, and entrepreneurial efforts are seen as fulfilling religious duties and pleasing Allah (Ramadani, Dana, Gërguri-Rashiti, & Ratten, 2016). Entrepreneurship is deeply rooted in Islamic culture, exemplified by Prophet Muhammad (PBUH) and his companions, and although Islam encourages innovation and entrepreneurship, many Muslims have unfortunately lost confidence over time despite the presence of successful Muslim entrepreneurs globally (Vargas-Hernández, Noruzi, & Sariolghalam, 2010). An ideal Muslim entrepreneur adopts a service-oriented, collectivist mindset focused on solving problems for all stakeholders rather than prioritizing profit maximization, maintains financial sustainability while avoiding systemic complexity, fosters a family-like atmosphere within the firm, and constructively engages with local stakeholders without disrupting local social structures (Javaid, 2021). By guaranteeing adherence to Islamic laws and principles, Islamic entrepreneurship closely resembles halal entrepreneurship in that it encourages moral and community-focused business activities. The propensity for halal entrepreneurship is significantly influenced by factors such as halal entrepreneurship principles, intrinsic motivation, opportunity-seeking effort, perceived desirability, peer influence, perceived feasibility, and perceived governmental support

(Soltanian, Zailani, Iranmanesh, & Aziz, 2016) which together contribute to create an ethical, fair, and sustainable business environment.

A pressing issue that needs attention is Islamic women entrepreneurship, which is often accompanied by various stereotypes and prejudices. The misconception regarding Muslim women entrepreneurs frequently implies that their prospects are limited by cultural and religious restrictions, falsely implying that their roles and aspirations are more limited than those of their male counterparts. Islam is used to ensure that religious norms and values take precedence over cultural ones, creating space for individualism, honor, and entrepreneurship, while also shaping diverse religious identities to expand the opportunities for female entrepreneurs and challenge traditional, dogmatic interpretations of Islam (Essers & Benschop, 2009).Islam is a dynamic religion that promotes women's agency even within a context dominated by deeply entrenched patriarchal norms and gender-based restrictions (Tlaiss & McAdam, 2021).With the backing of Islamic values and social structures, Muslim women can succeed in business on par with their male counterparts thanks to Islamic entrepreneurship, which offers equal chances and opportunities for men and women.

6.2.4 Future Trends and Directions in Islamic Entrepreneurship

The increasing global Muslim population has facilitated greater participation of Muslim entrepreneurs in the market, enabling them to engage in entrepreneurial activities while adhering to religious teachings (Harizan & Mustafa, 2020). Religion profoundly shapes individuals' attitudes, values, and behaviors, and as a comprehensive system, Islam governs all aspects of life by emphasizing the importance of its values and practices to seek Allah's blessings and mercy; in the business realm, this is reflected in the pursuit of both profit and the maximization of mashlahah (public interest), which together contribute to achieving genuine success (Rafiki & Wahab, 2014).

The Islamic economic system, a comprehensive and enduring framework, governs the entire production, distribution, and consumption processes according to Islamic principles to ensure justice, balance, freedom, and benefit, with entrepreneurship serving not just as a means to profit but as a crucial form of social service aimed at advancing civilization and societal development (Hamid & Sa'ari, 2011). For future trends and prospects in Islamic entrepreneurship, it is emphasized that innovation and technology will play a crucial role in shaping this future (Raimi, Adekunle, & Shabbir, 2023). According to (Ratten, 2022) emerging trends in entrepreneurship now include new opportunities brought about by digital transformation technologies such as the Internet of Things (IoT), 3D printing, cloud computing, automation, robotics, artificial intelligence, data analytics, digital platforms, and blockchain. Advances in mentioned digital technology, that are improving e-commerce and Sharia-compliant financial services, are expected to affect future trends in Islamic entrepreneurship. Because there is a rising need for socially conscious business models, there is a focus on combining ethical and sustainable operations. The growth of digital platforms and the heightened emphasis on education and skill development will also probably have an impact on how Islamic entrepreneurship develops.

6.3 Methodology

In social scientific research, a diverse array of methods is used to examine both numerical data and non-numerical insights (Neuman, 2014). The use of qualitative methods in this research was deemed beneficial by the authors for developing a richer and more nuanced understanding of strategic motivations and the extensive impacts of Islamic entrepreneurship in Kosovo. In qualitative research, conclusions are derived from a variety of diverse and sometimes contrasting observations, each illuminating different aspects of a problem (Gerring, 2017). To better understand people's experiences and perspectives, qualitative research is typically used to investigate phenomena or topics that are not well known (Antwi & Hamza, 2015) and that's also the reason for choosing this case for this scientific research. This study utilizes a qualitative approach to investigate the strategic motivations and extensive effects of Islamic entrepreneurship in Kosovo, concentrating on eight entrepreneurs from various sectors who adhere to Islamic business principles. As one of the last countries in the region to transition to a market economy, Kosovo relies heavily on SMEs, which are crucial for job creation, income growth, and fostering a competitive business environment, though these SMEs face significant environmental barriers (Krasniqi, 2007). Unstructured interviews were used to obtain data, giving the study method flexibility and adaptability. Because the interviews were unstructured, the questions and processes changed in response to the participants' answers and the themes that emerged throughout the process. An organic and engaging conversation between the interviewer and the subjects was made possible by this method. Every interview was audio recorded and lasted for around an hour. In qualitative research, audio recording is essential because it guarantees correct capture of all spoken information. To produce a written record of the talks, the audio recordings from the interviews were transcribed thereafter. After transcription, the data underwent a comprehensive analytical procedure. To guarantee the correctness and consistency of the data, logical verification was part of this process. In order to extract important themes and nodes from the text, the analysis concentrated on finding recurrent themes and noteworthy insights about the application of Islamic teachings in business. To get a group viewpoint from the participants, a focus group was held in addition to one-on-one interviews. The focus group gave them a forum to talk about the similarities and differences in their backgrounds and driving forces. The in-depth explanations from the focus groups and individual interviews assisted in identifying the fundamental drivers behind following Islamic business practices. The viewpoints and narratives of the participants were revealed through analysis and interpretation of the high-quality data gathered from open-ended questions. A greater comprehension of how Islamic beliefs impact their entrepreneurial activities and decision-making processes was made possible by this in-depth analysis of their comments. Rich, nuanced data was collected thanks to the utilization of audio recordings and direct participant interaction. The examination of these data points gave rise to insightful conclusions on the strategic drivers and effects of Islamic entrepreneurship, presenting a thorough picture of how these ideas are used and interpreted across various industries. Table 6.2 below provides essential information on the eight interviewed entrepreneurs respondents for this analyze, detailing their sector, year of establishment, and type of capital investment.

Table 6.2: Entrepreneur Profiles.

No	Respondent	Sector	Year of Establishment	Capital Structure
1	A	Services	2008	Private Capital
2	B	Trade	2000	Private Capital
3	C	Trade	2005	Shareholder
4	D	Services	2010	Private Capital
5	E	Manufacturing	2004	Shareholder
6	F	Manufacturing	2009	Private Capital
7	G	Services	2013	Private Capital
8	H	Trade	2006	Private Capital

Qualitative research in challenging environments improves understanding of entrepreneurs' experiences and provides rich data that quantitative methods often miss, especially in post-conflict areas like Kosovo. Participants were directly contacted, and interviews were recorded to capture their insights. This focused group represented a hidden subset of the population, resulting in a small sample size.

6.4 Findings

This section presents findings on Islamic entrepreneurship in Kosovo, emphasizing the motivations, challenges, and practices of Muslim entrepreneurs. The study explores how Islamic principles impact their business operations, motivations, and contributions to society through qualitative interviews with eight entrepreneurs. The subsequent results and discussion provide insights into their approaches to charity and social responsibility, the challenges encountered in adhering to Islamic financial regulations, and their commitment to religious obligations.

In this part, we explore the individual motivations of the respondents regarding their adherence to Islamic principles in business. It is noteworthy that they were not compelled by anyone to follow these principles, which inevitably impact their financial decisions, including the obligation to give zakat (charity) alongside tax payments to relevant state and local institutions.

In response to our first question about their regular practice of religious obligations, the majority reported being consistent in performing duties such as prayer, fasting, and zakat (6 out of 8), while only two mentioned being less frequent in their religious practices. This indicates that these entrepreneurs are well-rounded in both their private and public lives.

Regarding the question of whether they read the Quran and Islamic literature, 7 out of 8 affirmed they do so regularly, with only one respondent indicating they read less frequently. Respondent "D" stated, *"I start my day by reading a portion from the Quran. If I begin without reading, the day feels difficult."* This highlights that the respondents engage in self-directed reading, reducing the risk of indoctrination or exploitation by individuals seeking to misuse their charitable intentions.

When asked if they believe their business actions are influenced by Quranic teachings, 5 out of 8 responded positively, while the remaining three expressed ambivalence. Thus, their motivations to help others are significantly shaped by Quranic lessons.

Further, in response to whether Islamic business norms are compatible with local regulations, 7 out of 8 agreed, while only one responded somewhat negatively. Current legislation permits businesses to donate up to 5% of EBIT (earnings before interest and taxes) for charitable purposes, while Islamic principles require only 2.5% of profits. Respondent "B" remarked, *"No one forces you to take an interest-bearing loan if you have alternative options. Therefore, Islamic business principles can create a duality in the laws that entrepreneurs must consider, but they do not present a conflict between the two systems."*

When asked about their reasons for engaging in business, two respondents expressed a desire for stable income, compared to seasonal work, while six others, already in regular employment, sought higher earnings than a fixed salary. Respondent "H" shared, *"I was employed in public administration with good income, but the daily routine challenged me. With my degree in economic management, I was always drawn to starting my own business. In 2006, after some savings and loans from family, I started my private business. I refused to go into debt and now feel fulfilled, as I not only earn for myself but have also created 36 additional monthly salaries."*

In discussing the challenges, they faced when starting their businesses, one respondent cited a lack of managerial experience, another mentioned limited distribution channels, while six identified the absence of institutions offering interest-free loans and the stance of Islamic faith on interest.

When asked about their motivations for entering business, 3 out of 8 respondents stated that their goal was to improve their standard of living, while 5 indicated an interest in earning halal (permissible) profits while also benefiting society by creating jobs.

In response to whether Islamic principles influence their business practices, 6 out of 8 respondents answered positively, citing elements such as justice, accuracy, and fairness towards employees and clients. Two others noted that Islamic teachings promote social responsibility. Respondent "F," a producer of meat products, said, *"I never produce something I cannot consume myself."*

When inquiring about their charitable activities as businesses, 3 out of 8 respondents stated they give charity both secretly and openly, 2 exclusively openly, and 3 solely in private. Islamic teachings generally prefer that charity is given discreetly to avoid pride and seek God's pleasure. Respondent "E," a well-known agricultural producer, noted, *"I continue to contribute in both ways—secretly for divine reward and openly to encourage my fellow entrepreneurs to give. If we all contributed, the social conditions would improve, and fewer families would suffer from basic needs, without being a heavy burden for us."*

We also asked about their motivations for wealth accumulation, receiving varied responses: one cited personal motivation, three desired to be a success story in entrepreneurship, and four aimed to help others. Respondent "H" remarked, *"The day I give someone charity, I feel happier; I sit down with my family at dinner relieved. It feels like I have gained more that day. On days when I don't give, I struggle to enjoy my meal, thinking of those who go to bed hungry. It feels like I haven't done well that day."*

When asked if they believe that Islam encourages them to be socially responsible as entrepreneurs, two respondents cited giving zakat, three mentioned creating job opportunities, and three indicated using resources justly.

Further questions revealed that one respondent had taken an interest-bearing loan in extraordinary circumstances, such as cash shortages due to delayed payments from clients, while seven had never done so. Respondent "A" stated, *"I have never taken a loan because it is prohibited in Islam. Although taking a loan could allow me to buy necessary assets for international transportation and be more competitive, I decided to limit my family's luxuries until I can purchase needed assets without borrowing."*

When asked if they believe Islamic business principles offer viable alternatives by prohibiting interest, three respondents affirmed positively, while four acknowledged that while Islam provides good alternatives, they are not available in Kosovo, and one responded negatively. Respondent "E" added, *"I have researched literature and consulted theologians regarding Islamic financing alternatives. I concluded that while Islamic principles offer suitable alternatives, we lack an Islamic bank in Kosovo to provide these options. From personal experience, I recognize two non-bank financial institutions offering some financing products, but they mainly focus on household economies rather than SMEs."*

Subsequently, when asked if Islamic business principles are burdensome for entrepreneurs due to the requirement of paying zakat in addition to taxes, three respondents disagreed entirely, while five noted that they willingly give zakat, seeking to draw closer to God through their donations.

In response to whether they have ever considered evading tax or zakat payments, seven respondents stated they had never thought about such evasion. One respondent

(C) admitted to having considered evading tax but changed his mind after reading literature emphasizing that love for one's homeland is part of faith.

When asked if they have any products prohibited by Islamic principles, all respondents answered negatively. Regarding past agreements with unclear elements that are prohibited, five indicated they had never engaged in such actions, while three admitted to having done so previously without knowledge of its prohibition but now ensure all agreements are clearly defined.

Finally, when asked for examples of how Quranic and Islamic teachings have motivated them to take specific actions regarding employees or social responsibility, several responses emerged: two respondents stated they act consistently with Islamic teachings and periodically contribute to needy families, while four others were influenced by visual situations showcased in local media and participated in humanitarian efforts. Two respondents noted they are motivated by Islamic teachings to avoid exploiting workers, ensuring salaries are always paid on time.

These statements from the respondents were recorded during their interviews, conducted on various days and in different locations. While some respondents were more concise, others provided lengthy responses, we have distilled the essence of their declarations.

The raw data collected from the respondents are organized into meaningful categories that summarize the key points of their responses related to the posed questions. Table 6.3 summarizes the key findings from the responses of the eight interviewed entrepreneurs.

Table 6.3: Findings from entrepreneurs.

Theme	Findings
Religious Practices	Most respondents regularly practice religious obligations like prayer, fasting, and zakat. Some read the Quran daily; others do so less frequently.
Business Motivations	Key motivations include seeking stable income, job creation, and contributing to society. A few are driven by personal success or improving living standards.
Challenges	Common challenges include a lack of managerial experience, difficulties with distribution channels, and issues related to obtaining interest-free credit.
Compliance with Norms	Most respondents find Islamic business norms compatible with local regulations, though some see a partial conflict. Norms are seen as encouraging fair business practices and social responsibility.
Charity Practices	Varied approaches to charity: some give both secretly and openly, others only one way. The emphasis is on giving to help others and fulfilling religious duties.
Views on Interest-Free Finance	Some see Islamic principles as providing good alternatives to interest, while others feel that suitable financial products are lacking in Kosovo.
Perceptions of Burden	The majority do not view zakat as a burden but as a way to draw closer to God. Few have considered avoiding zakat or taxes but later adhered to the principles.

These findings shed light on how Islamic beliefs influence the financial decisions and social duties of Muslim entrepreneurs in Kosovo, as well as their business practices and motives. Notwithstanding difficulties and the have to comply with local laws, the answers demonstrate a genuine commitment to Islamic principles.

6.5 Conclusions and Recommendations

Our research has led us to a number of important conclusions. First of all, production and entrepreneurship are highly encouraged by the Islamic faith. It encourages people to make a positive impact on society by generating new employment possibilities and providing support in many forms. Islam also encourages money creation since it believes that managing wealth is a task that God has given to humans.

Within the Kosovo environment, Islamic entrepreneurship serves as an inspiration for entrepreneurs to consistently make beneficial contributions to relevant organizations and society. This was made clear by the Muslim entrepreneurs with whom we conducted qualitative interviews; all of them showed a strong sense of responsibility toward God and the Kosovo state institutions. Considering that the majority of Kosovars practice Islam, we have succeeded in offering crucial insights on Islamic entrepreneurship overall. Emphasizing the attributes of Islamic business was essential. Understanding their cultural background is also a big obligation for us because we have a lot of friends and possible investors from all over the world, including the East.

For future research, it is recommended to examine the long-term effects of Islamic business principles on entrepreneurial success and community impact, considering various contexts. Practitioners should focus on integrating Islamic principles into their business practices while ensuring ethical conduct and community involvement. Entrepreneurs could benefit from building supportive networks to share experiences and strategies related to Islamic entrepreneurship. Policymakers should consider developing regulations that support interest-free finance and align with Islamic business practices to better accommodate these principles in the local business environment.

Bibliography

Ahamed, G. T., & Ahammed, T. M. (2023). Exploring Islamic Entrepreneurship: Perceptions, Challenges, and Economic Contributions among Muslims in India. *World Academic Journal of Management, 11*(3), 01–16.

Antwi, S. K., & Hamza, K. (2015). Qualitative and Quantitative Research Paradigms in Business. *European Journal of Business and Management, 7*(3), 217–225.

Barman, R. P. (2022). Religion from Sociological Perspectives: An Overview. *Asian Journal of Social Sciences and Legal Studies, 4*(2), 24–31.

Bhutta, M. U., Li, C., Chaudhry, N., & Akhter, W. (2023). Does religion impact corporate innovation in developing countries? *Journal of Islamic Accounting and Business Research, 14*(6), 887–910.

Buren, H. J., Syed, J., & Mir, R. (2020). Religion as a macro social force affecting business: Concepts, questions, and future research . *Business & Society, 59*(5), 799–822.

Carsrud, A., Brännback, M., Elfving, J., & Brandt, K. (2017). Motivations: The Entrepreneurial Mind Motivations: The Entrepreneurial Mind and Behavior. In M. Brännback, & A. L. Carsrud, *Revisiting the Entrepreneurial Mind Inside the Black Box: An Expanded Edition* (pp. 185–209). Cham: Springer.

Dana, L.-P. (2010). *Entrepreneurship and Religion.* Cheltenham: Edward Elgar Publishing.

Dik, B. J., Daniels, D., & Alayan, A. J. (2024). Religion, Spirituality, and the Workplace: A Review and Critique. *Annual Review of Organizational Psychology and Organizational Behavior, 11*(1), 279–305.

Essers, C., & Benschop, Y. (2009). Muslim businesswomen doing boundary work: The negotiation of Islam, gender and ethnicity within entrepreneurial contexts. *Human relations, 62*(3), 403–423.

Fathonih, A., Anggadwita, G., & Ibraimi, S. (2019). Sharia venture capital as financing alternative of Muslim entrepreneurs: Opportunities, challenges and future research directions. *Journal of Enterprising Communities: People and Places in the Global Economy, 13*(3), 333–352.

Gerring, J. (2017). Qualitative Methods. *Annual review of political science, 20*(1), 15–36.

Grine, F., Fares, D., & Meguellati, A. (2015). Islamic spirituality and entrepreneurship: A case study of women. *The Journal of Happiness & Well-Being, 3*(1), 41–56.

Gümüsay, A. A. (2015). Entrepreneurship from an Islamic Perspective. *Journal of Business Ethics, 130(2),* 199–208.

Güneş, S. (2022). Religious Products, Product Design, Meanings and Economy of Religion. *Journal of Engineering and Architecture, 10*(2), 1–15.

Hamid, S. A., & Sa'ari, C. Z. (2011). Reconstructing Entrepreneur's Development Based on al-Qur'an And al-Hadith. *International Journal of Business and Social Science, 2*(19), 110–116.

Harizan, S. H., & Mustafa, M. S. (2020). Islamic Entrepreneurship: Analysis of Research Trend. *Islamiyyat, 42*(2), 71–84.

Hassan, M. K., & Hippler, W. (2014). Entrepreneurship and Islam: An Overview. *Econ Journal Watch, 11*(2), 170–178.

Henley, A. (2017). Does religion influence entrepreneurial behaviour? *International Small Business Journal, 35*(5), 597–617.

Javaid, O. (2021). An Islamic vision and approach for entrepreneurship: developing through a multi-stage comparative analysis of systems, ideologies and code of ethics. *International Journal of Ethics and Systems, 38*(1), 125–146.

Jones, J., Hymer, C., Roccapriore, A., & Smith, B. (2024). Does religion matter to angels? Exploring the influence of religion in entrepreneurial investor decision-making. *Small Business Economics, 62*(4), 1337–1360.

Kayed, R. N., & Hassan, M. K. (2010). Islamic entrepreneurship: A case study of Saudi Arabia. *Journal of Developmental Entrepreneurship, 15*(4), 379–413.

Khalique, M., Ramayah, T., Hina, K., & Shaari, J. A. (2020). Islamic Entrepreneurship: A Systematic Review of Future Challenges and Prospects of Pakistani SMEs. *International Journal of Economics, Management and Accounting, 28*(2), 277–295.

Krasniqi, B. (2007). Barriers to entrepreneurship and SME growth in transition: the case of Kosova. *Journal of Developmental Entrepreneurship, 12*(1), 71–94.

Kumara, S., Sahoo, S., Lim, W. M., & Dana, L.-P. (2022). Religion as a social shaping force in entrepreneurship and business: Insights from a technology-empowered systematic literature review. *Technological Forecasting and Social Change, 175(1),* 121393.

Landes, D. S., Mokyr, J., & Baumol, W. J. (2010). *The Invention of Enterprise Entrepreneurship from Ancient Mesopotamia to Modern Times.* Princeton, NJ: Princeton University Press.

Latifi, V., Ramadani, V., & Rexhepi, G. (2022). Women minority entrepreneurs: Motivational factors and challenges. *Strategic Change, 31*(2), 219–225.

Lisnawati, D., & Ahman, H. E. (2019). Relationship between Entrepreneurial Characteristics from Islamic Perspective and the Performance of Small and Medium-Sized Businesses (A Study of SMEs in Indonesia). *The 2nd International Conference on Islamic Economics, Business, and Philanthropy (2nd ICIEBP)* (pp. 576–593). KnE Social Sciences.

Mahmood, B., Khalid, S., Sohail, M. M., & Babak, I. (2012). Exploring the Motivation and Barriers in Way of Pakistani Female Entrepreneurs. *British Journal of Education, Society & Behavioural Science, 2*(4), 353–368.

Mebroui, T., & Mosbah, A. (2020). Islamic Entrepreneurship: Issues and Debates. *International Journal of Management and Commerce Innovations, 7*(2), 461–468.

Neuman, W. L. (2014). *Social research methods: Qualitative and quantitative approaches* (Seventh ed.). Harlow: Pearson.

Qayyum, U., Anjum, S., & Sabir, S. (2020). Religion and economic development: new insights. *Empirica, 47(1)*, 793–834.

Rafiki, A., & Wahab, K. A. (2014). Islamic Values and Principles in the Organization: A Review of Literature. *Asian Social Science, 10*(9), 1–7.

Rafiki, A., Hidayat, S. E., & Pananjung, A. G. (2023). Islamic Entrepreneurship Research Since 1990: A Systematic Literature Review. *Jurnal Ekonomi Islam, 12*(1), 39–56.

Rahman, S. S. (2023). Analysis of Opportunities and Threats for Muslim SMEs. *10th International Conference on Management and Muamalah*, (pp. 367–377). Bangi, Malaysia.

Raimi, L., Adekunle, S. M., & Shabbir, M. S. (2023). *Contemporary Discourse of Halal and Islamic Entrepreneurship Trends and Future Opportunities.* Singapore: Springer.

Ramadani, V., Dana, L.-P., Gërguri-Rashiti, S., & Ratten, V. (2016). *Entrepreneurship and Management in an Islamic Context.* Cham: Springer.

Ramadani, V., Dana, L.-P., Ratten, V., & Tahiri, S. (2015). The context of Islamic entrepreneurship and business: concept, principles and perspectives. *International Journal of Business and Globalisation, 15*(3), 244–261.

Ratten, V. (2022). *Cultural Entrepreneurship New Societal Trends.* Singapore: Springer.

Sadri, A. (2010). Science-Driven Entrepreneurship in the Islamic World. *International Journal of Information, 8*(1), 73–81.

Sandikci, O. (2021). Religion and everyday consumption ethics: a moral economy approach. *Journal of Business Ethics, 168*(2), 277–293.

Smith, B. R., Conger, M. J., McMullen, J. S., & Neubert, M. J. (2019). Why believe? The promise of research on the role of religion in entrepreneurial action. *Journal of Business Venturing Insights, 11(1)*, e00119.

Smith, B. R., McMullen, J. S., & Cardon, M. S. (2021). Toward a theological turn in entrepreneurship: How religion could enable transformative research in our field. *Journal of Business Venturing, 36*(5), 106139.

Soltanian, M., Zailani, S., Iranmanesh, M., & Aziz, A. A. (2016). Motivations of SME entrepreneurs to become halalpreneurs. *Journal of Science and Technology Policy Management, 7*(2), 173–189.

Tlaiss, H. A., & McAdam, M. (2021). Islam, Arab women's entrepreneurship and the construal of success. *International Journal of Entrepreneurial Behavior & Research, 27*(3), 821–844.

Vargas-Hernández, J. G., Noruzi, M. R., & Sariolghalam, N. (2010). An Exploration of the Affects of Islamic Culture on Entrepreneurial Behaviors in Muslim Countries. *Asian Social Science, 6*(5), 120–127.

Yixing, P. (2019). The Strength of Belief: Empirical Research on the Influence of Religion on Economy—An Analysis Based on the Panel Data of Yangtze River Delta Region in China. *International Relations, 136*(1), 377–383.

Zelekha, Y., Avnimelech, G., & Sharabi, E. (2014). Religious institutions and entrepreneurship. *Small Business Economics, 42(5)*, 747–767.

Naveed Yasin, Farooq Haq, Aidin Salamzadeh, Leo Paul Dana

Chapter 7
Faith-driven Enterprise: Navigating Modern Markets with Islamic Values in Contemporary Entrepreneurship

Abstract: This chapter explores the integration of Islamic values in contemporary entrepreneurship, examining how faith-driven businesses navigate modern market demands while upholding core religious principles. Through a selection of case studies of Al Baik in Saudi Arabia, Osmanli Oud, inspired by the globally popular series Diriliş: Ertuğrul in Turkiye, and My Salah Mat in the United Kingdom (UK), and J. from Pakistan, this chapter explores how Islamic values shape these enterprises. Each case provides insights into distinct industries, ranging from fast food and fragrance to educational technology, highlighting the ways in which Islamic principles like social responsibility, ethical transparency, and cultural authenticity contribute to competitive advantage and brand loyalty. This study is particularly relevant for scholars, policymakers, and practitioners interested in the intersection of faith and commerce in a globalised world.

Keywords: Islamic Business, Faith, International Cases, Traditions

7.1 Introduction

In the pursuit of building inclusive, culturally sensitive frameworks in higher education institutions (HEIs), there is a growing movement to decolonise the study of entrepreneurial businesses by recognising the role of diverse cultural and religious influences on the theory and practice in business and enterprise. While the decolonisation of higher education has predominantly been focused on reforms in the curriculum, greater research attention needs to be attributed to the material implications of colonialism and address newer forms of empires that have colonised HEIs (Enslin & Hedge, 2024). A similar emphasis was echoed by Everett (2023), outlining in a report published by the AACSB that Western business schools have historically benefited from imperialist structures that established their ideologies as dominant and privileged. Decolonising their curricula requires more than simply diversifying reading lists; it necessitates integrating knowledge and educational approaches from scholars of varied cultural and philosophical backgrounds. This inclusive approach would broaden perspectives within the field, enriching the discipline with greater diversity and deeper analysis, ultimately strengthening it. Based on this rationale, recognising the role of religion in

https://doi.org/10.1515/9783111575407-008

business and enterprise is relevant towards developing contextualised approaches to academic scholarship (Verver et al., 2019, 2020).

In the context of this chapter, the global presence of over 2.04 billion Muslims and the existence of 57 Muslim-majority countries underscores Islam's significant and diverse influence in the world. This widespread reach is not only a demographic reality but also impacts the economic, social, and cultural landscapes of these regions, including their entrepreneurial ecosystems. The Organisation of Islamic Cooperation (OIC), representing these nations, reflects a collective approach to aligning economic and social development with Islamic principles. Exploring Islamic values within business and entrepreneurship provides a meaningful framework for understanding ethical practices, community-focused business models, and sustainable growth strategies within Muslim-majority contexts (Haq, Yasin & Nair, 2023). This perspective enriches the study of entrepreneurship by introducing insights rooted in Islamic philosophy, expanding beyond traditional Western business models to include a broader, culturally diverse approach (Ramadani et al., 2015, 2016).

Islamic values and principles provide unique insights into business practices, emphasising ethical conduct, community well-being, and sustainable growth. This approach reshapes the understanding of entrepreneurship in predominantly Muslim regions and also introduces a valuable perspective into the global entrepreneurial context. By integrating Islamic concepts, such as fairness (ʿadl), ethical stewardship (Amanah), and social welfare (Maslaha), entrepreneurial businesses gain a framework that extends beyond profit, fostering practices that contribute positively to society. Islamic principles provide a comprehensive ethical and moral framework that can be applied to all aspects of life, including business and commerce. As the global Muslim population continues to grow worldwide, there is increasing interest in understanding how Islamic teachings and values can be integrated into modern business practices.

This chapter is structured to provide an in-depth examination of contemporary Islamic business practices by analysing prominent companies from Saudi Arabia, Qatar, Pakistan, and the UK. It begins with an overview of the foundational Islamic principles guiding ethical business practices, setting the stage for the detailed case studies that follow. Using secondary data, the chapter investigates the operations of companies to illustrate how these businesses blend Islamic values with modern entrepreneurial strategies. Each case study explores aspects of ethical frameworks, including sustainability, social responsibility, and stakeholder engagement, illustrating the balance these companies strike between tradition and innovation.

7.2 Interaction of Islam and Enterprise

Islam is a monotheistic religion that emerged in the 7th century CE in the Arabian Peninsula. Founded on the teachings of the Prophet Muhammad, who is considered the last Prophet in a long line of messengers, including figures from Judaism and Christianity. Islam emphasises submission to the will of Allah (God) as the path to achieving peace and purpose in life (Esposito, 2011). The Quran, Islam's sacred text, is believed by Muslims to be the literal word of God, as revealed to Muhammad over 23 years ago. Alongside the Quran, the Hadith, or recorded sayings and practices of the Prophet Muhammad, shape religious, social, and legal norms for Muslims (Waines, 2003).

Islam originated in the city of Mecca, in modern-day Saudi Arabia, during a period marked by tribal and polytheistic practices. Muhammad's message of monotheism, social justice, and moral reform initially met resistance but gained traction among followers who valued its call for unity and compassion (Lapidus, 2002). After Muhammad's migration (Hijra) to Medina in 622 CE, Islam grew rapidly, consolidating political and spiritual power. By the Prophet's death in 632 CE, Islam had become the primary religious and political force in the Arabian Peninsula. Over the next century, Islam expanded across the Middle East, North Africa, and parts of Europe and Asia through both conquest and trade, forming one of history's most significant empires, the Caliphate (Donner, 2010).

The spread of Islam catalysed a period of extensive intellectual, cultural, and scientific development known as the Islamic Golden Age (roughly the 8th to 14th centuries). The Abbasid Caliphate, based in Baghdad, became a hub of learning and culture, where Muslim scholars made groundbreaking contributions in fields like medicine, mathematics, astronomy, philosophy, and literature. Figures such as Al-Khwarizmi, Ibn Sina (Avicenna), and Al-Farabi integrated knowledge from Greek, Persian, Indian, and other traditions into Islamic thought, advancing scientific and philosophical understanding (Hodgson, 1974). During this period, Islamic civilisation established a thriving commercial network, connecting the Muslim world to Europe, Africa, and Asia through trade routes like the Silk Road (Lapidus, 2002).

By the 15th century, the political unity of the Islamic world began to fragment due to internal divisions and the rise of competing empires, such as the Ottomans, Safavids, and Mughals. The onset of European colonialism in the 18th and 19th centuries significantly impacted Muslim-majority regions, introducing Western cultural, economic, and political dominance, which disrupted traditional Islamic governance and institutions. The colonial era introduced modern nation-state borders and systems that often clashed with Islamic law and social customs, resulting in both tension and adaptation among Muslim societies (Esposito, 2011).

In the 20th century, the decolonisation process saw many Muslim-majority countries gaining independence and seeking ways to integrate Islamic principles within modern political and social frameworks. This led to a diversity of Islamic governance models, ranging from secular democracies to theocratic systems. The emergence of Islam as a political force during the mid-20th century brought renewed interest in Islamic law (Sharia) as a basis for governance, particularly in the Middle East and parts of South Asia (Lewis, 1998). At the same time, Muslims in diaspora communities around the world began to reinterpret Islamic principles to fit new social contexts, further diversifying Islamic thought and practice.

Today, Islam is the second-largest religion in the world, with over two billion adherents worldwide (Pew Research Center, 2017). The global Muslim community (ummah) includes diverse ethnic, linguistic, and cultural groups, with significant populations in the Middle East, South Asia, Southeast Asia, and Africa and growing numbers in Europe and North America. In response to globalisation, many Muslims strive to balance traditional Islamic values with contemporary challenges, such as secularisation, technological advancement, and globalised economic systems. This era has also seen the rise of movements advocating for Islamic values in fields like finance, social justice, and environmental sustainability (Moten, 2005).

Islamic thought has evolved to respond to various social, political, and economic challenges. For instance, Islamic finance emerged as a field in the 20th century to provide financial services that adhere to Sharia principles, such as the prohibition of interest (riba) and ethical investing (Iqbal & Mirakhor, 2007). Additionally, contemporary Islamic scholarship often addresses issues such as human rights, gender equality, and environmental stewardship within an Islamic framework, reflecting a dynamic engagement with modern concerns while upholding core religious principles (Haq, Yasin & Nair, 2023). Islam has undergone a complex journey from its origins in 7th-century Arabia to its current position as a global faith with diverse expressions (Dana, 2010; Ramadani, 2021). While its foundational teachings remain unchanged, interpretations and applications of Islamic principles continue to adapt to new contexts and challenges, underscoring the religion's capacity for renewal and relevance across centuries.

7.3 Literature Review

Islam is often perceived as an inherently "anti-modernist faith" that may not support entrepreneurship (Cooney et al., 2011). However, research suggests that Islam actually encourages entrepreneurship, viewing it as a dignified and honourable pursuit (Koehler, 2011; Rafiq, 1992; Vargas-Hernández et al., 2010). Rafiq (1992) highlights the significant role of culture and religion in shaping entrepreneurial choices, showing that for many Muslims, their cultural and religious values strongly influence the types of businesses they establish, often leading them to avoid sectors involving alcohol or non-halal products. This highlights that religious beliefs can shape not only the motivation to engage in entrepreneurship but also the specific sectors in which entrepreneurs choose to operate (Yasin and Hafeez, 2023; Yasin, 2020). Further, Basu and Altinay (2002) explored the relationship between culture and entrepreneurship within six immigrant communities in London, discovering that some groups exhibit a more pronounced connection between their cultural identity and entrepreneurial activities. They concluded that understanding the entrepreneurial behaviours of ethnic groups requires a community-level analysis, as these behaviours affect their economic resources, which in turn shape the scale and characteristics of their business endeavours.

In countries like Saudi Arabia, institutional structures are deeply influenced by Shariah law, which shapes the governance, regulations, and practices within both public and private sectors, including businesses and enterprises. Shariah, derived from Islamic legal sources such as the Quran, Hadith, and the consensus of scholars, outlines ethical guidelines and prohibitions, including the prohibition of interest (riba), unfair trading practices, and unethical labour conditions (Ahmad, 2018). These guidelines impact how businesses operate, mandating compliance with Islamic principles in financial transactions, employment practices, and corporate governance (El-Gamal, 2006). For example, in Saudi Arabia, businesses must adhere to halal standards, not only in product offerings but also in operational practices, to meet both regulatory requirements and consumer expectations in the predominantly Muslim society (Khan & Bhatti, 2008). Furthermore, Shariah law emphasises social welfare and community support, influencing corporate social responsibility policies, which are often designed to align with zakat (obligatory charity) and sadaqah (voluntary charity), further embedding Islamic values into the economic framework of the country (Grais & Pellegrini, 2006). These religiously rooted institutional frameworks create a distinct business environment where ethical and social obligations are as integral to business practices as profit motives.

Turkey offers a distinct contrast to Saudi Arabia regarding how Islamic principles influence its institutional structures, particularly in the business and financial sectors. Unlike Saudi Arabia, where Shariah law significantly shapes legal and business frameworks, Turkey operates under a secular legal system established by Mustafa Kemal Atatürk in the early 20th century. This secular foundation means that Turkey's official institutional structures are governed by civil law rather than Shariah, allowing for greater flexibility in terms of economic practices, such as permitting interest-based banking, which is prohibited in Shariah-compliant systems (Kuran, 2011). However, Turkey has seen an increased interest in Islamic finance and halal industries, particularly in the past two decades. For example, Islamic banking, known as "participation banking" in Turkey, has grown substantially, with government support for Shariah-compliant financial institutions to attract Middle Eastern investment and appeal to conservative Muslim consumers within Turkey (World Bank, 2015). Despite this, Islamic finance remains one component of a broader financial system, where conventional banking still dominates (Demirguc-Kunt et al., 2015).

Additionally, Turkey has a vibrant halal market and consumer base, with businesses voluntarily adopting halal standards to meet consumer demand rather than regulatory requirements, showing a more market-driven approach to integrating Islamic principles compared to Saudi Arabia's institutional enforcement (Ar, 2020). Thus, while Islamic values influence certain sectors, especially in finance and halal industries, Turkey's institutional structures remain largely secular, accommodating a blend of Shariah-compliant and conventional business practices (Anggadwita et al., 2021; Rafiki et al., 2024).

Pakistan presents a unique position between Turkey and Saudi Arabia in terms of how Islamic principles influence institutional and business frameworks. Like Saudi Arabia, Pakistan identifies itself as an Islamic Republic and integrates Islamic principles into its legal and financial systems; however, unlike Saudi Arabia, Pakistan operates under a hybrid system that combines Islamic and secular legal elements. Pakistan's constitution declares Islam as the state religion and Shariah principles are embedded within certain laws, particularly those governing family, inheritance, and finance (Ahmed & Khan, 2018). However, Pakistan's business environment is more flexible than Saudi Arabia's strict Shariah-compliant structure, allowing for a mix of conventional and Islamic practices, much like Turkey (Khan, 2019).

In the financial sector, Pakistan has a substantial Islamic banking industry, with a regulatory framework designed to support both Islamic and conventional banks. The State Bank of Pakistan promotes Islamic finance as an alternative, with Shariah-compliant banking capturing a significant market share. However, unlike Saudi Arabia, Pakistan's regulatory environment allows both Islamic and conventional banks to operate side-by-side, giving consumers a choice (Khan & Bhatti, 2008). This dual system is similar to Turkey, where traditional banking dominates, but Islamic banking options are available and expanding (Demirguc-Kunt et al., 2015).

Unlike Turkey, where secularism is constitutionally enshrined, Pakistan's policies often incorporate Islamic values, especially in social welfare and corporate governance, drawing upon principles like zakat and sadaqah for CSR initiatives. Additionally, Pakistan's halal industry has grown in response to both domestic demand and global halal markets, with businesses adhering to halal standards to appeal to consumers within Pakistan and abroad (Nasir & Pereira, 2008). Thus, Pakistan shares Saudi Arabia's religious influence on certain regulatory areas while also resembling Turkey's flexible, dual approach in sectors like finance and business, allowing both Islamic and conventional practices to coexist within a hybridised framework.

The following section presents four case studies—Al Baik from Saudi Arabia, Osmanli Oud from Turkey, J. from Pakistan, and My Salah Mat from the United Kingdom—to explore how Islamic values influence business practices across varied cultural and regulatory landscapes. Each case highlights unique adaptations of Islamic principles.

7.3.1 Case Study 1: Al Baik (Saudi Arabia)

Al Baik, a fast-food restaurant chain headquartered in Jeddah, Saudi Arabia, is known for its distinctive fried chicken and affordable menu, making it one of the most successful and popular brands in the country. Founded in 1974 by the late Shakour AbuGhazalah, Al Baik has expanded to over 120 branches across Saudi Arabia and has gained popularity beyond the Kingdom's borders. Unlike other fast-food chains, Al Baik's success story is not solely about efficient service or product quality; it is deeply intertwined with the Islamic values guiding its business practices. The company's commitment to community welfare, ethical practices, and service excellence reflects core Islamic principles, highlighting how faith can shape a successful business model that resonates with customers and broader society alike.

– ***Al Baik's Commitment to Community Welfare***

One of the defining characteristics of Al Baik is its emphasis on social responsibility, which is embedded in Islamic teachings. Islam places high importance on community welfare and charitable acts, such as zakat (obligatory charity) and sadaqah (voluntary charity). Al Baik's corporate philosophy aligns with these values by prioritising the welfare of its employees, customers, and the communities in which it operates.

Al Baik's community-oriented approach is evident in its extensive social initiatives, which address critical social issues in Saudi Arabia, such as youth unemployment and hunger. The company has supported youth development programs, offering training to young Saudis and creating job opportunities that empower the local workforce. Additionally, Al Baik engages in direct charitable acts, such as distributing free meals to underserved communities, a practice that gained heightened visibility during the COVID-19 pandemic. This community-focused ethos has earned Al Baik considerable respect and loyalty from the public, reflecting the Islamic values of compassion and care for others.

– ***Employee Welfare and Fair Treatment***

In Islam, the concept of justice and fairness ('adl) is a core value that extends to all aspects of life, including the treatment of workers. Al Baik's approach to employee welfare demonstrates a commitment to fair and ethical treatment of its staff, which is rare in an industry often criticised for poor working conditions. The company offers competitive wages, comprehensive training, and a supportive work environment that respects the dignity and rights of employees. Al Baik provides opportunities for growth and advancement, ensuring that employees feel valued and empowered.

Furthermore, Al Baik's hiring practices emphasise inclusivity and respect for diversity, reflecting the Islamic principle of equality. This dedication to fair treatment not only aligns with Islamic teachings but also enhances the company's reputation, making it an attractive employer and fostering a loyal, motivated workforce.

– ***Ethical Business Practices and Halal Standards***

Al Baik's adherence to ethical business practices is another key area where Islamic values are evident. As a business in Saudi Arabia, Al Baik operates in a society where halal standards are paramount. The company takes great care to ensure that all its products comply with halal requirements, from sourcing ingredients to preparing and serving food. This commitment reflects the Islamic dietary laws governing permissible (halal) and forbidden (haram) foods, which are crucial for gaining trust and maintaining a loyal customer base in predominantly Muslim regions.

Al Baik's focus on quality control and transparency further aligns with Islamic ethical principles. In Islamic business ethics, honesty and integrity are fundamental. Al Baik maintains rigorous quality control measures and ensures that customers receive what is promised. This dedication to quality, combined with the adherence to halal standards, fosters trust and loyalty among customers, distinguishing Al Baik from competitors and reinforcing its reputation as a reliable and principled brand.

– ***Environmental Responsibility and Islamic Stewardship***

Islamic teachings emphasise the concept of stewardship, where humans are considered caretakers of the Earth and are responsible for preserving the environment. Al Baik has demonstrated a commitment to environmental responsibility through various initiatives aimed at minimising its ecological footprint. For instance, the company has implemented waste reduction programs and sustainable packaging solutions, reducing the use of plastics and promoting environmentally friendly alternatives. Al Baik has also engaged in campaigns to raise environmental awareness, particularly among younger generations.

These efforts align with the Islamic principle of environmental stewardship and add a unique dimension to Al Baik's brand identity. In a region where environmental awareness is gradually increasing, Al Baik's proactive approach serves as a model for other businesses and reinforces its image as a responsible corporate citizen.

– ***Quality and Service Excellence: The Concept of Ihsan***

Another Islamic value reflected in Al Baik's business model is the concept of Ihsan, or excellence in all actions. Ihsan emphasises striving for the highest standard of quality and integrity, and this principle is evident in Al Baik's approach to customer service and product quality. Al Baik is renowned for the consistency of its offerings and the high quality of its food, which has been a key factor in its success. The company places a premium on customer satisfaction, providing efficient, courteous service that has set a standard in the fast-food industry within Saudi Arabia and beyond.

This commitment to excellence extends to every aspect of Al Baik's operations, from food preparation to customer interactions, embodying the Islamic ethos of Ihsan. By upholding this standard of quality and service, Al Baik not only meets customer expectations but also reinforces the Islamic value of striving for excellence, contributing to its lasting success in a competitive industry.

– ***Balancing Tradition and Innovation in a Globalized Market***

As Al Baik has expanded, it has faced the challenge of balancing its Islamic values with the demands of a rapidly globalising market. While Al Baik's growth has introduced it to new audiences, the company remains rooted in its Islamic principles, which shape its business decisions and strategic direction. For example, as Al Baik explores international expansion, it maintains its commitment to halal standards and ethical practices, ensuring that its brand identity remains authentic and consistent.

This balance between tradition and innovation reflects the flexibility of Islamic principles in adapting to contemporary challenges. By remaining true to its values, Al Baik not only appeals to Muslim consumers but also attracts a diverse customer base that appreciates the ethical foundation of its business model. This adaptability highlights how Islamic values can provide a solid foundation for navigating the complexities of a globalised market, showcasing Al Baik as a successful model of ethical entrepreneurship in the modern business world.

7.3.2 Case Study 2: Osmanli Oud: A Halal Turkish Perfume

Osmanli Oud, a halal perfume brand inspired by the globally popular Turkish series *Diriliş: Ertuğrul* (known internationally as *Ertugrul Ghazi*), has captured the essence of Islamic heritage and tradition through fragrance. The series, which depicts the story of the founding of the Ottoman Empire, resonated deeply with audiences across the Muslim world, sparking a renewed interest in Ottoman history, Islamic values, and traditional culture. Osmanli Oud capitalised on this cultural resurgence, positioning itself as a fragrance brand that not only offers halal-certified products but also reflects Islamic values in its business model. With a focus on ethically sourced ingredients, cultural authenticity, and community engagement, Osmanli Oud represents a compelling example of how Islamic-inspired branding can create a unique, successful niche in the global market.

– ***Drawing Inspiration from Islamic Heritage and Ottoman Culture***

Osmanli Oud was founded to celebrate the cultural legacy of the Ottoman Empire, and its connection to Islamic values is integral to its brand identity. The brand's name, Osmanli, refers to the Ottoman Empire, while Oud, a traditional fragrance ingredient valued in Islamic culture, is central to its products. Oud, derived from the resinous wood of the agar tree, is often referred to as "liquid gold" and has been treasured in the Middle East and South Asia for centuries for its deep, warm scent.

The influence of *Diriliş: Ertuğrul* has been significant in Osmanli Oud's branding and product development. The brand capitalised on the global popularity of the series, which highlighted values such as loyalty, bravery, faith, and community – qualities that resonate with Islamic and Ottoman cultural ideals. By evoking the spirit of Ertugrul Ghazi, Osmanli Oud taps into a nostalgic appeal, offering consumers a sensory connection to Islamic heritage through its fragrances. This alignment of product and brand with historical and religious values differentiates Osmanli Oud in a competitive fragrance market, appealing to consumers who identify with Islamic culture.

- ***Halal Certification and Ethical Sourcing***

A core aspect of Osmanli Oud's appeal is its commitment to halal certification, ensuring that all products meet Islamic guidelines. Halal certification is critical in Islamic business ethics, as it assures Muslim consumers that products are free from forbidden (haram) substances and processes. Osmanli Oud goes beyond halal requirements by ensuring that every step of production, from sourcing raw materials to manufacturing, adheres to strict ethical and halal standards. This dedication is particularly important in the fragrance industry, where alcohol and other non-halal ingredients are commonly used in perfumes.

Osmanli Oud's ethical sourcing practices also reflect the Islamic value of environmental stewardship. The brand sources its Oud and other ingredients sustainably, promoting fair trade and working with suppliers who share its commitment to ethical practices. This approach not only ensures the quality and purity of the ingredients but also builds a reputation for transparency and integrity, aligning the brand with Islamic teachings on environmental responsibility and social justice. By maintaining high ethical standards, Osmanli Oud has established itself as a trustworthy brand that respects both its consumers and the natural world.

- ***Commitment to Modesty in Marketing and Brand Messaging***

One of the defining characteristics of Osmanli Oud is its adherence to Islamic values in marketing and brand messaging. While many fragrance brands rely on glamorous or provocative advertising, Osmanli Oud has chosen a modest and culturally respectful approach, focusing on themes of tradition, purity, and heritage. The brand's advertising often depicts scenes inspired by Ottoman aesthetics, featuring classic motifs and historical references that appeal to consumers drawn to Islamic history and values.

By presenting its products through the lens of modesty and heritage, Osmanli Oud has successfully differentiated itself from mainstream fragrance brands. This marketing strategy aligns with the Islamic principle of modesty and reflects a respect for the cultural and religious sensibilities of its target audience. Through this approach, Osmanli Oud has cultivated a loyal customer base that appreciates the brand's dedication to cultural authenticity and its alignment with Islamic values.

- ***Promoting Islamic Values Through Community Engagement and Philanthropy***

In Islam, business is not solely a means of profit but also a platform for social good and community welfare. Osmanli Oud has embraced this principle by engaging in philanthropic activities and supporting social causes, such as funding education programs, sponsoring community events, and collaborating with charities. The brand's commitment to community engagement is a practical expression of *zakat* (obligatory charity) and *sadaqah* (voluntary charity), central tenets of Islamic financial ethics.

Osmanli Oud's philanthropic efforts are particularly impactful during Ramadan, a month of fasting, reflection, and charity in Islam. The brand frequently donates a portion of its profits to charitable organisations, supporting initiatives that benefit underserved communities. This commitment to giving back not only reflects the Islamic values of generosity and compassion but also strengthens Osmanli Oud's connection to its consumers, who value the brand's dedication to social responsibility. By aligning its business with the principles of charity and social welfare, Osmanli Oud enhances its brand identity as a values-driven business.

– ***Global Expansion and Maintaining Cultural Integrity***
Since its launch, Osmanli Oud has expanded beyond Turkey, establishing a presence in the Middle East, South Asia, Europe, and North America. This global reach has introduced the brand to diverse markets, allowing it to connect with Muslim consumers around the world who seek halal-certified, culturally authentic fragrances. Despite its expansion, Osmanli Oud has maintained a strong commitment to its cultural and religious roots, ensuring that its brand identity remains consistent across regions.

The brand's success in international markets demonstrates the demand for products that resonate with Islamic values and heritage. By staying true to its Islamic identity, Osmanli Oud has created a niche for itself, attracting consumers who appreciate the brand's authenticity and ethical foundation. This ability to balance global expansion with cultural integrity serves as a model for Islamic-inspired brands seeking to succeed in a competitive and diverse marketplace.

– ***Incorporating Ottoman and Islamic Values into Product Development***
Osmanli Oud's product line is not only a celebration of Oud as a fragrance ingredient but also an embodiment of Ottoman and Islamic cultural values. The brand draws inspiration from traditional Ottoman perfumes and Islamic botanical knowledge, infusing each fragrance with historical significance. Osmanli Oud frequently names its products after Ottoman figures, locations, or concepts, reinforcing its connection to Islamic history.

By incorporating these elements, Osmanli Oud offers consumers a multi-sensory experience that goes beyond fragrance. Each product is a reminder of the Islamic golden age, celebrating the historical contributions of Muslim civilisations to art, science, and culture. This connection to Islamic heritage adds depth to the brand, appealing to consumers who view fragrance as a personal expression of faith and identity.

7.3.2.1 Case Summary

Osmanli Oud's success is a testament to the potential of Islamic-inspired brands to thrive in the global market by adhering to ethical principles and celebrating cultural heritage. Through its commitment to halal certification, ethical sourcing, modest marketing, and community engagement, Osmanli Oud has built a brand that resonates deeply with consumers seeking products that align with their values. The influence of *Diriliş: Ertuğrul* has provided a cultural foundation for Osmanli Oud's identity, allowing the brand to connect with audiences who appreciate the legacy of Islamic history and the principles of integrity and compassion.

By blending Islamic values with modern entrepreneurship, Osmanli Oud has created a niche in the fragrance industry that appeals to a diverse, globally connected Muslim audience. This case study highlights how Islamic heritage can serve as a source of inspiration for the business, offering a model for entrepreneurs interested in developing brands that honour faith, culture, and social responsibility. As Osmanli Oud continues to grow, it stands as a powerful example of how Islamic values can guide business practices, creating a legacy of ethical, values-driven entrepreneurship that resonates in the modern world.

7.3.3 Case Study 3: "J." A Pakistan-based Islamic Business

Junaid Jamshed, a household name in Pakistan and beyond, is widely recognised for his unique journey from a celebrated pop music icon to a successful Islamic entrepreneur. Beginning his career as the lead vocalist of the popular Pakistani band Vital Signs, Junaid rose to fame in the late 1980s with hits like *Dil Dil Pakistan*, a patriotic anthem that remains cherished to this day. However, in a surprising turn of events, he left his music career at its peak, dedicating his life to Islamic values and entrepreneurship. Junaid's transformation and subsequent success in the fashion industry with his brand, J., embody a powerful example of how Islamic principles can guide entrepreneurial success. His journey reflects a harmonious balance between faith and business, inspiring Muslims worldwide to pursue ventures aligned with their values.

– ***Transition from Music to Faith***

Junaid Jamshed's decision to leave the music industry stemmed from a personal spiritual awakening. After years in the limelight, Junaid sought a deeper sense of purpose, eventually embracing a path of Islamic faith and religious practice. This transition marked a significant lifestyle change, with Junaid distancing himself from music and dedicating his life to Islamic teachings and philanthropy. His decision resonated with audiences in Pakistan and across the Muslim world, who saw in him a model of repentance, faith, and resilience.

During this period, Junaid became actively involved in Dawah (Islamic preaching) and aligned himself with prominent religious scholars in Pakistan. His transition was not merely a personal transformation but also a shift in his public persona, as he used his influence to promote Islamic values and encourage ethical living. This commitment laid the foundation for his entrepreneurial endeavours, rooted firmly in Islamic principles.

– ***The Launch of J.: An Islamic Approach to Fashion***

Junaid Jamshed's foray into entrepreneurship began in 2002 with the establishment of J., a clothing brand that quickly gained popularity in Pakistan and abroad. Founded with the aim of providing modest, culturally relevant fashion, J. embodies Junaid's vision of Islamic values in the business world. The brand focuses on traditional attire, including shalwar kameez and abayas, designed to appeal to a Muslim audience seeking modest and elegant clothing options.

By promoting Islamic modesty through fashion, J. filled a gap in the market and struck a chord with Muslim consumers who valued both style and spirituality. Junaid's influence and credibility as a public figure lent authenticity to the brand, establishing it as a respected name in the industry. This approach not only gave J. a strong identity rooted in Islamic principles but also allowed it to differentiate itself from other brands, aligning fashion with faith in a way that was both modern and culturally resonant.

– ***Commitment to Ethical Business Practices***

In Islam, honesty, integrity, and fairness are fundamental principles governing all aspects of life, including business. Junaid Jamshed was dedicated to ensuring that J. operated ethically and transparently, upholding Islamic values at every level. From sourcing materials to providing fair wages to employees, Junaid emphasised ethical standards that would honour both his faith and his commitment to his customers.

By maintaining strict quality control and transparency in production, J. gained a reputation as a trustworthy brand, echoing the Islamic value of ihsan (excellence) in every product and service. Junaid's adherence to these ethical practices helped build customer trust, further establishing J. as a brand that valued its consumers beyond mere commercial transactions. This ethical approach fostered customer loyalty and demonstrated that Islamic business values can contribute positively to brand reputation and business growth.

– ***Sustainability and Social Responsibility***

Junaid Jamshed's approach to social responsibility was grounded in the Islamic concepts of charity and social welfare. Throughout his life, Junaid engaged in philanthropic activities, dedicating a portion of J.'s profits to charitable initiatives. These included supporting educational institutions, orphanages, and other social welfare programs in Pakistan. Junaid's commitment to social responsibility is reflective of zakat (obligatory charity) and sadaqah (voluntary charity), essential aspects of Islamic financial ethics that emphasise supporting those in need. J. became known not only for its high-quality clothing but also for its contributions to the welfare of the community. Junaid's dedication to using business as a force for good resonated with consumers, who appreciated the brand's focus on giving back. This alignment with Islamic social values enhanced the brand's image, creating a business model that served both economic and social goals.

– ***Modesty in Marketing and Brand Messaging***

One of the unique aspects of J.'s business strategy was its adherence to modesty in marketing and brand messaging. In a world where fashion brands often rely on provocative or glamorous advertising to appeal to consumers, J. took a different approach, choosing to market its products in a respectful manner and line with Islamic teachings. The brand's advertisements focused on family values, tradition, and modesty, appealing to customers who valued Islamic principles in both style and lifestyle. By taking this approach, J. built a brand that felt authentic and trustworthy, gaining the support of consumers who shared Junaid's vision of modesty and ethical living. This approach also differentiated J. in a competitive market, allowing it to capture a loyal customer base that appreciated its values-driven approach.

– ***Global Expansion and Islamic Identity***

With the growing demand for modest fashion worldwide, J. successfully expanded its reach beyond Pakistan, opening stores in the Middle East, the UK, and the US. This expansion introduced Islamic fashion to new audiences, giving Muslim consumers access to clothing that honoured their cultural and religious identity. Despite the challenges of entering new markets, J. retained its commitment to Islamic principles, ensuring that its brand identity remained consistent.

Junaid's influence extended beyond fashion; his brand's success symbolised the potential for Islamic values to thrive in the global business landscape. By remaining true to his principles, Junaid demonstrated that an Islamic business could compete internationally without compromising its ethical foundation. This commitment to cultural integrity while embracing global expansion served as an example for other entrepreneurs interested in aligning business with faith.

– ***Legacy and Influence***

Tragically, Junaid Jamshed passed away in 2016, yet his legacy endures through the continued success of J. and his impact on Islamic entrepreneurship. His journey from pop icon to Islamic entrepreneur left a lasting impression on the Muslim community, inspiring others to pursue businesses that reflect their values. Junaid's success story highlights the possibility of creating brands rooted in Islamic principles that appeal to modern consumers, contributing positively to society while building a profitable enterprise.

The success of J. illustrates how Islamic values can shape a distinctive, competitive, and socially responsible business model. Junaid's journey inspires entrepreneurs to consider how faith can guide not only personal transformation but also business practices that serve communities and align with ethical standards. His legacy serves as a testament to the enduring power of faith-driven entrepreneurship in an increasingly globalised world.

7.3.3.1 Case Summary

Junaid Jamshed's transformation from a musician to an Islamic entrepreneur reflects a remarkable journey of faith, resilience, and purpose. Through the establishment of J., he demonstrated that business can be a means of embodying and promoting Islamic values. His commitment to ethical practices, modesty, and social responsibility allowed J. to grow into a successful, values-driven brand that resonated with Muslim consumers and expanded globally.

Junaid's legacy illustrates the potential for Islamic entrepreneurship to thrive in today's business landscape, offering a model for how faith and business can work together to create a meaningful impact. His story continues to inspire individuals worldwide to pursue entrepreneurship that not only seeks profit but also serves a higher purpose, integrating values of faith into every aspect of business.

7.3.4 Case Study 4: My Salah Mat UK-based Islamic Enterprise

My Salah Mat originated in the United Kingdom and was created by Kamal Ali in 2018 to support young Muslims in learning and engaging with Salah (Islamic prayer) through an interactive educational tool. The *My Salah Mat* is an interactive prayer mat designed to help children learn and engage with the practice of Salah, the Islamic ritual prayer. Developed by Kamal Ali in 2018, this innovative product uses technology to teach young Muslims the steps, phrases, and positions of Salah in a way that is both engaging and educational. My Salah Mat is a prime example of Islamic entrepreneurship that not only meets a practical need but also promotes Islamic values through an accessible, child-friendly format. By integrating educational technology with faith-based learning, My Salah Mat bridges the gap between tradition and modern pedagogy, empowering the next generation to connect with their faith meaningfully.

– ***The Need for Accessible Islamic Education***

In Islam, Salah is a foundational pillar and a core component of a Muslim's daily life. However, teaching young children to perform Salah can be challenging for parents, especially for those in non-Muslim-majority countries with limited access to religious education resources. Recognising this gap, Kamal Ali sought to create a tool that would make learning Salah easy and enjoyable for children, fostering a love for prayer and encouraging consistent practice from a young age.

My Salah Mat was developed to address this need by using an interactive approach to introduce children to prayer. The mat's design, with built-in audio guidance and visual prompts, simplifies the learning process, allowing children to learn at their own pace. This approach is particularly valuable for parents who want to teach their children about Salah in a way that aligns with modern educational practices while still preserving Islamic traditions. The mat has become widely popular among Muslim families globally, illustrating the potential for faith-based products to meet community needs in innovative ways.

– ***Product Design: Blending Technology with Tradition***

The design of My Salah Mat reflects a thoughtful blend of traditional Islamic education and modern technology. The mat is embedded with touch-sensitive sensors that trigger audio instructions in several languages, guiding children through Salah's steps. Each position, from standing (Qiyam) to bowing (Ruku) and prostration (Sujood), is accompanied by recorded recitations and instructional prompts, allowing children to learn the correct postures and phrases in a structured, interactive way.

While there is a growing emphasis on incorporating technology in entrepreneurial business ventures (Hyams-Ssekasi and Yasin, 2022), this fusion of technology and tradition makes My Salah Mat an effective educational tool, appealing to children's natural curiosity and engagement with technology. The mat's colourful, kid-friendly design is also intended to make learning appealing, creating a positive association with Salah. By using technology to make religious learning accessible, My Salah Mat addresses a common educational challenge while maintaining the integrity of Islamic practices, embodying the Islamic principle of *ihsan* (excellence in all actions).

– ***Promoting Cultural and Religious Identity***

In a world where young Muslims are often exposed to diverse cultural influences, maintaining a connection to their Islamic identity is increasingly important. My Salah Mat reinforces this identity by providing a tool that familiarises children with one of the core aspects of Islamic practice. By engaging children with Salah interactively and enjoyably, the mat fosters a sense of pride in their faith, contributing to a positive Islamic identity from a young age.

My Salah Mat also includes features that make it accessible to Muslim families from various cultural backgrounds, as it offers audio instructions in 15 different languages, including English, Arabic, Urdu, and French. This multilingual approach underscores the brand's inclusivity and commitment to supporting diverse communities, allowing children worldwide to learn Salah in their preferred language. This inclusivity resonates with the Islamic value of *ummah*, or community, ensuring that the product is accessible and relevant to Muslims across the globe.

– ***Ethical Production and Halal Certification***

The production of My Salah Mat is guided by ethical principles, aligning with Islamic values of fairness, integrity, and social responsibility. Kamal Ali emphasises that the mat is produced with high-quality materials, ensuring safety and durability for young users. The product is also certified as halal, assuring parents that it adheres to Islamic standards in both its content and production process. This attention to quality and ethical standards reflects the Islamic emphasis on transparency and trustworthiness in business, qualities that have contributed to My Salah Mat's positive reception among Muslim families.

Islamic scholars have reviewed the mat's design and content to ensure accuracy in representing the steps and phrases of Salah. This scholarly involvement underscores the brand's dedication to authenticity, ensuring that children learn Salah correctly and with respect to Islamic teachings. This approach not only builds trust among consumers but also upholds the value of *amanah* (trust) in business, emphasising ethical responsibility in both product design and messaging.

– ***Educational Impact and Faith-Based Learning***

My Salah Mat represents a unique approach to faith-based learning, merging Islamic education with interactive technology to enhance understanding and retention. Research in educational psychology suggests that children learn best through interactive, hands-on experiences, and My Salah Mat leverages this by allowing children to practice Salah with guided feedback. The audio prompts and visual cues support auditory, visual, and kinesthetic learning styles, making it easier for children to internalise each step of prayer.

By providing a structured learning experience, My Salah Mat allows parents to introduce religious education in a way that is both comprehensive and engaging. This interactive model also helps reinforce daily prayer habits, encouraging consistency in a practice that can be challenging for young learners to develop. The mat thus serves as a bridge between Islamic education and modern pedagogy, illustrating the potential for innovative products to enhance faith-based learning for children.

– ***Community Engagement and Social Impact***

Beyond its educational impact, My Salah Mat reflects a broader commitment to the Muslim community. Kamal Ali, the creator, has expressed a dedication to making Islamic education accessible, regularly collaborating with mosques, Islamic schools, and community organisations to distribute the mat to families who might otherwise lack access to such resources. Additionally, during Ramadan and other significant Islamic occasions, the brand often runs charity drives and promotions, making the mat available to underprivileged families.

This community-focused approach aligns with the Islamic values of *sadaqah* (charity) and *zakat* (obligatory almsgiving), reinforcing the brand's commitment to social welfare. By contributing to community initiatives and supporting Islamic education, My Salah Mat has earned a reputation as a values-driven brand that goes beyond commercial interests to make a meaningful impact. This focus on social responsibility strengthens the brand's connection with Muslim families, who appreciate its dedication to supporting the community.

– ***Global Reach and Cultural Relevance***

Since its launch, My Salah Mat has gained popularity not only in Muslim-majority countries but also among diaspora communities in North America, Europe, and Australia. Its global reach highlights the demand for products that help young Muslims connect with their faith, particularly in multicultural settings where access to Islamic educational resources may be limited. The product's success demonstrates how Islamic entrepreneurship can address specific community needs while appealing to a diverse, international market.

By promoting Islamic education in a culturally relevant format, My Salah Mat supports Muslim parents in fostering a connection to faith within a modern, globalised world. The brand's success also reflects the broader trend of culturally conscious entrepreneurship, where products serve to reinforce identity and promote inclusivity in faith-based education.

7.3.4.1 Case Summary

My Salah Mat is a powerful example of how Islamic values can drive meaningful innovation in educational products. Through its commitment to interactive learning, cultural inclusivity, and community engagement, the mat provides a valuable tool for young Muslims to learn Salah in a way that is both engaging and rooted in tradition. By blending technology with Islamic teachings, My Salah Mat has created a model for faith-based entrepreneurship that prioritises ethical production, educational impact, and social responsibility. The case of My Salah Mat highlights the potential for Islamic entrepreneurship to address academic needs within the Muslim community, offering a product that resonates with consumers' faith and cultural identity. As the brand continues to expand its reach, it stands as a testament to the power of innovative, values-driven entrepreneurship in fostering a meaningful connection to faith in the modern world.

7.3.5 Islamic Entrepreneurship: A Comparative Analysis

This chapter underscores the importance of recognising how Islamic principles shape business practices beyond the traditional scope of Shariah-compliant finance. While Islamic finance has often been the focus of Islamic business practices, there is a growing need to appreciate the wider application of Islamic values across a broad range of operations, products, and services. Through the four case studies—Al Baik (Saudi Arabia), Osmanli Oud (Turkey), J. (Pakistan), and My Salah Mat (United Kingdom)—this chapter illustrates that Islamic values can effectively influence diverse aspects of business, from product offerings to operational ethics and community engagement, within both Muslim-majority and secular markets (See Figure 7.1).

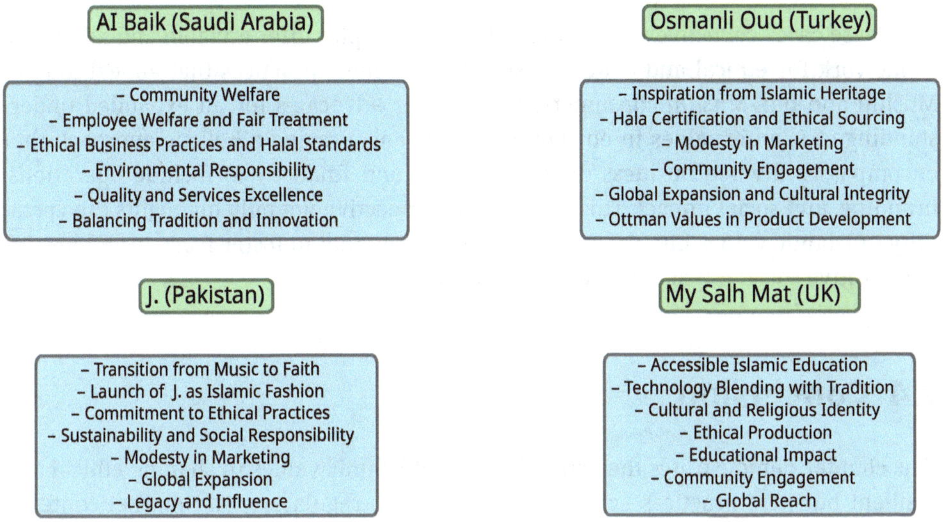

Figure 7.1: Features of the used cases in this chapter.
Source: Authors.

The influence of Islamic values extends far beyond financial practices, impacting how companies engage with social responsibility, ethical sourcing, environmental stewardship, and community welfare. For example, Al Baik in Saudi Arabia operates within a Shariah-governed environment where Islamic principles guide business ethics comprehensively, informing decisions on employee welfare, environmental responsibility, and community involvement. This broad integration of Islamic values goes beyond studies on Islamic finance, creating a holistic framework that shapes customer perception and builds brand loyalty within culturally aligned regulatory contexts. In contrast, Osmanli Oud in Turkey showcases how Islamic-inspired branding and product offerings, such as halal-certified perfumes, can thrive in a secular legal environment. The brand's commitment to halal standards and cultural authenticity speaks to consumer demand rather than regulatory enforcement, emphasising the adaptability of Islamic values in meeting market expectations voluntarily.

Similarly, J. in Pakistan operates within a hybrid system that allows for both Islamic and secular practices, applying Islamic values to its marketing, product design, and corporate social responsibility efforts. This flexibility enables J. to maintain a strong Islamic identity while expanding in local and international markets. In the United Kingdom, My Salah Mat demonstrates the application of Islamic values within a non-Muslim-majority context, where faith-based entrepreneurship meets the needs of Muslim consumers by offering modern technology in the development of educational tools aligned with Islamic principles. This case illustrates that Islamic entrepreneurship can resonate in secular, multicultural markets by focusing on inclusivity, ethical production, and community support, which appeal to a wide audience while fulfilling specific religious requirements.

These cases collectively show that Islamic principles offer a viable and adaptable framework for ethical and culturally sensitive business practices that appeal to both Muslim and non-Muslim consumers. The chapter advocates for an expanded understanding of Islamic values in entrepreneurship, encouraging a holistic approach that encompasses diverse business dimensions—beyond finance—to include operations, branding, and social impact. This broadened perspective not only highlights the versatility of Islamic values but also showcases their potential to foster trust, brand loyalty, and positive social impact in diverse market contexts.

7.4 Conclusion

This chapter demonstrates the expansive role of Islamic values in shaping ethical and resilient business practices across varying cultural, regulatory, and market contexts, moving beyond the narrow lens of Sharia-compliant finance. Through the cases of Al Baik (Saudi Arabia), Osmanli Oud (Turkey), J. (Pakistan), and My Salah Mat (United Kingdom), it is evident that Islamic principles hold broad applicability across industries, including ethical sourcing, environmental stewardship, and culturally attuned branding in a digital age. These cases emphasise the adaptability of Islamic values in both Muslim-majority and secular settings, highlighting their potential to foster ethical integrity, customer loyalty, and social impact in a globalised marketplace.

The chapter advocates for integrating Islamic values into entrepreneurial frameworks as a competitive advantage, appealing to a diverse consumer base by aligning business with ethical and cultural authenticity. This approach challenges the Western-centric models prevalent in business studies, contributing to the decolonisation movement by emphasising diverse cultural and religious frameworks. Recognising faith-based values as fundamental to business practices enriches our understanding of global entrepreneurship and encourages further exploration into how these values can inform ethical, future-focused business models. This expanded perspective not only advances Islamic entrepreneurship but also invites scholars and educators to foster a more inclusive, globally representative academic landscape.

Future research on faith and entrepreneurship among Muslims can deepen our understanding by exploring how Islamic principles uniquely shape entrepreneurial identity, decision-making, and resilience across diverse socio-cultural contexts. Qualitative studies can investigate how Muslim entrepreneurs interpret and integrate values like tawakkul (trust in God), Ihsan (excellence), and Amanah (trustworthiness) in their business practices and how these values impact ethical behaviour, business growth, and community engagement. Cross-cultural comparisons, for example, between Muslim-majority and minority settings, can provide insight into the adaptability of Islamic ethics in varying market environments. Additionally, longitudinal studies on the role of faith in entrepreneurial resilience amid economic challenges would illuminate how faith-based practices influence sustainability and innovation over time. By focusing on in-depth interviews, ethnographic studies, and case analyses, future qualitative research can offer nuanced perspectives that capture the lived experiences of Muslim entrepreneurs, contributing richly to the decolonisation of entrepreneurship studies and fostering a more inclusive, culturally diverse body of knowledge.

References

AACSB. (2023). Decolonising the business school curriculum. Retrieved October 27, 2024, from https://www.aacsb.edu/insights/articles/2023/02/decolonizing-the-business-school-curriculum.

Ahmad, A. (2018). Islamic law and finance: Protecting the integrity of Islamic finance in Saudi Arabia.

Anggadwita, G., Dana, L. P., Ramadani, V., & Ramadan, R. Y. (2021). Empowering Islamic boarding schools by applying the humane entrepreneurship approach: the case of Indonesia. *International Journal of Entrepreneurial Behavior & Research*, *27*(6), 1580–1604.

Dana, L. P. (Ed.). (2010). *Entrepreneurship and religion*. Edward Elgar Publishing.

Donner, F. M. (2010). Muhammad and the believers: At the origins of Islam. Harvard University Press.

El-Gamal, M. (2006). Islamic finance: Law, economics, and practice. Cambridge University Press.

Enslin, P., & Hedge, N. (2024). Decolonising higher education: The university in the new age of Empire. Journal of Philosophy of Education, 58(2–3), 227–241. https://doi.org/10.1093/jopedu/qhad052

Esposito, J. L. (2011). What everyone needs to know about Islam. Oxford University Press.

Grais, W., & Pellegrini, M. (2006). Corporate governance and Shariah compliance in institutions offering Islamic financial services. World Bank Policy Research Working Paper.

Haq, F., Yasin, N., & Nair, G. (2023). Envisioning the Future of Heritage Tourism in the Creative Industries in Dubai: An Exploratory Study of Post COVID-19 Strategies for Sustainable Recovery. Heritage, 6(6), 4557–4572.

Hodgson, M. G. S. (1974). The venture of Islam: Conscience and history in a world civilisation. University of Chicago Press.

Hyams-Ssesaki, D.H., & Yasin, N. (2022) Technology and Entrepreneurship: Adopting Creative Technologies in Entrepreneurship Education. Palgrave Macmillan/Springer. ISBN 978-3-030-84291-8 (Print Version) ISBN 978-3-030-84292-5 (e-book version)

Iqbal, Z., & Mirakhor, A. (2007). An introduction to Islamic finance: Theory and practice. Wiley.

Khan, M. M., & Bhatti, M. I. (2008). Development in Islamic banking: A financial risk-allocation approach. The Journal of Risk Finance, 9(1), 40–51.

Lapidus, I. M. (2002). A history of Islamic societies. Cambridge University Press.

Lewis, B. (1998). The multiple identities of the Middle East. Schocken Books.

Moten, A. R. (2005). Modernity, tradition, and identity: The battle for the hearts and minds of Muslims. Islamic Studies, 44(2), 193–210.

Pew Research Center. (2017). The future of world religions: Population growth projections, 2010–2050. Pew Research Center.

Rafiki, A., Ramadani, V., Dana, L. P., & Hidayat, S. E. (Eds.). (2024). *Strategic Islamic Business and Management: Solutions for Sustainability*. Springer Nature.

Ramadani, V. (2021). Islamic entrepreneurship. In *World Encyclopedia of Entrepreneurship* (pp. 457–470). Edward Elgar Publishing.

Ramadani, V., Dana, L. P., Gërguri-Rashiti, S., & Ratten, V. (2016). An introduction to entrepreneurship and management in an Islamic context. In *Entrepreneurship and management in an Islamic context* (pp. 1–5). Cham: Springer International Publishing.

Ramadani, V., Dana, L. P., Ratten, V., & Tahiri, S. (2015). The context of Islamic entrepreneurship and business: concept, principles and perspectives. *International Journal of Business and Globalisation*, *15*(3), 244–261.

Times Prayer. (2024). Muslim population 2024. Retrieved October 27, 2024, from https://timesprayer.com/en/muslim-population

Verver, M., Passenier, D., & Roessingh, C. (2019). Contextualising ethnic minority entrepreneurship beyond the West: Insights from Belize and Cambodia. International Journal of Entrepreneurial Behavior & Research, 25(5), 955–973. https://doi.org/10.1108/IJEBR-03-2019-0190

Verver, M., Roessingh, C., & Passenier, D. (2020). Ethnic boundary dynamics in immigrant entrepreneurship: A Barthian perspective. Entrepreneurship & Regional Development, 32(9–10), 757–782. https://doi.org/10.1080/08985626.2020.1757160

Waines, D. (2003). An introduction to Islam. Cambridge University Press.

Yasin, N. (2022) Cold Grass or Hot Sands: A Comparative Study of Immigrant Punjabi-Pakistani Entrepreneurs in London and Dubai. Strategic Change: Briefings in Entrepreneurial Finance. Special Issue 31(4) 1–10

Yasin, N., and Hafeez, K. (2023). Three Waves of Immigrant Entrepreneurship. A Cross-National Comparative Study, Small Business Economics: An Entrepreneurship Journal. 60(1) pp.1281–1306 doi: 10.1007/s11187-022-0065z

Aidin Salamzadeh, Ali Esmaeil Zadeh, Sama Hosseini, Seyed Morteza Mortazavi, Morteza Hadizadeh

Chapter 8
Islamic Business Ecosystems: UAE's Innovation Incentives and Iran's Knowledge-driven Approach

Abstract: This work investigates how governance frameworks shape business environments, focusing on strategic incentives, policy directives, and alignment with national priorities. It examines the economic impact of governance ideas rooted in Islamic principles on business practices across diverse socio-political contexts. Islamic business models align economic activities with Sharia principles as those in the United Arab Emirates and Iran, two nations with distinct governance models based on Islamic values. Despite differences in geography, history, and demographics, the study centers on how each country's governance idea influences alignment with state values in business environments. In the UAE, governance promotes innovation and global integration, encouraging businesses to adopt advanced technologies and align with national priorities. Government incentives drive economic diversification through support for sectors like technology, tourism, and trade. In Iran, however, the governance model emphasizes self-reliance and knowledge-based development, guiding enterprises toward science-driven and knowledge-based business sectors. Policies are designed to reduce dependency on external resources and reinforce national objectives. Through this comparative analysis, the work highlights the critical role of government in shaping business ecosystems and fostering economic growth. It underscores how Islamic governance structures adapt to promote sustainable development and alignment with national principles.

Keywords: Islamic governance, Islamic sustainable development, Islamic innovation and entrepreneurship, regulatory framework, knowledge-based development, economic diversification, United Arab Emirates

8.1 Introduction

Acknowledging governance as a crucial factor in shaping the business environment is vital for comprehending the alignment of business practices with national objectives. Circo (2007) believes that the government actively pushes the private sector to enhance product output. Advocate for ethical practices and maintain alignment with state values. An entity possessing extensive societal significance dictates how it attains

https://doi.org/10.1515/9783111575407-009

its objectives. Remarkably when grounded in Islamic principles (Alam Choudhury & Ziaul Hoque, 2006)

Recognizing the government's role is crucial for evaluating how national policy directs the private sector in achieving its economic objectives. Several studies (e.g., Brammer, Jackson, and Matten, 2012) demonstrate that these policies affect the growth and development of organizations by establishing standards that promote business practices aligned with national development. Although the geographic differences in history and demographics are significant, the United Arab Emirates (UAE) and the Islamic Republic of Iran exemplify the impact of regulatory frameworks on Islamic business development as they employ two different approaches to governing. (Yusuf, Nabeshima, & Perkins, 2006).

The Islamic business model prioritizes ethical standards and social responsibility by Shariah principles. maintaining Islamic principles, These models demonstrate the adaptability of Islamic business ideas to various regulatory systems. It underscores the significance of governance models in shaping Islamic businesses' developmental trajectory and strategic approach.

This chapter highlights the influence of governmental ideology on business activities. It examines how the regulatory framework directs the private sector toward national objectives. Instead of performing a comprehensive comparison, Moradi (2020) indicates that analyzing these frameworks demonstrates how regulatory approaches directly influence the structure and trajectory of business activities.

The Islamic regime's governance framework and policy initiatives directly impact business strategy, guaranteeing that the organization aligns with the state's articulated values and long-term objectives. Burrone et al. (2019) contend that the regulatory framework significantly influences economic growth by utilizing Islamic principles to formulate policy. A governance model framework is crucial for economic development as it emphasizes innovation, efficiency, and global integration to Foster a business environment that incentivizes organizations to adopt advanced technology and sustain competitiveness. Within the United Arab Emirates, The government prioritizes advancing innovation and modernization. By the nation's ambition to thrive in the Arab and Muslim domains (Luomi, 2015), policies in the UAE endorse multiple sectors, including technology. Tourism and trade enhance economic diversity and ecosystems that foster innovation and responsible governance (Tallman, Luo, & Buckley, 2018).

On the other hand, Iran's governmental structure prioritizes knowledge significantly. Self-reliance inspired by Imam Ali's teachings: "Knowledge is power." Iran's economic strategy prioritizes self-sufficiency and the advancement of scientific progress (Morady, 2020). The Iranian government promotes knowledge-driven development. Regulate commercial practices to reduce reliance on foreign entities. Moreover, enhancing critical sectors such as Islamic finance and technology. Several studies (e.g., Circo, 2007) indicate that this approach has facilitated the global integration and modernization of the UAE; alternatively, the centralization of the nation under Islamic governance reveals varying interpretations.This chapter analyzes the influence of diverse regulatory frameworks on advancing Islamic business and economic growth. It underscores the significant role of government in influencing the business environment through foundational principles (Alam et al., 2006).

8.2 Literature Review

8.2.1 The Role of Governance in Shaping Business Environments

Governments substantially impact the business environment through their fundamental regulatory framework (Wanyama et al., 2009). Governance's influence goes beyond basic regulations. This directly impacts business operations by aligning activities with national objectives (Levy & Fukuyama, 2010). The regulatory framework establishes strategic guidance for both the public and private sectors. Fostering an environment that supports enterprises Assists in attaining holistic economic objectives (Abbott, 2012). The government employs economic incentives. Regulatory framework and policy directives to orient private sector entities by governmental priorities. Encourage innovation, ethical practices, and productivity (Haufler, 2013). Incentives include tax advantages, subsidies, or advantageous regulations. Frequently employed to synchronize business operations with governmental objectives (Price et al., 2005), these incentives motivate private entities to embrace practices corresponding to fundamental governance principles. These cover sustainability, transparency, and ethical accountability (Graham & Woods, 2006). By establishing strong incentives, the government ensures that organizations are incentivized to foster innovation, invest in essential sectors, and foster sustainable economic growth aligned with the state's core values and strategic objectives (Bradshaw & Blakely, 1999). This dynamic underscores the crucial role of government in fostering a productive and compliant business environment.

8.2.2 Nation Branding and Government Marketing

Nation branding and government marketing are critical strategies employed by countries to cultivate their global image. These strategies aim to influence perceptions and generate positive impressions internationally. By utilizing cultural products and strategic messaging, governments can construct a unique national identity that highlights their economic strengths, cultural heritage, and political values (Dinnie, 2015; Aronczyk, 2013). This process allows nations to develop soft power, draw investment, forge alliances, and elevate their cultural and political influence globally. Effective nation branding transcends superficial advertising methods; it necessitates significant, impactful actions and policy accomplishments that resonate on a global scale. Efforts to establish a national brand without substantive enhancements in governance, economy, and cultural involvement are inadequate. A sustainable reputation relies on authentic advancements in innovation, human rights, and societal progress. Effective nation branding, therefore, necessitates strategic governance and sustained efforts that convey a nation's authentic value. This secures a nation's position in the global community through substantive and esteemed achievements rather than mere superficial perceptions. Multicultural marketing and cultural diplomacy are essential instruments for promoting international respect, comprehension, and enduring relationships (Lee, 2015).

8.2.3 Multicultural Marketing and Cultural Diplomacy

Cultural diplomacy, in contrast to traditional marketing, prioritizes authentic exchange rather than mere promotion. This allows nations to interact through shared cultural activities that foster deeper connections and transcend stereotypes, enhancing respect, tolerance, and cooperation (Moon, 2007; Zamorano, 2016; 2018; Hadizadeh et al, 2024). As a result, this strategy enhances the credibility of a nation's image and reinforces connections in commerce, collaboration, and culture. In the contemporary interconnected world, multicultural marketing complements cultural diplomacy by fostering cross-cultural understanding and inclusivity, aligning with soft power goals (Ryniejska–Kiełdanowicz, 2009; Amin & Bashir, 2023). Countries foster intercultural dialogue through cultural exchanges, educational initiatives, and artistic engagements. These efforts bridge cultural divides and enhance personal influence on a global scale (Zaharna, 2019). By emphasizing common values and customizing communications to various cultural contexts, nations can improve diplomatic relations and solidify their position in an increasingly multicultural global environment.

8.2.4 Organizational Excellence and Governance Models (GEM)

Establishing organizational excellence and implementing Governance Excellence Models (GEM) are crucial for improving a nation's reputation and credibility internationally (Talwar, 2011). Effective governance, characterized by transparency, accountability, and integrity, demonstrates a nation's dedication to maintaining high standards and aligning its operations with national objectives and cultural values. By adopting GEM, governments can organize their operations to consistently provide high-quality services. This cultivation of trust among citizens and international stakeholders is vital for a nation's stability and attractiveness to foreign investors (Herrington & Coduras, 2019). The GEM frameworks facilitate these objectives by enhancing efficiency and responsiveness to societal demands. These governance models also enhance a nation's soft power, showcasing its dedication to excellence and dependability while fostering effective international collaborations (Pamment, 2014). Through GEM principles, nations can exemplify their commitment to innovation, integrity, and service, solidifying their status as competent and reliable global participants.

8.2.5 Tourism Potential and Structural Challenges

Tourism promotion, unlike nation branding, entails marketing specific destinations and experiences without fundamentally changing a country's national identity (Goldstone, 2001). A thriving tourism sector can elevate a country's visibility and draw visitors, but it only bolsters national reputation if these experiences correspond with favorable perceptions of the nation's values and overall image.Nevertheless, nations frequently encounter substantial structural obstacles that may impede the development and sustainability of their tourism potential. Challenges such as infrastructure constraints, regulatory obstacles, and inadequate promotion can hinder the effective presentation of cultural and natural assets (Chandra & Idrisova, 2011). Mitigating these challenges necessitates significant investment in both physical and digital infrastructure to enhance visitor experiences while safeguarding environmental sustainability (Hussin, 2018). By addressing these issues, nations can establish a tourism sector that enhances soft power, promotes economic development, and encourages global interaction.

8.2.6 Effective Governance

The caliber of governance is a crucial factor influencing a nation's global reputation and significantly impacts its capacity to draw foreign investment, tourism, and international collaborations (Backer, 2011). Nations that uphold stringent standards in human rights, environmental stewardship, transparency, and accountability are more likely to earn respect and exert influence in the global sphere. Effective governance exemplifies a nation's dedication to responsible administration, democratic principles, and public service. This commitment attracts foreign investments and strengthens diplomatic relations, enhancing a country's strategic allure and global stature (Cheema, 2005; 2018; Salamzadeh et al, 2023). By adhering to principles esteemed by other nations and international entities, a country can significantly improve its credibility and demonstrate its commitment to the welfare of its populace and the stability of its economy (Hathaway, 2005).

8.2.7 Innovation and Export Challenges

In a progressively interconnected world, a nation's capacity to innovate and sustain the relevance of its exports is essential for preserving global stature and economic resilience. Countries that significantly address critical global issues, such as technological progress or human rights, augment their influence and reputation internationally (Fiksel & Fiksel, 2015). Nations that neglect meaningful engagement or fail to maintain high export standards jeopardize their credibility and relevance. Establishing a robust innovation ecosystem necessitates substantial investment in research and development, a proficient workforce, and a conducive regulatory framework (Sykes, 1995). Nations must consistently adapt to global demands to effectively promote and distribute their products, exacerbated by export challenges including market access restrictions, logistical difficulties, and intense competition. By surmounting these obstacles and promoting innovation, nations can diversify their economies, augment economic influence, and convey a dynamic and progressive image, establishing enduring connections and enhancing their soft power through creativity and technological expertise (Nicita, Ognivtsev, & Shirotori, 2013).

8.2.8 Economic Diversification and Global Competitiveness

Economic diversification is essential for countries aiming to bolster resilience and sustain global competitiveness. Diversifying across various sectors diminishes dependence on individual industries, thus alleviating risks associated with global market volatility and commodity price fluctuations (Hvidt, 2013). This comprehensive strategy fosters innovation, draws foreign investment, and provides various pathways for growth, reinforcing a nation's foundation for sustained prosperity. By cultivating a stable and flexible economy, nations enhance their international reputation, thereby increasing their soft power and attractiveness to global investors and partners (Li & Worm, 2011). This strategic diversification enables countries to adeptly manage economic fluctuations, positioning themselves as flexible, progressive entities in a globalized environment and enhancing their reputation for sustainable growth within a competitive international arena (Williams & Vorley, 2017).

8.2.9 Cultural Heritage and Identity in Global Marketing

Advocating for cultural heritage and national identity via global marketing fortifies a nation's image, amplifies its soft power, and cultivates international admiration (Van de Port & Meyer, 2018). By highlighting distinctive cultural assets—such as traditional arts, historical landmarks, and indigenous practices—countries create a persuasive narrative that sets them apart globally, appealing to both domestic and international audiences (Aronczyk, 2013; 2018; Salamzadeh et al, 2024).

This strategic emphasis on cultural identity not only draws tourists and enhances exports of cultural products but also strengthens cultural and diplomatic relations with other countries. Incorporating these elements into global marketing fosters pride and unity among citizens, creating a cohesive and authentic representation that challenges stereotypes and enhances a nuanced, positive perception of the nation's values and societal identity (Milakovich, 2012).

8.2.10 Digital Transformation and E-Governance

Digital transformation and e-governance are fundamentally altering governmental operations and citizen engagement, resulting in efficient, transparent, and accessible public services (Dahlman, Mealy, & Wermelinger, 2016). By adopting digital technologies, governments augment service efficiency, decrease operational expenses, and elevate citizen satisfaction via secure data management, online public services, and enhanced communication with the populace (Lim, Jørgensen, & Wyborn, 2018; Mohammadhosseini et al., 2021). These advancements cultivate confidence in governmental institutions and indicate a dedication to modernization and innovation. Digital governance enhances domestic administrative efficiency and boosts a nation's global competitiveness, thereby attracting foreign investment and fostering collaboration in the international digital economy (McGiffert, 2009). By implementing digital governance, nations establish themselves as progressive and technologically adaptable, fostering a business-friendly environment and enhancing the quality of life for their citizens (Hvidt, 2013).

8.3 UAE: A Framework for Strategic Expansion and International Competitiveness

In today's globalized world, nation branding and government marketing are essential tools for countries seeking to enhance their international standing and achieve sustainable development. A nation brand can be defined as the total sum of all perceptions of a nation in the mind of global stakeholders that may contain some of the following elements: people, place, culture/ language, history, food, fashion, famous faces (celebrities), global brands, etc. (Hassan & Mahrous, 2019). A significant point to consider is that a nation's "brand" exists, with or without any conscious efforts by its governance, as each country has a current image for its international audience. Still, by effectively managing their brand and engaging with target audiences, governments can make a positive, lasting impression on their nation (Hassan & Mahrous, 2019; 2018; Salamzadeh et al, 2024). Simon Anholt, who coined the term, refers to nation branding as "the systematic process of aligning the actions, behaviors, investments, innovations, and communications of a country around a clear strategy for achieving a strengthened competitive identity"(Anholt, 2008). He also introduces a framework for assessing and evaluating a country's brand image. By analyzing six aspects: tourism, exports, people, culture and heritage, inward investment, and governance, the model provides insights into how a nation is perceived globally (Morgan et al., 2012).

Before starting, it is advisable to define the scope of the research more clearly. In a comprehensive analysis of the UAE's remarkable journey to becoming the third most powerful brand in the world in 2016, a pivotal role is played by the flagship project-Dubai. Despite Abu Dhabi's status as the capital city, Dubai has emerged as a powerful nation brand, developed in successive layers. Dubai policymakers have reacted quickly by recognizing the need for economic diversification and reducing reliance on oil (Zeineddine & Nicolescu, 2018; Salamzadeh et al, 2024). Therefore, our focus will primarily be on the actions of the state of Islamic bussiness in Dubai.

Leaders from Dubai are concerned about their factual standing in international affairs, particularly their involvement in humanitarian cases, and are working on cultural diplomacy. The leaders have acknowledged the importance of communication in the global context. They use multicultural marketing and cultural diplomacy as tools to showcase their nation's rich cultural heritage, exert a powerful influence without resorting to military might, create a solid cultural brand in tourism, and ultimately foster cooperation and economic ties with other nations (Ang, 2018). With strategic planning, policymakers have initiated a plan to enrich the business ecosystem through trade, tourism, and real estate development.

Not only are the fundamental actions of governance crucial, but the public's perception of the government is also of great importance and can significantly shape the nation's brand. M. Al Zaabi in "Driving an Ambitious Vision with Excellence the UAE Government Excellence Model" presented by the Sheikh Khalifa Government Excellence Program, Prime Minister's Office, mentions a model called The GEM, which embodies the philosophy of organizational excellence and the leadership mindset that regards quality and organizational excellence as essential for attaining leadership and fostering effective, positive governance to influence the future. "The GEM helps advance management thinking beyond the achievement of an end target. It considers the organization as an open system with dynamic inter-related activities supported by smart connected systems that transcend the closed borders of traditional management to help build multiple business models in government work." (Zaabi, 2019)

The UAE has achieved a new global breakthrough with the help of this model. Three pillars are taken into consideration; the first is "Vision achievement," with the aim to achieve the highest levels of satisfaction and happiness through integration and collaboration with other government entities, the private sectormostly Islamic businesses, and the community. Second, "Innovation" looks to the future, seeking to achieve continuous innovation and drive new and creative services in creative ways, and finally, "Enablers" commitment to the highest standards of transparency, integrity, governance, effective management, and operation risk to benefit all human resources and stakeholder (Zaabi, 2019).

Again, by looking at Anholt's model, he explains tourism as a factor that affects the quality of a nation's brand. It is wise to delve into the role of government in this industry (Anholt, 2008). Scholars within the field of tourism have devised a range of methodologies aimed at comprehending and bolstering the sustainable competitiveness of tourism destinations. In the realm of tourism destination planning, there has been a concerted effort to embrace a spatial perspective and infrastructure as integral components. This endeavor has also involved the integration of diverse development objectives within the framework of tourism concepts and guidelines, accompanied by a sophisticated business orientation influenced by strategic management. Moreover, the concept of strategic tourism destination leadership aims to enhance the structural and procedural facets of destination governance by acknowledging the significance of emotion, creativity, and values in shaping tourism destinations (Alseiari, 2019).

The Dubai government's aim for 2020 was to reach a peak of 20 million tourists per year. Most of the visitors (86%) to Dubai fall into the 20–40 age group and are internationally exposed, demonstrating the potential of Dubai as a destination brand. In 2012, tourism accounted for 31% of Dubai's GDP.

Compared to most Gulf countries, Iran possesses more diverse tourist attractions. However, it has not effectively implemented regional planning and employment focus in free, industrial, and economic zones, unlike the United Arab Emirates. The management systems of many cities and free zones in Iran are dealing with economic, social, and structural challenges. These include a lack of necessary capital, high unemployment, poverty, and the rapid growth of urbanization. These issues have directly or indirectly impacted the tourism industry, especially sports tourism, which presents a sustainable opportunity for economic development in Iran (Pirjamadi, 2022).

8.4 Iran: Governance Issues and Unexploited Economic Opportunities

Iran possesses significant potential in the tourism industry due to its diverse natural attractions, including mountains, plains, and deserts, as well as historical sites, tourism-friendly villages, and coastal cities. Domains including sports tourism, coastal and marine tourism, cultural and rural tourism, and health tourism can significantly contribute to the economic and cultural advancement of Iran. Consequently, the presence of the aforementioned competitive advantages in the tourism sector has garnered the attention of policymakers to enhance economic activities within this domain. The importance of addressing this issue is underscored by the 20-year Vision Document and the Seventh Five-Year Development Plan of the Islamic Republic of Iran, which emphasize government policies in the tourism sector through supportive measures such as incentive policies, the provision of essential infrastructure for tourist destinations, and the facilitation of business license issuance to enhance domestic tourism and attract foreign visitors. Consequently, despite the government's focus on the tourism industry, innovative business initiatives within this sector have been overlooked. Furthermore, within the executive sector, the existence of specific tourism impediments has resulted in subpar performance and insufficient exploitation of this industry.

The Iranian Cultural Heritage, Handicrafts and Tourism Organization's statistical yearbook indicates that the number of incoming tourists in 2018 was 7,804,113, and in 2019, it was 8,832,050, with 4.79 percent associated with the tourism sector. This issue suggests that, despite the rising trend in tourist attraction, these statistics are inadequate for Iran's ambition to attain a prominent status in regional tourism and to establish itself as a global tourism hub. Consequently, it can be asserted that policymaking in the tourism sector, besides developing diverse policies, must emphasize implementation and be supplemented by oversight and assessment throughout the execution phase.

Research in this domain has identified several impediments, including inadequate lodging options like hotels, a deficiency of specialized tourism personnel, a lack of a coherent strategy within the tourism sector, and insufficient collaboration among organizations. Additional concerns encompass inadequate urban and rural transportation infrastructure, insufficient private sector involvement in tourism, challenges in obtaining financial resources for tourism-related enterprises, a dearth of entrepreneurial initiatives within the tourism sector, a lack of awareness among residents in tourist regions regarding its significance, ineffective promotion of Iran's tourist attractions, subpar management of historical site preservation and maintenance, and insufficient oversight and assessment. Consequently, proactive strategies to mitigate these challenges can substantially enhance Iran's tourism sector.

Strategic foresight, in conjunction with environmental dynamics, clarifies the driving forces of progress through stakeholder engagement and diverse actors, offering robust strategies for alternative and procedural futures to assess actions. Consequently, comprehending the impactful forces, including laws and regulations, financial incentives aimed at enhancing the motivation of both domestic and foreign investors in this sector, the modernization of the tourism industry through the adoption of contemporary technologies in service delivery, strategic advertising, and the introduction of a business ecosystem model for tourism-centric enterprises are regarded as significant catalysts for the tourism industry.

Governance encompasses a framework of normative principles and interactions that link the government, various state institutions, the private sector, and civil society to tackle social issues or generate associated social opportunities. (Azadi et al., 2022; Meuleman & Niestroy, 2015). The objective of effective governance is to enhance service delivery and Islamic businesses accountability by fostering participation, consensus orientation, transparency, responsiveness, effectiveness, efficiency, and adherence to the rule of law. (Handoyo, 2023; Karunia et al., 2023; Felekech & Guohua, 2020). In the absence of sound governance, numerous governments struggle to deliver public services efficiently. Obstacles persist and prospects are forfeited. (Lustrilanang et al., 2023, p. 2).

Research indicates that effective governance establishes a basis for the attainment of sustainable development strategies and objectives (Chien & Thanh, 2022; Omri & Mabrouk, 2020), improves national well-being (Helliwell et al, 2018) and quality of life

(Cárcaba et al, 2017), boosts tourism revenue (Detotto et al, 2021), and fosters a positive correlation with citizen trust. Yousaf et al. (2016). The results demonstrate that effective governance positively influences organizational health (Azad-Baf and Rajabi Farjad, 2019), employee job satisfaction (Hijazi, 2021), organizational performance (Beyene et al., 2023), and public satisfaction levels (Chien & Thanh, 2022).

Consequently, effective governance is a paramount priority for governments. (Hwang & Akdede, 2011; Haliah, 2021; Chien & Thanh, 2022). In Iran, indicators of effective governance, as indicated by various studies and the World Bank's report, are not in a favorable condition (Komijani and Iyozi, 2021: 431; Gholipour Soteh et al., 2020: 136; Moghadam Firouzabad, 2019: 298; Ahani et al., 2019: 111; Emamgholipour and Asmaneh, 2016: 96). Challenges include inadequate public oversight, the prevalence of ineffective NGOs, subpar media performance in fulfilling their responsibilities, and insufficient education necessary for achieving good governance (Arai et al., 2017).

This issue may result in suboptimal performance (Ghoochanian and Fashai, 2022: 5; Shahbazi et al., 2015: 31). A thorough examination of the core elements influencing effective governance and the development of suitable strategies is crucial, as it establishes a foundation for enhancing governance indicators and, in turn, improving its effects on the attainment of public sector policies and strategic objectives. In this context, Iran has concentrated on enhancing governance indicators, with initiatives evident in the section on administrative system reform within the Seventh Five-Year Development Plan of the Islamic Republic of Iran.

The export performance of Iran is a crucial indicator of its creativity and innovation capabilities. The 2023 report by the World Intellectual Property Organization (WIPO) indicates that Iran is ranked 62nd among 132 global economies regarding innovation in science and technology. The nation's distinct rankings illustrate its diverse strengths and weaknesses: it ranks 131st in the Institutions index, 60th in Human Capital and Research, 97th in Infrastructure, 19th in Market Sophistication, 117th in Business Sophistication, 55th in Knowledge and Technology Outputs, and 43rd in Creative Outputs, encompassing intangible assets, creative goods, services, and online creativity. Furthermore, in the domain of research and development, a crucial aspect of human capital, Iran is positioned 49th. The rankings reveal that Iran possesses certain strengths, notably in market sophistication and creative outputs; however, its overall innovation performance is moderate, positioning it in the second quartile globally.

8.5 Conclusion

Governance is pivotal in influencing business environments, directing both public and private sectors through regulatory frameworks, incentives, and alignment with overarching national goals. This chapter comparestwo islamic countries governence , illustrating how they affect business practices by utilizing incentives to foster innovation, productivity, and ethical standards.Islamic Governance models that emphasize innovation and global integration foster competitive, progressive Islamicbusiness environments. In these models, governments utilize incentives, such as tax advantages and regulatory assistance, to promote the adoption of modern technologies and practices by businesses. These policies promote economic diversification and expansion in critical sectors including technology, tourism, and trade. Businesses are incentivized to align with national development objectives while complying with governance principles that foster sustainability and ethical behavior. This method underscores the capacity of governance to effectively cultivate a dynamic and innovative private sector that advances national development. governance models that prioritize self-sufficiency, knowledge-based development, and ethical principles underscore enduring resilience and sustainable advancement. These frameworks foster sectors such as Islamic finance, technology, , urging Islamic businesses to diminish dependence on foreign entities and function within ethical parameters. Incentives are intended to encourage business practices that correspond with national goals of self-sufficiency, equity, and ethical governance.

Islamic business framework, shaped by governance models like those in the UAE and Iran, shows how Islamic governance approaches can promote different development paths. The UAE's focus on innovation and global integration promotes a competitive business environment. On the other hand, Iran emphasizes self-reliance and independence, knowledge-based enterprises as well as revealing and adjusting business practices to align with national priorities.

These governance strategies guarantee that private sector development aligns with the nation's overarching objectives of economic autonomy and sustainable progress. Both governance strategies emphasize the essential function of Islamic government in guiding Islamic business ecosystems and influencing economic development. These models illustrate that governments, through their fundamental philosophies, significantly influence the business sector by either encouraging global integration and innovation or advocating for self-reliance and ethical governance. The comparison underscores the influence of distinct governance frameworks, shaped by Islamic principles, on business development and the economic sustainability of nations. Governance is essential for aligning business practices with national priorities, facilitating sustainable economic growth and upholding core values.

References

Ahani, M., Musakhani, N., Najafbeigi, A., & Afsharkazemi, M. (2019). Cluster analysis of Iran's position in the world and future trends based on the components of good governance. *Management Future Research, 116*(30), 118–99.

Alseiari, H. A. S. M., Khalifa, G. S., & Bhaumick, A. (2019). Tourism destination competitiveness in UAE: The role of strategic leadership and strategic planning effectiveness. *International Journal of Recent Technology and Engineering (IJRTE), 8*(4), 860–865.

Amin, S., & Bashir, S. (2023). Cultural diplomacy: Fostering cross-cultural understanding and cooperation. *International Journal of Art, Culture and Communication, 2*(1), 45–55.

Ang, I., Isar, Y. R., & Mar, P. (2018). Cultural diplomacy: Beyond the national interest?. In *Cultural diplomacy: Beyond the national interest?* (pp. 11–27).

Anholt, S. (2008). Place branding: Is it marketing, or isn't it? *Place Branding and Public Diplomacy, 4*(1), 1–6.

araei, V., Ghasemi, A., & Moeininfar, Y. (2018). Policy recommendations about barriers of good governance in public affairs (Case study: Governorate and Municipality of Minoodasht). *Strategic Studies of Public Policy, 7*(25), 113–133.

Aronczyk, M. (2013). *Branding the nation: The global business of national identity*. Oxford University Press, USA.

Azadi, B., Hamidi, K., Eslambolchi, A., Niknafs, J., & Bayat, B. (2022). Identifying and prioritizing the challenges of implementing participatory governance in the Ministry of Health, Treatment and Medical Education of the country. *Iranian Journal of Educational Sociology, 5*(2), 166–181.

Backer, L. C. (2011). On the evolution of the United Nations protect-respect-remedy project: The state, the corporation and human rights in a global governance context. *Santa Clara Journal of International Law, 9*, 37.

Beyene, E., Benti, A., Mohamed, S., Edao, A., & Kitessa, W. (2023). The effect of good governance on organizational performance: A study of public offices in Gudeya Bila District, East Wollega Zone, Oromia, Ethiopia. *Journal of Survey in Fisheries Sciences, 10*(4S), 1378–1404.

Cárcaba, A., González, E., Ventura, J., & Arrondo, R. (2017). How does good governance relate to quality of life? *Sustainability, 9*(4), 631.

Chandra, A., & Idrisova, A. (2011). Convention on Biological Diversity: A review of national challenges and opportunities for implementation. *Biodiversity and Conservation, 20*, 3295–3316.

Cheema, G. S. (2005). *Building democratic institutions: Governance reform in developing countries*. Kumarian Press.

Chien, N. B., & Thanh, N. N. (2022). The impact of good governance on the people's satisfaction with public administrative services in Vietnam. *Administrative Sciences, 12*(1), 35.

Dahlman, C., Mealy, S., & Wermelinger, M. (2016). Harnessing the digital economy for developing countries.

Detotto, C., Giannoni, S., & Goavec, C. (2021). Does good governance attract tourists? *Tourism Management, 82*, 104155.

Dinnie, K. (2015). *Nation branding: Concepts, issues, practice*. Routledge.

Felekech, T., & Guohua, W. (2020). Service delivery and good governance in public sectors: A review of literature. *International Journal of Academic Multidisciplinary Research (IJAMR), 4*(11), 128–135.

Fiksel, J., & Fiksel, J. R. (2015). *Resilient by design: Creating businesses that adapt and flourish in a changing world*. Island Press.

Ghochanian, M., & Fashaee, M. (2022). Water resources management indicators focusing on governance. *Journal of Water and Sustainable Development, 9*(1), 1–10. doi: 10.22067/jwsd.v9i1.2110.1086

Goldstone, P. (2001). *Making the world safe for tourism*. Yale University Press.

Hadizadeh, M., Ghaffari Feyzabadi, J., Fardi, Z., Mortazavi, S. M., Braga, V., & Salamzadeh, A. (2024). Digital platforms as a fertile ground for the economic sustainability of startups: Assaying scenarios, actions, plans, and players. *Sustainability, 16*(16), 7139.

Haliah, H. (2021). A study of performance model development and good governance budgeting. *International Journal of Law and Management, 63*(3), 301–319.

Handoyo, S. (2023). Worldwide governance indicators: Cross country data set 2012–2022. *Data in Brief, 51*, 109814.

Hassan, S., & Mahrous, A. A. (2019). Nation branding: The strategic imperative for sustainable market competitiveness. *Journal of Humanities and Applied Social Sciences, 1*(2), 146–158.

Hathaway, O. A. (2005). Between power and principle: An integrated theory of international law. *The University of Chicago Law Review, 72*, 469–536.

Helliwell, J. F., Huang, H., Grover, S., & Wang, S. (2018). Empirical linkages between good governance and national well-being. *Journal of Comparative Economics, 46*(4), 1332–1346.

Herrington, M., & Coduras, A. (2019). The national entrepreneurship framework conditions in sub-Saharan Africa: A comparative study of GEM data/national expert surveys for South Africa, Angola, Mozambique and Madagascar. *Journal of Global Entrepreneurship Research, 9*(1), 60.

Hijazi, H. A. (2020). The impact of applying good governance principles on job satisfaction among public sector employees in Jordan. *Open Journal of Business and Management, 9*(01), 1.

Hussin, H. (2018). Gastronomy, tourism, and the soft power of Malaysia. *SAGE Open, 8*(4), 2158244018809211.

Hvidt, M. (2013). Economic diversification in GCC countries: Past record and future trends.

Hwang, J., & Akdede, S. H. (2011). The influence of governance on public sector efficiency: A cross-country analysis. *The Social Science Journal, 48*(4), 735–738.

Imam Qolipour Sara, A., & Asamene, Z. (2016). Governance index in Islam and its impact on health outcomes in Iran. *Journal of Islamic Economics and Banking, 5*(15), 93–108.

Karunia, R. L., Darmawansyah, D., Dewi, K. S., & Prasetyo, J. H. (2023). The importance of good governance in the government organization. *HighTech and Innovation Journal, 4*(1), 75–89.

Komijani, A., & Eivazi, M. (2021). The profile of good governance in Iran: From capacity to opportunity. *Strategy, 30*(3), 427–465.

Lee, J. T. (2015). Soft power and cultural diplomacy: Emerging education hubs in Asia. *Comparative Education, 51*(3), 353–374.

Li, X., & Worm, V. (2011). Building China's soft power for a peaceful rise. *Journal of Chinese Political Science, 16*, 69–89.

Lim, M. M., Jørgensen, P. S., & Wyborn, C. A. (2018). Reframing the sustainable development goals to achieve sustainable development in the Anthropocene—a systems approach. *Ecology and Society, 23*(3).

Lustrilanang, P., Suwarno, Darusalam, Rizki, L. T., Omar, N., & Said, J. (2023). The role of control of corruption and quality of governance in ASEAN: Evidence from DOLS and FMOLS test. *Cogent Business & Management, 10*(1), 2154060.

McGiffert, C. (Ed.). (2009). *Chinese soft power and its implications for the United States: Competition and cooperation in the developing world: A report of the CSIS Smart Power Initiative*. CSIS.

Meuleman, L., & Niestroy, I. (2015). The 2030 agenda for sustainable development: The role of good governance in realizing the agenda. *Sustainable Development, 23*(4), 233–240.

Mitra, S. (2018). The role of entrepreneurship in the global economy: A comparative analysis. *Journal of Business Studies Quarterly, 10*(4), 23–35.

Mofidi, M., & Ebrahimi, N. (2023). Quality of governance and public-private partnerships: An exploratory study in developing countries. *International Journal of Public Administration, 46*(9), 927–936.

Mokhber, M., Mohamad, M. H., & Nasr, A. M. (2023). Governance framework for sustainable tourism development in Malaysia: The case of Penang. *Sustainability, 15*(3), 1621.

Moussa, M. (2020). Good governance and urban development in Egypt: Towards sustainable and resilient cities. *Sustainable Cities and Society, 54*, 101998.

Ojo, A. T., & Ojo, E. (2021). Good governance, quality of life and social capital: An analysis of urban Nigeria. *Social Indicators Research, 152*(1), 187–205.

Olufemi, S. T. (2023). The impact of good governance on socio-economic development in Nigeria: An empirical analysis. *Economics and Finance, 11*(1), 45–62.

Pallavi, M., & Pramod, K. S. (2021). Role of tourism in enhancing good governance in the states of India: A comparative study of selected states. *Tourism Management Perspectives, 39*, 100842.

Qadri, F. (2023). An exploratory study on good governance and development in Pakistan: Policy implications. *Asian Journal of Political Science, 29*(2), 217–234.

Rahman, A. (2016). Cultural governance and development: A case study of rural Bangladesh. *Development in Practice, 26*(4), 452–467.

Rehman, H. U., Ali, A., & Faheem, M. (2017). Good governance and its impact on economic growth: A case study of Pakistan. *Global Journal of Management and Business Research, 17*(3), 1–8.
Rivera, J. F. (2022). Tourism and sustainable development: The role of cultural diplomacy in Latin America. *Journal of Sustainable Tourism, 30*(5), 917–935.
Rodríguez, R. (2021). Good governance as a catalyst for sustainable development: Insights from Mexico. *Development Policy Review, 39*(6), 837–854.
Sanusi, Z. (2018). *Governance and development in Nigeria: The role of public policy*. Unilag Press.
Saldaña, M. C. M. (2018). Factors influencing good governance in developing countries: A systematic review of the literature. *Journal of Policy Modeling, 40*(6), 1035–1051.
Shakibaei, A., & Lankarani, M. (2023). A conceptual framework for good governance and its relationship with service quality: A systematic literature review. *Public Sector Management, 26*(1), 1–16.
Siddique, R., & Bader, M. (2022). Building better governance in the post-COVID world: Lessons learned from the crisis. *International Journal of Public Administration, 45*(2), 134–143.
Sturges, D. L. (2018). Fostering cooperation between China and the United States: Governance and engagement in the digital age. *The International Journal of Sino-American Studies, 15*(2), 51–69.
Suwaileh, A. M., Al-Tarawneh, M., & Atta, M. (2022). The impact of good governance on tourism development: Evidence from Jordan. *International Journal of Tourism Research, 24*(5), 911–920.
Taleb, A., & Aamer, F. (2021). Nation branding: An analysis of tourism promotion in Saudi Arabia. *International Journal of Business and Management, 16*(2), 66–76.
Teh, P. L., & Chia, Y. J. (2022). The role of local governance in promoting sustainable tourism: A study of the Malaysian Penang island. *Sustainable Cities and Society, 75*, 103333.
Tussle, T., & Orgun, M. (2021). Good governance and its impact on community participation in local government. *International Journal of Public Sector Management, 34*(5), 455–473.
Van der Meer, F., & Geys, B. (2016). Good governance and public service delivery: A systematic review of the evidence. *Public Management Review, 18*(3), 393–415.
Vo, A. T., & Tran, D. H. (2020). Factors affecting good governance and its impact on socio-economic development: Evidence from Vietnam. *Journal of Management Development, 39*(1), 115–130.
Wang, Y., & Wei, J. (2022). The impact of good governance on tourism competitiveness: Evidence from China. *Tourism Management, 87*, 104381.
Yusof, S. M., & Shafee, N. N. (2023). Tourism governance: A systematic literature review of the last two decades. *Journal of Travel Research, 62*(3), 445–463.
Zaman, S. (2017). Towards good governance: The role of the legal profession in Pakistan. *Journal of Law, Policy and Globalization, 60*, 1–9.
Ziemann, L., & Verheijen, T. (2020). Good governance in the digital age: Towards a new paradigm of public sector management. *International Review of Administrative Sciences, 86*(4), 622–639.

Mahameru Rosy Rochmatullah & Hasan Mukhibad

Chapter 9
Performance Banking Baselines Under Maqashid Sharia

Abstract: This chapter reviews the maqashid sharia as a proper roadmap for managing business in Islamic banking. In the introduction, this chapter explains the scope of Islamic banking, religious views on the purpose of establishing Islamic banks, and the performance of Islamic banking based on maqashid sharia. This chapter further explains the broader scope of Islamic banking based on existing literature. This section describes the structure of Islamic banking stakeholders who believe in God, governance and performance structures, asset management, performance measures based on the Maqashid Sharia index (MSI), and the experimental results of MSI on 12 Islamic banks in Indonesia. Performance assessment using MSI includes three essential elements: banking managerial education, social justice, and public interest. Interestingly, the experimental results show that the average MSI score still needs to be higher (31.64%), implying that Islamic banking management tends not to follow maqashid sharia. Further analysis shows that the tight competition between banks (both conventional and sharia) causes the Sharia supervisory board and the board of commissioners to play Islamic banking like conventional banking. In addition, managerial compliance with Sharia principles in managing bank assets still needs to improve. In the last section, this chapter concludes that MSI is a proper measure of Sharia banking performance to assess the extent to which Sharia bank management follows sharia principles. This chapter recommends that Islamic banking authorities use performance measurement tools based on maqashid sharia. This chapter also shows the need for further research to develop MSI in non-Islamic countries.

Keywords: Performance, Maqashid sharia, Stakeholder arrangement, Governance structure, Islamic banking

9.1 Introduction

The establishment of Islamic banking reflects Muslim preferences for financial transactions devoid of usury, maysir, gharar, and other haram behaviors. Islamic banking management adheres to Islamic governance, emphasizing ethics, morals, and virtuous qualities as delineated in Islamic law (Hidayah et al., 2019). The creation of Islamic banking in a country signifies an endeavor to integrate spiritual concepts into macroeconomic activities (Mohammed et al., 2015). The presence of Islamic banking in a nation serves significant purposes: facilitating the halal allocation of wealth (Hudaefi &

https://doi.org/10.1515/9783111575407-010

Badeges, 2022), enhancing ethical standards and sharia principles in commercial practices (Hudaefi, 2014; Bedoui, 2012), integrating Islamic values into the national economy (Asutay, 2012), and elevating the global perception of the Islamic community (Laldin & Furqani, 2014).

The principles of Islamic theology assert that the primary purpose of establishing Islamic banking is to achieve "Falah," which refers to prosperity in both this life and beyond (Abdul-Baki & Uthman, 2017). The notion suggests that the governance of Islamic banks prioritizes socio-economic justice, an orientation towards al-falah, the public interest, and the principle of monotheism (Tauhid). Nevertheless, scholarly examinations concerning the successful operation of Islamic banks frequently need to be more explicit about the foundational principles of Falah, resulting in a presentation of findings that may seem skewed. For instance, numerous international studies employ standard banking financial ratios to assess the performance of Islamic banks in comparison to conventional banks (See e.g., Fah & Hassani, 2014; Qian & Velayutham, 2017; Milhem & Istaiteyeh, 2015; Zarrouk et al., 2016). Several other studies similarly employ conventional bank financial ratios to assess the efficiency levels of Islamic banks (see e. g., Hisham Yahya et al., 2012; Pradiknas & Faturohman, 2015; Ismail et al., 2013; Sakti & Mohamad, 2018; Shawtari et al., 2019). This tendency suggests that Falah often becomes obscured when examining Islamic banking.

Syafii et al. (2012) have proposed a commendable alternative for assessing the performance of Islamic banking, grounded in the principles of maqashid sharia. The study elaborates that the notion of maqashid facilitates entities in attaining the well-being of all individuals, both in this life and beyond (Falah). From a more expansive perspective, Falah aligns with the triple bottom line concept, which emphasizes the importance of environmental, social, and economic well-being. The notion of maqashid interprets falah as an impetus to attain rahmatun lil'alamin, encompassing the welfare of the entire universe, which includes environmental, social, and economic dimensions. It aligns with the divine revelation to humanity articulated in the Al-Qur'an, specifically in Surah As-Sajdah verse 5. This verse can signify that the order and blessings throughout the universe are compelling evidence of the omnipotence and singularity of the divine. Consequently, the notion of maqashid sharia establishes the triple bottom line as a standard for evaluating the efficacy of Islamic banking, emphasizing the importance of environmental sustainability, societal welfare, and permissible profit (Halal).

A study by Kholid & Bachtiar (2015) examines the application of maqashid sharia in evaluating the performance of Islamic banks. The results indicate that performance metrics based on maqashid sharia improve Islamic entities' governance structure, as evidenced by a rise in the number of independent commissioners. Nonetheless, other studies contest these findings by demonstrating that an increased number of boards may lead to free-riding, which diminishes supervision effectiveness (Coles et al., 2008; Farag et al., 2018). The findings from these three studies suggest that the assessment of Islamic banking performance through the lens of maqashid remains a topic of scholarly discussion. This chapter addresses the ongoing debate by examining the efficacy of maqashid-based performance measurement (Maqashid Sharia index/MSI) through three key indicators: board effectiveness, board education level, and cross-membership. This chapter offers novel ideas on maqashid-based Islamic performance, potentially reconciling discussions from earlier studies.

9.2 Stakeholder Structure for Islamic Banking

Stakeholder theory suggests that a business entity that effectively manages its relationships with stakeholders—including customers, suppliers, owners, creditors, employees, and the community—exerts a considerable influence on business goodwill (Freeman et al., 2010). The primary duty of management is to ensure that the demands of all stakeholders are consistently addressed (Freeman, 2017). Nonetheless, this theory cannot be entirely implemented in Islamic banking, which is governed by two primary regulations: the laws of the country and the rules of faith (sharia). The prior study demonstrates that the primary responsibility in managing Islamic business lies with God, specifically in adhering to Sharia laws, while stakeholders' interests follow in importance (Mukhibad, 2019). In the Sharia framework, adherence to God's law should be prioritized above all other considerations. Thus, Islamic banking has two primary responsibilities: adhering to Sharia law to generate value for God (Habluminallah) and addressing the preferences of Muslims to enhance value for stakeholders (Habluminannas).

The fundamental difference between Islamic and conventional banks lies in the principal stakeholders' identity. Islamic banking is founded on principles that emphasize ethical and moral considerations, prioritizing social justice, community cohesion, and the welfare of individuals as central objectives (Akbar & Siti-Nabiha, 2022). It indicates that God serves as the primary stakeholder in Islamic banking. The primary focus for Muslim stakeholders is to achieve welfare and financial gain, which are considered the next priorities in this context. Therefore, the performance measurement of Islamic banking is distinct from that of conventional banking, which primarily emphasizes economic profit (Syafii et al., 2012). Additional studies confirm this perspective, indicating that evaluating the performance of Islamic banking through the same financial ratios applied to conventional banks is inappropriate. This approach reflects the performance metrics of non-Islamic entities that do not align with the maqashid sharia (Hartono & Sobari, 2017; Mukhibad, 2019).

9.3 Governance Structure and Performance of Islamic Banks

9.3.1 Sharia Supervisory Board

The governance structure of Islamic financial institutions is notably defined by the presence of a sharia supervisory board (SSB) responsible for overseeing and coaching managers (Farook & Lanis, 2011; Almutairi & Quttainah, 2017). The SSB monitoring process seeks to align banking operations with maqashid sharia, whereas SSB coaching focuses on enhancing the quality of financial reports (Rini, 2014), reducing earnings management (Mersni & Ben Othman, 2016), and improving profitability (Shittu et al., 2016; Nomran et al., 2017). The performance of Islamic banking is significantly influenced by the frequency of meetings between SSB and managers, the educational qualifications of the SSB members, and the presence of cross-membership SSB.

The increased discussions between SSB and banking management during the consultation and supervision process profoundly influence performance under maqashid sharia. Hameed et al. (2004) articulated that the frequency of SSB meetings is a compelling indicator to assure stakeholders of aligning bank operations with sharia principles. Furthermore, the educational attainment of SSB serves as the second determinant influencing the efficacy of Islamic banking. According to stakeholder theory, the supervisory board's academic background is essential in enhancing company performance in alignment with established regulations (Freeman, 2010). This theory posits that aligning SSB education with the requisite competencies enhances the quality of performance of Islamic banking. Previous studies (Nomran et al., 2017; Nomran et al., 2018; Nurkhin, 2018) have examined SSB education, revealing that the educational background of SSB positively impacts zakat performance and business profitability.

SSB members with higher education qualifications are considered notable institutional assets that influence financial performance and practices (Gray et al., 1988). More specifically, Berger et al. (2014) revealed that board members with advanced education exhibit superior analytical thinking, leading to more effective decision-making and enhanced monitoring of risk-taking behavior. Furthermore, the risks associated with operational and bank bankruptcy will diminish as qualifications related to SSB educational background improve (Valls et al., 2016; Safiullah & Shamsuddin, 2018; Khan et al., 2024).

Cross-membership of SSB indicates that the board handles several (more than one) Islamic banks. The cross-membership of SSB can provide valuable insights when there are differences of opinion on sharia compliance because they have better knowledge, skills, and experience (Hillman et al., 2009). Cross-membership of SSB enhances efficiency by augmenting expertise and experience, improving service quality, and subsequently elevating the bank's performance. El-Halaby & Hussainey (2016) have proven that cross-membership of SSB can compare knowledge obtained from other companies to make decisions more accurate. Other studies reveal that the cross-membership of SSB positively affects financial performance as measured by the return on asset ratio (ROA/ Nomran et al., 2018).

9.3.2 Board of Commissioners

The board of commissioners ensures that the board of directors adheres to the results and recommendations provided by the sharia supervisory board concerning the bank's operational compliance with Islamic sharia. The board of commissioners is tasked with offering guidance and overseeing the duties and responsibilities of the board of directors concerning the bank's operations. According to Patro et al. (2004), a larger board of commissioners facilitates access to a broader range of information regarding issues that impact the company, including markets, technology, relevant regulations, and more. This information will significantly aid the board of directors in their advisory and maintenance roles.

The board of commissioners is responsible for ensuring that banking performance continues to improve, as they should oversee all regulations applicable to the company. Therefore, Islamic banks with more commissioners demonstrate improved performance (Quttainah et al., 2011). The growing presence of boards of commissioners is expected to lower agency costs and enhance coordination among them while diminishing information asymmetry (Nawaz, 2019). These two studies imply that the board of commissioners reduces the information asymmetry inherent in the banking organizational structure. Many commissioners increase the effectiveness of a more comprehensive supervisory mechanism and diversify strategic decision-making perspectives. In this theoretical framework, the board of commissioners has a fundamental responsibility to ensure compliance with internal and external regulations and optimize institutional performance through a systematic supervisory mechanism. The implication is that Islamic banks with a more significant number of boards of commissioners have the potential to have superior supervisory and governance capacity (Ali et al., 2023).

A diverse group of commissioners facilitates knowledge exchange, enhancing their collective understanding. Additional effects will undoubtedly enhance bank performance. Nonetheless, a significant number of commissioners will face coordination costs, potentially leading to free riders and increased complexity in coordination (James & Joseph, 2015). If this occurs, the significant number of commissioners adversely affects performance (Guest, 2009; Bukair et al., 2015). It is important to consider the possible diseconomies of scale that could result from a vast board structure. The challenges of intricate coordination and the potential for free rider behavior may diminish the effectiveness of oversight and negatively impact organizational performance. Thus, optimizing the size of the board of commissioners necessitates a balanced approach that considers quantitative and qualitative factors in the governance of Islamic banks.

Although the number of commissioners has been considered to decrease firm performance, Coles et al. (2008) contend that a larger board size is associated with improved firm performance in times of financial crises. Diversified and highly leveraged firms might gain advantages from having a larger board (Pathan & Faff, 2013). In Islamic banking, an expanded board of commissioners is crucial for managing intricate firm operations (Mollah & Zaman, 2015; Mollah et al., 2017).

Independent commissioners have been recognized as essential in promoting a transparent, accountable, and equitable corporate governance framework. Commissioners also play a role in supervision and consultation. This consultation takes place in a meeting involving commissioners and management. Following an excessive number of meetings held by the board of commissioners, a practical supervisory function is essential to evaluate the decisions made by the board of directors. Regular board of commissioner meetings will mitigate fraud by providing solutions to significant issues, particularly regarding the quality of financial reporting (Fauzyyah & Rachmawati, 2018). The significant frequency of meetings suggests that the commissioners have fulfilled their responsibilities. The frequency of commissioner meetings serves as a metric for evaluating the effectiveness of supervision and consultation provided by the commissioners (Carausu, 2015).

The more frequently the board of commissioners interacts with management, the more they supervise. Supervisory meetings are not just procedural; they help implement accountability and openness. By interacting often, commissioners and directors can create a positive discussion space for information exchange, performance audits, and strategic decision-making. Thus, the board of commissioner meeting frequency and quality can indicate corporate governance effectiveness and organizational performance potential. Many studies have linked board of commissioner meetings to firm performance (Kent & Stewart, 2008; Jizi et al., 2014).

9.4 Asset Management Under Maqashid Sharia

In banking, assets signify the resources a company can utilize to conduct its business operations. An organization's assets illustrate the intricacies of its strategic ability to generate economic value and foster sustainable economic growth. A bank can diversify its portfolio, reduce risk, and enhance profit potential by managing significant assets. Furthermore, substantial assets enhance the efficacy of banking strategies to optimize eco-friendly projects, foster the economic empowerment of small communities, and aid in sustainable development (Wuttichindanon, 2017; Magnanelli & Izzo, 2017). The amount of assets is closely associated with the profitability and performance of banks (Hirindukawshala, 2017; Hakimi et al., 2018).

Financial assets are one of the indicators that determine the size of a bank. Kibet Alex (2018) stated that the size of a bank measured financially has a significant impact on its financial performance. However, the perspective of maqashid sharia provides a different dimension in interpreting the size of banking and performance. The maqashid sharia approach assesses a bank's size from its financial capacities, such as total assets, profitability, or capital growth, and its substantive contribution in realizing falah. This concept emphasizes that the size of a sharia bank must be viewed from its ability to create welfare (welfare) for the wider community, not just creating profits for shareholders. Therefore, maqashid sharia presents a holistic benchmark in assessing bank performance. This approach encourages the transformation from a profit-oriented paradigm to a value-driven one, where the success of a sharia financial institution is measured by its ability to create a balance between economic, social, and spiritual interests. This is the essence of sharia banking, which is not just an alternative but a comprehensive solution in the modern financial system.

9.5 Maqashid Sharia Index

Islamic theology characterizes maqashid sharia as the commitment to achieve the intended goals of Islamic law (Soleh, 2016). The implementation of maqashid sharia is beneficial for safeguarding the faith of Muslims (din), desires (nafs), intellect ('aql), progeny (nasi), and wealth (mal) (Asutay & Harningtyas, 2015; Mohammad & Shahwan, 2013; Mohammed et al., 2015; Rusydiana, 2016; Shinkafi et al., 2017; Widarjono, 2017; Syafii et al., 2012; Tarique & Ahmed, 2017). Consequently, the assessment of Islamic banking performance must align with maqasid sharia to ensure that corporate activities comply with Islamic law (Hurayra, 2015; Mohammed et al., 2015). Performance assessment grounded in maqashid sharia extends beyond financial measures to encompass economic empowerment and the satisfaction of the community's spiritual requirements. Performance assessment utilizing maqashid sharia is a sophisticated and comprehensive methodological framework for evaluating the efficacy of Islamic banking in attaining falah.

Previous studies have established the maqashid sharia index (MSI) to evaluate the efficacy of Islamic banking by maqashid sharia (Asutay & Harningtyas, 2015; Mukhibad et al., 2020). MSI converts the theoretical notion of maqashid sharia into a tangible framework that can be quantified and examined. MSI evaluates Islamic banking performance by sharia governance disclosure indicators and financial ratios (Mohammed et al., 2008; Rusydiana & Parisi, 2016; Hartono & Sobari, 2017; Syafii et al., 2012; Kholid & Bachtiar, 2015). Disclosure indicators determine the managerial quality of Islamic banking when implementing Islamic governance principles within the maqashid sharia framework (Khomsatun et al., 2021). These ideas encompass justice, individual education, and the public interest. The financial ratio indicator assesses Islamic banks' performance and adherence to Islamic principles in financial procedures (Olson & Zoubi, 2008). The MSI operation is elaborated in Table 9.1 and Formulas 1, 2, 3, and 4.

Table 9.1: Maqashid Sharia Index Indicators and Items.

Indicators	Disclosure Items and Weight	Financial Ratio Items and Weights
	ED1: Education Grants (0.120)	ED5: Educational grant expenditure (0.120)
	ED2: Research (0.135)	ED6: Research expenditure/Total expenditure (0.135)
A. Education (ED)	ED3: Training (0.130)	ED7: Training expenditure/ /Yotal expenditure (0.130)
	ED4: Publication (0.115)	ED8: Publication expenditure /Total expenditure (0.115)
	JT1: Fair Return (0.150)	JT4: Net profit/Shareholders' equity (0.150)
B. Justice (JT)	JT2. Functional distribution (0.150)	JT5: Profit sharing/Total financing (0.150)
	JT3. Non-Interest Bank Products (0.200)	JT6: Margin/Total revenue (0.200)
	WF1: Profitability (0.165)	WF4: Sharia profit/Total assets (0.165)
C. Public Interest (WF)	WF2: Revenue Transfer (0.150)	WF5: Zakat/Net Profit (0.150)
	WF3: Real sector investment (0.185)	WF6: Real sector investment/Total investment (0.185)

Source: Olson & Zoubi (2008); Asutay & Harningtyas (2015): Mukhibad et al. (2020); Khomsatun et al. (2021).

ED weighted value = 30% $\left(\sum_{i=1}^{8} ED_i \times W_i\right)$ ....**Formula 1**

JT weighted value = 41% $\left(\sum_{i=1}^{6} JT_i \times W_i\right)$ ....**Formula 2**

WF weighted value = 29% $\left(\sum_{i=1}^{6} WF_i \times W_i\right)$ ....**Formula 3**

MSI = ED weighted value + JT weighted value +WF weighted value...................**Formula 4**

Source: Mukhibad et al., (2020).

Note(s): Wi denotes the weight of each item. EDi indicates the education indicator for the i item; JTi signifies the justice indicator for the item of – i; WFi represents the welfare indicator for the item of – i; MSI is the cumulative score of MSI.

9.6 Maqashid Sharia Index Eksperiment

In this chapter, the authors experimented to demonstrate the compatibility of MSI with Islamic banking principles. The project occurred in Indonesia, a nation with the largest Muslim population globally (RISSC, 2023). The study involved a thorough examination of how the characteristics of the sharia supervisory board—such as the frequency of meetings, educational qualifications, and cross-membership—alongside the attributes of commissioners, including the ratio of independent commissioners, total membership, and meeting frequency, impact the performance of Islamic banks as measured by MSI. The study involved a cohort of 12 banking institutions, analyzed over five years, specifically from 2014 to 2018. The sample selection was conducted utilizing the purposive sampling method, facilitating the systematic identification of analysis units according to specific predetermined criteria. This study employs the panel data regression method utilizing the fixed effect model (FEM) approach, meticulously chosen through a comprehensive series of statistical tests for rigorous analysis of the data. The process of selecting a model involves the application of the Chow test and the Hausman test, designed to identify the most suitable estimation model and yield precise and dependable parameter estimates relevant to the ongoing research. This examination incorporates a variety of factors, including:

6.1. The performance of Islamic banking (PS) is measured by the maqashid sharia index (MSI).
6.2. The frequency of SSB meetings (MS) is quantified by the count of such meetings held annually.
6.3. The educational attainment of SSB (ED) is assessed dichotomously with scores of 1 (bachelor's degree), 2 (master's degree), and 3 (Doctorate/Ph.D). The aggregate score of each bank is derived from the mean of the Education scores of all SSBs.
6.4. SSB cross-membership (CM) is quantified by the average number of SSB members occupying simultaneous positions.
6.5. The ratio of independent commissioners to the total number of commissioners is used to assess independent commissioners (IC).
6.6. The board size (BZ) is quantified by the number of commissioners at each bank.
6.7. The number of commissioner meetings (MK) is determined by the annual occurrence of such meetings.
6.8. Size (SZ) is measured by the number of assets transformed in logarithmic form (Log).

Table 9.2 shows that the PS variable exhibits a mean value of 31.60%, as determined by statistical analysis. The data indicates that banking performance regarding maqashid sharia remains relatively low, suggesting that Islamic banking still needs to fully align its operations with sharia principles. In the interim, the average value of the MS variable stands at 13.717, indicating that SSB has engaged in monitoring and coaching a minimum of 13 times within a year. Nonetheless, the MS variable presents a probability value (p-value) exceeding the significance threshold of 0.10, indicating that SSB monitoring and coaching do not significantly impact performance as measured by maqashid sharia (PS). The average value of the CM variable stands at 3.211, accompanied by a p-value of 0.832, which exceeds the significance threshold of 0.10, indicating that the relationship between CM and PS lacks significance. The data suggests that, on average, a single SSB is associated with more than three Islamic financial institutions; however, this association does not influence performance concerning maqashid sharia. The dual position of SSB inhibits the transfer of knowledge and best practices among companies that facilitate sharia banking operations in alignment with maqashid sharia.

Table 9.2: Eksperimental Results.

Variabel	Min	Max	Mean	St. Dev	β	St. Error	t-Stat	p-value
PS	12.639	48.903	31.604	9.419				
MS	6.000	30.000	13.717	4.043	-0.003	0.002	-1.564	0.127
CM	1.500	5.500	3.211	0.985	0.002	0.010	0.213	0.832
ED	1.000	3.000	2.342	0.471	-0.044	0.025	-1.817	0.077
IC	0.000	1.500	0.672	0.251	-0.073	0.037	-1.997	0.053
BZ	2.000	6.000	3.750	0.968	0.009	0.014	0.623	0.537
MK	2.000	23.000	9.883	5.511	-0.002	0.001	-1.563	0.126
SZ	6.62E+11	9.83E+13	1.88E+13	2.37E+13	0.065	0.052	1.253	0.218
C					-0.352	0.667	-0.528	0.600

Note(s): Min (minimum value); Max (maximum value); Mean (average value); St.Dev (standard deviation); β (coefficient value); St. Error (standard error); t-Stat (t-statistic); p-value (probability value); Islamic banking performance assessed by the maqashid sharia index (PS); Quantity of Sharia supervisory board meetings (MS); Educational attainment of the Sharia supervisory board (ED); cross membership of the Sharia supervisory board (CM); Independent Commissioner (IC); Board Size (BZ); Number of Commissioner Meetings (MK); Company Size (SZ); Constant (C).

Furthermore, Table 9.2 illustrates that the ED variable exhibits a mean value of 2.342, accompanied by a negative coefficient value and a p-value below the significance threshold of 0.10, indicating statistical significance. This outcome suggests that, on average, SSB possesses a considerable level of education; however, it simultaneously creates a divergence between Islamic banking and the foundational principles of maqashid. There is a propensity for SSB to emphasize the management of Islamic banks in a manner akin to that of the conventional sector. In a similar vein, the average value of the IC variable stands at 0.672, accompanied by a negative coefficient and a p-value that falls below 0.10, indicating statistical significance. This outcome suggests that a significant majority of the commissioners (67%) are independent; however, it raises concerns regarding the management of Islamic banking in alignment with the principles of maqashid sharia.

The results of the BZ variable presented in Table 9.2 indicate a mean value of 3.750, with a p-value exceeding the significance threshold of 0.10, suggesting that the relationship between BS and PS lacks significance. This finding indicates that the mean count of independent commissioners within Islamic banking exceeds three individuals; however, it fails to substantiate the operational framework of Islamic banking under maqashid sharia. In the interim, the MK variable exhibits a mean value of 9.883, accompanied by a p-value exceeding the significance threshold of 0.10, indicating that the relationship between MK and PS lacks statistical significance. This statistic demonstrates that the oversight and guidance provided by independent commissioners occurs a minimum of nine times within a year; however, it needs to align with the operational principles of Islamic banking. Moreover, Table 9.2 indicates that the SZ variable presents a p-value exceeding the significance threshold of 0.1, suggesting that the relationship between SZ and PS lacks statistical significance. The findings indicate that company assets do not influence the performance of Islamic banking. Methodologically, these experimental results offer compelling evidence that MSI serves as a metric for evaluating the performance of Islamic banking, particularly in assessing the board's ability to fulfill its responsibilities in alignment with Islamic principles. Furthermore, MSI can determine the efficacy with which Islamic banking employs its assets in alignment with Islamic principles.

The results of this experiment corroborate the conclusions drawn by Kholid and Bachtiar (2015), indicating an absence of correlation between the board and the performance of maqashid sharia. In the context of Islamic banking in Indonesia, it is evident that most financial ratios employed to assess the realization of maqashid sharia remain comparatively low. This phenomenon reveals a significant disparity between the normative idealism of maqashid sharia and the actual practices within banking, wherein the financing mechanisms have yet to fully embody the principles of justice, economic empowerment, and comprehensive welfare distribution. For instance, regarding the financing structure provided by Islamic banks in Indonesia, murabahah financing continues to prevail, characterized by a fixed income (Anisykurlillah & Mukhibad, 2018). This financing structure yields a predominance of high financing derived from fixed income, while the financing based on profit and loss sharing (PLS) remains comparatively low. Consequently, Islamic banks apply Islamic law somewhat superficially (Hidayah et al., 2019).

This phenomenon suggests no distinction between Islamic and conventional banks (Chong & Liu, 2009). Fixed-income financing prevails primarily due to risk considerations. PLS-based financing possesses a higher risk profile than fixed-income financing instruments, prompting Islamic banks to exercise caution in implementing this scheme.

Islamic banks possessing SSB with advanced educational backgrounds ought to enhance their operational frameworks, thereby striving for superior performance aligned with sharia principles in the economic sphere. The possession of established intellectual capacity and academic proficiency indicates a heightened potential for strategic contributions to enhance Islamic financial institutions' governance. The indicators of education, alongside ongoing training and development, as well as welfare dimensions manifested in the execution of zakat and investment in the real sector, illustrate a nuanced and interdependent relationship within the economic performance of Islamic financial institutions. A profound grasp of human resource capabilities, underpinned by a comprehensive understanding of Islamic economic principles, can foster a more efficient, transparent, and sustainable institutional framework. Consequently, an advanced level of SSB education, coupled with a comprehensive understanding of sharia principles, is pivotal in enhancing economic performance and fulfilling the socio-economic objectives that define Islamic financial institutions.

The findings of the experiment indicate that all metrics employed to assess the efficacy of the board of commissioners in fulfilling their responsibilities (such as the frequency of meetings, the total number of commissioners, and the proportion of independent commissioners) do not, in general, exert a favorable influence on the performance of maqashid sharia. The results presented here contradict the conclusions drawn by Kholid and Bachtiar (2015), who asserted that an increased number of boards of commissioners positively influences maqashid sharia. The distinction in these findings is rooted in the methodology employed for data analysis. The study utilized regression, specifically a common effect model, which often overlooks data variations among banks. In contrast, this experiment employs a panel regression – fixed effect model (FEM) that considers the data variations between banks. According to the findings of the chow test, the author determined that the fixed effects model is superior to both the random and common effects models.

The experimental findings further indicate that the ratio of independent commissioners harms the performance of maqashid Syariah. This outcome suggests that most of the indicators employed to assess maqashid Syariah are those that, when implemented, tend to diminish the short-term economic performance of banks, which stands in opposition to the foundational principles of maqashid Syariah. The impetus to satisfy shareholder expectations, the structure of compensation systems, and a constrained comprehension of the principles of maqashid sharia may serve as pertinent factors. Moreover, the inclusion of independent commissioners serves to mitigate agency conflicts between majority and minority owners, thereby emphasizing the bank's economic performance in the short term. The disparity in motivation between majority and minority owners adds complexity to the situation. Minority owners typically prioritize immediate investment returns, whereas majority owners adopt a more strategic and sustainable outlook. The ratio of independent commissioners may adversely affect the performance of maqashid Syariah, stemming from a constrained comprehension and emphasis on conventional financial metrics that only partially correspond with the comprehensive principles of sharia.

An examination of Islamic banking assets indicates that the size of the bank does not positively influence the performance of maqashid sharia. This observation suggests that the governance of Islamic banks remains a significant factor in attaining economic performance that needs to be aligned with maqashid principles. This situation is further emphasized by the traits of customers who prioritize economic factors, alongside the rivalry between Islamic banks and conventional banks in Indonesia (dual system banking), which compels Islamic banks to enhance their economic performance to remain competitive. The competitive dynamics presented by traditional banking institutions catalyze Islamic banks to enhance their operational efficiency and economic viability. While the principles of maqashid sharia aim to foster comprehensive welfare, contemporary banking practices remain primarily influenced by traditional economic factors.

9.7 Conclusion

This chapter elucidates the principles of effectively managing Islamic banking through the lens of maqashid sharia. This chapter elucidates the significant aspects of banking management as informed by maqashid sharia. This chapter underscores the primacy of monotheism as the foundational principle for establishing Islamic banking, thereby positioning God and His laws as the principal stakeholders. Consequently, Islamic banking must adhere to Islamic jurisprudence (fiqh), which is reflected in the governance of institutions in alignment with maqashid sharia. The efficacy of the governance framework is paramount to the success of Islamic banking in achieving the objectives of maqashid sharia.

This chapter delineates various indicators that signify the efficacy of the governance framework, encompassing the oversight and mentorship provided by the supervisory board to bank managers, the dual roles assumed by the supervisory board, the educational credentials of the supervisory board members, and the oversight and guidance offered by independent commissioners to bank managers. Furthermore, the administration of assets or wealth in alignment with maqashid sharia significantly contributes to the efficacy of Islamic banking in realizing falah. In this instance, the allocation of assets within Islamic banking is undoubtedly directed towards attaining substantial growth and profitability; however, this pursuit must be harmonized with the principles of maqashid sharia, which prioritize the welfare of the Muslim community.

This chapter reveal a significant benchmark for assessing the performance of Islamic banking, grounded in the principles of maqashid sharia. The standard is represented by the "Maqashid Sharia Index/ MSI." The performance of Islamic banking, as indicated by this index, centers on three fundamental components: the education of banking managers, the principle of social justice, and the consideration of public interest. This index is assessed through the lens of disclosure and financial ratios.

The findings from the experiments indicate that the MSI score associated with Islamic banking remains comparatively low. It is attributed to the presence of a supervisory board and a board of commissioners, alongside the management of banking assets, which do not contribute positively to the performance of Islamic banks when evaluated through the maqashid sharia framework. This setback arises from the intense competition posed by conventional banking institutions. The findings exemplify the imperative for Muslims to oversee Islamic banking in alignment with maqashid sharia; however, this endeavor presents considerable challenges when contending with the competitive landscape posed by non-Islamic financial entities. Nevertheless, these findings pertain exclusively to Islamic banking within non-Islamic nations, exemplified by Indonesia, which encounters significant competition from conventional banking institutions. These outcomes might vary in Islamic nations, where the governance of all financial entities adheres to the principles of Islamic sharia.

This chapter enhances the comprehension of the efficacy of the established maqashid Syariah (Mohammed et al., 2008). This model remains conceptual and requires further deliberation with regulators, stakeholders, and SSB. It is because dialogues surrounding the maqashid syariah indicators as a framework for assessing bank performance remain in progress. Consequently, the advancement of the concept and the instruments for measuring maqashid syariah may be undertaken through the subsequent activities:

1. Perform an extensive validation of maqashid sharia indicators utilizing a collaborative approach that engages regulators, scholars, banking professionals, and SSB.
2. Formulate a hybrid measurement framework synthesizing maqashid sharia indicator with traditional accounting metrics to deliver a thorough and all-encompassing performance evaluation.
3. Undertake a thorough comparative analysis to discern the significance and comparative benefits of maqashid sharia-based metrics versus conventional accounting indicators within the framework of Islamic banking in non-Islamic nations.

References

Abdul-Baki, Z., & Uthman, A. B. (2017). Exploring The “Social Failures” Of Islamic Banks: A Historical Dialectics Analysis. *Journal of Islamic Accounting and Business Research*, 8(3), 250–271.

Akbar, T., & Siti-Nabiha, A. (2022). Objectives and measures of performance of Islamic microfinance banks in Indonesia: the stakeholders’ perspectives. *International Journal of Islamic Finance, 14*(2), 124–140.

Ali, M., Khan, S. M., Puah, C., Mubarik, M. S., & Ashfaq, M. (2023). Does stakeholder pressure matter in Islamic banks’ corporate social responsibility and financial performance? *International Journal of Ethics and Systems, 39*(2), 236–263.

Hudaefi, F. A., & Bisyri, A. (2020). Pool of Funds Approach and Asset Allocation Approach in Sharia’s Perspective (A Literature Review). *Jurnal Ekonomi Dan Perbankan Syariah*, 2(1), 4–25.

Almutairi, A. R., & Quttainah, M. A. (2017). Corporate governance: Evidence from Islamic banks. *Social Responsibility Journal, 13*(3), 601–624.

Anisykurlillah, I., & Mukhibad, H. (2018). Empirical Proof of Traditional Market Trader Readiness in Preparing Financial Statement as a Mudharabah Transaction Media. *Australian Journal of Islamic Finance and Business, 4*(1), 11–18.

Asutay, M. (2012). Conceptualising and Locating the Social Failure of Islamic Finance:Aspirations of Islamic Moral Economy vs the Realities of Islamic Finance. *Asian and African Area Studies, 11*(2), 93–113.

Asutay, M., & Harningtyas, A. F. (2015). Developing Maqashid al-Shari’ah Index to Evaluate Social Performance of Islamic Banks: A Conceptual and Empirical Attempt. *International Journal of Islamic Economics and Finance Studies, 1*(1), 5–64.

Bedoui, H. E. (2012). *Ethical Competitive Advantage for Islamic Finance Institutions: How should They Measure Their Performance Houssem eddine BEDOUI The Islamic Development Bank.* In Tenth Harvard University Forum on Islamic Finance. 24–25.

Berger, A. N., Kick, T., & Schaeck, K. (2014). Executive board composition and bank risk taking. *Journal of Corporate Finance, 28* (october 2014), 48–65.

Bukair, A. A., & Abdul Rahman, A. (2015). Bank performance and board of director attributes by Islamic banks. *International Journal of Islamic and Middle Eastern Finance and Management, 8*(3), 291–309.

Carausu, N. (2015). Monitor and Control in Companies: an Agency Theory Approach. *Journal of Public Administration, Finance and Law, 6*(special issue 2), 46–60.

Chong, B. S., & Liu, M. H. (2009). Islamic banking: Interest-free or interest-based? *Pacific Basin Finance Journal, 17*(1), 125–144.

Coles, J. L., Daniel, N. D., & Naveen, L. (2008). Boards: Does one size fit all? *Journal of Financial Economics, 87*(2), 329–356.

El-Halaby, S., & Hussainey, K. (2016). Determinants of Compliance with AAOIFI Standards by Islamic Banks. *International Journal of Islamic and Middle Eastern Finance and Management, 9*(1), 143–168.

Fah, C. F., & Hassani, A. (2014). A Study of Islamic and Conventional Banks in Malaysia. *JKAU: Islamic Econ, 27*(1), 73–99.

Farag, H., Mallin, C., & Ow-Yong, K. (2018). Corporate governance in Islamic banks: New insights for dual board structure and agency relationships. *Journal of International Financial Markets, Institutions and Money, 54* (May 2018), 59–77.

Farook, S., M, K. H., & Lanis, R. (2011). Determinants of Corporate Social Responsibility Disclosure: The Case of Islamic Banks. *Journal of Islamic Accounting and Business Research, 2*(2), 114–141.

Fauzyyah, R., & Rachmawati, S. (2018). The Effect of Number of Meetings of The Board of Commissioners, Independent Commissioners, Audit Committee and Ownership Structure Upon the Extent of CSR Disclosure. *The Accounting Journal of Binaniaga, 3*(2), 41–54.

Freeman, R. E. (2017). Five Challenges to Stakeholder Theory: A Report on Research in Progress. *Stakeholder Management (Business Society 360, 1),* Emerald Publishing Limited, Leeds, 1–20.

Freeman, R. E., Harrison, J. S., Wicks, A. C., Parmar, B., & Colle, S. de. (2010). *Stakeholder Theory – The State of The Art (1st ed.).* United States of America by Cambridge University Press.

Gray, R., Dave, O., & Maunders, K. (1988). Corporate social reporting: emerging trends in accountability and the social contract. *Accounting, Auditing and Accountability Journal, 1*(1), 6–20.

Guest, P. M. (2009). The impact of board size on firm performance: Evidence from the UK. *European Journal of Finance, 15*(4), 385–404.

Hakimi, A., Rachdi, H., Mokni, R. B. S., & Hssini, H. (2018). Do board characteristics affect bank performance? Evidence from the Bahrain Islamic banks. *Journal of Islamic Accounting and Business Research*, 9(2), 251–272.

Hameed, S., Wirman, A., Alrazi, B., Nazli, M., & Pramono, Sigit. (2004). *Alternative Disclosure and Performance Measures for Islamic Banks.* Second Conference on Administrative Sciences: Meeting the Challenges of the Globalization Age, King Fahd University of Petroleum & Minerals, Dhahran, Saudi Arabia, 19–21.

Hartono, S., & Sobari, A. (2017). Sharia Maqashid Index as a Measuring Performance of Islamic Banking: a More Holistic Approach. *Corporate Ownership and Control, 14*(2), 193–201.

Hidayah, N. N., Lowe, A., & Woods, M. (2019). Accounting and pseudo spirituality in Islamic financial institutions. *Critical Perspectives on Accounting, 61*, 22–37.

Hillman, A. J., Withers, M. C., & Collins, B. J. (2009). Resource dependence theory: A review. *Journal of Management, 35*(6), 1404–1427.

Hirindukawshala, K. (2017). The Factors Effecting on Bank Profitability. *International Journal of Scientific and Research Publications, 7*(2), 212–216.

Hisham Yahya, M., Muhammad, J., & Razak Abdul Hadi, A. (2012). A comparative study on the level of efficiency between Islamic and conventional banking systems in Malaysia. *International Journal of Islamic and Middle Eastern Finance and Management, 5*(1), 48–62.

Hudaefi, F. A., & Badeges, A. M. (2022). Maqāṣid al-Sharīʿah on Islamic banking performance in Indonesia: a knowledge discovery via text mining. *Journal of Islamic Marketing, 13*(10), 2069–2089.

Hurayra, M. A. (2015). Achievement of Maqashid-al-Shari'ah in Islamic Banking: An Evaluation of Islami Bank Bangladesh Limited. *Global Journal of Computer Science and Technology: A Hardware & Computation, 15*(1), 8–15.

Ismail, F., Shabri Abd. Majid, M., & Rahim, R. Ab. (2013). Efficiency of Islamic and conventional banks in Malaysia. *Journal of Financial Reporting and Accounting, 11*(1), 92–107.

James, B. J., & Joseph, C. (2015). *Corporate Governance Mechanisms and Bank Performance: Resource-based View.* International Accounting and Business Conference (IABC), 31(2015), 117–123.

Jizi, M. I., Salama, A., Dixon, R., & Stratling, R. (2014). Corporate Governance and Corporate Social Responsibility Disclosure: Evidence from the US Banking Sector. *Journal of Business Ethics, 125*(4), 601–615.

Kent, P., & Stewart, J. (2008). Corporate governance and disclosures on the transition to International Financial Reporting Standards. *Accounting and Finance, 48*(4), 649–671.

Khan, I., Khan, I. U., Uddin, M. J., Khan, S. U., & Marwat, J. (2024). Diversity of Shari'ah supervisory board and the performance of Islamic banks: evidence from an emerging economy of Pakistan. *Journal of Islamic Accounting and Business Research, 15*(1), 1–31.

Kholid, M. N., & Bachtiar, A. (2015). Good corporate governance dan kinerja maqashid syariah bank syariah di Indonesia. *Jurnal Akuntansi & Auditing Indonesia, 19*(2), 126–136.

Khomsatun, S., Rossieta, H., Fitriany, F., & Nasution, M. E. (2021). Sharia Disclosure, Sharia Supervisory Board and the Moderating Effect of Regulatory Framework: The Impact on Soundness of Islamic Banking. *International symposia in economic theory and econometrics, 28*(January 2021), 291–321.

Kibet Alex, M. (2018). Effect of Firm Size on Financial Performance on Banks: Case of Commercial Banks in Kenya. *International Academic Journal of Economics and Finance, 3*(1), 175–190.

Laldin, M. A., & Furqani, H. (2014). The Foundations of Islamic Finance and the Maqāṣid Al-Sharīʿah Requirements. *Journal of Islamic Finance, 2*(1), 31–37.

Magnanelli, B. S., & Izzo, M. F. (2017). Corporate Social Performance and Cost of Debt: The Relationship. *Social Responsibility Journal, 13*(2), 250–265.

Mersni, H., & Ben Othman, H. (2016). The impact of corporate governance mechanisms on earnings management in Islamic banks in the Middle East region. *Journal of Islamic Accounting and Business Research,* 7(4), 318 - 348.

Milhem, M. M., & Istaiteyeh, R. M. S. (2015). Financial performance of islamic and conventional banks: evidence from jordan. *Global Journal of Business Reseacrh, 9*(3), 27–41.

Mohammad, M. O., & Shahwan, S. (2013). The objective of islamic economic and islamic banking in light of maqashid al-shariah: A critical review. *Middle East Journal of Scientific Research, 13*(special issue 13: Research in Contemporary Islamic Finance & Wealth Management), 75–84.

Mohammed, M. O., Razak, D. A., & Taib, F. M. (2008). *The Performance Measures of Islamic Banking Based on the Maqashid Framework.* IIUM International Accounting Conference (INTAC IV), 1–17.

Mohammed, M. O., Tarique, K., & Islam, R. (2015). Measuring The Performance of Islamic Banks Using Maqāṣid -Based Model. *Intellectual Discourse, 23*(special issue 1), 401–424.

Mollah, S., Hassan, M. K., Farooque, O. Al, & Mobarek, A. (2017). The Governance, Risk-taking, and Performance of Islamic Banks. *Journal of Financial Services Research, 52*(2), 1–29.

Mollah, S., & Zaman, M. (2015). Shari' ah supervision , corporate governance and performance : Conventional vs Islamic banks. *Journal of Banking & Finance, 58*(September 2015, 418–435.

Mukhibad, H. (2019). The Role of Sharia Supervisory Boards in Meeting Maqashid Syariah – Study on Islamic Banks in Indonesia. *European Journal of Islamic Finance*, 13(August 2019), 1–10.

Mukhibad, H., Rochmatullah, M. R., Warsina, W., Rahmawati, R., & Setiawan, D. (2020). Islamic corporate governance and performance based on maqashid sharia index– study in Indonesia. *Jurnal Siasat Bisnis, 24*(2), 114–126.

Nawaz, T. (2019). Exploring the Nexus Between Human Capital, Corporate Governance and Performance: Evidence from Islamic Banks. *Journal of Business Ethics, 157*(2), 567–587.

Nomran, N. M., Haron, R., & Hassan, R. (2017). Bank Performance and Shari'ah Supervisory Board Attributes of Islamic Banks : Does Bank Size Matter ? *Journal of Islamic Finance, 6*(special issue 1), 174–187.

Nomran, N. M., Haron, R., & Hassan, R. (2018). Shari'ah supervisory board characteristics effects on Islamic banks' performance: Evidence from Malaysia. *International Journal of Bank Marketing, 36*(2), 290–304.

Nurkhin, A., Rohman, A., Rofiq, A., & Mukhibad, H. (2018). The role of the Sharia Supervisory Board and corporate governance mechanisms in enhancing Islamic performance-evidence from Indonesia. *Banks and Bank Systems, 13*(4), 85–95.

Olson, D., & Zoubi, T. A. (2008). Using accounting ratios to distinguish between Islamic and conventional banks in the GCC region. *The International Journal of Accounting, 43*(1), 45–65.

Pathan, S., & Faff, R. (2013). Does board structure in banks really affect their performance? *Journal of Banking and Finance, 37*(5), 1573–1589.

Patro, S., Lehn, K., & Zhao, M. (2004). *Determinants of the Size and Structure of Corporate Board : 1935–2000.* Working Paper Pitsburgh : Katz Graduate School of Business, University of Pitsburgh.

Pradiknas, T. Y., & Faturohman, T. (2015). Efficiency of Islamic Banking Compared to Conventional Banking: Eveidence from Indoensian Banking Sector. *Journal of Business and Management, 4*(5), 540–551.

Qian, D. J., & Velayutham, S. (2017). Conventional Banking and Islamic Banking: Do the Different Philosophies Lead to Different Financial Outcomes? *Journal of Wealth Management & Financial Planning, 4*(June), 3–14.

Quttainah, M. A., Song, L., & Wu, Q. (2011). *Do Islamic Banks Employ Less Earnings Management ? Do Islamic Banks Employ Less Earnings Management ?* Politics and Conomics Development ERF 17th Annual Conference 2011.

Rini. (2014). The Effect of Audit Committee Role and Sharia Supervisory Board Role on Financial Reporting Quality at Islamic Banks in Indonesia. *Journal of Economics, Business, and Accountancy Ventura, 17*(1), 145–156.

Rusydiana, A. (2016). The Measurement of Islamic Bank Performance : A Study Using Maqashid Index and Profitability. *Global Review of Islamic Economics and Business, 4*(1), 1–14.

Rusydiana, A. S., & Parisi, S. Al. (2016). The Measurement of Islamic Bank Performance: A Study Using Maqashid Index and Profitability. *Global Review of Islamic Economics and Business, 4*(1), 1–14.

Safiullah, M., & Shamsuddin, A. (2018). Risk in Islamic Banking and Corporate Governance. *Pacific-Basin Finance Journal 47*(February 2018), 129–149.

Sakti, M. R. P., & Mohamad, A. (2018). Efficiency, stability, and asset quality of Islamic vis-à-vis conventional banks: Evidence from Indonesia. *Journal of Islamic Accounting and Business Research, 9*(3), 378–400.

Shawtari, F. A., Ariff, M., & Razak, S. H. A. (2019). Efficiency and bank margins: a comparative analysis of Islamic and conventional banks in Yemen. *Journal of Islamic Accounting and Business Research, 10*(1), 50–72.

Shinkafi, A. A., Ali, N. A., & Choudhury, M. (2017). Contemporary Islamic Economic Studies on Maqashid Shari'ah : A Systematic Literature Review. *Humanomics, 33*(3), 315–334.

Shittu, I., Ahmad, A. C., & Ishak, Z. (2016). Board Characteristics and Earnings Per Share of Malaysian Islamic Banks. *International Journal of Economics and Financial Issues, 6*(S6), 135–137.

Soleh, I. (2016). The Impact of Maqashid Syariah and Core Competency on Performance of Islamic Bank. *International Journal of Economics, Commerce and Management, 4*(10), 872–880.

Widarjono, A. (2017). Islamic Bank Performance : Between Maqashid Sharia and Camels Model. *International Journal of Economics, Business and Management Research, 1*(04), 562–574.

Syafii, M., Sanrego, Y. D., & Taufiq, M. (2012). An Analysis of Islamic Banking Performance: Maqashid Index Implementation in Indonesia and Jordania. *Journal of Islamic Finance, 1*(1), 12–29.

Tarique, K., & Ahmed, M. U. (2017). Maqashid al-Shariah in CSR Practices of the Islamic Banks : A Case Study of IBBL. *Journal of Islamic Economics, Banking and Finance, 13*(3), 47–63.

Valls, V., González-Romá, V., & Tomás, I. (2016). Linking educational diversity and team performance: Team communication quality and innovation team climate matter. *Journal of Occupational and Organizational Psychology, 89*(4), 751–771.

Wuttichindanon, S. (2017). Corporate social responsibility disclosure—choices of report and its determinants: Empirical evidence from firms listed on the Stock Exchange of Thailand. *Kasetsart Journal of Social Sciences, 38*(2), 156–162.

Zainuldin, M. H., Lui, T. K., & Yii, K. J. (2018). Principal-agent relationship issues in Islamic banks: a view of Islamic ethical system. *International Journal of Islamic and Middle Eastern Finance and Management, 11*(2), 297–311.

Zarrouk, H., Jedidia, K. Ben, & Moualhi, M. (2016). Is Islamic bank profitability driven by same forces as conventional banks? *International Journal of Islamic and Middle Eastern Finance and Management, 9*(1), 46–66.

Putri Ayu Puspieta Wardhani, Cicilia Larasati Rembulan

Chapter 10
Examining Self-Congruity among Muslim Consumers: The Intersection of Islamic Beliefs and Beauty Brand Attributes

Abstract: Indonesia, home to one of the largest Muslim populations globally, has experienced a growing demand for halal and Islamic-oriented industries, including the beauty sector. While halal certification has traditionally been the cornerstone of Islamic branding, the attributes of Islamic branding may differ in the context of beauty products. Previous research on Islamic branding in Indonesia has primarily employed quantitative methods, focusing on correlations between branding factors and variables such as customer satisfaction and religiosity. However, the specific elements of Islamic branding remain underexplored, particularly from the perspective of consumer values rather than product attributes. This study aims to address the gap in research examining self-congruity in the consideration of choosing beauty products among Muslim consumers. It also aims to identify brand attributes perceived as elements of Islamic branding by Muslim consumers. A Qualitative study with a concurrent nested strategy was employed using open-ended questionnaires distributed to 112 Muslim consumers in emerging adulthood. Participants reflected on the factors influencing their purchases and how these aligned with their Islamic values. To broaden the view, the quantitative analysis was conducted using two single-item measures to assess the impact of self-religiosity on purchasing behavior. Results reveal that Islamic branding encompasses more than halal certification; narrative elements such as the use of Muslim representatives, social media campaigns, and ethical business practices significantly influence consumer perceptions. Practical factors, such as price and accessibility, also play a critical role. Regression analysis highlights that higher self-religiosity predicts a preference for more religiously aligned beauty products. However, Muslim consumers actively validate product claims, ensuring congruity with their Islamic idenfity through detailed scrutiny of labels, ingredients, and ethical business processes. These findings suggest that both Islamic and secular attributes are important, highlighting the need for beauty brands to integrate holistic narratives and ethical practices into their branding strategies. Managerial implications and recommendations for future research are discussed.

Keywords: Islamic self-congruity, Islamic Brand Attributes, Beauty products, Indonesia muslim consumers

https://doi.org/10.1515/9783111575407-011

10.1 Introduction

As one of the largest Muslim populations in the world, Indonesia has significant potential to develop its national halal industry and Islamic economy. The Coordinating Minister for Economic Affairs stated that Indonesia's halal expenditure reached USD 184 billion and is projected to increase to USD 281.6 billion by 2025 (Coordinating Ministry for Economic Affairs (Ekon), 2022). Among the growing demands for halal and Islamic-oriented industries, the beauty sector has emerged as a leading industry. Susilowati et al. (2023) noted that halal cosmetics have been a rapidly expanding market since 2020, with consumption reaching USD 4.19 billion in Indonesia. This highlights that the demand for halal products is not limited to food and beverages but extends to personal care items such as face creams, base makeup, decorative cosmetics, hair dyes, and more. However, research on halal beauty products remains limited, with most studies focusing on food and beverages (Sudarsono & Nugrohowati, 2020; Millatina et al., 2022) and pharmaceuticals (Herdiana & Rusdiana, 2022) in Indonesia. This gap needs to be addressed, as the beauty sector differs from food and pharmaceuticals due to the emotional and personal connections consumers have with beauty products. Furthermore, the dilemmas faced by consumers when choosing beauty products extend beyond halal certification.

When choosing products, Muslims consider the Islamic attributes within them, evaluating whether certain brands align with their Islamic beliefs. This evaluation process can create dilemmas. The psychological process through which consumers compare their perception of a brand's personality or brandings with their actual or ideal self is known as self-congruity (Sop, 2020). The theory of self-congruity, as developed by Sirgy (1985), suggests that self-congruity is higher when a brand's image and attributes align closely with a consumer's self-concept. This theory highlights that purchasing decisions are often motivated by an expression of one's identity rather than solely fulfilling physical needs. For Muslim consumers, their identity as Muslims represents their ideal self, and Islamic self-congruity influences their purchase behavior as a means of reinforcing that identity. Shalihin et al. (2023) further emphasized that Muslim millennials prioritize religiosity as a core foundation when selecting and purchasing products.

The self-congruity theory has been applied across various domains, including purchasing luxury cars (Birdwell, as cited in Sop, 2020), travel choices (Sirgy & Su, 2000), and retail store preferences (Ibrahim & Najjar, 2017). These studies suggest that self-congruity can serve as a bias in purchasing behavior. For instance, individuals who perceive a brand as highly aligned with their self-concept tend to form positive impressions of its products or services, potentially influencing their evaluation of functional attributes. However, the application of self-congruity in the context of Islamic identity among Muslims remains underexplored. Most studies have narrowly focused on religiosity as a determinant of purchasing behavior in specific domains, such as fashion (Shalihin et al., 2023), hospitality in luxury hotels (Zainol et al., 2024), and retail (Aji et al., 2020). Eventhough, It is noteworthy that Islamic Shariah Law has been influencing consumer choices (Floren et al., 2019), leaving the broader implications of Islamic self-congruity largely unexamined, especially in beauty products.

10.2 Present Study

This study focuses on Islamic self-congruity in beauty products among emerging adults in Indonesia. Unlike the food and beverage or pharmaceutical industries, where products are directly consumed, beauty products are considered indirect and secondary necessities. The use of beauty products serves broader purposes beyond basic skin and body care. These purposes include enhancing appearance, boosting confidence and quality of life (Draelos, 2021), and acting as a form of self-expression (Smith et al., 2021) among consumers. This becomes an intriguing area of exploration when Islamic beliefs are introduced into the decision-making process. Muslim consumers often reflect on how their self-expression through beauty products aligns with their Islamic values, raising questions about the extent to which these values influence their purchasing decisions.

Moreover, the influence of brand image on consumer perceptions cannot be overlooked. Islamic branding—defined as any brand or marketing activity that serves products or services for Muslims, whether derived from Muslim or non-Muslim countries (Alserhan, 2010)—acts as a medium for companies to introduce their products. However, as noted by Ismail et al. (2022), the concept of Islamic branding remains conventional, often limited to engaging Muslim consumers through branding strategies and failing to capture broader Islamic principles. This highlights the need to explore the specific brand attributes that resonate with Islamic principles as perceived by Muslim consumers, particularly in the context of beauty products.

The purpose of this research is to examine Islamic self-congruity of Muslim consumers in consideration when choosing beauty products. Additionally, it seeks to identify the beauty product attributes perceived by Muslim consumers as the elements of Islamic branding. By employing a qualitative approach, this study provides an in-depth understanding of how religious values intertwine with consumer behavior in the beauty sector. This study expands the understanding of self-congruity theory in the religious domain and integrates it with Islamic attributes concepts, extending the future research in religious consumer behavior in Indonesia. The insights gained from this research also offer practical implications. For beauty brands, the findings can inform more inclusive and culturally sensitive marketing strategies in Indonesia, aligning their marketing attributes with the religious and personal values of Muslim consumers.

10.3 Methods

This study employed a qualitative approach with a concurrent nested strategy to explore Islamic self-congruity. The method combined primary data collection through qualitative open-ended questions with a nested quantitative analysis, allowing for a broader perspective on the research topic (Terrell, 2015). The research design addressed two key questions: (1) the extent to which Islamic congruity influences Muslim consumers' decisions when purchasing beauty products, and (2) the attributes of beauty brands perceived as the primary drivers for Muslim consumers' purchase decisions. Data were collected through an online open-ended questionnaire, which allowed participants to freely express their thoughts without being influenced or led by the researchers (Jain, 2021). The online questionnaire was distributed to 130 emerging adult Muslim consumers in Indonesia. After eliminating irrelevant answers and disqualifying participants, 112 responses were deemed eligible for analysis. To ensure data anonymity and participant consent, respondents were required to complete an informed consent form before filling out the questionnaire. Later, the qualitative data was analyzed and coded using thematic analysis to interpret the dataset into categories and sub-categories.

As additional exploration, the study incorporated a quantitative component by including a single-item measure to assess participants' perceptions of their own religiosity and the religiosity attribute of the beauty products they purchase. Single-item measures can reliably and validly assess conceptually narrow constructs (Matthews et al., 2022). The first item was, "How religious are you?" and the second item was, "How religious are the attributes of the beauty products that you purchased?" Both items were measured on a 5-point Likert scale, where 1 represented "Not religious at all" and 5 represented "Truly religious." Regression analysis conducted using JASP software, was employed to examine the self and the perceived purchased religiosity, thereby, exploring the degree of Islamic self congruity. This method aligns with Sirgy's framework (in Sop, 2020), which emphasizes capturing an individual's perception of product or brand image in relation to their self-image. This qualitative study with concurrent nested strategy provides both in-depth qualitative insights and quantitative validation, offering a comprehensive exploration of the role of Islamic self-congruity in Muslim consumers' beauty product choices.

10.4 Result

Table 10.1 provides an overview of the participants in the study.

Table 10.1: Distribution of Data Demography.

Demography Data	Category	COUftt	Percentage
Age	Less than 18 yrs old	1	0.9%
	18–20 yrs old	82	73.2%
	20–22 yrs old	29	25.9%
Gender	Male	6	5.4%
	Female	106	94.6%
Occupation	Undergraduate Students	102	91.1%
	Part time workers	2	1.8%
	Fulltime workers	1	0.9%
	Others	7	6.3%
Average expense on Beauty Products in every month	Less than 100.000 IDR (6 USD)	19	17%
	1o1.000–300.000 IDR (6 USD–18 USD)	63	56.3%
	301.000–500.000 IDR (18 USD–30 USD)	25	22.3%
	501.000–700.000 IDR (30 USD–43 USD)	5	4.5%

From Table 10.1, it shows the majority of participants were aged 18–20 years old (73.2%) and predominantly female (94.6%), with only a small proportion of males using beauty products. Most participants were undergraduate students (91.1%), reflecting the typical demographic of emerging adults in Indonesia. Regarding monthly beauty product expenses, 56.3% of participants spent between 101,000–300,000 IDR (approximately 6–18 USD) and 22.3% spent 301,000–500,000 IDR (18–30 USD). This indicates that the majority of participants were students with limited monthly budgets.

To address the first research question regarding self-congruity in the consideration of choosing beauty products among Muslim consumers, Table 10.2 presents the categorization of participants' Islamic beliefs that serve as considerations.

The results indicate that there are four main categories in the beliefs of Muslim consumers that inform their considerations when selecting beauty products (see Table 10.2). The first category pertains to the Islamic belief in ethical consumption. Halal products are aligned with prior studies (Fathoni et al., 2022; Susilowafi et al., 2023), which underscore the significance of this aspect for all Muslim consumers. Surprisingly, there are also concerns about the benefits or functions of the products. When choosing beauty products, Muslim consumers also consider the functionality of these products, believing that this reflects the correct approach to ethical consumption in Islam. It also relates to the Islamic principle of Wasathiyah or moderation in all things (Hanapi et al., 2019). Consequently, they prefer brands that do not promote excessive Tabarruj, avoid overdressing and advocate for moderation in usage.

The second important consideration is the ethical stance of the brand company itself. Muslim consumers hold the belief that they should support ethical businesses, in accordance with the trade practices of Prophet Muhammad (SAW), particularly the

Table 10.2: The Islamic Beliefs in the Self-Congruity to Purchase Beauty Products.

Main Category	Sub-category 1	Open-end Citation
Belief in Ethical Consumption	Use Halal products	"Because it is a halal products," (S9)
	Use functional products	"Good for the face and skin," (S97)
	Consume in moderation (Wasathiyah)	"Using product with the intention of avoiding excessive use," (S54)
Belief to support a Ethical Business Practices	Support honest business (Siddiq)	"(A business that) applies ethical business, such as honesty. . ." (S11)
	Support trustworthy business (Amanah)	"(A business that) is already trusted. . ." (S36)
	Support environmentally responsible business (Maslahah)	". . .doesn't exploit human or environment (in the manufacturing process)," (S16)
Belief to align with Prophet's Guidance	Use ingredients suggested in Hadith	". . .using Zaitun that is mentioned in Hadith," (S8)
Belief to support personal worship	Use products that easy to purify (Thaharah)	"The product should be wudhu-friendly (easy to clean) for muslimah," (S51)
	Use product that promote cleanliness (Nazafah)	"Need cleaning product because clean is a part of Iman," (S112)

principles of Siddiq (truthfulness), Amanah (trustworthiness), and Maslahah (public interest). Muslim consumers often view their consumption practices as acts of worship similar to the conduct of Prophet Muhammad (SAW) way of conducting business. This perspective leads them to support businesses that are truthful, trustworthy, and that do not exploit the environment in their operations. In alignment with these values, they seek to adhere to the teachings of the Prophet by selecting ingredients recommended in Hadith, such as Zaitun (olive oil) and Siwaq (tooth-stick).

The final category relates to personal worship practices. Muslim consumers believe that beauty products should not hinder their prayer times. Thus, they choose products that are easy to clean, enabling them to perform Thaharah (purihcation), such as Wudhu before daily praying. This preference aligns with findings from a previous study (Ilmi et at., 2024), which indicates that Muslims tend to favor non-waterproof products. Furthermore, as beauty products also include items designed to enhance cleanliness (such as facial washes and shampoos), Muslim consumers believe that their use of these products contributes to their Iman (faith). A hadith reported by Abu Malik al-Ash'ari mentions that Prophet Muhammad (SAW) said, "Cleanliness is half of faith," emphasizing that cleanliness is an integral component of Iman.

Regarding the second research question about brand attributes, Table 10.3 highlights the Islamic attributes of brands that contribute to Muslim consumers' purchasing decisions.

There are several components of brand attributes identified in the results (see Table 10.3). The first is the brand's compliance with halal standards. For Muslim consumers, halal remains the primary driver when purchasing a brand, particularly beauty products. This aligns with previous studies (Fathoni et at., 2022), confirming it as a widely recognized fact. However, this study further categorizes halal compliance into three subcategories: halal certification, alcohol-free tags, and ritual impurity (Najis)-free tags. Despite local producers often using halal ingredients, the official certification from organizations, such as the Indonesian Ulama Council (MUI), is crucial. Additionally, some consumers prefer to check the ingredients themselves. Labels such as "najis-free" or "alcohol-free" reassure Muslim consumers that the product is "safe" for their use.

The second attribute relates to product safety and purity. This is distinct from halal compliance, which focuses on ingredient permissibility. Safety and purity refer to the product's original purpose—being safe to use as beauty products. This attribute is emphasized in studies by Lee & Kwon (2022), applicable to all consumers, not just Muslims. Safety is validated through certification by the Indonesian Food and Drug Authority (BPOM) or tags such as "clinically tested" or "mercury-free." This aligns with the Islamic concept of *thayyib*, or consuming what is good, as mentioned in the Quran (QS. Al-Baqarah, 2: 172). Interestingly, many Muslim consumers equate nature-based ingredients with *thayyib*, believing that natural products inherently represent goodness.

Table 10.3: The Brand Attributes Driving Muslim Consumers' Beauty Brand Purchases.

Main Category	Sub-category 1	Open-end Citation
Compliance with Halal Standards	Halal Certified	"The product is halal-certified," (S22)
	Alcohol Free	"The product is free from alcohol," (S95)
	Ritual-Impurities (Najis) Free	"The production process is free from Najis," (S28)
Products' Safety & Purity (Thayyib)	Safety Certified	". . .Already BPOM-certified so it is safe," (S17)
	Clinically tested	". . .Already clinically tested," (S39)
	Free from Harmful Ingredients	"Using the ingredients that is not dangerous for skin," (S32)
	Using Nature-based Ingredients	"Made from natural ingredients," (S36)
Using Faith-Aligned Ingredients	Ingredients mentioned in Hadith	". . .using Zaitun that is mentioned in Hadith," (S8)
	Ingredients Adviced by Islamic Teaching	"Using the suggested ingredients from Islam (teachings)," (S80)

Table 10.3 (continued)

Main Category	Sub-category 1	Open-end Citation
Moderation-in -Use Products	Temporary impact on appearance	"Doesn't change what Allah made for us," (S16)
	Promote simplicity (avoid Tabarruj)	"The product is supporting simplicity and natural beauty," (S11)
Ethical Business Practices	Honesty in Product Label	"The ingredients were shown all in the label (of the products). . ." (S67)
	Trusworthy production Process	"The production process were following Islamic Qaida (rules)," (S78)
	Environmentally Responsible	"They show ethical practice and are environmentally saved. . ." (S11)
Islamic Brand Narratives	Brand Name/Tagline	"Using the name (for the brand) derived from Arabic. . ." (S22)
	Narratives in Advertising (e.g. in TV Commercials & Social Media)	"The commercials seems Islamic," (S32)
		"Their (sounding in) Social Media is promoting Islamic products," (S34)
	Representation of Hijab Women in Marketing (e.g. as models and salesperson)	"The commercials show models in Hijab. . ." (S40)
		"Their SPGs (Sales Promotion Girls) were all showing Islamic appearance," (S20)

The third and fourth attributes, less explored in prior literature (see Floren et al. (2019) for a literature review), highlight religiously inspired preferences. Consumers value ingredients mentioned in the Hadith and Quran, such as *zaitun* (olives) (QS. AI-Mu'minun, 23:20) and *siwak* (tooth-cleaning twig) (as mentioned in Hadith cited by HR. Bukhari), which were used by Prophet Muhammad (SAW). Furthermore, Islamic teachings discourage extravagance, promoting simplicity and modesty instead (Floren et al., 2019). As a result, Muslim consumers often favor brands that emphasize simplicity over those with glamorous branding, aligning with Islamic values like avoiding *tabarruj* (excessive adornment). They also expressed a preference for beauty brands that do not promote permanent alterations, such as tattoos or plastic surgery, aligning with their religious beliefs.

The fifth attribute concerns the business process itself. Muslim consumers actively observe whether a company operates in a manner that aligns with Islamic ethics. Prophet Muhammad (SAW), a merchant himself, emphasized honesty, trustworthiness, and responsibility in business. Companies demonstrating ethical practices, such as contributing to environmental and social causes, are viewed favorably. This belief stems from the concept of *Rahmatan lil alamin* (divine blessings for the universe). This aligns with Bukhari and Isa (2019), which highlights ethical business as one of the key drivers for consumer loyalty, though its connection to Islamic consumers is less explored.

This result also shows the key indicator that a beauty brand possesses Islamic attributes lies in the narrative of its brand persona. This includes the use of Arabic or Islamic-related names in taglines and product names, the incorporation of Islamic narratives in advertisements, and the overall marketing communication. It has been noted that consumers perceive the Islamic attributes of certain brands based on their advertising on social media and TV commercials. A beauty brand is considered Islamic when its commercials feature hijabi models, and its sales promotion girls (SPGs) wear hijabs while advertising the products. This emphasizes that narratives in advertising and marketing significantly influence consumers' perception of a brand in relation to their branding appeals. Furthermore, this study revealed that a particular brand with strong Islamic attributes, from the name of the brand to the advertising, was mentioned more frequently in the open-ended questionnaire responses, reflecting the alignment of its Islamic narrative elements, such as SPGs and associate social media influencers, with consumer perceptions.

Interestingly, beyond the Islamic attributes, this study found that participants also considered secular attributes as deciding factors when purchasing beauty products, as shown in Table 10.4.

This study also identifies considerations beyond beauty brand religious attributes. The first factor is social validation. In a collectivistic culture, external validation plays a significant role in decision-making (Susilowati et al., 2023), including purchasing behavior. The findings indicate that this validation may come from influential figures, such as religious leaders and social media personalities. Consumers may also rely on heuristic thinking, assuming a product is safe if it is widely used by the general population, whether Muslim or not. This may be further influenced by Indonesia's Muslim-majority population, where such products are often presumed to be safe for Muslim consumers.

Interestingly, although this study focuses on Islamic branding in beauty products, the results indicate that secular aspects of branding remain important to Muslim consumers. Product functionality, such as compatibility with skin type and personal preferences, continues to be a major consideration. Other factors, such as the product's practicality, price, and accessibility, also play a significant role. This aligns with the findings of Hecht et al. (2020), who noted that the classic 4Ps of marketing—product, place, price, and promotion—remain fundamental to ensuring a product's market success.

Table 10.4: Other Considerations Influencing Muslim Consumers.

Main Category	Sub-category 1	Sub-category 2	Open-end Citation
Social Validation	Recommendation from Influential Figures	Religious Leader	"Widely used by religious leader," (S23)
		Social Media Personalities	". . .was mentioned by a lot of influencers (as Islami Products)," (S61)
	Consumed by Majority	By general consumers	"Widely used by other consumers," (S110)
		By Muslim Consumers	". . .saw many Muslims use it," (S10)
Non-religious Product Attributes	Alignment with personal consideration	Compatibility with skin type	". . .whether it is good or not for my skin type," (S4)
		Compatibility with preference	"Because it is good on my face, comforting, and suit me," (S61)
	Affordable price		"It is cheap and comfortable," (S112)
	Ease of Use		"Easy to apply and use it," (S90)
	Products Accessibility		"It is easy to find (the brand and purchase)," (S28)

To better understand the extent of Islamic self and the brand religious attributes perceived by consumers, a regression analysis was conducted, as shown in Table 10.5.

Table 10.5: Regression analysis for Perception of self-Religiosity and Purchased-Product Religiosity Attribute.

Model	R	R^2	Standardized	F (1,110)	P-value
H1 : Perception of Self-Religiosity Level and Purchased Product Religiosity Attribute	0.351	0.123	0.351	15.467	< 0.001

Table 10.5 indicates that the hypothesis is accepted (p-value < 0.001), underscoring the significant role of self-religiosity levels as predictors of the religiosity of purchased products. The standardized score of 0.351 highlights a positive impact, suggesting that the higher an individual's perception of their religiosity level, the more religious the products they purchase, with R^2 0.123 shows the 12.3% influence of self-religiosity on the religiosity attributes of the purchased products. This finding demonstrates the presence of Islamic self-congruity. It aligns with Fahrullah et al. (2024) and Andini and Rufaidah (2018), who also noted that religiosity significantly influences purchasing decisions among Muslim consumers.

10.5 Discussion

To address the first research question regarding the extent of self-congruity's influence on Muslim consumers' consideration to choose beauty products, this study found that Islamic belief plays a significant role in shaping their perceptions. However, it is not the sole deciding factor, as evidenced by the inclusion of secular attributes (see Table 10.4) alongside Islamic attributes (see to Table 10.3). Its influence extends beyond halal certification to include broader religious beliefs, such as the belief in ethical consumption, the belief in supporfing ethical business practices, the belief in aligning with the Prophet's guidance, and the belief in enhancing personal worship through product usage. While halal certification is widely mentioned, these additional values reflect a multidimensional view of Islamic congruity in beauty brand purchases. Yet, contrary to findings from previous research (Fahrullah et al., 2024; Zainol et al., 2024), Muslim consumers do not make trade-offs between Islamic branding and other factors. Instead, they consider practical elements of beauty products, such as price, accessibility, and skin compatibility, alongside religious considerations. This indicates that practical elements, along with Islamic branding attributes, are considered by Muslim consumers. Therefore, especially in Indonesia, beauty brands need to adopt a holistic approach, balancing religious factors with practical considerations to effectively promote their products. The findings from the regression analysis (see Table 10.5) confirm that religiosity significantly predicts consumers' preferences for beauty products. Highly religious individuals tend to favor products with stronger Islamic attributes, emphasizing the alignment of their consumption choices with their religious values. This reinforces the importance of Islamic attributes in brand selection among devout Muslim consumers.

The second research question explores the attributes Muslim consumers seek when selecting beauty products.While Islamic attributes remain significant to Muslim consumers, the findings indicate that, in Indonesia, they prioritize a combination of religious, practical, and narrative attributes as key considerations. Religious aspects, such as compliance with halal standards, product safety and purity (thayyib), the use of faith-aligned ingredients, and moderation in product use, are foundational. However, religious branding extends beyond these elements. Brand narratives also need to be recognized as integral Islamic attributes, as they play a crucial role in making consumers aware of the Islamic aspects of the branding.

These narratives are often conveyed through social media, brand taglines, and advertisements, enhancing the visibility of a product's Islamic branding (Fathoni et al., 2022). Media exposure increases consumer awareness of a product's halal certification and alignment with Islamic principles. Moreover, despite the importance of this narrative component, it remains underexplored in Indonesia. Existing studies primarily focus on measuring Islamic branding's relationship with religiosity (Andini & Rufaidah, 2018), the brand's religiosity aura (Wahyuni & Fitriani, 2017), or its direct effect on purchasing decisions (Ambarwati & Sari, 2023).

This study identifies several narrative strategies perceived by consumers as defining elements of an Islamic brand. Brands often emphasize their Islamic identity by featuring Muslim representatives, such as models or hijabi influencers, to promote and review their products. The use of sales promotion girls (SPGs) wearing hijabs further reinforces these narratives. Additionally, incorporating the Arabic language in branding and advertisements is perceived as a strong selling point, as it aligns with the cultural and religious identity of Muslim consumers. These narrative strategies highlight how brands can create a deeper connection with their target audience while promoting Islamic principles. The depth of knowledge consumers acquire about how Islamic a brand is becomes a vital factor, enabling them to form stronger religious associations (Bukhari & Isa, 2019).

Furthermore, the reputation of the brand and its alignment with Islamic principles significantly contribute to its appeal. These findings suggest that Muslim consumers evaluate beauty brands hoIistJcaIIy in terms of their Islamic branding. This evaluation goes beyond the products themselves, encompassing the company's ethical business practices. As highlighted by Bukhari and Isa (2019), consumers perceive initiatives such as corporate social responsibility (CSR) as a successful implementation of Islamic branding principles. While previous studies have primarily proposed the antecedents of this perception, the present study provides evidence that consumers actively assess a company's ethical practices. For instance, environmentally responsible actions and the avoidance of animal testing are considered important markers of alignment with Islamic values. These insights underscore the growing importance of ethical considerations in Muslim consumers' evaluation of brands, further expanding the understanding of Islamic branding's scope and impact.

Besides that, Muslim consumers also consider practical factors such as product functionality, price, accessibility, and ease of use. These findings demonstrate that both Islamic and secular-practical attributes are key considerations for Muslim consumers. Interestingly, this result provides a slightly different perspective compared to previous studies, such as Zainol et al. (2024), which suggested that Islamic self-congruity could mediate purchase intentions even in the context of luxury services. This difference may be linked to the nature of the participants, who are primarily mid-economic class and undergraduate students. Their purchasing decisions are influenced by financial constraints, as they must balance their spending on beauty products with other daily expenses. The majority of participants reported spending under 500,000 IDR per month (only 10% from the average salary) on beauty products, reflecting the perception of such items as secondary necessities rather than primary ones. It is noteworthy that even in building an Islamic branding, the basic secular marketing strategies also remained as important factors in Indonesia consumers' decision making process.

10.6 Conclusion

Alongside examining self-congruity, this study took an exploratory approach to investigate Muslim consumers, particularly regarding their preferences for beauty products. The findings highlight that, while Islamic self-concept and belief are significant factors, consumers also emphasize their consideration on external validation and secular attributes, such as price. The novelty of this study lies in its detailed exploration of attributes. Previous research often simplified Islamic attributes in branding to Halal certification, whereas this study demonstrates that Islamic narrative attributes play a critical role. The strength of narrative marketing lies in its ability to enhance brand awareness and foster deeper connections with Muslim consumers. Effective narratives, such as those emphasizing ethical business practices aligned with Prophet Muhammad's (SAW) principles, resonate with consumers' values.

This study also found that consumers actively seek to validate their choices to ensure alignment with their identity. Muslim consumers assess the validity of labels, ingredients, and ethical business practices to confirm that their beauty products do not hinder religious observances, such as prayer. This finding challenges the traditional perception of consumers as passive recipients of information, shedding new light on their active role in seeking and verifying information to align their purchases with their beliefs and values.

This study has several limitations. Firstly, The quantitative approach used serves only as an additional exploration. The single-item measures used to assess perceived self-religiosity and Islamic attributes also lack validity and reliability testing. Future research should develop more robust instruments to measure Islamic self-congruity. Secondly, the study is limited to emerging adults and predominantly women, despite the diversity of Muslim consumers. The next research should include a broader age range to allow for comparisons and explore male consumers, who are an emerging market for beauty products.

Lastly, as the managerial implication, Products/services that target Muslim consumers should recognize the dual importance of secular and Islamic aspects of their business. Islamic narratives can go beyond simple markers, such as hijabs or Halal labels, to include more profound elements like ethical business practices and corporate social responsibility (CSR). Highlighting CSR initiatives in line with Islamic values could strengthen brand positioning. Businesses can also leverage recommendation strategies and narrate their ethical processes to appeal to consumers' desire for congruity with their religious and personal identifies.

References

Aji, H. M., Husin, M. M., & Muafi, M. (2020). The role of self-congruity in the retail store patronage model: The case of Islamic retail stores in Indonesia and Malaysia. *Journal of International Studies, 13(2)*, 62–80. https://doi.org/10.14254/2071-8330.2020/13-2/5

Alserhan, B. A. (2010). Islamic branding: A conceptualization of related terms. *Journal of Brand Management, 18(1)*, 34–49. https://doi.org/10.1057/bm.2010.18

Ambarwati, R., & Sari, D. K. (2023). Experiential marketing and Islamic branding: A new perspective on college decision in Islamic higher education. *Journal of Islamic Marketing, 15(3)*, 745–776. https://doi.org/10.1108/jima-08-2022-0207

Andini, A. L., & Rufaidah, P. (2018). The influence of Islamic branding and religiosity on brand image. *AFEBI Islamic Finance and Economic Review*, J(02), 31. https://doi.org/10.47312/aifer.v2i02.111

Bukhari, S. N. Z., & Isa, S. M. (2019). Islamic branding: Insights from a conceptual perspective. *Journal of Islamic Marketing, 11(6)*, 1743–1760. https://doi.org/10.1108/jima-02-2018-0035

Coordinating Ministry for Economic Affairs (Ekon). (2022, December 9). *Not only has a large domestic market, but Indonesia also has the opportunity to become the world's leading halal producer.* Kementerian Koordinator Bidang Perekonomian Republik Indonesia. https://www.ekon.go.id/publikasi/detail/4969/not-only-has-a-large-domestic-market-but-i ndonesia-also-has-the-opportunity-to-become-the-worlds-leading-halal-producer

Draelos, Z. D. (2021). The use of cosmetic products to improve self esteem & quality of life. *Essential Psychiatry for the Aesthetic Practitioner, 11(1)*, 34–41. https://doi.org/10.1002/9781119680116.ch3

Fahrullah, A., Zulfa, F. L., Anwar, Moch. K., Ridlwan, A. A., & Yasin, Ach. (2024). The influence of Islamic branding , religiousity, and fashion trends on Islamic fashion purchase decisions. *IQTISHODUNA: Jurnal Ekonomi Islam, 13(1)*, 59–80. https://doi.org/10.54471/iqtishoduna.v13i1.1894

Fathoni, M. A., Suryani, S., & Sumilir, S. (2022). Determinant of consumer awareness toward halal food during the covid-19 pandemic: Evidence from Indonesia. *IQTISHODUNA.' Jurnal Ekonomi Islam*, 11(1), 67. https://doi.org/10.54471/iqtishoduna.v11i1.1319

Floren, J., Rasul, T., & Gani, A. (2019). Islamic marketing and consumer behaviour: A systematic literature review. *Journal of Islamic Marketing, 11(6)*, 1557–1578. https://doi.org/10.1108/jima-05-2019-0100

Hanapi, M. S., Mastura, S., & Doktoralina, C. M. (2019). Wasatiyyah-Consumerism ethics in AI-Qur'an. *International Journal of Financial Research, 10(5)*, 204. https://doi.org/10.5430/ijfr.v10n5p204

Hecht, A. A., Perez, C. L., Polascek, M., Thorndike, A. N., Franckle, R. L., & Moran, A. J. (2020). Influence of food and beverage companies on retailer marketing strategies and consumer behavior. *International Journal of Environmental Research and Public Health*, 17(20), 7381. https://doi.org/10.3390/ijerph17207381

Herdiana, Y., & Rusdiana, T. (2022). Indonesian Halal Pharmaceutical: Challenges and market opportunities. *Indonesian Journal of Pharmaceutics*, 3(3), 99. https://doi.org/10.24198/idjp.v3i3.37660

IImi, M. N., Rahmani, R. A., Dwi Yanti, T., & Faqihuddin, A. (2024). The challenges faced by muslim female students in maintaining appearance and validity of wudhu: A study on the use of waterproof makeup. *eL-HIKMAH: Jurnal Kajian Dan Penelitian Pendidikan Islam, 18(2)*, 123–143. https://doi.org/10.20414/elhikmah.v18i2.11575

Ismail, M. S. I., Harun, T. W. R., Ismail, S., Aziz, A., & Ibrahim, M. A. (2022). Definition of Islamic Brand: A Study From Islamic Conjuction and its Findings. *International Journal of Academic Research in Business and Social Sciences, 12(8)*. https://doi.org/10.6007/ijarbss/v12-i8/14731

Jain, N. (2021). Survey versus interviews: Comparing data collection tools for exploratory research. *The Qualitative Report, 26(2)*. https://doi.org/10.46743/2160-3715/2021.4492

Lee, J., & Kwon, K. H. (2022). Sustainable changes in beauty market trends focused on the perspective of safety in the post-coronavirus disease-19 period. *Journal of Cosmetic Dermatology*, 21(7), 2700–2707. https://doi.org/10.1111/jocd.14493

Matthews, R. A., Pineault, L., & Hong, Y.-H. (2022). Normalizing the use of single-item measures: Validation of the single-item compendium for organizational psychology. *Journal of Business and Psychology, 37*(4), 639–673. https://doi.org/10.1007/s10869-022-09813-3

Millatina, A. N., Hakimi, F., Budiantoro, R. A., & Arifandi, M. R. (2022). The impact of Halal label in Halal food buying decisions. *Journal of Islamic Economic Laws, 5(1),* 159–176. https://doi.org/10.23917/jisel.v5i1.17139

Shalihin, N., Darmaiza, Sholihin, M., & Yusuf, M. (2023). Muslim millennials fashion self-congruity: How The religiosity and spiritual well-being affect? *Cogent Social Sciences,*
9(1). https://doi.org/10.1080/23311886.2023.2194110

Sirgy, M. J. (1985). Using self-congruity and ideal congruity to predict purchase motivation. *Journal of Business Research, 13(3),* 195–206. https://doi.org/10.1016/0148-2963(85)90026-8

Sirgy, M. J., & Su, C. (2000). Destination image, self-congruity, and travel behavior: Toward an integrative model. *Journal of Travel Research, 38(4),* 340–352. https://doi.org/10.1177/004728750003800402

Smith, R. K., vanDellen, M. R., & Ton, L. A. N. (2021). Makeup who you are: Self-Expression enhances the perceived authenticity and public promotion of beauty work. *Journal of Consumer Research, 48(1),* 102–122. https://doi.org/10.1093/jcr/ucaa066

Sop, S. (2020). Self-congruity theory in tourism research: A systematic review and future research directions. *European Journal of Tourism Research, 26,* 2604. https://doi.org/10.54055/ejtr.v26i.1935

Sudarsono, H., & Nugrohowati, R. N. I. (2020). Determinants of the intention to consume halal food, cosmetics and pharmaceutical products. *The Journal of Asian Finance, Economics and Business,* Z(10), 831–841. https://doi.org/10.13106/jafeb.2020.voI7.no10.831

Susilowati, F. D., Ridlwan, A. A., Fikriyah, K., & Timur, Y. P. (2023). Instagram halal cosmefics reviews: Emotion polarity and presentation modality effects on information quality and purchase intention. *IQTISHODUNA: Jurnal Ekonomi Islam, 12(2),* 471–486. https://doi.org/10.54471/iqtishoduna.v12i2.2610

Terrell, S. (2015). Mixed-Methods research methodologies. *The Qualitative Report,* 1Z(1). https://doi.org/10.46743/2160-3715/2012.1819

Wahyuni, S., & Fitriani, N. (2017). Brand religiosity aura and brand loyalty in Indonesia Islamic banking. *Journal of Islamic Marketing, 8(3),* 361–372. https://doi.org/10.1108/jima-06-2015-0044

Zainol, Z., Noor, N., & Tong, A. (2024). Faithful and luxurious: Mediating halal with luxury through self-congruity. *Journal of Global Fashion Markenng, 15(4),* 422–439. https://doi.org/10.1080/20932685.2024.2346841

Muhammad Rizky Prima Sakti, Thuraya Saleh Al-Qarni

Chapter 11 The Critical Success Factors and Challenges of Women-Run and Owned Businesses in Contemporary Saudi Arabia: A Perspective on Islam and Modernity

Abstract: This study examines the role of women-run and women-owned business in the contemporary Saudi Arabia, underscoring their contribution the nation's modernization under Vision 2030. A qualitative thematic analysis was conducted with ten Saudi women entrepreneurs to explore the critical success factors and challenges they face in the contemporary Saudi's business landscape. The findings reveal that family and personal networks, strong government support on women-business, and importance of Shariah are pivotal role in shaping women-entrepreneurial journeys. Additionally, the notable challenges facing by women-run and owned business, including socio-cultural norms, lack of opportunities, and legal complexities under Sharia law and broader commercial legal frameworks. Its also clear that these women entrepreneurs recognize the importance of acquiring knowledge about Sharia law to navigating the business landscape in the Saudi Arabia. The findings of this study are crucial not only for women-entrepreneurs but also for policy makers aiming to empower and accelerate the success of women entrepreneurship in the Kingdom. The insights gained can inform initiatives designed to break down barriers, foster growth, and contribute to the broader goals of Vision 2030

Keywords: Women, Business, Entrepreneurship, Saudi Arabia, Islam, Vision 2030

11.1 Introduction

In Saudi Arabia, as well as in other developing economies across the Middle East, an increasing number of women are taking the reins of their own businesses. This trend is not limited to the region, as women worldwide are recognizing the significant impact on both society and the economy. More and more women are pursuing careers in entrepreneurship, understanding that it not only enhances their financial security but also improves their overall quality of life. As a result, the number of women choosing entrepreneurship as a career path continues to rise. Saudi Arabia has successfully diversified its economy away from its reliance on oil and gas sector, resulting in rapid economic improvement. Under the leadership of His Majesty King Salman and Crown Prince Mohammed bin Salman, the country's economic transformation has gained momen-

https://doi.org/10.1515/9783111575407-012

tum. Historically, women in Saudi Arabia faced legal restrictions that prevented them from pursuing jobs outside the home, but in recent years, these restrictions have gradually been relaxed.

Researchers have noted that Saudi Arabia's unique cultural context, shaped by Arab and Islamic values, significantly influences the entrepreneurial paths of business owners. These values have been crucial in shaping the growth and development of Saudi Arabia, given its role as the birthplace of both Arab and Islamic traditions. Previous studies have explored the impact of family support, self-confidence, risk-taking, and a lack of business skills on women's productivity (Nanda & Sorensen, 2008, Postigo, 2021). The success of women-owned businesses is influenced by several factors, including government policies, access to financial resources, cultural norms, and regulations (Postigo, 2021; Yadav & Umi, 2016). This study seeks to explore of both internal and external factors on the success of women-owned businesses in Saudi Arabia, where religious, cultural, and societal dynamics often differ from those in developed nations. High levels of economic and political uncertainty pose significant challenges for female entrepreneurs, with government policies and environmental factors potentially affecting employee motivation and confidence.

The primary objective of this study is to identify the critical success factors and barriers faced by female business owners in Saudi Arabia. Many entrepreneurship scholars come from western countries, raising questions about the relevance, biases, and applicability of their perspectives to Arab countries. Despite the wealth of theoretical literature, the practical implications for developing economies, such as Saudi Arabia, remain unclear. This research is crucial for understanding the environment in which women-owned businesses operate, providing valuable insights for policymakers, female entrepreneurs, and community leaders to further research and develop strategies for empowering female business owners.

11.2 Previous Studies on Entrepreneurship

Women business owners are recognized as a key driver of growth in the small and medium-sized business sector, significantly contributing to the expansion and modernization of free enterprise in developing and transitional economies. However, most current theoretical frameworks regarding women-owned businesses are primarily based on the experiences of women in Western countries. While research on female entrepreneurs has been conducted in other developing and transitional economies, the Arab world has received less scholarly attention.

One of important aspect in elevate entrepreneurship is education. Entrepreneurship education aims to cultivate an entrepreneurial mindset by exposing students to business practices and providing opportunities for hands-on learning. Studies by Galloway et al. (2005) show that individuals with formal entrepreneurship training are more likely to pursue business ventures and identify market opportunities. Research by Souitaris et al. (2007) found that students who participated in entrepreneurship courses were more likely to start businesses after graduation. Similarly, Wilson et al. (2007) demonstrated that exposure to entrepreneurship education increases interest in business ownership, while Turker and Selcuk (2009) found that higher education fosters entrepreneurial thinking among Turkish university students.

Work experience or an entrepreneurial background is also a critical factor. Previous job experiences often shape one's entrepreneurial perspective. Kolvereid (1996) found that individuals with prior business experience exhibited higher entrepreneurial intentions compared to those without such experience. Drennan et al. (2013) noted that individuals with a positive perception of a family business are more likely to want to start their own enterprise.

Relational support, which refers to financial and emotional encouragement from close contacts during the startup phase, also plays a crucial role (Türker & Selçuk, 2009). Nanda and Sorensen (2008) emphasized the importance of social networks when making career decisions, while Postigo et al. (2021) suggested that role models provide valuable guidance for entrepreneurs. Among young Australians, peer pressure has been identified as a significant factor in entrepreneurial decisions (Nanda & Sorensen, 2008).

Women entrepreneurs strive to grow their businesses beyond mere survival. Yadav & Unni (2016) discovered that women-led businesses often face greater challenges in the early stages of development. Factors such as limited capital, difficulty scaling, time constraints, role juggling, inadequate record-keeping, price fluctuations, weather-related challenges, lack of business training, and insufficient education can hinder business success. While some of these challenges are common to businesses led by both men and women, this study focuses on the unique obstacles faced by women-owned enterprises.

A baseline understanding of women in business in the Arab is needed to compare and contrast the experiences of Arab women entrepreneurs with those of their global counterparts. Tlaiss and McAdam (2021) revealed that Islam has a pivotal role that influence the success of Arab Muslim women entrepreneurs, and Islam supports the women's agency in business landscape. This has echoed the earlier study by Dechant and Lamky (2005) who found that Arab women entrepreneurs in Bahrain and Oman are infused with Arab and Islamic values.

11.3 Data, Sampling, and Analysis

11.3.1 Data and Sample

This study explores the experiences of women business owners in Saudi Arabia. To answer the research questions, qualitative data was collected through interviews with ten women entrepreneurs who operate their own businesses across four different cities within the Kingdom of Saudi Arabia. The selection of these women entrepreneurs was based on the researcher's professional knowledge and judgment of their influence in the business community. Rather than being randomly selected, the participants were deliberately chosen to align with the objectives of the study. As such, the most appropriate sampling method employed is judgmental sampling, also known as purposive or authoritative sampling.

11.3.2 Thematic Analysis

Thematic analysis is a widely used method of qualitative data analysis that involves identifying, analyzing, and interpreting patterns within selected qualitative data (Braun & Clarke, 2014). This method enables researchers to recognize specific themes and structures in the data, offering a comprehensive understanding of the underlying meaning. A key strength of thematic analysis is its flexibility, as it can be applied to a variety of data types, research questions, study designs, and sample sizes (Marks & Yardley, 2004). This makes it particularly valuable for research across different disciplines and contexts.

In the context of this study, thematic analysis is essential for ensuring that the research objectives are aligned with the data and that the themes are coherently connected to the overall content. It allows for a systematic approach to interpreting the experiences, behaviors, and thoughts represented in the data, helping to maintain consistency throughout the analysis process (Braun & Clarke, 2014). By employing thematic analysis, the researcher can gain a deeper understanding of the topic, while also preparing to address any emerging complexities. This approach not only enhances the clarity of the research findings but also ensures that the analysis remains nuanced and precise.

11.4 Findings

11.4.1 Interviewee's Profile

For this research, ten Saudi Arabian women were interviewed to compare their experiences in establishing businesses with those of women in both developed and developing nations (*see* Table 11.1). The interviews revealed that both the length of experience in business and educational background play significant roles in determining business success. Throughout the interviews, the participants demonstrated a clear understanding of the intricacies of running a business. Each participant had varying levels of experience and education.

Interviewee A has three years of experience and holds a high level of education. Interviewee B has been in business for 2.5 years and holds a BA in Business Administration. Interviewee C, with only six months of experience, has no formal business education. Interviewee D has been in business for 10 years, possesses basic education, but plans to update her skills through additional business courses. Interviewee E has almost seven years of experience and holds a BA in Business Administration, while Interviewee F has been running her business for six years and also has a BA in Business Administration. Interviewee G has been in business for three years and holds an MA in Business Administration. Interviewee H, with 15 years in business, has no formal business education but is eager to expand her knowledge of business development and the Saudi economy over the next five years. Interviewee I, with almost two years of experience, holds an MA in Business Administration. Finally, Interviewee J has been in business for seven years and has a BA in Business Administration.

Despite their varying levels of experience and education, all participants expressed a strong desire to gain more knowledge about business practices and better understand the workings of the Saudi Arabian economy. While some are newcomers to business, others are seasoned entrepreneurs who have navigated numerous challenges and successes throughout their journeys.

Table 11.1: Profile of Interviewees.

No	Interviewee's	Lengths of Experience in Business	Education Levels
1.	A	3 years	Higher Level of Business Education
2.	B	2.5 years	BA in Business Administration
3.	C	6 months	No formal education
4.	D	10 years	Basic education
5.	E	7 years	BA in Business Administration
6.	F	6 years	BA in Business Administration
7.	G	3 years	MA in Business Administration
8.	H	15 years	No formal education
9.	I	2 years	MA in Business Administration
10.	J	7 years	BA in Business Administration

11.4.2 Motivation of Women Entrepreneurs-run a Business in Saudi Arabia

Women entrepreneurs often have the support of their families, but their motivations for starting businesses can vary. In some cases, it is a necessity driven by circumstances; in others, it is the influence of a family business. More frequently, it stems from a personal desire to do something meaningful, create a distinct place for themselves in society, and contribute to the larger community. As the world evolves, both women and entrepreneurs have recognized the importance of playing an active role in building a stronger, better society—for themselves and the women who will follow in their footsteps.

Interviewee A started her business out of necessity, as she could not find a suitable job. She wanted to pursue something she loved and was passionate about, stating,

"To be honest, I did not find a job, and I tried to create an opportunity for myself by doing something I love. Maybe in the future, I will never give up."

Interviewee B, motivated by her strong business skills and desire for financial independence, aimed to bring a unique brand to life and expand her business activities. Interviewee C, driven by her ambition to enter business management, was determined to establish her own company. Interviewee D opened her business in line with her childhood dream of becoming an entrepreneur and contributing to the welfare of her country. She also has plans to expand her business within the Gulf region, sharing, "*The reason for starting my business is that I had a childhood dream of becoming a woman entrepreneur and doing something that contributes to the welfare of the country. Maybe in the future, I will expand my business to the Gulf region.*"

Interviewee E embarked on her entrepreneurial journey with a goal to contribute to the improvement of Saudi Arabia's economy. Interviewee F, faced with a salary that didn't cover her expenses, turned to entrepreneurship as a financial solution. Interviewee G started her business with the same goal of enhancing the Saudi economy. Interviewee H, passionate about becoming an expert in women entrepreneurship and a female leader, expressed, "*The reason for starting my business is that I wanted to become an expert in women entrepreneurship and a woman leader.*" Interviewee I's motivation was to contribute to the progress and economic development of her country, a sentiment shared by Interviewee J.

While each interviewee had her unique reason for starting a business, common threads emerged: they are all (i) committed to becoming successful entrepreneurs, (ii) expanding their businesses, and (iii) strengthening their country's economy. These women are not only focused on personal success but also on contributing to the broader societal and economic landscape.

11.4.3 Critical Success Factors of Women Entrepreneurs in Saudi Arabia

The success of a business often depends on the hard work and dedication of the entrepreneurs, but several other factors also contribute to the achievements of women entrepreneurs in Saudi Arabia. The interviewees provided various insights into the support systems that played a crucial role in their success. Some attributed their achievements to the strong support from their parents, while others credited their husbands, friends, and relatives. Based on the interviews, several common factors emerged that have contributed to the success of women entrepreneurs in Saudi Arabia:

- Family and friend support
- Timing of Launching the Project
- Modernization of Saudi and Government Support under Vision 2030
- Importance of shariah law

Most of the interviewees emphasized that family support is a critical element in the success of their businesses. Interviewee A, for instance, shared, "*My parents have always encouraged me. Their belief in me gave me the confidence to keep pushing forward, even when I faced obstacles.*" Interviewee B echoed this sentiment, saying, "*My husband has been a pillar of support. His encouragement and belief in my ideas helped me start my business, especially when the challenges seemed too much to handle.*" Similarly, Interviewee F noted, "*I couldn't have made it without the support of my close friends and relatives—they've been a constant source of advice and motivation.*"

However, support extends beyond family and friends. Some interviewees identified the timing of their project launch and the work plan as significant factors in their success. Interviewee C mentioned, "*The timing of my business launch aligned well with the growing demand in the market, which gave me an edge. I also made sure to have a solid business plan in place.*" Interviewee G stressed the importance of ongoing learning and personal growth, saying, "*Continuous learning and self-control have been key to staying competitive. I always seek out new knowledge to improve my business practices.*"

The women also acknowledged the positive impact of the Saudi government's policies on their entrepreneurial journeys. Interviewee D explained, "*The 2030 Vision has opened many doors for women entrepreneurs. There are now fewer restrictions, and the government's support through various initiatives has been invaluable in helping me grow my business.*" Interviewee H noted, "*I've benefited greatly from the facilities provided by the Saudi government, especially financial support and training programs that have been tailored to women entrepreneurs.*" Moreover, Interviewee G shared, "*The modernization of Saudi Arabia has greatly contributed to my success as a businesswoman. The government's push for Vision 2030 has made it easier for women to access resources and networks that were previously unavailable. This shift towards modernity empowers women to excel and expand their businesses.*"

Moreover, many of the interviewees highlighted the importance of Shariah law in shaping their entrepreneurial journeys. Shariah law, which governs various aspects of life in Saudi Arabia, plays a critical role in business operations, particularly for women entrepreneurs. Several interviewees mentioned how they have navigated the intersection of business and Shariah principles in their ventures. Interviewee A, for example, shared, "*In my business, I always make sure to comply with the ethical guidelines set by Shariah law. This has helped me build trust with my customers, who appreciate knowing that my business operates according to Islamic principles.*" Similarly, Interviewee B discussed the challenge of balancing entrepreneurship with religious guidelines: "*While I am focused on expanding my business, I ensure that my practices align with Shariah. It's important for me to maintain transparency and fairness in all my dealings, as this resonates well with both my clients and partners.*" Interviewee D also noted, "*Shariah law encourages fair trade and ethical business, which has helped me make decisions that are both profitable and morally sound.*"

In conclusion, while family and personal networks are essential to their success, the broader support & modernization from the Saudi government and importance of

Shariah law in shaping women-entrepreneurial journeys play a pivotal role in their achievements.

11.4.4 Challenges Facing Women Entrepreneurs in Saudi Arabia

There has been considerable progress made by women entrepreneurs in Saudi Arabia, but despite these advancements, they continue to face significant social, cultural, educational, and technological barriers. These barriers are especially prominent when launching, growing businesses, and accessing economic resources. As women-led businesses expand, they encounter even greater challenges. Several barriers were common across the interviewees' responses:

- Lack of awareness about available opportunities: Many interviewees mentioned that they were not fully aware of the entrepreneurial opportunities available to women in Saudi Arabia. This lack of awareness often led to delays in decision-making and business development.
- Access to financing and investors: The ability to secure funding is a critical issue, with women often finding it harder to access the financial resources needed for growth compared to their male counterparts. Interviewee I noted, *"The most challenging aspects of running a business as a woman in Saudi Arabia were keeping up with the market, planning ahead, and managing cash flow. Access to capital is limited for women, and financial planning is often a challenge, especially when dealing with unpredictable market conditions and delayed government payments."*
- Balancing work and family life: Several entrepreneurs expressed how difficult it was to juggle their business responsibilities with family expectations, a challenge often compounded by socio-cultural norms.
- Shariah Islamic law and extensive commercial law: One of the notable challenges noted by Interviewee E was navigating the legal framework, which is heavily influenced by Shariah law. As she explained, *"The most challenging aspect of running a business as a woman in Saudi Arabia was the legal system of Saudi Arabia, which is based on Shariah Islamic Law. This system is unique in the region and must be understood thoroughly. Commercial law is extensive, and a woman entrepreneur must know how to operate within it. Most legal processes are conducted by Saudis, and everything is done in Arabic.* "Additionally, the constraints imposed by Shariah law were mentioned by several interviewees. Interviewee B remarked, *"While Shariah law ensures fairness, it also adds layers of complexity. For example, finding financing options that comply with Islamic law can be difficult, as interest-based loans are not permissible.*
- Socio-Cultural Norms: Another challenge discussed in the interviews was the socio-cultural norms that often restrict women's roles in business. Interviewee H shared, *"In Saudi Arabia, there is still a traditional view of women being primarily responsible for family roles, which makes it difficult for women to be fully accepted*

in the business world. It's not always easy to prove yourself when society has preconceived notions about what women should or shouldn't do." This reflects the broader societal norms that still place limitations on women's participation in economic activities, despite the ongoing efforts to empower them through reforms like Saudi Vision 2030.

Despite these significant barriers, women entrepreneurs in Saudi Arabia continue to push forward, striving to overcome challenges related to Shariah law, socio-cultural norms, and limited opportunities. While there are still obstacles to be faced, the ongoing development of legal frameworks and government support are helping women to succeed in the business world, contributing to Saudi Arabia's economic growth.

11.4.5 Accelerate Women Entrepreneurs in Saudi Arabia

The acceleration of women entrepreneurship in Saudi Arabia is achievable with a robust support system involving family, friends, acquaintances, and, most importantly, government support. This comprehensive support is seen as a key enabler for women to expand their businesses and achieve sustainable success.

The women entrepreneurs interviewed expressed high optimism for their business growth over the next five years. They believe that with the right support and strategies, their businesses will flourish both personally and financially. Some participants anticipate a 5% revenue growth, while others are more ambitious, expecting a 9% to 10% increase in revenue. Despite these varying expectations, all the interviewees—ranging from Interviewee A to Interviewee J—are confident that revenue will rise within the next five years, underscoring their optimism and ambition for the future.

Furthermore, these entrepreneurs are also placing significant value on formal business education. While most of the interviewees are already highly educated and have considerable experience, a few have only basic education. However, all of them are committed to enhancing their knowledge by pursuing higher education or professional training in the coming years. They recognize that business education is not just supplementary but a critical key to long-term success. Many of the participants expressed interest in gaining expertise in key areas such as Sharia law and understanding the complexities of running a business successfully in Saudi Arabia. As Interviewee G stated, *"I am fully committed to improving my knowledge in both business management and the legal nuances of operating a business under Saudi laws, especially Sharia law."*

Most of the women entrepreneurs are also focused on formalizing their businesses and enhancing their professional credibility by obtaining a commercial register. This is seen as a crucial step towards securing their rights and expanding their ventures. Interviewee C shared, *"I am definitely thinking of getting a commercial register in the future because it guarantees my rights to work and makes my project official and recognized by the Ministry of Commerce. I am confident that my business will see significant growth in the next five years, and I will also have gained invaluable experience in managing special projects."*

This forward-thinking attitude highlights the entrepreneurs' commitment to long-term success. Despite not having formal business education at the start, Interviewee C and others are determined to elevate their business acumen through online entrepreneurship courses in the coming years. The overarching theme among the interviewees is a shared belief in continuous self-improvement, both personally and professionally. As they look ahead, they are not only aiming for success but are actively planning to expand their businesses, open multiple branches across the Kingdom, and increase their revenue streams, contributing significantly to the growing female entrepreneurial presence in Saudi Arabia.

11.5 Conclusion and Recommendations

Women entrepreneurs in Saudi Arabia have shown considerable progress in the contemporary era of Saudi Arabia. They have recognized their strengths and the importance of perseverance in realizing their dreams. While they are aware of the challenges, including socio-cultural norms, lack of opportunities, and legal complexities under Sharia law, they remain determined to find solutions and succeed. Many women-entrepreneurs in the Kingdom rely on the support of their families, friends, and government resources to fuel their business ambitions. Looking ahead, the interviewed women expressed strong optimism about the future, under Saudi Vision 20230. They anticipate revenue growth in the next five years, with some expecting a 5% increase, while others are more ambitious, projecting 9–10% growth. Moreover, they recognize the value of learning about Sharia law and other nuances essential to navigating the business landscape in Saudi Arabia.

Future research should focus on the impact of Sharia law on female entrepreneurship in Saudi Arabia, exploring how legal frameworks influence business operations. Additionally, examining the role of government policies and family support systems in empowering women entrepreneurs can offer insights into further accelerating their success.

References

Braun, V., & Clarke, V. (2014). What can "thematic analysis" offer health and wellbeing researchers?. *International journal of qualitative studies on health and well-being*, *9*(1), 26152.

Dechant, K., & Lamky, A. A. (2005). Toward an understanding of Arab women entrepreneurs in Bahrain and Oman. *Journal of Developmental Entrepreneurship*, 10(02), 123–140.

Galloway, L., & Anderson, M., & Brown, W., & Wilson, L. (2005). Enterprise skills for the economy. Education + Training, 47.

Kolvereid, L. (1996). Prediction of employment status choice intentions. Entrepreneurship.

Marks, D. & Yardley, L. (2004). Research methods for clinical and health psychology. SAGE

Nanda, R., & Sørensen, J. B. (2008). *Peer effects and entrepreneurship*. Boston: Harvard Business School.

Postigo, Á., Cuesta, M., García-Cueto, E., Prieto-Díez, F., & Muñiz, J. (2021). General versus specific personality traits for predicting entrepreneurship. *Personality and Individual Differences*, *182*, 111094.

Souitaris, V., & Zerbinati, S., & Al-Laham, A. (2007).The effect of learning, inspiration and resources. *Journal of Business Venturing*, 22, 566–591.

Tlaiss, H. A., & McAdam, M. (2021). Islam, Arab women's entrepreneurship and the construal of success. *International Journal of Entrepreneurial Behavior & Research*, 27(3), 821–844.

Turker, D., & Selcuk, S.S. (2009). Which factors affect entrepreneurial intention of university students? *Journal of European Industrial Training*.

Wilson, F., & Kickul, J., & Marlino, D. (2007). *Gender, Entrepreneurial Self-Efficacy, and Entrepreneurial Career Intentions: Implications for Entrepreneurship Education*.

Yadav, V., & Unni, J. (2016). Women entrepreneurship: research review and future directions. *Journal of Global Entrepreneurship Research*, *6*, 1–18.

Amirul Afif Muhamat, Nurul Syifaa Mohd Shakil, Nur'asyiqin Ramdhan, Shahsuzan Zakaria, Roslina Mohd Shafi, Mohamad Nizam Jaafar & Arief Wibisono Lubis

Chapter 12 Determinants of Enterprise Risk Management (ERM) Adoption Amongst the Shariah-Compliant Construction Companies in Malaysia

Abstract: This study delves into the determinants of Enterprise Risk Management (ERM) adoption among publicly listed Malaysian construction companies that adhere to Shariah principles. The research spans the period from 2007 to 2016, a timeframe marked by significant government initiatives and projects aimed at bolstering the construction sector. Notably, this period witnessed the launch of the East Coast Rail Link (ECRL), a monumental infrastructure project stretching 665 kilometers from Port Klang, Selangor to Wakaf Bahru, Kelantan. Additionally, the Klang Valley Mass Rapid Transit (KVMRT) project, which commenced in 2011 and reached completion in 2016, further underscores the dynamic developments within this period. The study employs a sample of Malaysian construction enterprises that comply with Shariah principles as outlined by Bursa Malaysia. Utilizing logistic regression analysis, the research identifies several key factors that influence the adoption of ERM. These factors include the scale of the company, financial leverage, the reputation of foreign auditors, and profitability. Interestingly, the analysis reveals that stock price volatility and board independence do not exhibit statistical significance in influencing ERM adoption. The findings of this study hold significant implications for regulators. By leveraging these insights, regulators can develop strategies to incentivize Shariah-compliant construction companies to adopt ERM practices. Such measures would enhance transparency and governance within the sector, ultimately contributing to its sustainable growth and stability.

Keywords: Shariah-compliant, construction companies, enterprise risk management

Acknowledgement: We would like to extend our heartfelt gratitude to the Research Management Centre (RMC) UiTM for generously awarding us the research grant under file number 600-RMC 5/3/GPM (110/2022). Our sincerest appreciation also goes to the Faculty of Business and Management UiTM for their unwavering support throughout this research project. Additionally, we wish to express our deep thanks to Nur Faziera Mohamed Nassir and Siti Aisyah Abdul Mutalib for their invaluable contributions and active involvement in this endeavour.

https://doi.org/10.1515/9783111575407-013

12.1 Introduction

Enterprise Risk Management (ERM) serves as a crucial governance tool, particularly in times of rising corporate scandals, to address agency issues and enhance organizational resilience (Desender, 2011). Lundqvist and Vilhelmsson (2016) highlight that ERM can significantly reduce a company's default risk by improving information retrieval and monitoring processes, thereby mitigating agency risk. Furthermore, ERM facilitates access to capital and essential resources necessary for the seamless operation of a business (Nocco & Rene, 2022). In the context of Oman, ERM has been suggested to contribute to sustainability and financial performance, underscoring its broader benefits (Khan, Alkathiri, Alhaddad & Alnajjar, 2021).

However, Kurbonov and Saidov (2022) note that practitioners often face challenges due to a lack of comprehensive information on ERM management. This study focuses on Shariah-compliant construction companies in Malaysia, a sector notably plagued by integrity issues (The Star Online, 2014). The Shariah-compliant status of these companies mandates adherence to moral and ethical standards in line with Islamic precepts (Muhamat, Jaafar & Basri, 2017; Muhamat, Basri et al., 2023).

This chapter is structured as follows: it begins with a brief discussion on economic crime and the imperative role of ERM in combating it. This is followed by an exploration of Shariah-compliant companies and a review of previous ERM studies. The chapter concludes with a detailed discussion of the research findings and their implications, providing a comprehensive understanding of the factors influencing ERM adoption in Shariah-compliant construction companies in Malaysia.

12.2 Economic Crime

Economic crime, defined as the illegal acquisition of monetary gain or privilege, poses a significant threat to business integrity and economic stability (Tan, Viksnins & Kumar, 2018). The primary objective of such crimes is to secure financial gain through unethical means. The 2018 Global Economic Crime and Fraud Survey (Figure 12.1) highlights the alarming prevalence of economic crime in Malaysia, revealing that 41% of Malaysian companies reported involvement in economic crime over the past two years, a substantial increase from 28% in 2016. This data underscores the pervasive nature of fraud and corruption within the business sector.

According to Tan, Viksnins, and Kumar (2018), a majority of business leaders have identified fraud and corruption as critical risks to their operations. Despite the ongoing prevalence of these issues, many businesses continue to exhibit lax internal controls, which exacerbate the problem. To effectively combat economic crime and ensure long-term organizational stability, it is imperative for companies to fully adopt and implement Enterprise Risk Management (ERM). ERM provides a structured framework for identifying, assessing, and mitigating risks, thereby enhancing transparency, accountability, and governance within organizations.

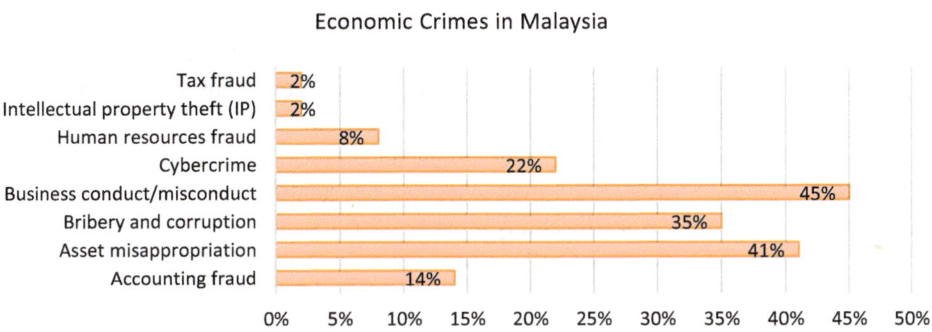

Figure 12.1: Economic Crimes in Malaysia.
Source: Global Economic Crime and Fraud Survey 2018 (Malaysia Report).

The construction industry is widely regarded as one of the most hazardous and high-risk sectors globally (Gonzalez Fajardo, Solis Carcano & Juan, 2018). The inherent dangers of the industry, often encapsulated by the "3D" descriptor—dangerous, difficult, and dirty—are compounded by the involvement of a diverse array of stakeholders, including suppliers, clients, workers, and financial institutions. These multifaceted interactions introduce a spectrum of risks that can significantly impact the overall performance of construction firms if not adequately managed.

The complexity and dynamic nature of construction projects further exacerbate these risks, introducing significant unpredictability. The industry is vulnerable to a variety of hazards, encompassing technical, socio-political, and economic risks. Despite the critical importance of risk management, the adoption of Enterprise Risk Management (ERM) within the construction sector remains relatively informal. While listed firms in Malaysia are mandated to implement ERM, the primary challenge lies in the effective execution of ERM strategies.

Financial and contractual risks are particularly detrimental to the successful completion of construction projects. Financial risks pertain to the availability of funds necessary for procuring raw materials and compensating subcontractors and employees. Contractual risks, on the other hand, involve the relationships between project stakeholders, inadequate record-keeping, and imprecise contract structuring (Akintoye & MacLeod, 1997). These risks underscore the necessity for robust ERM practices to ensure the successful and timely completion of construction projects.

Given the critical importance of fostering an ERM culture within the construction sector, this study aims to address this need comprehensively. The specific objectives of this research are twofold:

i. Investigate the adoption of ERM by Shariah-compliant construction companies: This objective seeks to understand the extent to which Shariah-compliant construction firms in Malaysia have integrated ERM practices into their operations. By examining the adoption rates and identifying the factors that facilitate or hinder this process, the study aims to provide a clear picture of the current state of ERM within these companies.

ii. Evaluate the impact of ERM determinants on Shariah-compliant construction companies: This objective focuses on assessing how various determinants influence the adoption and effectiveness of ERM in Shariah-compliant construction firms. Key determinants include company scale, financial leverage, the reputation of foreign auditors, profitability, stock price volatility, and board independence. By evaluating the impact of these factors, the study aims to offer insights into the conditions that promote or impede successful ERM implementation.

Through these objectives, the study aspires to contribute valuable knowledge to the field of risk management, particularly within the context of Shariah-compliant construction companies in Malaysia. The findings are expected to inform both industry practitioners and regulators, guiding efforts to enhance transparency, governance, and overall risk management practices in the sector.

12.3 Enterprise Risk Management (ERM)

Enterprise Risk Management (ERM) is a comprehensive process undertaken by a company's board of directors, management, and employees to achieve strategic objectives, such as enhancing financial performance through cost-effective measures. ERM can be defined as the strategic utilization of resources to gain a competitive advantage (Yang, Muhammad & Anwar, 2018). It serves as a "trigger mechanism" for organizations to anticipate and mitigate future events that could jeopardize their operations or financial performance. Risk management solutions should be tailored to align with the company's risk tolerance (Shad & Lai, 2015).

Shamsuddin (2018) posits that ERM provides a structured framework for risk management, which typically involves identifying specific events or circumstances relevant to a company's goals (both risks and opportunities), assessing their likelihood and potential impact, determining appropriate response strategies, and continuously monitoring the process. The company's annual report is often the primary vehicle for communicating the ERM practices that have been implemented.

According to Zainuddin, Togok, and Isa (2015), there are three primary techniques for identifying ERM adopters and their levels of adoption. One approach is to establish a specialized managerial position, such as a Chief Risk Officer (CRO), as evidence of ERM programs. Another method involves conducting surveys to assess the degree of ERM adoption. Additionally, financial reports, newswires, and other media sources can be examined for indications of ERM activities. Their findings indicate that 29 out of 46 construction enterprises have implemented ERM. A recent study involving over 300 construction firms in China demonstrated that proper ERM implementation significantly influences organizational performance (Wangyanwen, Senathirajah & Haque, 2023).

12.4 Shariah-Compliant Construction Companies

The Securities Commission of Malaysia has established criteria to determine whether a company is Shariah-compliant. For listed companies, the Shariah Advisory Council of the Securities Commission Malaysia (SAC of SC) employs a two-tier quantitative approach, which includes business activity benchmarks and financial ratio benchmarks, to assess Shariah compliance (Khouildi et al., 2017; SAC SC, 2022).

According to the business activity benchmarks, the contribution of Shariah non-compliant activities to the group's revenue and profit before taxation must be less than 5% for activities such as conventional banking and lending, conventional insurance, gambling, liquor and liquor-related activities, non-halal food and beverages, tobacco and tobacco-related activities, interest income from conventional accounts and instruments, dividends from Shariah non-compliant investments, Shariah non-compliant entertainment, and other activities deemed non-compliant according to Shariah principles. For activities such as share trading, stockbroking, rental income from Shariah non-compliant activities, and other similar activities, the benchmark is set at less than 20%.

The financial ratio benchmarks are designed to measure *riba* (interest) and *riba*-based elements within a company's financial statements, with a threshold of less than 33%. The financial ratios used include cash over total assets (where cash includes only cash placed in conventional accounts and instruments) and debt over total assets (where debt includes only interest-bearing debt).

In addition to the quantitative criteria, qualitative screening is also conducted to ensure that the company's public perception or image is favourable from a Shariah perspective. Achieving Shariah-compliant status can attract investment from both Muslim and non-Muslim investors. However, in Malaysia's parallel financial system, non-Shariah-compliant businesses face no legal consequences, although devout Muslims may avoid investing in such firms. As of the end of 2021, nearly 80% of the firms listed on the Malaysian bourse are Shariah-compliant.

12.5 Determinants of Enterprise Risk Management (ERM)

This section explores the significant determinants of ERM adoption as discussed in previous studies. While the factors influencing ERM adoption can be generalized across most companies, it is essential to consider industry-specific issues. For instance, ERM practices in financial institutions differ from those in construction companies due to the unique risks and exposures each industry faces (Ali, Alasan & Khan, 2021).

i. Firm Size (FS)
Firm size, measured by the net asset value of the business, is a critical determinant of ERM adoption (Yegon, Mouni & Wanjau, 2014). As the size of an organization increases, the nature, timing, and scale of the events that threaten it will vary (Desender, 2007; Golshan & Abdul Rasid, 2012). Larger organizations can allocate more resources to ERM implementation, leading to a significant positive association between firm size and ERM adoption (Beasley, Clune & Hermanson, 2005; Golshan & Abdul Rasid, 2012; Gatzert & Martin, 2015). The necessity of having sufficient assets and utilizing firm revenue to fund ERM programs was also emphasized in the study conducted by Pagach and Warr (2007).

ii. Financial Leverage (LEV)
Financial leverage refers to the amount of debt a firm uses to acquire additional "productive" assets. It is employed to minimize the reliance on equity for funding operations (Jaba, Robu & Balan, 2017). When a company leverages, it borrows money to purchase assets that facilitate its growth and operations. Other financial instruments, such as options and futures, can also generate leverage. The primary goal of leveraging is growth. However, excessive financial leverage increases the risk of bankruptcy due to high debt levels, especially during financial distress or economic downturns (Yazid, Razali & Hussin, 2012). Consequently, a leveraged company must manage bankruptcy risk or remain in financial difficulty. This necessity encourages companies to implement ERM.

Pagach and Warr (2007) suggest that companies practicing leverage should adopt ERM. Firms with high leverage are more likely to be concerned about ERM. Liebenberg and Hoyt (2003) further state that such companies are more inclined to appoint a Chief Risk Officer (CRO). Golshan and Rahid (2009) argue that companies with high financial leverage depend more on debt to meet their obligations and may face bankruptcy risks. Therefore, these companies are more likely to use ERM to mitigate bankruptcy risks. Conversely, Gatzert and Martin (2015) found that companies with lower financial leverage tend to implement ERM despite perceived lower financial risks.

Interestingly, Hoyt and Liebenberg (2011) discovered a significant negative relationship between financial leverage and ERM adoption, indicating that companies with high financial leverage are less likely to adopt ERM. This finding contrasts with the earlier studies by Liebenberg and Hoyt (2003) and Golshan and Rahid (2009), which found a positive relationship between leverage and ERM adoption.

iii. Prominence of International Auditors (BIG4)
Several studies have identified a significant positive relationship between ERM adoption and the choice of a company's auditor, specifically the "Big Four" audit firms (Lechner & Gatzert, 2018). The "Big Four" refers to KPMG, Ernst & Young, Deloitte, and Pricewa-

terhouseCoopers (Simunic & Biddle, 2019). The presence of these auditors is likely to influence companies to implement ERM due to their global reputation for expertise and experience in ensuring transparency and accuracy in annual reports. Lechner and Gatzert (2018) emphasize that the Big Four audit firms are renowned for maintaining their international reputation through rigorous auditing standards. Additionally, there is a positive relationship between risk management and audit fees, which tend to be higher when a company engages one of the Big Four auditors (Kneche & Willekens, 2006).

iv. Stock Price Volatility (SPV)
Pagach and Warr (2011) suggest that stock price volatility is a significant determinant influencing ERM adoption. However, Golshan and Abdul Rasid (2012) challenged this claim based on their findings, which may be attributed to differences in sample sizes. Pagach and Warr (2011) focused on 26 companies, while Golshan and Abdul Rasid studied 90 companies. Another study by Liebenberg and Hoyt (2003) also described stock price volatility as insignificant. Companies with higher stock price volatility are more likely to adopt ERM due to its impact on reducing stock price and income volatility, lowering external capital costs, increasing capital efficiency, and creating synergies between various risk management activities.

Construction company managers must use risk profiles to evaluate risk-return trade-offs in investment decisions within the firm's risk appetite. A holistic approach to risk management can reduce the volatility of income, cash flow, and stock prices. Higher stock price volatility signifies that a company faces more significant risks, and adopting ERM can provide substantial benefits (Gatzert & Martin, 2015).

v. Independence of Board of Directors (BOD)
The term "independence of the board of directors" refers to a management board with no material or financial ties to the company (Golshan & Rasid, 2012). Desender (2011) asserts that the independence of the board of directors drives comprehensive risk management and auditing, as the presence of non-executive directors promotes complete control, risk management, and audit processes, reducing the likelihood of fraudulent reporting. Mohd Sanusi et al. (2017) emphasize that the independence of the board motivates them to undertake more extensive risk management and auditing to fulfil their responsibilities effectively.

vi. Profitability (ROA)
Yazid, Razali, and Hussin (2012) highlight that profitable companies use their profits for various purposes to sustain operations and ensure good returns. One effective way to achieve this is by implementing ERM to reduce, avoid, or transfer risks. There is a positive link between profitability and ERM adoption. Lechner and Gazert (2018) state that a company's profitability, measured by its return on assets (ROA), shows a positive relationship with ERM adoption. This finding is echoed by Mafrolla, Matozza, and D'Amico (2016), who found that earnings are often used to fund ERM initiatives within companies.

12.6 Research Methodology

This study focuses on Shariah-compliant construction companies in Malaysia, examining a sample of 39 such firms over a 10-year period from 2007 to 2016. Notably, this period witnessed the launch of the East Coast Rail Link (ECRL), a monumental infrastructure project stretching 665 kilometers from Port Klang, Selangor to Wakaf Bahru, Kelantan. Additionally, the Klang Valley Mass Rapid Transit (KVMRT) project, which commenced in 2011 and reached completion in 2016, further underscores the dynamic developments within this period. The research employs logistic regression analysis to determine the factors influencing the adoption of Enterprise Risk Management (ERM). The dependent variable in this analysis is the adoption of ERM, categorized as either adopted or not adopted.

Data for this study were meticulously gathered from multiple sources, including annual reports, DataStream, and Bursa Malaysia. These sources provided comprehensive and reliable data necessary for the analysis. The list of Shariah-compliant construction companies included in the sample is presented in Table 12.1, offering a detailed overview of the firms under study.

By leveraging logistic regression, the study aims to identify the determinants that significantly influence ERM adoption among Shariah-compliant construction companies. This methodological approach ensures a robust analysis, providing valuable insights into the factors that drive or hinder the implementation of ERM practices within this specific sector.

Table 12.1: List of *Shariah* Compliant Construction Companies in Malaysia as at 2019.

No.	Construction Companies in Malaysia	No.	Construction Companies in Malaysia
1.	Ahmad Zaki Resources Bhd	18.	Kerjaya Prospek Group Bhd
2.	Benalec Holding Bhd	19.	Kimlun Corporation Bhd
3.	Bina Puri Holdings Bhd	20.	Lebtech Bhd
4.	Crest Builder Holdings Bhd	21.	Melati Ehsan Holdings Bhd
5.	DKLS Industries Bhd	22.	Merge Energy Bhd
6.	Econpile Holdings Bhd	23.	MGB Bhd
7.	Ekovest Bhd	24.	Metrajaya Holdings Bhd
8.	Fajarbaru Builder Group	25.	MTD ACPI Engineering (M) BHD
9.	Gabungan AQRS Bhd	26.	Mudajaya Group Bhd
10.	Gadang Holdings Bhd	27.	Muhibbah Engineering (M) Bhd
11.	Gamuda Bhd	28.	Pesona Metro Holdings
12.	Ho Hup Construction Company Bhd	29.	Pintras Jaya Bhd
13.	Hock Seng Lee Bhd	30.	Prinsiptek Corporation Bhd
14.	IJM Corporation Bhd	31.	Protasco Bhd
15.	Ikhmas Jaya Group Bhd	32.	Sunway Construction Group Bhd
16.	Ireka Corporation Bhd	33.	Sycal Ventures Bhd
17.	Jaks Resources Bhd	34.	TRC Synergy Bhd

Table 12.1 (continued)

No.	Construction Companies in Malaysia	No.	Construction Companies in Malaysia
35.	TSR Capital Bhd	38.	Zecon Bhd
36.	WCE Holdings Bhd	39.	Zelan Bhd
37.	WCT Holdings Bhd		

Table 12.2 provides a comprehensive overview of the dependent and explanatory variables utilized in this study, along with the corresponding measurement methods and data sources. This detailed presentation ensures clarity and transparency in the research methodology, facilitating a thorough understanding of the factors influencing ERM adoption among Shariah-compliant construction companies in Malaysia.

The dependent variable in this study is the adoption of Enterprise Risk Management (ERM), which is measured as a binary outcome—whether ERM is adopted (1) or not adopted (0). The explanatory variables encompass a range of factors that are hypothesized to influence ERM adoption. These include firm size, financial leverage, the presence of prominent international auditors (Big Four), stock price volatility, board independence, and profitability.

Each variable is meticulously measured using specific metrics. For instance, firm size is quantified by the natural logarithm of total assets, while financial leverage is calculated as the ratio of total debt to total assets. The presence of Big Four auditors is represented as a binary variable, indicating whether a company is audited by one of the Big Four firms. Stock price volatility is measured by the difference between new and old stock prices, and board independence is assessed by the ratio of independent board members to the total number of board members. Profitability is measured by the return on assets (ROA).

Data for these variables were sourced from annual reports, DataStream, and Bursa Malaysia, ensuring a robust and reliable dataset for the analysis. This methodological rigor underpins the study's findings, providing valuable insights into the determinants of ERM adoption in the context of Shariah-compliant construction companies.

Table 12.2: Variables and proxies.

VARIABLES	MEASUREMENTS	SOURCES
ERM adoption	Dummy variable ERM adopted= 1 ERM not adopted= 0	Annual report of *Shariah-compliant* construction companies
Firm size	Ln (Total assets)	Datastream
Financial leverage	Total debt/Total asset	Datastream

Table 12.2 (continued)

VARIABLES	MEASUREMENTS	SOURCES
Presence of prominent international auditors (BIG4)	Dummy variable. Audited by KPMG, Ernst&Young, PWC or Deloitte Touche =1 Not audited by KPMG, Ernst&Young, PWC or Deloitte Touche =0	Annual report of *Shariah-compliant* construction companies
Stock price volatility (RM)	Differences between new and old stock price	Datastream
Independence board of director	Number of independent members of the board/total numbers of BOD	Annual report of *Shariah-compliant* construction companies
Profitability (%)	Return on assets	Datastream

– **Model Specification**

The logit model for this study is:

$$In\ \frac{ERM}{(1-ERM)} = \alpha 0 + \beta 1\ FSit + \beta 2\ LEVit + \beta 3\ BIG4 + \beta 4\ SPVit + \beta 5\ BODit + \beta 6\ ROAit$$

Where:

ERM = Enterprise Risk Management adoption; *FS* = Firm size; *LEV* = Financial leverage; *BIG*4 = Big four auditors; *SPV* = Stock price volatility; *BOD* = Independence board of directors and *ROA* = Profitability. The dependent variable, Enterprise Risk Management adoption, reflects a dummy variable. Value of 1 or 0 as follows: ERM = 1 if there is disclosure on the adoption of ERM in the annual reports, and ERM = 0 otherwise. The independent variables are firm size (FS), financial leverage (LEV), presence of big four auditors (BIG4), stock price volatility (SPV), independent board of directors (BOD) and profitability (ROA).

12.7 Findings

Table 12.3: Descriptive Analysis.

VARIABLES	MEAN	MEDIAN	STD DEV	MINIMUM	MAXIMUM
Enterprise Risk Management (ERM)	0.819149	1.000000	0.385579	0.000000	1.000000
Firm Size (FS)	13.37056	13.21054	1.221527	10.46133	16.79132

Table 12.3 (continued)

VARIABLES	MEAN	MEDIAN	STD DEV	MINIMUM	MAXIMUM
Financial Leverage (LEV)	0.207157	0.190398	0.167772	0.000000	1.072165
Big 4 Auditor (BIG4)	0.372340	0.000000	0.484288	0.000000	1.000000
Stock Price Volatility (SPV)	0.571656	0.430000	0.507716	0.050000	3.755000
Board of Directors (BOD)	0.475813	0.444444	0.121095	0.272727	0.857143
Profitability (ROA)	−0.387114	−0.139520	6.731965	−78.20000	46.85714

Table 12.3 presents the descriptive statistics for the variables used in this study, highlighting the central tendencies and variations within the data set. The analysis reveals key insights into the adoption of Enterprise Risk Management (ERM) among Shariah-compliant construction companies in Malaysia. The mean and median ratios for ERM adoption are 0.82 and 1.00, respectively, indicating that, on average, 82% of the Shariah-compliant construction companies have adopted ERM. This high adoption rate underscores the importance of ERM practices within the sector.

The independent variables examined in this study include Firm Size (FS), Financial Leverage (LEV), Big Four Auditor (BIG4), Stock Price Volatility (SPV), Board of Directors (BOD), and Profitability (ROA).

i. Firm Size (FS): The mean firm size, measured by the natural logarithm of total assets, is 13.37, with a median of 13.21. This suggests that larger firms are more likely to adopt ERM, as they have the resources and capacity to implement comprehensive risk management practices.
ii. Financial Leverage (LEV): The mean and median ratios for financial leverage are 0.21 and 0.19, respectively. These figures indicate that most Shariah-compliant construction companies finance their assets through borrowings, highlighting the importance of managing financial risks.
iii. Big Four Auditor (BIG4): The mean and median ratios for the presence of Big Four auditors are 0.37 and 0.00, respectively. This suggests that a significant proportion of Shariah-compliant construction companies in Malaysia are audited by prominent firms such as KPMG, Ernst & Young, Deloitte, and PricewaterhouseCoopers, which may influence their ERM adoption.
iv. Stock Price Volatility (SPV): The mean and median ratios for stock price volatility are RM0.57 and RM0.43, respectively, indicating relatively low stock price volatility among these companies. Lower volatility suggests reduced risk, which may impact the necessity and approach to ERM.
v. Board of Directors (BOD): The average proportion of independent board members is 48%, with a median of 44%. This reflects the governance structure of Shariah-compliant construction companies, where nearly half of the board members are independent, potentially influencing ERM practices.

vi. Profitability (ROA): The mean and median ratios for return on assets (ROA) are -0.39 and -0.14, respectively. These negative values indicate that many Shariah-compliant construction companies experienced low profitability and high operating costs during the observation period, which may affect their ability to invest in ERM.

These descriptive statistics provide a foundational understanding of the variables influencing ERM adoption among Shariah-compliant construction companies in Malaysia, setting the stage for further analysis and discussion.

– Multicollinearity

Table 12.4: Variance Inflation Factor (VIF).

VARIABLES	CENTERED VIF
FS	1.228478
LEV	1.109969
BIG4	1.105730
SPV	1.105730
BOD	1.199004
ROA	1.002983

The variance inflation factor (VIF) test was used to test whether the variables have multicollinearity issues or vice-versa. Table 12.4 reveals the VIF for each variable that is close to 1. This indicates an absence of multicollinearity amongst the variables in this study.

– Logistic Regression

Table 12.5: Logistic Regression.

VARIABLE	COEFFICIENT
C	-0.548814
FS	0.270280*
LEV	-2.864662***
BIG4	-0.891209***
SPV	-0.075341
BOD	-0.984889
ROA	-0.087447**

*significant at 5% level
**significant at 10% level
***significant at 1% level

Table 12.5 reveals that the coefficients for financial leverage and the presence of prominent international auditors are negative and statistically significant at the 1% level. This indicates strong evidence that financial leverage decreases and firms become less dependent on the services of prominent international auditors when adopting ERM. Consequently, ERM contributes to cost savings, as companies allocate fewer funds to borrowing and audit fees (Lundqvist, 2015). These savings can be redirected to enhance ERM implementation.

Additionally, the coefficient for profitability (ROA) is negative and statistically significant at the 10% level. This suggests that lower profitability increases the likelihood of ERM adoption, as companies seek to manage risks and improve their financial performance. Manyo (2013) notes that construction companies may prioritize other uses for their profits, such as research and development (R&D) or purchasing raw materials, over ERM. The coefficient for firm size is positive and statistically significant at the 10% level, implying that larger companies are more likely to adopt ERM. This is due to the complexity of their operations, which involve numerous branches, employees, clients, and suppliers. Previous research by Pagach and Warr (2007) supports this finding, highlighting the importance of sufficient assets to support ERM initiatives.

The study finds that stock price volatility (SPV) has a negative and insignificant relationship with ERM adoption. The movement of stock prices is beyond management's control, and investor appetite is often unpredictable (Briston, 2017). The results also indicate that the independence of the board of directors (BOD) does not significantly influence ERM adoption. Desender (2007) suggests that separating the roles of CEO and chairman can lead to better ERM adoption. Fraser, Quail, and Simkins (2022) recommend assigning ERM supervision to the strategic planning unit rather than internal audit to focus on distinct issues. However, they suggest that these roles can be combined for micro, small, and medium enterprises (MSMEs).

12.8 Conclusion

The construction industry is characterized by complexity and risk, necessitating effective risk management practices. ERM is touted to improve business performance in terms of cost of capital, profitability, and shareholder value. It is crucial to foster a culture of ERM within the construction industry. Adequately trained staff are essential to assess and manage the risks these companies face. The industry must establish guidelines to identify risks, assess their magnitude and impact, and make informed decisions to be shared with management. However, implementing an adequate risk assessment and management system remains challenging for industry practitioners.

The status of Shariah-compliant construction companies listed on the Malaysian bourse does not guarantee proper ERM adoption, despite the alignment of ERM benefits with Islamic precepts. This discrepancy is evident when comparing Shariah-compliant construction companies to Shariah-compliant financial institutions, which have more stringent governance requirements. The presence of a Shariah committee in financial institutions, mandated by the central bank, is a key component of their governance structure. In contrast, Shariah-compliant construction companies are primarily governed by the Securities Commission's screening process for business activities, without mandatory Shariah governance requirements.

To address this gap, the Securities Commission could consider mandating the appointment of a Shariah officer in Shariah-compliant construction companies. This officer would ensure compliance with Shariah requirements and oversee ERM aspects. While this suggestion may seem radical, it warrants further discussion and consideration.

The study's limitations include its focus on construction companies and a single industry, which may limit the generalizability of the findings to other sectors such as finance, services, and manufacturing. Future research could incorporate other listed Shariah-compliant companies from different sectors on the Malaysian bourse or conduct cross-comparisons between conventional and Shariah-compliant construction companies regarding ERM adoption. Additionally, comparative studies on ERM adoption in construction firms across different countries could provide valuable insights.

References

Akintoye, A., & MacLeod, M. (1997). Risk analysis and management in construction. *International Journal of Project Management*, 31–38.

Ali, W., Ibrahim Alasan, I., Hussain Khan, M., Ali, S., Cheah, J.-H. and Ramayah, T. (2021),

Competitive strategies-performance nexus and the mediating role of enterprise risk management practices: a multi-group analysis for fully-fledged Islamic banks and conventional banks with Islamic window in Pakistan, *International Journal of Islamic and Middle Eastern Finance and Management*, Vol. ahead-of-print No. ahead-of-print. https://doi.org/10.1108/IMEFM-06-2020-0310.

Beasley, M. S., Clune, R., & Hermanson, D. R. (2005). Enterprise risk management: An empirical analysis of factors associated with the extent of implementation. *Journal of accounting and public policy*, 521–531.

Briston, R. J. (2017). *The stock exchange and investment analysis*. Routledge.

Desender, K. (2007). On the Determinants of Enterprise Risk Management Implementation. *Managing Worldwide Operations & Communications with Information Technology*, 115–119.

Desender, K. (2011). *On the determinants of enterprise risk management implementation.* IGI Global.

Fraser, J. R. S., R. Quail, et al. (2022). "Questions asked about enterprise risk management by risk practitioners." Business Horizons 65(3): 251–260.

Gatzert, N., & Martin, M. (2015). Determinants and value of enterprise risk management: Empirical evidence from the literature. *Risk Management and Insurance Review*, 29–53.

Golshan, N. M., & Abdul Rasid, S. (2012). Determinants of enterprise risk management adoption: An empirical analysis of Malaysian public listed firms. *International Journal of Social and Human Sciences*, 119–126.

Golshan, N., & Rahid, S. (2009). Determinants of ERM adoption: An empirical analysis of Malaysian public listed companies. *J. Strat. Fin. Bus*, 123.

Gonzalez-Fajardo, J. A., Solis-Carcaño, R. G., & Be-Garcia, J. A. (2018). ERM in Construction Companies in the Mexican Southeast. *International Journal of Construction Engineering and Management*, 153–161.

Hoyt, R., & Liebenberg, A. (2011). The value of enterprise risk management. *Journal of Risk and Insurance*, 795–822.

Jaba, E., Robu, I.-B., & Balan, C. (2017). Panel data analysis applied in financial performance assessment. *Romanian Statistical Review*.

Khan, M. A. I., Alkathiri, M. A. M. A., Alhaddad, H. A., & Alnajjar, F. M. (2021). Impact of ERM on sustainability and financial performance of enterprises in the Gulf Cooperation Council: Case Study of Oman. *International Journal of Management (IJM)*, *12*(1).

Khouildi, M. Y., Bengana, M., Rakibi, M., Riad, M. R., & Aldirchawi, S. (2017). Shariah screening methodologies: SAC-SC vs DJIM Comparative study and impact assessment on their performance. *Global Review of Islamic Economics and Business*, *5*(2), 068–082.

Kneche, W. R., & Willekens, M. (2006). The role of risk management and governance in determining audit demand. *Journal of Business Finance & Accounting*, 1344–1367.

Kurbonov, S. A., & Saidov, S. (2022). Enterprise risk management: review, critique, and research directions. Science and Education, 3(1), 1054–1061.

Lechner, P., & Gatzert, N. (2018). Determinants and value of enterprise risk management: Empirical evidence from Germany. *The European Journal of Finance*, 867–887.

Liebenberg, A., & Hoyt, R. (2003). The determinants of enterprise risk management: Evidence from the appointment of chief risk officers. *Risk management and insurance review*, 37–52.

Lundqvist, S. A., & Vilhelmsson, A. (2016). Enterprise risk management and default risk: Evidence from the banking industry. *Journal of Risk and Insurance*.

Mafrolla , E., Matozza, F., & D'Amico, E. (2016). Enterprise risk management in private firms: Does ownership structure matter? *Journal of Applied Business Research*, 671.

Manyo, S. (2013). Does cash conversion cycle have impact on return on assets of Nigerian firm? Journal of Finance and Accounting.

Muhamat, A. A., et al. (2023). "Efficiency of general takaful operators in Malaysia: Post implementation of IFSA 2013." Iranian Economic Review 27(3): 895–913.

Muhamat, A. A., Jaafar, M. N., & Basri, M. F. (2017). Corporate social performance (CSP) influences on Islamic bank's financial performance. *Journal of International Business, Economics and Entrepreneurship (JIBE)*, *2*(1), 11–16.

Mohd Sanusi, Z., Motjaba Nia, S., Roosle, N., Sari, R., & Harjitok, A. (2017). Effects of corporate governance structures on enterprise risk management practices in Malaysia. *International Journal of Economics and Financial Issues*, 6–13.

Nocco, B. W., & Stulz, R. M. (2022). Enterprise risk management: Theory and practice. Journal of Applied Corporate Finance, 34(1), 81–94.

Pagach, D. P., & Warr, R. S. (2007). The effects of enterprise risk management on firm performance. *Available at SSRN 1155218*.

Pagach, D. &Warr, R. 2011. The characteristics of firms that hire chief risk officers. Journal of Risk and Insurance.

Securities Commission Malaysia, List of Shariah-Compliant Securities by the Shariah Advisory Council of the Securities Commission Malaysia dated 25 November 2022. Retrieved at: https://www.sc.com.my/development/icm/shariah-compliant-securities/list-of-shariah-compliant-securities

Shad, M. K., & Lai, F. W. (2015). Enterprise risk management and firm performance validated through economic value-added factors. *International Journal of Economic and Statistics*.

Shamsuddin, A. (2018). Company's characteristics and risk management disclosure: Evidence from the top 100 public listed companies in Malaysia. *Global Business & Management Research, 10*.

Simunic, D. A., & Biddle, G. C. (2019). The big four: The curious past and perilous future of the global accounting monopoly.

Tan, A., Viksnins, P., & Kumar, R. (2018). *Global economic crime and fraud survey 2018 (Malaysian Report).* PWC.

The Star Online (2014). State director says corruption in construction industry at serious level. Retrieved at: https://www.thestar.com.my/news/community/2014/04/25/state-director-says-corruption-in-construction-industry-at-serious-level/. Accessed date 3 July 2019.

Wangyanwen, L., et al. (2023). "Influence of enterprise risk management (ERM) on perceived organizational performance: Evidence from Chinese-based organizations." International Journal of Operations and Quantitative Management 29(1): 68–82.

Yang, S., Muhammad, I. and Anwar, M. (2018), "Enterprise risk management practices and firm performance, the mediating role of competitive advantage and the moderating role of financial literacy", Journal of Risk and Financial Management, Vol. 11 No. 3.

Yazid, A., Razali, A., & Hussin, M. (2012). Determinants of enterprise risk management (ERM): A proposed framework for Malaysian public listed companies. *International Business Research*, 80.

Yegon, C. K., Mouni, J. G., & Wanjau, K. (2014). Effects of firm size on enterprise risk management of listed firms in Kenya. *Journal of Business and management*, 86–95.

Zainuddin, S., Togok, S., & Isa, C. (2015). ERM adoption in Malaysia: A disclosure approach. *Proceedings of the Asia Pacific Conference on Business and Social Sciences.*

Fitriani Tobing, Ja'far Hamzah Pulungan, Yessy Agustia Lestari,
Dewi Santri, Hery Syahrial

Chapter 13
The Role of Artificial Intelligence in Developing Halal Cosmetic

Abstract: The phenomenon of the use of Artificial Intelligence technology is bringing fundamental changes to the cosmetic products being developed, exploring ways in which artificial intelligence can be used to improve product safety and quality as well as meeting the needs of consumers who are increasingly aware of the legitimacy of the products they buy. This research was conducted using qualitative descriptive methods and content analysis based on a literature review of academic research journals or articles, websites, electronic databases (secondary data) and other relevant sources. Artificial intelligence plays a role in clarifying information on Optimisation of good cosmetic formulas, Identification of Halal Cosmetic Ingredients, Explaining Challenges and Strategies for Halal Cosmetics and Opportunities for Halal Cosmetics in the World, Artificial Intelligence technology has made it possible to conduct innovative research in the discovery of cosmetic components that comply with validity. Artificial intelligence contributes to the process of ensuring that each product meets the established safety and validity criteria by performing sensor analysis and accurately identifying ingredients. This helps companies create effective marketing campaigns, increasing their competitiveness in the global market.

Keywords: Artificial intelligence, Halal Cosmetics, Halal Industry, Consumer Behavior

13.1 Introduction

The halal industry is currently a global phenomenon as evidenced by the continuous growth in its prospects from year to year. Based on the report State of The Global Islamic Report (2019) it was found that the number of halal industry consumers reached around 1.8 billion Muslims. Halal industry consumers spend 2.2 trillion dollars annually, with an increase of 5.2 percent annually. The projected average annual growth rate (CAGR) of the halal industry is expected to reach 6.2% from 2018 to 2024. In addition, total consumer spending in the halal industry is expected to reach USD 3.2 trillion by 2024. (Adamsah & Subakti, 2022) . This data clearly shows that the future of the halal industry is bright (State of The Global Islamic Report, 2019). With 2.4 billion Muslim customers worldwide, the demand for halal cosmetic products continues to increase (Sugibayashi *et al.*, 2019). Worldwide consumption of halal cosmetics increased by 4.9% in 2018 and totaled 64 billion dollars; the largest consumer, Indonesia, spent 4 billion dollars. (Sholikhah *et al.*, 2021).

https://doi.org/10.1515/9783111575407-014

Indonesia has great potential to advance the halal industry, which is largely driven by its significant Muslim population. The country accounts for about 12.7% of the total Muslim population worldwide. With a total population of around 278 million in 2020, around 86.7% of Indonesia's population is Muslim, according to (World Population Review, 2023). This large presence makes the demand for halal products in Indonesia very high, so Indonesia is often considered as the embodiment of the global halal industry market. In 2017, the total expenditure spent by Indonesians on halal products reached USD 218.8 billion, demonstrating the huge economic potential of the halal industry in the country (Ministry of Finance of the Republic of Indonesia, 2019).

Artificial Intelligence technology has emerged today as one of the most important innovations in the world of technology. *Artificial Intelligence* acts as a link between data science and data analysis involving very large amounts of data that cannot be handled quickly by humans. (Pangkey *et al.*, 2019). *Artificial Intelligence* technology has transcended technological boundaries, bringing significant changes in various sectors, including the cosmetics industry. At a time when consumers are increasingly concerned about the quality, ethics and safety of the products they use, the cosmetics industry has undergone rapid development. One of the most striking changes is the increasing popularity of halal cosmetics around the world. In this context, the role of *Artificial Intelligence* in the halal cosmetics industry is not only important, but also changes the dynamics of the evolving beauty products.

Artificial Intelligence is becoming increasingly common in various industries. Every country has at least 50% of industries using artificial intelligence in their commercial operations (Vasiljeva *et al.*, 2017). Businesses consider many advantages of *Artificial Intelligence* so they continue to develop and cooperate in their business processes. AI technology is used to perform operational procedures (Pillai *et al.*, 2020) to understand customers and to predict their demand (Arifin, 2019). AI is also used in product marketing to improve the customer's buying experience. (Abyan Ramadhana & Hussein, 2022). The ability to customize items to meet individual customer needs is one of the benefits generated by AI. One of the sectors that use AI to improve customer shopping experience is the cosmetics business (Kristi & Kusumawati, 2021). AI is used by the beauty industry, particularly in the sale of skincare and makeup items, to assist customers in making product choices. (Zhong *et al.*, 2021).

This research specifically analyzes the phenomenon that the use of *Artificial Intelligence* technology brings fundamental changes in the cosmetic products developed, exploring ways in which *Artificial Intelligence* can be used to improve product safety and quality and meet the needs of consumers who are increasingly aware of the halalness of the products they buy. Halal cosmetics have been made by many well-known companies, but whether the use of *Artificial Intelligence* technology has been properly utilized by the company to increase profits. Because consciously using AI technology through the website can help decisions to be made and due to the security of data from users about halal cosmetics to be purchased, this can design a more effective marketing campaign. All cosmetic information will help customers in finding data, so that the human-centered Society 5.0 balances solutions to social problems with existing technological advances.

13.2 Literature Review

13.2.1 Development of *Artificial Intelligence*

The thinking ability of *Artificial Intelligence* technology is the result of knowledge created by human information and then processed through simulation of its reasoning process to solve problems (Kusumawati, 2018). *Artificial Intelligence* also includes fields such as natural language processing, which allows computers to understand and communicate in human language. This opens up vast opportunities in the development of applications in various fields, including language processing and the increasing popularity of the use of chatbots. (Huang, 2010).

The development of *Artificial Intelligence* has undergone a profound transformation in the industrial structure of companies, having a significant impact on operational efficiency, decision-making, and innovation capabilities. *Artificial Intelligence is* becoming an important pillar in various sectors, increasing productivity and providing smarter solutions.

Table 13.1: Role of *Artificial Intelligence* in various Industry Sectors.

No	Industry	The role of *Artificial Intelligence*	Reference
1	Manufacturing	- Optimizing the supply chain - Conducts machine performance monitoring - Forecasting maintenance needs	(Davenport & Ronanki, 2018)
2	Finance	- Risk Analysis - Fraud detection - Investment portfolio management	(Ngai *et al.*, 2019)
3	Health	- Medical diagnosis - Drug development - Patient data management	(Topol, 2019)
4	Creative	- Processing Images and Designs - Data Analysis and Prediction - Virtual dan Augmented Reality (VR/AR) - Content Personalization	(Hanifa *et al.*, 2023)
5	Cosmetics	- Marketing Beauty Products - Cosmetic ingredient analysis - Provide experience for potential customers - Minimize inappropriate products	(Dwinata & Pambudi, 2023) (Kumar & Srivastava, 2020) (Wang *et al.*, 2019)

Source: Data Processed.

The development of *Artificial Intelligence* has had a significant impact on the cosmetics industry sector. This reflects the role of *Artificial Intelligence* in penetrating various industries, enriching innovation and supporting efforts to provide more targeted services.

13.2.2 Current Developmet of Halal Cosmetic

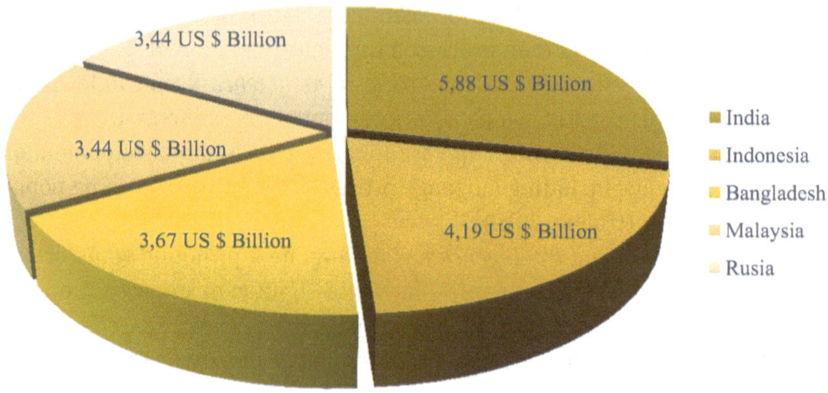

Figure 13.1: Consumption of Halal Cosmetics in the World.
Source: Dinar Standard (2021).

This growth in consumption of halal cosmetics can be caused by several factors, first, the use of halal labeling in business. (Choirunnisa & Firmansyah, 2021)second, halal certification (Shakirah & Sapir, 2021), and third, the level of consumer religiosity (Mudi Awalia & Bin Lahuri, 2021). The view of some parties is that halal cosmetics are not just an element of beauty, but also prioritize the health aspect, which is reflected in the view of a halal lifestyle. (Adinugraha & Sartika, 2019). This is in line with Islamic teachings, as taught by the Prophet Muhammad, who emphasized the importance of a halal lifestyle in maintaining health, including in terms of cosmetics. (Aziz & Ahmad, 2018)Therefore, the teachings of the Prophet Muhammad Saw. regarding halal cosmetics need to be deepened and studied further to enrich understanding in the Islamic treasury

13.2.3 The Role of *Artificial Intelligence* in the Halal Cosmetics Industry

Artificial Intelligence is playing an increasingly important role in the cosmetics industry, especially in the effort to develop halal-compliant cosmetic products. In recent years, research has highlighted the contribution of *Artificial Intelligence* in the process of identifying halal-compliant cosmetic ingredients. For example, it has been shown that *Artificial Intelligence* can be used to analyze data from various sources, including cosmetic ingredient databases, with a high degree of accuracy. (Attila *et al.*, 2022).This allows cosmetic companies to ensure that the ingredients used meet halal requirements properly.

In addition, *Artificial Intelligence* also plays a role in the formulation process of cosmetic products that meet halal requirements to detail how machine learning algorithms can be used to create ingredient combinations that comply with halal standards while maintaining product quality and performance. (Rahman, 2020)In the quality control of halal cosmetic products, *Artificial Intelligence* also has a very important role that *Artificial Intelligence* allows the development of automated systems capable of detecting haram components or inappropriate ingredients, thus ensuring that cosmetic products continue to meet halal standards (Ali *et al.*, 2020).

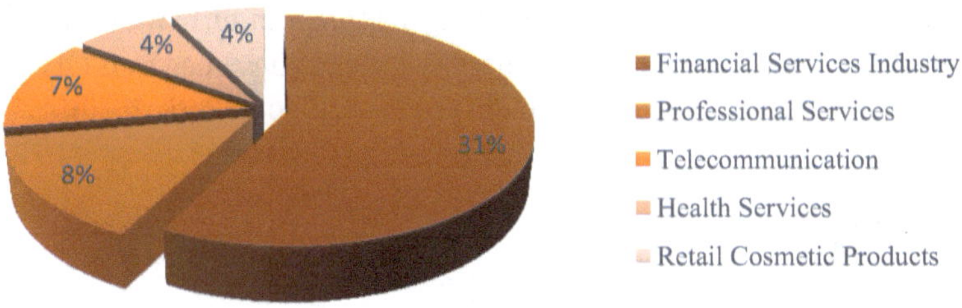

Figure 13.2: Proportion of AI Use in Product Development in the Industrial Sector.
Source: Mckinsey & Company (2022).

The cosmetics industry, often referred to as the beauty industry, refers to an economic sector focused on the production, marketing and sale of beauty products. In the literature, the cosmetics industry is often identified as a broad and dynamic sector, involving a variety of products such as skincare, makeup, and hair and body care products. For example, Grădinaru *et al.* (2022) have discussed various aspects of the industry, including market trends, product innovations, and evolving marketing strategies in the context of the beauty industry.

Innovation in the cosmetics industry has occurred through cosmetic products that meet halal standards, with a focus on high quality and adherence to strict scientific guidelines. (Khan *et al.*, 2020). Today, the cosmetics and personal care products segment has become one of the most prominent and fast-growing ones (Shahid *et al.*, 2018). This progress is in line with the growing Muslim population and increasing awareness of halal products. In addition, halal cosmetic products also attract non-Muslim consumers who seek better safety, hygiene, and product quality (Rafiki *et al.*, 2022).

Halal cosmetics refer to the understanding of beauty products that adhere to halal standards in Islam. According to Sugibayashi *et al*, (2019), halal cosmetics are defined as beauty products that are manufactured, processed, and formulated in accordance with Sharia principles. This includes the use of ingredients that are considered halal, keeping products away from forbidden contaminants, and involving production processes that comply with halal values. This definition reflects the cosmetics industry's efforts to meet the demands and preferences of halal-concerned consumers, illustrating the growing importance of this market segment in the beauty world. Further research by Rahim *et al.* (2015) highlighted that sustainability and sanctity of halal cosmetic products is a major concern in this industry. This study may provide further insight into the critical aspects that need to be considered in an effort to maintain the integrity of halal cosmetic products, including aspects of sustainability and maintenance of product sanctity during the entire production chain.

The quality and suitability of halal cosmetic products is an important issue in the cosmetic industry today. Research conducted by (Septiarini *et al.*, 2023) emphasizes the significance of *Artificial Intelligence* in verifying cosmetic products to comply with halal requirements, including permitted ingredients and production processes that meet halal standards. *Artificial Intelligence* not only helps in checking the composition of the product, but also enables tracking of the product from its source to the end consumer, thus ensuring transparency in the supply chain of halal cosmetic products. (Choi & Park, 2020)

13.3 Methodology

This study was conducted using descriptive qualitative method and content analysis based on literature review from journals or academic research articles, websites, electronic databases (secondary data) and other relevant sources. From the sources of previous research sources, this argumentation and discussion is created.

13.4 Discussion

The role of AI is very important for industries, one of which is halal cosmetics. AI is used in various ways, such as product formula optimization and identification of halal cosmetic ingredients. AI can help cosmetic companies in product development by analyzing consumer data to help them innovate and lead in the digital era. AI can also analyze consumers' skin characteristics through selfies and recommend skincare products that suit their individual needs. Although AI has many benefits, there are some challenges and strategies to encourage the halal cosmetics industry to use it.

1. Cosmetic Formula Optimization

Optimization of cosmetic formulations by utilizing artificial intelligence (AI) is an innovative approach that is rapidly growing in the beauty industry, especially in the context of developing halal cosmetics. (Penlington & Chen, 2020). Making halal cosmetics does not only require critical sources of ingredients to be considered halal. A similar concept is also applied in the production process of various cosmetic products (Sugibayashi *et al.*, 2019).

To ensure product quality and safety, the production of halal cosmetics needs to comply with *current Good Manufacturing Practice* (cGMP) and other quality standards. It is recommended to establish specialized staff trained in handling and manufacturing halal cosmetics. (Sugibayashi *et al.*, 2019).

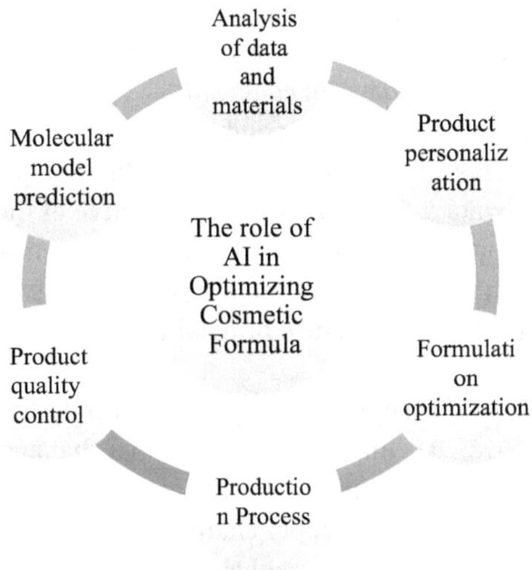

Figure 13.3: The Role of Artificials in Cosmetic Formula Optimization.
Source: Data Processed.

Table 13.2: Suggestions in Halal Cosmetics Production.

–	A place that is clean and free from contaminated places such as pig farms
–	Halal cosmetics production equipment must be sterile and clean
–	Not using water contaminated with substances such as recycled water from unclean wastes
–	Cleaning materials in the maintenance of production equipment must also be guaranteed to come from animal sources in accordance with halal principles

Source: *Good Manufacturing Practice (2016)*

One aspect that is considered in the production of halal cosmetics is packaging materials. Materials used in the manufacture of main and ancillary packaging must comply with halal standards. In general, packaging materials are usually derived from halal sources, although it is important to raise awareness about the origin of animal materials used as supports in the packaging manufacturing process. (Sugibayashi *et al.*, 2019). Manufacturers of halal cosmetics need to ensure that they source packaging materials from reputable packaging suppliers that adhere to halal principles (Talib & Johan, 2012).

Application tools and other product accessories must be confirmed to come from sources free of human, pork, or other illegal substances. An efficient distribution system must also be established to guarantee that halal cosmetic products can be sold while maintaining their halal status and avoiding contamination by illegal or impure ingredients. (Sugibayashi *et al.*, 2019).

2. Identification of Halal Cosmetic Ingredients

Cosmetics manufactured in accordance with the principles of the halal system and using ingredients from approved sources are halal products. These products are intended to be applied to different parts of the body, either as a wash or as a residual, to protect, beautify, and alter the appearance of the body. (Sugibayashi *et al.*, 2019).

Cosmetics contain a number of diverse components, involving elements such as water, oils, surfactants, polymers, organic solvents, colorants, proteins, vitamins, plant extracts, preservatives, and antioxidants. (Iwata & Shimada, 2013). The source of these ingredients plays a crucial role in determining the outcome and overall performance of a cosmetic product. It is important for manufacturers, not regulators, to provide safety evidence related to the ingredients used in the manufacture of halal cosmetics. (Sugibayashi *et al.*, 2019).

Manufacturers need to collaborate with their suppliers to ensure that only halal-certified ingredients are used. (Dent *et al.*, 2018). It is important to remember that active ingredients, raw materials, and excipients must all come from halal-certified sources. This collaborative effort promotes transparency in the supply chain and ensures that halal cosmetic products meet high halal standards. (Sugibayashi *et al.*, 2019).

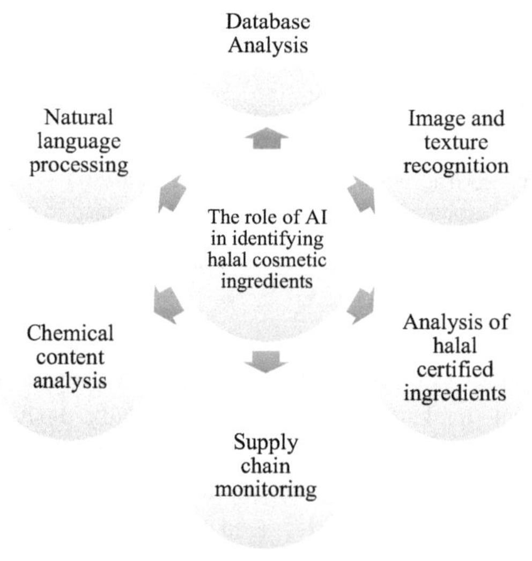

Figure 13.4: Role of AI in Identification of Halal Cosmetic Ingredients.
Source: Data Processed.

2.1 Permitted Halal Cosmetic Ingredients

Halal cosmetic ingredients refer to all ingredients obtained from plants, soil, water, animals recognized as halal through the slaughter process in accordance with Islamic principles, marine animals considered halal, and synthetic ingredients that have been proven safe for consumers. (Sugibayashi *et al.*, 2019).

Table 13.3: Halal Cosmetic Ingredients.

Category	Material	Reference
Skin Whitening	*4-potassium methoxysalicylate (4-MSK)*	(Y. Li *et al.*, 2016) (Ito & Wakamatsu, 2015)
	Arbutin	(Ivica & Litvi´c, 2008)
	Ferulic acid	(Maeda & Fukuda, 1996)
	Tranexamic acid	(Z. Li *et al.*, 2015)
	Vitamin B3	(Everts, 2008)
	Vitamin C	(Linster & Van Schaftingen, 2007)
Thickener	*Carboxymethyl cellulose*	(Shui *et al.*, 2017)
	Carnauba wax	(Yu *et al.*, 2017)
	Carrageenan	(Zia *et al.*, 2017)
	Petrolatum	(Battarjee *et al.*, 1999)
Dyes	*Carotene (merah-jingga)*	(Iwata & Shimada, 2013) (M. Yusuf *et al.*, 2017)
	Lithospermum purple (violet)	
	Paprika (kuning, jingga, merah)	
	Safflower (kuning, merah)	
	Turmeric (kuning)	
Solvent	*Safflower oil*	(Han *et al.*, 2000)
	Water	(E. Yusuf & Yajid, 2017)
	Avocado oil	(Qin & Zhong, 2016)
	Corn oil	(Ni *et al.*, 2016)

Source: Data Processed.

The cosmetic ingredients are considered halal because it is ensured that they are not contaminated or adulterated with haram ingredients after being obtained and produced from halal sources.

2.2 Non-allowed Non-Halal Cosmetic Ingredients

Cosmetic ingredients that are considered haram include ingredients such as blood, prohibited human body parts, animals or insects, and chemicals that can be harmful or dangerous to consumers.

Table 13.4: Non-Halal Cosmetic Ingredients.

Category	Material	Reference
Restricted Chemicals	*Chloroform* *Halogenated Salicylanilides* *Hexachlorophene* *Mercury compounds* *Methylene chloride* *Prohibited cattle materials* *Vinyl chloride*	(Prohibited and Restricted Chemicals in Cosmetics, 2022)
Insect derived Materials	*Carmine dye (Cochineal; E 120 or Natural Red)* *Crimson dye (fromKermes vermilio)* *Laccaic acid*	(Iwata & Shimada, 2013) (M. Yusuf *et al.*, 2017)
Human derived Materials	*Amniotic fluid* *Growth factors* *Placenta*	(E. Yusuf & Yajid, 2017)

Source: Data Processed.

2.3 General Guidelines for Halal and Non-Halal Cosmetic Ingredients

Halal cosmetics certification requirements are regulated by several manuals. Cosmetic manufacturers are required to comply with the set standards and applicable cosmetic standards.

Table 13.5: List of Cosmetic Production Guidelines.

Guidelines	Description	Reference
ISO 22716:2007	Good Manufacturing Practices (GMP) Guidelines for Cosmetics Standards and Metrology Institute for Islamic Countries as a Requirement for Halal Cosmetics	(International Organization for Standardization, 2007)
LPPOM MUI: HAS23000:1	Association MUI Halal Certification Requirements of Southeast Asian Nations Guide	(LPPOM MUI, n.d.)
ASEAN Cosmetic Directives	Guidelines for Cosmetics Manufacturers and Consumers of Halal Cosmetics	(ASEAN Guidelines, n.d.)
CH Guidelines Q7: 2016	International Council for Harmonization Guidelines on GMP	(Good Manufacturing Practice, 2016)

Source: Data Processed.

3. Challenges and Strategies for the Halal Cosmetics Industry

The progress of the halal cosmetics industry is showing notable developments. However, to encourage the growth of this sector, a careful strategic approach is needed (Imam & Khoirul, 2020). To achieve this goal, the right first step is to find the strengths, weaknesses, challenges and strategies of the industry.

3.1 Factors that are the strength of the Halal Industry in Indonesia

– Government Support in Halal Industry

The Indonesian government has provided significant support in the development of the halal industry. Several strategic initiatives have been carried out, including the establishment of halal industrial zones (KIH) such as Modern Halal Valley, Halal Industrial Park Sidoarjo, and Bintan Inti Halal Hub. In addition, the government also encourages program collaboration between ministries and institutions in the regions to strengthen the halal industry ecosystem.

– Existence of a Certification Body that has Survived

In Indonesia, there are certification bodies known as the Indonesian Ulama Council (MUI) and the Halal Product Guarantee Agency (BPJPH). MUI initially regulated halal certification on a voluntary basis, but since the enactment of Law 33 of 2014 concerning Halal Product Guarantee (JPH), as well as the Job Creation Law and Government Regulation No. 39 of 2021 concerning the Implementation of Halal Product Guarantee, halal certification has become *mandatory*.

– Halal Product Campaign

The Indonesian government has conducted significant campaigns to encourage halal product certification. For example, the Ministry of Religious Affairs has organized a mandatory halal certification campaign at 1,000 points throughout Indonesia to remind that halal certification is officially mandatory. This campaign involves all stakeholders of halal product assurance from the center to the regions, as well as all levels of society, including micro, small, medium, and large businesses, and consumers.

– Significant Halal Trends from Muslims and Non-Muslims

In various sectors, by both Muslims and non-Muslims. The halal industry transcends many sectors, including food and beverages, cosmetics, pharmaceuticals, banking, tourism and more. This halal trend shows that halal products are becoming an increasing necessity in various sectors, both by Muslims and non-Muslims.

3.2 Factors that Weaken the Halal Industry in Indonesia

– Low Awareness of Consumers and the Public about the Importance of Halal Aspects

Consumers and the public's awareness of the importance of halal aspects can be influenced by various factors, including education, information, and religious beliefs. Education on halal aspects, law enforcement, and related sanctions can increase awareness of the importance of halal compliance. In addition, the provision of clear and transparent information regarding the halal status of a product can also help increase public awareness.

– Lack of Cooperation between Industry Sectors

Lack of cooperation between fellow industrial sectors can be one of the obstacles in industrial development. This can be reflected in the limited business network of cooperation between small entrepreneurs, as well as a less conducive business climate. To overcome this, efforts are needed to build better cooperation between industrial sectors, including small industries and creative industries. In addition, government programs such as the Import Substitution Program and the Domestic Production Improvement Program (P3DN) can also be a step to encourage cooperation between industrial sectors.

– Policy Framework and Protection Product Guarantees Not Yet Established

The framework of protection product policies and warranties should usually be carefully drafted by the responsible party. The initial step involves identifying risks, defining the scope of protection, and determining terms and conditions. This process involves collaboration between insurance experts and relevant parties to ensure clarity and fairness in the policy.

– Lack of Halal Certified Companies

The lack of companies that have halal certification can be an obstacle in meeting the needs of consumers who pay attention to the halal aspects of the product. There is a need for incentives and approaches that support companies to obtain halal certification, including counseling and technical assistance. Authorities can also raise awareness of the importance of halal certification for companies to expand markets and meet religious standards.

Table 13.6: Challenges of Halal Cosmetics Industry.

–	Challenge
–	Muslim and non-Muslim countries develop halal cosmetics industry
–	Product quality that lacks competitiveness
–	The rise of non-halal products and the circulation of non-halal ingredients
–	Low awareness about the use of non-halal ingredients, especially for small-scale producers
–	No halal standardization
–	SARA issues are still quite strong

Source: (Imam & Khoirul, 2020).

The strategy to optimize the halal industry, especially the halal cosmetics industry, is further strengthened by involving various sectors and increasing synergy between all related elements. Thus, the strategies that can be applied will be more focused and able to operate optimally in accordance with market conditions and consumer needs:

Table 13.7: Halal Cosmetics Industry Strategy.

Strategy
Increase socialization and education on the importance of halal certification for the Indonesian people and industry players, both small and large
– Strengthen legal certainty
– The government needs to optimize plans and disseminate halal information on industrial estates to improve the quality of halal products.
– Improve the quality of halal industrial products, especially the halal cosmetics industry, so that they can compete in the domestic and international markets.

Source: (Imam & Khoirul, 2020).

4. Halal Cosmetics Industry Opportunities

Halal cosmetics are products made using ingredients that comply with the principles of Islamic law. These products are guaranteed to be free from ingredients prohibited in Islam and do not contain animal or genetically modified ingredients. The rapid growth in the halal cosmetics market can be attributed to the increasing Muslim population worldwide. This phenomenon is further intensified by the entry of Muslim women into the cosmetic and fashion industry as professionals, which significantly increases the demand for halal cosmetic products.

Table 13.8: Halal Cosmetics Market Share by Region (2022).

Region	Market Share 2022 (%)
North America	5,9%
Asia Pacific	74%
Europe	11,6%
Latin America	5,5%
ASEAN Economic Community (AEC)	3%

Source: *Precendece Research (2023)*

A huge demand for halal cosmetics exists in developing and developed countries around the world, with significant markets in North America, Europe, and Asia Pacific. Notably, the Asia Pacific region is dominant in the halal cosmetics market, providing a large product base to cater to global needs. Multinational players are involved in this industry as they see huge growth potential in various regions.

The increase in demand for halal cosmetics is mainly due to the fulfillment of halal certification and the growing population of the Muslim community. This creates a significant demand pool for halal cosmetic products. Major players in the cosmetics industry are also actively entering this market, recognizing the opportunities that exist. Interestingly, halal products are not only in demand by the Muslim population, but also by non-Muslim women and men. These products are considered a symbol of cleanliness,

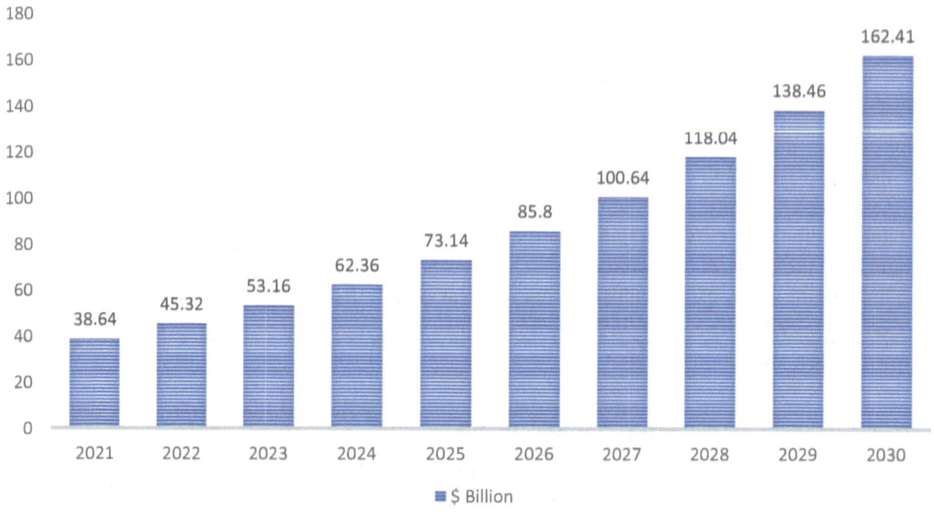

Figure 13.5: Halal Cosmetics Market Share Opportunities 2021–2030.
Source: Precendece Research (2023).

purity and safety. Moreover, the need for hygiene extends not only to the production of halal cosmetics but also to the packaging of the products.

The growth of the halal cosmetics market has a great opportunity as it is increasing every year, especially in regions with a majority Muslim population. The growth rate from 2021–2030 has a CAGR of 12.1%. Countries such as Saudi Arabia, United Arab Emirates, Indonesia, Turkey, and Malaysia are experiencing a significant increase in demand for halal cosmetic products, due to the large number of Muslims on a global level. Projections indicate that the industry will continue to grow, with increased production of Shariah-compliant products. India, as the country with the third largest Islamic population, is also experiencing significant growth in the halal cosmetics market. Factors such as rising living standards and rapid urbanization are the main drivers of this growth. The growing demand for shariah-compliant or halal-certified products marks a positive trend in the cosmetics industry in the World.

13.5 Conclusions

Artificial Intelligence technology has made it possible to conduct innovative research on the discovery of halal-compliant cosmetic components. Cosmetics manufacturers now can discover and confirm substances that meet validity standards thanks to artificial *intelligence* and advanced algorithms and data analysis. *Artificial Intelligence* also accelerates product formulation, allowing cosmetics manufacturers to produce more efficient goods that meet the demands of a rapidly evolving market. In this regard, the integration of AI technology into the halal cosmetics sector improves compliance with validity criteria, which is important for customers, in addition to increasing efficiency. *Artificial Intelligence* contributes to the process of ensuring that each product meets the set safety and validity criteria by performing sensor analysis and identifying ingredients precisely. By using this technology, the possibility of contamination is reduced and customers can use halal cosmetics with confidence that there will be no adverse health effects.

The use of *Artificial Intelligence* is essential for halal cosmetics manufacturers to understand consumer preferences and emerging trends. *Artificial Intelligence also* plays a role for Muslim and non-Muslim consumers to identify halal cosmetics that do not only focus on technical aspects. *Artificial Intelligence* also provides a great opportunity to win world market share by meeting the demands of global consumers. It helps companies create more effective marketing campaigns and build product portfolios that match consumer needs and wants, increasing their competitiveness in the global market.

References

Abyan Ramadhana, M., & Hussein, A. S. (2022). Pengaruh Penggunaan Artificial Intelligence Terhadap Customer Loyalty Dengan Citra Merek Sebagai Variabel Mediasi. *Manajemen Pemasaran Dan Perilaku Konsumen*, *1*(4), 522–531. http://dx.doi.org/10.21776/jmppk.2022.01.4.11.

Adamsah, B., & Subakti, G. E. (2022). Perkembangan Industri Halal Terhadap Pertumbuhan Ekonomi. *Indonesian Journal of Halal, 5(1)*, 71–75.

Adinugraha, H. H., & Sartika, M. (2019). Halal Lifestyle Di Indonesia. *An-Nisbah: Jurnal Ekonomi Syariah, 5(2)*, 57–81.

Ali, A., Sherwani, M., Ali, A., Ali, Z., & Sherwani, M. (2020). Investigating the antecedents of halal brand product purchase intention: an empirical investigation. *Journal of Islamic Marketing*, *12*(7), 1339–1362.

Arifin, S. (2019). *Pemasaran era Millenium*.

ASEAN Guidelines. (n.d.). *ASEAN Guidelines for Cosmetic Good Manufacturing Practice*. Retrieved December 5, 2023, from https://ww2.fda.gov.ph/attachments/category/197/Appendix VI_CosmeticGMP

Attila, S., Wei, Y., Gyulavári, T., Syahrivar, J., Gaczek, P., & Dr.Hofmeister, Á. (2022). The e-WOM intention of artificial intelligence (AI) color cosmetics among Chinese social media influencers. *Asia Pacific Journal of Marketing and Logistics, 25(3)*. https://doi.org/10.1108/APJML-04-2022-0352

Aziz, N. I. A., & Ahmad, F. A. (2018). The Halal Lifestyle of Muslim Working Women. *International Journal of Academic Research in Business and Social Sciences*, *8*(5), 1121–1129. https://doi.org/10.6007/ijarbss/v8-i5/4489

Battarjee, S. M., Abd El-Azim, W. M., & Mohamed, A. (1999). A. Preparation of medicinal petroleum jelly using local petroleum waxes. *Lubr. Sci*, *12*, 89–104.

Choi, Y. J., & Park, J. W. (2020). Investigating factors influencing the behavioral intention of online duty-free shop users. *Sustainability (Switzerland)*, *12*(17), 1–20. https://doi.org/10.3390/su12177108

Choirunnisa, R., & Firmansyah, E. A. (2021). Muslim Consumer Behavior and Purchase Decisions of Halal Cosmetic Products. *Journal of Economic Studies*, *5*(1), 11–30. https://creativecommons.org/licenses/by-sa/4.0/

Davenport, T. H., & Ronanki, R. (2018). Artificial intelligence for the real world. *Harvard Business Review, 6(1)*, 108–116.

Dent, M., Amaral, R. T., Silva, P. A., Ansell, J., Boisleve, F., Hatao, M., Hirose, A., Kasai, Y., Kern, P., Kreiling, R., & Al., E. (2018). Principles underpinning the use of new methodologies in the risk assessment of cosmetic ingredients. *Comput. Toxicol, 7*, 20–26.

DinarStandard. (2021). *Indonesia Halal Market Reports*. Dinar Standard. https://isef.co.id/indonesia-halal-market-report/

Dwinata, P. W., & Pambudi, Y. J. (2023). Penggunaan Teknologi Artificial Intelligence dalam Pemilihan Produk Kecantikan oleh Konsumen Wanita. *E-Jurnal Manajemen, 12(7)*, 733–752.

Everts, S. (2008). Green chemistry environmentally friendly synthesis of niacin generates less inorganic waste. *Chem. Eng. News, 86*, 15.

Good Manufacturing Practice. (2016). *Q7 Good Manufacturing Practice Guidance for Active Pharmaceutical Ingredients. Guidance for Industry.International Council for Harmonization*. https://www.fda.gov/media/71518

Grădinaru, C., Obadă, D. R., Grădinaru, I. A., & Dabija, D. C. (2022). Enhancing Sustainable Cosmetics Brand Purchase: A Comprehensive Approach Based on the SOR Model and the Triple Bottom Line. *Sustainability (Switzerland), 14*(21), 9–11. https://doi.org/10.3390/su142114118

Han, X., Cheng, L., Zhang, R., & Bi, J. (2000). Extraction of safflower seed oil by supercritical CO2. *J. Food Eng, 96*, 370–376.

Hanifa, Sholihin, A., & Ayudya, F. (2023). Peran AI terhadap Kinerja Industri Kreatif di Indonesia. *Journal of Comprehensive Science, 2(7)*, 2159–2170.

Huang, L. F. (2010). Artificial intelligence. In *2010 The 2nd International Conference on Computer and Automation Engineering, ICCAE 2010* (Vol. 4). https://doi.org/10.1109/ICCAE.2010.5451578

Imam, F. K., & Khoirul, M. M. (2020). Halal Industry in Indonesia; Challenges and Opportunities. *Journal of Digital Marketing and Halal Industry, 5*(1), 55–64.

International Organization for Standardization. (2007). *Cosmetics–Good Manufacturing Practices (GMP)–Guidelineson Good Manufacturing Practices*.

Ito, S., & Wakamatsu, K. (2015). A convenient screening method to differentiate phenolic skin whitening tyrosinase inhibitors from leukoderma-inducing phenols. *J. Dermatol. Sci., 80*, 18–24.

Ivica, C., & Litvi´c, M. (2008). Simple and efficient synthesis of arbutin. *Arkivoc, 2*, 19–24.

Iwata, H., & Shimada, K. (2013). Developing the formulations of cosmetics. In Formulas, Ingredients and Production of Cosmetics: Technology of Skin-and Hair-care Products in Japan. *Springer: Tokyo, Jepang*, 21–86.

Khan, N., Sarwar, A., & Tan, B. C. (2020). Determinants of purchase intention of halal cosmetic products among Generation Y consumers. *Journal of Islamic Marketing, 12(1)*, 1461–1476. https://doi.org/https://doi.org/10.1108/JIMA-11-2019-0248

Kristi, K., & Kusumawati, N. (2021). *Technology Acceptance and Customer Perception of Augmented Reality (AR) in Indonesian Beauty Industry*. https://doi.org/10.4108/eai.22-7-2020.2307916

Kumar, A., & Srivastava, M. (2020). A survey on chatbot implementation in customer service industry using deep learning. *Journal of Ambient Intelligence and Humanized Computing, 11(10)*, 4289–4315.

Kusumawati, R. (2018). Kecerdasan Buatan Manusia (Artificial Intelligence); Teknologi Impian Masa Depan. *ULUL ALBAB Jurnal Studi Islam, 9*(2), 257–274. https://doi.org/10.18860/ua.v9i2.6218

Li, Y., Dong, C., Cun, D., Liu, J., Xiang, R., & Fang, L. (2016). Lamellar liquid crystal improves the skin retention of 3-O-ethyl-ascorbic acid and potassium 4-methoxysalicylate in vitro and in vivo for topical preparation. *AAPS PharmSciTech, 17*, 767–777.

Li, Z., Fang, L., Dong, L., Guo, Y., & Xie, Y. (2015). An improved and practical synthesis of tranexamic acid. *Org. Process. Res. Dev, 19*, 444–448.

Linster, C. L., & Van Schaftingen, E. (2007). Biosynthesis, recycling and degradation in mammals. *FEBS J, 274*, 1–24.

LPPOM MUI. (n.d.). *General Guidelines of Halal Assurance System*. Retrieved December 5, 2023, from https://www.halalcertifiering.se/newwebsiteimages/ebookhashaki.pdf (

Maeda, K., & Fukuda, M. (1996). Arbutin: Mechanism of its depigmenting action in human melanocyte culture. *J. Pharmacol. Exp. Ther*, *276*, 765–769.

Mckinsey & Company (2022). *AI Index Report 2022*. https://aiindex.stanford.edu/report/

Mudi Awalia, F. T., & Bin Lahuri, S. (2021). The Influence of Religiosity On Consumer Behavior in Purchasing Halal Label Cosmetics. *Ijtihad : Jurnal Hukum Dan Ekonomi Islam*, *15*(1), 63–90. https://doi.org/10.21111/ijtihad.v15i1.5760

Ngai, E., Moon, W., K. K. Riggins, F., & Yi, C. Y. (2019). Artificial intelligence chatbot research: A bibliometric study. *Expert Systems with Applications*, 56–67.

Ni, S., Zhao, W., Zhang, Y., Gasmalla, M. A. A., & Yang, R. (2016). Efficient and eco-friendly extraction of corngerm oil using aqueous ethanol solution assisted by steam explosion. *J. Food Sci. Techno*, *53*, 2018–2116.

Pangkey, F. M., Furkan, L. M., & Mulyono, L. E. H. (2019). Pengaruh Artificial Intelligence dan Digital Marketing terhadap Minat Beli Konsumen. *Jmm Unram – Master of Management Journal*, *8*(3), 258–269. https://doi.org/10.29303/jmm.v8i3.448

Penlington, A., & Chen, L. (2020). AI in Cosmetics: Opportunities and Challenges. *Journal of Artificial Intelligence in Beauty*, *12(3)*, 189–204.

Pillai, R., Sivathanu, B., & Dwivedi, Y. K. (2020). Shopping intention at AI-powered automated retail stores (AIPARS). *Journal of Retailing and Consumer Services*, *57*. https://doi.org/10.1016/j.jretconser.2020.102207

Precendece Research. (2023). *Halal Cosmetics Market (By Product Type: Personal Care Products, Color Cosmetics, Fragrances; By Application: Skin Care, Face Care Hair Care, Beauty Care; By Distribution Channel: Offline, Online) – Global Industry Analysis, Size, Share, Growth, Trends, R*. https://www.precedenceresearch.com/halal-cosmetics-market/amp *Prohibited and Restricted Chemicals in Cosmetics*. (2022).

QIn, X., & Zhong, J. (2016). A review of extraction techniques for avocado oil. *J. Oleo Sci*, *65*, 881–888.

Rafiki, A., Tobing, F., Suryani, W., Syahrial, H., & Clarissa, J. (2022). Consumer purchase intention of halal cosmetic: a systematic literature review. *Islamic Banking, Accounting and Finance International Conference*, 421–426.

Rahim, N. F. binti, Shafii, Z., & Shahwan, S. (2015). Awareness and Perception of Muslim Consumers on Halal Cosmetics and Personal Care Products. *International Journal of Business, Economics and Management*, *2*(1), 1–14. https://doi.org/10.18488/journal.62/2015.2.1/62.1.1.14

Septiarini, D. F., Ratnasari, R. T., Salleh, M. C. M., Herianingrum, S., & Sedianingsih. (2023). Drivers of behavioral intention among non-Muslims toward halal cosmetics: evidence from Indonesia, Malaysia, and Singapore. *Journal of Islamic Accounting and Business Research*, *14*(2), 230–248. https://doi.org/10.1108/JIABR-02-2021-0064

Shahid, S., Ahmed, F., & Hasan, U. (2018). A qualitative investigation into consumption of halal cosmetic products: the evidence from India. *Journal of Islamic Marketing*, *9*(3), 484–503. https://doi.org/DOI:10.1108/JIMA-01-2017-0009

Shakirah, A., & Sapir, M. (2021). Halal Cosmetic Awareness Among College Students in Malaysia Malezya'da Üniversite Öğrencileri Arasında Helal Kozmetik Farkındalığı. *International Journal of Business & Economic Studies Year: 2021*, *3*(1), 17–26. https://orcid.org/0000-0002-7454-7645

Sholikhah, B., Fitri, R., & Mahanani, Y. (2021). Analisis Pengambilan Keputusan Pembelian Kosmetik Berlabel Halal MUI pada Generasi Millenial. *Al Maal: Journal of Islamic Economics and Banking*, *2(2)*, 193–211.

Shui, T., Feng, S., Chen, G., Li, A., Yuan, Z., Shui, H., Kuboki, T., & Xu, C. (2017). Synthesis of sodium carboxymethyl cellulose using bleached crude cellulose fractioned from cornstalk. *Biomass Bioenergy*, *105*, 51–58.

State of Global Islamic Economy Report 2019. DinardStandard https://cdn.salaamgateway.com/special-coverage/sgie19-20/full-report.pdf

Sugibayashi, K., Yusuf, E., Toda, H., Dahlizar, S., Sakdiset, P., Arce, F. J., & See, G. L. (2019). Halal Cosmetics: A Review on Ingredients, Production, and Testing Methods. *Cosmetics, 6(37).*

Talib, M. S. ., & Johan, M. R. . (2012). Issues in halal packaging: A conceptual paper. *Int. Bus. Manag., 5,* 94–98.

Topol, E. J. (2019). High-performance medicine: the convergence of human and artificial intelligence. *Nature Medicine, 25(1),* 44–56.

Vasiljeva, T., Shaikhulina, S., & Kreslins, K. (2017). Cloud Computing: Business Perspectives, Benefits and Challenges for Small and Medium Enterprises (Case of Latvia). *Procedia Engineering, 178,* 443–451. https://doi.org/10.1016/j.proeng.2017.01.087

Wang, Z., Zheng, X., Hu, Q., & Zhou, M. (2019). A novel cosmetics recommendation system based on user preferences. *Multimedia Tools and Applications, 78(6),* 6923–6942.

Yu, X., Wang, N., Zhang, R., & Zhao, Z. (2017). Simple synthesis hydrogenated castor oil fatty amide wax and its coating characterization. *J. Oleo Sci, 66,* 659–665.

Yusuf, E., & Yajid, M. S. (2017). A. Related topic: Halal Cosmetics. In Skin Permeation and Disposition of Therapeutic and Cosmeceutical Compounds. *Springer: Tokyo, Japan,* 101–107.

Yusuf, M., Shabbir, M., & Mohammad, F. (2017). Natural colorants: Historical, processing, and sustainable prospects. *Nat. Prod. Bioprospect, 7,* 123–145.

Zhong, Y., Oh, S., & Moon, H. C. (2021). Service transformation under industry 4.0: Investigating acceptance of facial recognition payment through an extended technology acceptance model. *Technology in Society, 64.* https://doi.org/https://doi.org/10.1016/j.techsoc.2020.101515

Zia, K. M., Tabasum, S., Nasif, M., Sultan, N., Aslam, N., Noreen, A., & Zuber, M. (2017). A review on synthesis, properties and applications of natural polymer based carrageenan blends and composites. *Int. J. Biol. Macromol, 96,* 282–301.

Mohammad Mominul Islam

Chapter 14 The Strategic Aspects of the Resource-based View (RBV) of Halal Certification for Halal Marketing

Abstract: Halal certification encompasses both physical assets displaying the halal (حلال) logo and immaterial assets that foster a spiritual connection. As per the resource-based view (RBV), organizational assets meeting the criteria of being valuable, rare, inimitable, and non-substitutable (VRIN) can lead to a competitive advantage (CA). Thus, halal certification exemplifies VRIN standards that bolster the knowledge-based perspective (KBV) of Islamic shariah. This chapter explores the strategic aspects of RBV, KBV, and CA concerning Islamic principles. By following Islamic principles, comprehensive guidelines can be developed to make marketing mixes VRIN for halal competitive advantage (HCA). Moreover, the KBV of Islamic principles emphasizes knowledge seeking, integration, application, and dissemination, which can be leveraged to support the RBV. Ultimately, HCA is derived from the integration of Islamic knowledge with RBV and KBV. Therefore, it is essential to use scholarly insights to change mindsets and adopt the theoretical lenses of Islamic marketing originating from the Quran and authentic Sunnah. By using Islamic principles as a theoretical underpinning, halal certification can be managed as an economic resource with spiritual significance.

Keywords: Halal certification, Halal competitive advantage, the resource-based View, the Knowledge-based View, Strategic Islamic marketing, Marketing mix

14.1 Introduction

"Halal" is an Arabic term that refers to actions and behaviors that are permitted according to Islamic law. It is defined in the Quran and includes permissible affairs and strategic business practices. "Haram" is the opposite of "Halal" and refers to conduct that is forbidden. In Islam, individuals must only engage in permissible (halal) conduct and must avoid any forbidden (haram) actions (Islam et al., 2024). This understanding has greatly extended to various aspects of daily life, including commerce. For instance, in Chapter 2, verse 275 of the Noble Quran, Allah has decreed the trading of permissible goods.

Global halal certification bodies follow their criteria for certification (Latif et al., 2014). The certification bodies identify various categories for awarding halal certificates and the common categories include checking the halal status of raw materials,

https://doi.org/10.1515/9783111575407-015

country of origin, production process, workers' condition, halal and haram contamination, logistics, halal knowledge, and supply chain. The halal certifiers comprise the Muslim majority countries namely halal certification for the Gulf countries, Organization of the Islamic Cooperation (OIC), Saudi Arabia halal center, Brunei halal, and halal certification in Malaysia, Indonesia, Pakistan, and Bangladesh are the noted ones. The non-Muslim halal certification countries include Majlis Ugama Islam Singapura (Muis), American Halal Foundation, Halal Australia, and Halal India. These global halal certification bodies are accredited by one another and certify different halal foods and services.

Halal certification is a strategic resource for halal marketers considering halal certification a resource base (Islam et al., 2024). The Resource-Based View (RBV) is applied to test an organization's performance through its value, rarity, inimitability, and non-substitutability (VRIN) of resources. An organization's resources are the key determinants of its sustained competitive advantage (Barney & Hesterly, 2020). The resources must be a capability unique to the organization and a point of differentiation from its competitors. The VRIN intent of RBV can be applied by individuals and groups of organizations (Das & Teng, 2000). The intent suggests that firms must take care of their resources, create them, and make efforts to distinguish them. Eventually, RBV will yield economic returns in terms of sales, profits, and a strong brand image.

According to RBV, companies must have unique resources to succeed. Halal certification can be one of those resources that allow businesses to tap into the rapidly growing halal market. The certification measures the reliability of halal assurance systems, which can enhance a company's resource-based view and protect its halal certification from unexpected drawbacks (Abd Rahman et al., 2017). Further, halal certification boosts business performance for halal producers proving the resource-based of halal certification (Ab Talib et al., 2017). Thus, halal certification is a unique resource and a source of competitive advantage that other firms may lack. Producers with valid halal certification have greater confidence and protection against potential halal fraud compared to those without certification and enhance sales. As a result, halal stakeholders can showcase their halal certification on product labels, packaging, and promotional campaigns to leverage it as a brand image, which is an intangible resource in business.

14.1.1 Problem Statement

The RBV has been further developed in the form of the knowledge-based view (KBV) of the firm (Curado & Bontis, 2006). It states that firms can have a competitive advantage by creating, absorbing, integrating, and sharing knowledge (Balogun & Jenkins, 2003). Knowledge about RBV associated with halal certification needs a call for striving Islamic knowledge about halal and Tayyib according to the Noble Quran and Sunnah or prophetic traditions. This further requires not only learning halal knowledge to function halal certification but also connecting Islamic principles with KBV. Arguably, the lenses of RBV and KBV are conventional, and sourcing the required Islamic knowledge to advance conventional theories is a pressing need in academia.

While knowledge-based capabilities are key success factors in creating and sustaining competitive advantage for contemporary organizations (Whicker, 2004), gaining Islamic knowledge and its practice are the prerequisites to benefit from halal certification-focused organizations (Wannasupchue et al., 2023). In gaining a firm's crucial resource to improve an organization's competitiveness, knowledge management (KM) is imperative (Chiang et al., 2011). Nonetheless, merely possessing knowledge itself would not be enough to guarantee a competitive advantage if the possessed knowledge is not transmitted (Szulanski, 2000). It is evident that both the conventional and Islamic views of knowledge gaining, absorbing, and transmitting (KBV) to benefit the RBV are significant. Creating, integrating, applying, and disseminating knowledge of KBV about halal certification for halal competitive advantage is very scarce in halal research.

14.1.2 Aim and Objective

The core components of halal certification, which result in a competitive edge, hinge predominantly on a deep comprehension of the resource-based view, coupled with a knowledge-based perspective. The strategic dimensions of RBV, KBV, and CA can be delved into by adhering to Islamic principles to render marketing mixes VRIN for halal certification. Within this context, this chapter seeks to analyze the resource-based view and its correlation with halal certification, elucidating the Islamic principles governing halal marketing.

14.2 Literature Review

14.2.1 Halal Certification as a Resource

The previous research on halal logistics acknowledges halal certification as a resource but highlights that the successful execution of halal logistics operations remains to be fully realized, and the mechanism for achieving Halal logistics competence is still evolving. Hence, an approach rooted in Islamic principles, as outlined in the Al-Quran and Hadith, has been adopted to examine the fundamental factors of Halal services, particularly Halal logistics services (Karia et al., 2015). The objective of the study was to pinpoint the key determinants of halal logistics competence in delivering Halal products and services, particularly by third-party logistics firms. Consequently, the research delineates Halal, Tayyib, and piety-based standards derived from Islamic principles to ensure that suppliers, especially third-party agents of main suppliers, are Halal certified.

The study also concentrates on suppliers and supply chains within the framework of RBV and halal certification, to construct a theoretical model that elucidates the relationship between halal certification and logistics performance and identifies avenues for further research. The proposed model is grounded in the resource-based view (RBV) management theory (Ab Talib et al., 2016). The authors contend that the effective utilization of resources, including halal certification, can positively influence logistics performance. Furthermore, they argue that governmental factors may serve as moderators in the relationship between halal certification and logistics performance or can directly impact logistics performance. In addition to using halal certification as a means to enhance business credibility, the paper guides logistics service providers on leveraging halal certification to enhance organizational and logistics performance. The study emphasizes the certification of logistics as halal within the context of RBV.

Apart from intangible resources, tangible and dedicated resources like warehousing and packaging are crucial for halal integrity in the halal food industry. Among the dedicated resources, the product attached to the packaging is the main, and logistics like warehousing is the secondary importance of the RBV (Azhar & Tu, 2021). Logistics and halal certifications are recognized in another comprehensive research aiming to identify the various theories used in halal logistics (HL) and halal supply chain (HSC) by reviewing literature from 2007 to 2020 (Nee & Mohamad, 2022). As a result, halal certification is connected to logistics and finished products understanding RBV from the pursuit of tangibility.

Scandals involving food products within the halal supply chain have brought to light deficiencies in various food quality standards, certifications, and audits designed to ensure food safety. The study conducted by Ali et al. (2022) seeks to investigate how supply chain integration (SCI) influences the integrity of the halal food supply chain and its impact on food quality. Drawing on the resource-based view (RBV) theory, the study examines internal, supplier, and customer integrations to discern their significant effects on different aspects of halal food supply chain integrity, ultimately influencing halal food safety and quality. Emphasizing the significance of SCI in the halal food supply chain, the study offers managers valuable insights into its practical implementation within the industry. By analyzing the repercussions of SCI on both halal food supply chain integrity and food quality, the study enriches the limited existing research within the context of the halal industry.

Halal certification is important for ensuring that food is appropriate for consumption by those who follow Islamic dietary laws. The Resource-Based View (RBV) has been used to safeguard halal certification by proposing separate certification for the entire supply chain. This ensures that halal integrity is integrated throughout the value-creation process. The RBV helps to resolve scandals and fraud associated with halal certification in the food industry. The producers, suppliers, and consumers are the key stakeholders who ensure the RBV's effectiveness. However, the RBV's important components

(VRIN) have not received adequate attention from producers and suppliers, and the KBV of RBV has been overlooked in the study.

RBV outlines that the intangibility of resources like international orientation and marketing capability significantly affect the export performance of halal products. Hence, the product showcases the base, followed by exporting capability and international marketing promotion to cater to global customers (Ahmad-Fauzi & Md Saad, 2023). As such, halal certification holds some invisible power to capture international market share compared with the base of RBV.

According to a recent systematic literature review, business researchers mainly use the Resource-Based View (RBV) theory to recommend that producers in the halal industry obtain halal certification as an economic resource (Islam et al., 2024). The study delved into the halal competitive advantage by outlining marketing strategies based on Islamic teachings and offered a conceptual framework for how the RBV could be applied to halal competitive advantage.

The existing literature on Resource-Based Views (RBV) in halal business research highlights that halal certification is a valuable resource for halal logistics and supply chains. The studies emphasize the involvement of producers, suppliers, customers, and the government to leverage the halal products' integrity. The researchers suggest that RBV can be viewed both proactively to leverage future benefits, as well as reactively to address halal fraud through embracing halal certification. However, the core components of RBV, particularly the understanding of VRIN and knowledge-based view (KBV) are yet to be fully developed.

14.2.2 Resource-based View (RBV) Underpins Knowledge-based View (KBV)

KBV assumes that knowledgeable employees are the most valuable and dynamic resources of an organization and that knowledge has value, rarity, inimitability, and non-substitutability (VRIN) according to the RBV when it comes to phenomena like halal certification, which is cultivated from Islamic principles. Islamic principles are based on the Holy Quran, the final revelation from Allah, which is a comprehensive guideline for believers and humankind (The Noble Quran, 2:185). The guideline is easy to follow (The Noble Quran, 54:32). Then, the last messenger was authorized to explain the guideline, and the believers must accept the prophetic traditions for better clarification (The Noble Quran, 59:7). Although scholars might argue in understanding halal certification issue, Shariah and the prophetic traditions are the rules of thumb to stop arguing on Islamic jurisprudence (The Noble Quran, 4:59, 65; 33:21) associated with halal products, certification, and other issues on CA in business.

Halal product depicts the first input for cultivating CA. Allah has instructed Muslims and mankind to consume halal and tayyib. Halal and tayyib refer to the basic rules for consumption of the Muslims' dietary and provisions for halal certification. The market coverage of halal is the key to the CA of halal certification. The Noble Quran outlines clearly on halal. Allah says:

يَاأَيُّهَا ٱلنَّاسُ كُلُواْ مِمَّا فِي ٱلأَرْضِ حَلاَلاً طَيِّباً وَلاَ تَتَّبِعُواْ خُطُوَاتِ ٱلشَّيْطَانِ إِنَّهُ لَكُمْ عَدُوٌّ مُّبِينٌ

"O humanity! Eat from what is lawful and good on the earth and do not follow Satan's footsteps. He is truly your sworn enemy" (The Noble Quran, 2:168). It also says:

يَاأَيُّهَا ٱلَّذِينَ آمَنُواْ كُلُواْ مِن طَيِّبَاتِ مَا رَزَقْنَاكُمْ وَٱشْكُرُواْ لِلَّهِ إِن كُنْتُمْ إِيَّاهُ تَعْبُدُونَ

"O believers! Eat from the good things We have provided for you. And give thanks to Allah if you truly worship Him alone" (The Noble Quran, 2:172).

The market coverage of halal products is wide and comprehensive, catering to Muslim and non-Muslim consumers. A product can only be considered halal when it has been certified, a process that requires trust, responsibility, and authority from various stakeholders. The certification process starts when producers apply to certifiers or authorized personnel. Certifiers then visit the production process and plants to ensure Shariah compliance. They report their findings to Islamic scholars who evaluate the certification process using their knowledge of Islamic principles. Upon a satisfactory investigation, the certification is issued, and consumers trust the Islamic scholars and certifiers. Finally, the certifiers, producers, and Islamic scholars work together to ensure a seamless halal certification process. The authorized people must take a lesson from the verse that says:

إِنَّ ٱللَّهَ يَأْمُرُكُمْ أَن تُؤدُّواْ ٱلأَمَانَاتِ إِلَىٰ أَهْلِهَا وَإِذَا حَكَمْتُمْ بَيْنَ ٱلنَّاسِ أَن تَحْكُمُواْ بِٱلْعَدْلِ

"Indeed, Allah commands you to return trusts to their rightful owners; and when you judge between people, judge with fairness" (The Noble Quran, 4:58). Accordingly, certifiers and auditors must show fairness to the certification applicant and properly return the certification. Then, the producers must be submissive toward the authoritative entities of halal certification according to the teaching of the verse saying:

يَا أَيُّهَا ٱلَّذِينَ آمَنُواْ أَطِيعُواْ ٱللَّهَ وَأَطِيعُواْ ٱلرَّسُولَ وَأُوْلِي ٱلأَمْرِ مِنْكُمْ

"O believers! Obey Allah and obey the Messenger and those in authority among you" (The Noble Quran, 4:59). Accordingly, halal producers must be obedient toward the government, halal certification board, Islamic scholars, and other experts associated with halal certification. Then, inspection must be in an authentic way considering the verse depicting:

يَاأَيُّهَا ٱلَّذِينَ آمَنُوۤاْ إِن جَآءَكُمْ فَاسِقٌ بِنَبَإٍ فَتَبَيَّنُوۤاْ أَن تُصِيبُواْ قَوْمًا بِجَهَالَةٍ فَتُصْبِحُواْ عَلَىٰ مَا فَعَلْتُمْ نَادِمِينَ

"O believers, if an evildoer brings you any news, verify it so you do not harm people unknowingly, becoming regretful for what you have done" (The Noble Quran, 49:06). As Islamic knowledge is the key to halal certification, producers, auditors, and certifiers must ask Islamic scholars about Islamic rulings followed by the Holy verse:

فَاسْئَلُوۤاْ أَهْلَ ٱلذِّكْرِ إِن كُنتُمْ لاَ تَعْلَمُونَ

"Then ask those who know if you do not know" (The Noble Qur'an 16: 43; 21: 7).

Overall, all stakeholders namely the applicant, auditors, authority, and Islamic scholars of halal certification are responsible for the entire halal certification process. It is an *Amanah* (ٱلأَمَانَات) and Allah will ask the individual involved in the halal certification process. The prophetic tradition says:

أَلَا كُلُّكُمْ رَاعٍ وَكُلُّكُمْ مَسْئُولٌ عَنْ رَعِيَّتِه

> "Every one of you is a shepherd and is responsible for his flock" (Ṣaḥīḥ al-Bukhārī, 7138, Ṣaḥīḥ Muslim, 1829).

The gravity of being held accountable on the Day of Judgment can facilitate a smooth and credible halal certification process. Halal certifications and logos serve as trusted markers for consumers who rely on certifying bodies. These bodies, along with Shariah boards, function as trustworthy agents for consumers. The general public often depends on knowledgeable and authoritative individuals regarding the halal status of products.

The Shariah board typically comprises Islamic scholars and governmental representatives, providing a resource for consumers seeking further clarification and placing their trust in their expertise. According to Islamic principles, members of the Shariah board are responsible for verifying the halal production process and offering assurance to the public regarding halal certification.

Regarding *halal* and *haram* concerns, the certification board must avoid suspicion. Allah says:

ٱلْحَقُّ مِن رَّبِّكَ فَلَا تَكُونَنَّ مِنَ ٱلْمُمْتَرِين

> "This is the truth from your Lord, so do not ever be one of those who doubt" (The Noble Quran, 2:147). Islam guides establishing a board through Shura, which involves consultation among stakeholders to address issues related to halal certification. Shura, meaning consultation, allows stakeholders to form a Shariah board. This board for halal certification counseling may include government officials, product specialists, and scholars in Islamic marketing. Therefore, halal certification, serving as a source of resources, trust, and spiritual significance, stems from Shariah's knowledge, the board's expertise, and followers of Shariah. According to Islamic principles, members of the Shariah board are tasked with verifying the halal production process and providing assurance to the public regarding halal certification. Allah says:

وَشَاوِرْهُمْ فِى ٱلْأَمْرِ فَإِذَا عَزَمْتَ فَتَوَكَّلْ عَلَى ٱللَّهِ إِنَّ ٱللَّهَ يُحِبُّ ٱلْمُتَوَكِّلِي

> "And consult with them in conducting matters. Once you make a decision, put your trust in Allah. Surely Allah loves those who trust in Him" Notably, Islam outlines guidelines to form a halal certification board" (The Noble Quran, 3:159).

وَأَمْرُهُمْ شُورَىٰ بَيْنَهُم

> "Conduct their affairs by mutual consultation" (The Noble Quran, 42:38).

Mutual consultation among the certification stakeholders can help mitigate communication gaps and enhance the credibility of halal certification. Besides, spirituality and religious sensitivity are the cornerstones of halal certification sustainability. As such, halal certification is merely not a means of bread and butter, not a tool for economic gain, it is the ticket to the afterlife success for the Muslim stakeholders. This spiritual and religious sentiment can help boost halal certification's credibility and sustainability. Eventually, a competitive advantage will be the product of halal certification.

The Holy Quran says to compete in good deeds and not help in sinful acts. Competition for money, market share, and profit may generate hostility among the firms in the industry. However, cooperation from the industry, suppliers, consumers, and individual firms can create a congenial business environment and advantageous position for all. Obeying halal norms and encouraging other firms to follow need to be the norms of cooperation. Islam suggests cooperation instead of competition in business. Allah says:

وَتَعَاوَنُوا عَلَى ٱلْبِرِّ وَٱلتَّقْوَىٰ وَلَا تَعَاوَنُوا عَلَى ٱلْإِثْمِ وَٱلْعُدْوَانِ وَٱتَّقُوا ٱللَّهَ إِنَّ ٱللَّهَ شَدِيدُ ٱلْعِقَابِ

"Cooperate in goodness and righteousness, and do not cooperate in sin and transgression. And be mindful of Allah. Surely Allah is severe in punishment" (The Noble Quran, 5:2).

The basis of cooperation among the industry players may consist of halal pricing, halal distribution channels, and halal promotional activities to boost the sales of halal products. Alternatively, involvement with haram business activities must be avoided as Allah banned haram activities. Surely, haram harms that cannot result in favor or advantageous to Allah. As such, practicing halal and refraining from haram must guard the welfare of the individual business and society. This requires submission of will to Allah. Allah says:

يَٰأَيُّهَا ٱلَّذِينَ ءَامَنُوا ٱدْخُلُوا فِى ٱلسِّلْمِ كَآفَّةً وَلَا تَتَّبِعُوا خُطُوَٰتِ ٱلشَّيْطَٰنِ إِنَّهُ لَكُمْ عَدُوٌّ مُّبِينٌ

"O believers! Enter into Islam wholeheartedly and do not follow Satan's footsteps. Surely, he is your sworn enemy" (The Noble Quran, 2:208). Arguably, halal business affairs must be conducted in a manner that is pure and free from any suspicion of impurity. The principles of Islamic law dictate to avoid impure and prohibited practices. Therefore, the crucial issue in the halal business is to accept only halal and pure (tayyib) products, while rejecting anything that is haram (prohibited), impure (khabith), suspicious (mushabbah), and disliking affairs (makruh) in Islamic teachings.

According to the teachings of the Glorious Quran, halal products, pricing, place, promotion, process, physical evidence, and people are all essential components for achieving an advantageous position in the competitive halal market. First, halal pricing means setting prices for halal products without any interest or riba. Interest can increase product prices many times over, leading to inconvenience for consumers and reduced value and welfare. Instead, lowering costs can increase the value for consumers. Allah has made interest prohibited by saying:

وَأَحَلَّ ٱللَّهُ ٱلْبَيْعَ وَحَرَّمَ ٱلرِّبَا

"But Allah has permitted trading and forbidden interest" (The Noble Quran, 2:275). Then it says:

يَمْحَقُ ٱللَّهُ ٱلرِّبَا وَيُرْبِى ٱلصَّدَقَاتِ وَٱللَّهُ لَا يُحِبُّ كُلَّ كَفَّارٍ أَثِيمٍ

"Allah has made interest fruitless and charity fruitful. And Allah does not like any ungrateful evil-doer" (The Noble Quran 2: 276). Next it depicts:

يَا أَيُّهَا ٱلَّذِينَ آمَنُوا۟ لَا تَأْكُلُوا۟ ٱلرِّبَا أَضْعَافاً مُّضَاعَفَةً وَٱتَّقُوا۟ ٱللَّهَ لَعَلَّكُمْ تُفْلِحُون

"O believers! Do not consume interest, multiplying it many times over. And be mindful of Allah, so you may prosper" (The Noble Quran, 3:130). As esteemed consumers are to bear the final burden of interest, it significantly contributes to increasing customer suffering. Further, interest-based marketers benefit, which The Quran has prohibited. Allah says:

فَإِن لَّمْ تَفْعَلُوا۟ فَأْذَنُوا۟ بِحَرْبٍ مِّنَ ٱللَّهِ وَرَسُولِهِ وَإِنْ تُبْتُمْ فَلَكُمْ رُؤُوسُ أَمْوَالِكُمْ لَا تَظْلِمُونَ وَلَا تُظْلَمُون

"If you do not, then beware of a war with Allah and His Messenger! But if you repent, you may retain your principle- neither inflicting nor suffering harm" (The Noble Quran, 2:279). Therefore, pricing without riba denotes halal pricing and welfare for the marketers and consumers. Accordingly, riba-free pricing indicates a vital variable for competitive advantage. Similarly, halal pricing covers fair price, no unjustified price manipulation, no predatory pricing, no hoarding, no switch and bait, and no restriction in trade other unfairness. Overall, businesspeople must not eat the resources of other people in an invalid way. In this regard, Allah says:

يَا أَيُّهَا ٱلَّذِينَ آمَنُوا۟ لَا تَأْكُلُوٓا۟ أَمْوَالَكُمْ بَيْنَكُمْ بِٱلْبَاطِلِ إِلَّآ أَن تَكُونَ تِجَارَةً عَن تَرَاضٍ مِّنكُم

If any party does an unfair act, it will affect the individual and others. This is called golden rule said by the Noble Quran:

لَا تَظْلِمُونَ وَلَا تُظْلَمُون

About injustice, unfairness, and harming others, the prophetic traditions say that:

لَا ضَرَرَ وَلَا ضِرَار

"Do not cause harm or return harm" (Sunan Ibn Mājah, 2340).

Interest (riba), injustice or unfairness, and no-harming principles can result in halal pricing. This halal pricing can ensure the welfare, and protection of self, resources, and society. Eventually, CA can be gained among the halal business stakeholders through halal pricing. Second, producers must manage raw materials, manufacture finished products, and distribute the product to the consumers' hands following halal integrity. Integration of all networks of production and distribution is a halal supply chain in Islamic marketing. The Noble Quran has outlined the process by saying it is tayyib (The Noble Quran, 2:275). The Noble Quran also has an *Ayat* or sign on the halal distribution in chapter 18:19, depicting empirical evidence.

فَٱبْعَثُوٓا۟ أَحَدَكُم بِوَرِقِكُمْ هَٰذِهِۦٓ إِلَى ٱلْمَدِينَةِ فَلْيَنظُرْ أَيُّهَآ أَزْكَىٰ طَعَاما

"So, send one of you with these silver coins of yours to the city, and let him find which food is the purest, and then bring you provisions from it" (The Noble Quran, 18:19). The verse signals consumers-based halal distribution focusing on halal retailing, halal products, and halal integrity. Therefore, handling raw materials, production processes, shipment, and transportation by the suppliers need to be halal. This halal distribution can make a difference for halal marketers. Wholesomeness, halal retailing, halal products, and halal integrity are the key variables of distribution to receive a competitive advantage.

Halal distribution contributes to creating place utility, while competitive advantage can be attained through halal promotion, which involves advertising halal products under Islamic principles to boost sales and profitability. Halal promotion serves to generate knowledge utility. In the realm of halal advertising, the content of messages, choice of models, and selection of media play a crucial role in conveying to consumers that non-halal options are absent from advertisements. The message conveyed in halal product promotion must remain authentic.

Allah says:

يَٰٓأَيُّهَا ٱلَّذِينَ ءَامَنُوا۟ ٱتَّقُوا۟ ٱللَّهَ وَقُولُوا۟ قَوْلًا سَدِيدًا

"O believers! Be mindful of Allah and say what is right" (The Noble Quran, 33: 70).

The promotional message must be free from falsehood and exaggeration. Allah also says:

وَلَا تَلْبِسُوا۟ ٱلْحَقَّ بِٱلْبَاطِلِ وَتَكْتُمُوا۟ ٱلْحَقَّ وَأَنتُمْ تَعْلَمُو

"Do not mix truth with falsehood or hide the truth knowingly" (The Noble Quran, 2:42). Moreover, the message in promotion must be effective. Allah further says:

وَقُولُوا۟ لِلنَّاسِ حُسْنًا

"Speak good to people" (The Noble Quran, 2: 83).

In essence, halal marketers should lay out promotional messages according to The Quranic guidelines. The guidelines imply communicating right, avoiding falsehood, and following kindness. The designed advertisement and the models used in the advertisement have to be Islamic. As Allah guides:

وَقُل لِّلْمُؤْمِنَاتِ يَغْضُضْنَ مِنْ أَبْصَارِهِنَّ وَيَحْفَظْنَ فُرُوجَهُنَّ وَلَا يُبْدِينَ زِينَتَهُنَّ إِلَّا مَا ظَهَرَ مِنْهَا

"And tell the believing women to lower their gaze and guard their chastity, and not to reveal their adornments except what normally appears" (The Noble Quran, 24:31). Again, Allah says:

يَٰٓأَيُّهَا ٱلنَّبِىُّ قُل لِّأَزْوَٰجِكَ وَبَنَاتِكَ وَنِسَآءِ ٱلْمُؤْمِنِينَ يُدْنِينَ عَلَيْهِنَّ مِن جَلَٰبِيبِهِنَّ ذَٰلِكَ أَدْنَىٰٓ أَن يُعْرَفْنَ فَلَا يُؤْذَيْنَ

"O Prophet! Ask your wives, daughters, and believing women to draw their cloaks over their bodies. In this way it is more likely that they will be recognized as virtuous and not be harassed" (The Noble Quran, 33:59).

Shariah's compliant promotional activities with reasonable and economic halal product-based advertisements will be another source of competitive advantage for marketers. Truth, avoidance of false with truth, effectiveness, and questionable presentation of the female in the promotion are the crucial variables of halal promotion resulting in competitive advantage. The female-related Islami principles got the focus of this study as cosmetics producers tend to prioritize them in their advertisements. So, Islamic advertisements will leverage halal certification and halal products.

Halal and tayyib are important principles that guide cooperation and competitive advantages in comparison to non-halal certification. Halal certification ensures that products comply with Islamic dietary laws, and the tayyib principle refers to the purification process that ensures products' good and wholesome status. For halal integrity, resources such as physical evidence, transportation, logistics, warehousing, and working environment, among other tangible environmental issues, are required. Halal certification and competitive advantage are followed by the 7Ps (halal product, price, distribution, promotion, physical evidence, process, and people), involving producers, employees, certifiers, Islamic scholars, and other halal stakeholders. Competitive advantages of halal certification include halal consumption by consumers, halal distribution by suppliers, easy access to halal certification for producers in the halal industry, and voluntary exit from the industry if any firm does not wish to continue halal.

Halal certification is guided by Islamic rulings, which act as guiding principles for halal certification and a knowledge-based view. The process of acquiring, understanding, following, and transferring knowledge is outlined in Islam, and halal producers must sense the process of a knowledge-based view of Islam and the purpose of knowledge. Allah says:

ٱقْرَأْ بِٱسْمِ رَبِّكَ ٱلَّذِى خَلَقَ
خَلَقَ ٱلْإِنسَانَ مِنْ عَلَقٍ
ٱقْرَأْ وَرَبُّكَ ٱلْأَكْرَمُ
ٱلَّذِى عَلَّمَ بِٱلْقَلَمِ
عَلَّمَ ٱلْإِنسَانَ مَا لَمْ يَعْلَمْ

> "Read, O Prophet, in the Name of your Lord Who created. created humans from a clinging clot. Read! And your Lord is the Most Generous, Who taught by the pen. taught humanity what they knew not" (The Noble Quran, 96:1–5). The first five verses of the Quran were revealed to gain knowledge through reading and writing. Reading and writing signify the basic approach to gathering knowledge. Islamic principles also focus on hearing, watching, and thinking for knowledge achievement. Allah says:

وَلَا تَقْفُ مَا لَيْسَ لَكَ بِهِۦ عِلْمٌ إِنَّ ٱلسَّمْعَ وَٱلْبَصَرَ وَٱلْفُؤَادَ كُلُّ أُولَٰٓئِكَ كَانَ عَنْهُ مَسْـُٔولًا

> "Do not follow what you have no sure knowledge of Indeed, all will be called to account for their hearing, sight, and intellect" (The Noble Quran, 17:36).

When Islamic knowledge is achieved, it is time to absorb it. The Quranic verses are not hard and complex but easy to remember. Therefore, Allah repeats the same verse four times so that mankind can absorb the teachings of the Noble Quran in real-life situations, including personal, social, and business contexts. Allah says:

وَلَقَدْ يَسَّرْنَا ٱلْقُرْءَانَ لِلذِّكْرِ فَهَلْ مِن مُّدَّكِرٍ

> "And We have certainly made the Quran easy to remember. So, is there anyone who will be mindful?" (The Noble Quran 54:17,22,32,40).

After Islamic knowledge is contemplated, the gifted knowledge resource of Allah must be followed. The ultimate objective of heavenly revelation is to guide mankind. Hence, following the knowledge refers to the focal object of collecting knowledge. The magnitude of obeying heavenly knowledge has been promoted several times in the Noble Quran. It outlines:

ٱتَّبِعُواْ مَآ أُنزِلَ إِلَيۡكُم مِّن رَّبِّكُمۡ وَلَا تَتَّبِعُواْ مِن دُونِهِۦٓ أَوۡلِيَآءَۗ قَلِيلٗا مَّا تَذَكَّرُونَ

"Follow what has been sent down to you from your Lord, and do not take others as guardians besides Him. How seldom are you mindful"! (The Noble Quran 7:3). By following Shariah principles, individuals can transmit knowledge to benefit both the individual and society. Islamic principles are not solely resources for Muslims but for all mankind (The Noble Quran, 2:185). Therefore, knowledgeable individuals need to disseminate Islamic knowledge to others as instructed by Allah. It says:

يَٰٓأَيُّهَا ٱلرَّسُولُ بَلِّغۡ مَآ أُنزِلَ إِلَيۡكَ مِن

"O Messenger! Convey everything revealed to you from your Lord" (The Noble Quran, 5:67).

Prophetic tradition has also emphasized the transmission of knowledge. An authentic hadith says:

بَلِّغُوا عَنِّي وَلَوْ آيَة

"Convey from me, even a single verse" (Ṣaḥīḥ al-Bukhārī, 3461).

However, the precaution in suggesting to others is that individuals must practice what they preach. Transmitting knowledge without self-implementation is in vain. The purpose of heavenly knowledge is to bring about change on both the micro and macro levels (The Noble Quran, 13:11). Therefore, the spiritual guidelines motivate believers to first practice the knowledge and then preach it. It says:

يَٰٓأَيُّهَا ٱلَّذِينَ ءَامَنُواْ لِمَ تَقُولُونَ مَا لَا تَفۡعَلُونَ

كَبُرَ مَقۡتًا عِندَ ٱللَّهِ أَن تَقُولُواْ مَا لَا تَفۡعَلُونَ

"O believers! Why do you say what you do not do? How despicable it is in the sight of Allah that you say what you do not do!" (The Noble Quran, 61:2–3).

Halal, being a Quranic word, means that halal users such as producers, certifiers, and scholars must comprehend the significance of acquiring Islamic knowledge, contemplate it, follow it, and transfer it. These four tasks can fulfill the completeness of the KBV, and the absence of any task will limit the KBV of halal. Attaining competitive advantage (CA) from halal certification depends on how tactfully the halal producers view and manage Islamic knowledge. In essence, knowledge base in Islam is categorized as *Ilmal yaqiin* (عِلۡمَ ٱلۡيَقِينِ), *Eyenal yaqiin* (عَيۡنَ ٱلۡيَقِينِ), and *Haqqul yaqiin* (حَقُّ ٱلۡيَقِينِ) in the Noble Quran 102:5, 7 and 56:95 respectively. Knowledge through reading, writing, watching, perceiving, and getting involved in the practical world as reality can trigger the KBV for RBV and HCA linked with halal certification in the halal markets.

14.3 Methods

This chapter focuses on understanding the halal competitive advantage through the Resource-based view (RBV), knowledge-based view (KBV), and Islamic principles. The selected Quranic verse and authentic Sunnah help conceptualize the competitive advantage for halal certification, focusing on halal producers who use halal resources upstream. The chapter follows a qualitative approach and inductive reasoning. The existing literature on RBV and KBV is synthesized with Islamic principles. Then, thematic analysis is accomplished to ground the RBV and KBV, resulting in a halal competitive advantage for halal marketing. The qualitative software ATLAS.ti was used to delve into the analysis, while manual content analysis of RBV and KBV set the groundwork for the thematic analysis.

14.4 Findings

The thematic analysis table illustrates the elements, and propositions of RBV and KBV and their corresponding themes summarized from the extant literature. VRIN results from RBV to create and sustain organizational resources. Seeking, integrating, applying, and transferring (SIAT) knowledge ground the KBV for sustaining the distinctive resources for CA. Apart from the conventional views of RBV, halal product, price, place, promotion, and people (5Ps) must be attended to, and then defended from the haram norms in the business environment. The issues of taking care of halal resources and protecting them from haram contamination are subjected to adhering to Ilmal, Eyenal, and Haqqul (IEH) yaqiin of KBV.

Table 14.1: Thematic analysis table.

Theories	Propositions	Elements	Sub-themes	Theme
RBV	Distinctive resources	Valuable, Rare, Inimitable, Non-substitutable (VRIN) resource	Conventional competitive advantage (CCA)	Halal certification (HC) is viewed as RBV for HCA of halal marketing (HM)
KBV	Focusing knowledge	Seeking, Integrating, Applying, Transferring (SIAT) knowledge		
RBV with Islamic principles	Defending halal resources from Haram	Halal product, price, place, promotion, people (5Ps)	Halal competitive advantage (HCA)	
KBV with Islamic principles	Focusing Islamic knowledge	Ilmal, Eyenal, Haqqul (IEH) yaqiin		

As such, KBV with halal norms can produce a halal competitive advantage for RBV from an Islamic perspective, while conventional competitive advantages are deemed to emerge from the simplistic VRIN. Since HC reveals Islamic resources recognized as RBV from the Shariah lens, RBV implies to HC for HCA of halal marketing (HM).

The literature review regarding RBV and KBV has been analyzed with the help of ATLAS.ti to focus on the content and concept in Figure 14.1 showing the results of the analysis.

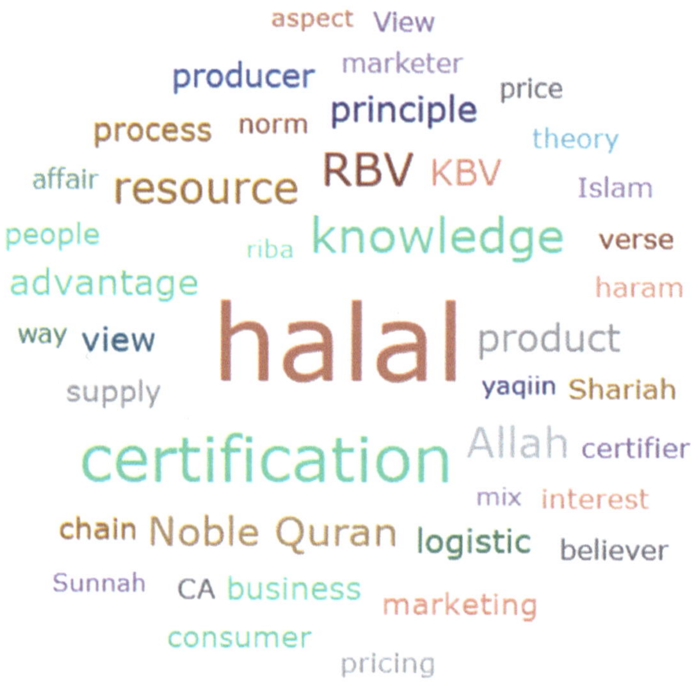

Figure 14.1: Content analysis to navigate thematic analysis.

Halal was the focal concept in the literature review. The halal concept is associated with certification, the resource-based view, and the knowledge-based view to producing competitive advantages. The closer the concepts are to halal, the more they are connected and significant. The concept and contents are the basis of the thematic analysis portrayed in the thematic analysis map shown in Figure 14.2.

Accordingly, RBV gives birth to VRIN of resource, and KBV produces SIAT of knowledge where RBV denotes the fundamental of KBV. CA originates from RBV and KBV in conventional strategic management. For strategic Islamic management, the 5Ps can logically be compared with the VRIN aspects of resources guarded against haram contamination. Since haram will not produce growth (barakah), pure RBV can only be generated by safeguarding 5Ps from haram integrity.

As such, halal integrity can be shaped to leverage the KBV focusing on IEH. In essence, HC signifies the application of RBV and KBV associated with Islamic Shariah to produce HCA. HCA is much more strategic since conventional strategic management cannot replicate it. Only HM can capitalize HCA linked with IEH.

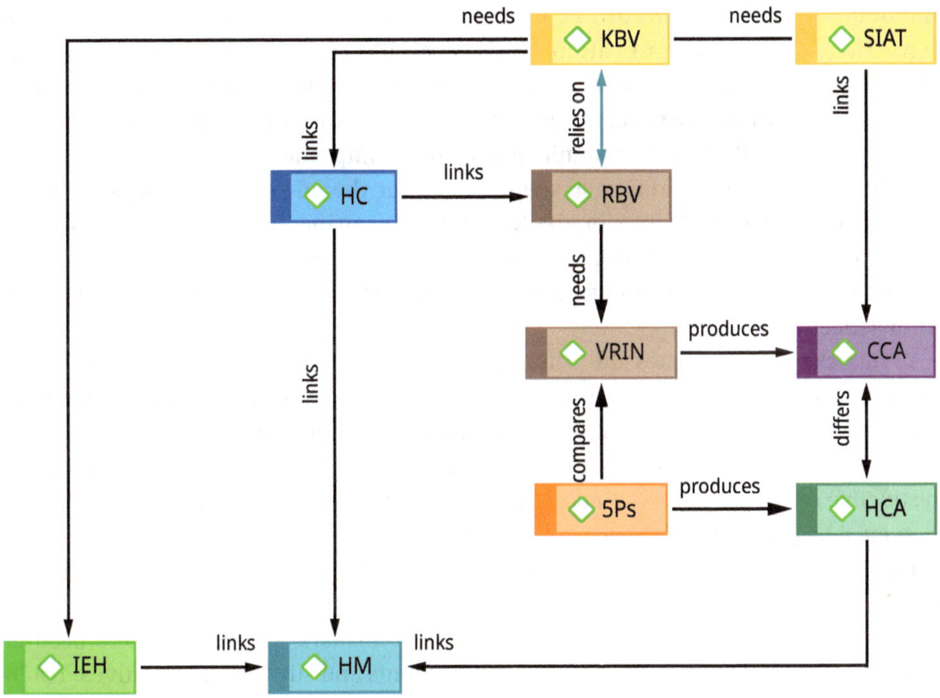

Figure 14.2: The strategic views of RBV with HC.

Islamic marketing, rooted in Islamic principles, prioritizes spirituality over materialism (Islam, 2021a). This spiritually driven approach extends its reach to a broad audience, encompassing both Muslims and non-Muslims (Islam, 2021b), and exploring global marketing opportunities (Islam, 2022a). Thus, Islamic marketing, besides focusing on spirituality and material aspects, also embraces strategic elements (Islam, 2022b). While the Halal and Haram guidelines serve as constraints in Islamic marketing (Islam, 2022c; Islam et al., 2024), these limitations can be effectively managed through consensus (Islam et al., 2023). Positioned against the backdrop of resource constraints, Islamic marketing stands out with its adherence to Halal and Haram standards, bolstered by moral and social considerations for institutionalizing Halal marketing (Islam, 2023). Ultimately, this approach, steered by Islamic norms, has the potential to enhance the HCA of HC associated with RBV, and KBV for HM.

14.5 Conclusion

Halal certification encompasses both tangible elements, such as the Halal logo, and intangible aspects that foster spiritual connection. According to the Resource-Based View (RBV), organizational resources meeting the criteria of having value, rarity, inimitability, and non-substitutablity (VRIN) can lead to a competitive advantage (CA). Therefore, halal certification serves as an illustration of VRIN principles that reinforce the Knowledge-Based View (KBV) rooted in Islamic Shariah. This chapter explores the strategic aspects of RBV, KBV, and CA within the framework of Islamic principles. By adhering to Islamic principles, comprehensive guidelines can be developed to make marketing strategies VRIN for the advantage of Halal competitive advantage (HCA). Moreover, the KBV of Islamic principles highlights the significance of knowledge acquisition, integration, application, and dissemination, which can complement the RBV to ensure that HCA emerges from the fusion of Islamic knowledge.

This chapter elucidates the components and propositions of RBV and KBV and their respective themes derived from existing literature. VRIN principles originating from RBV facilitate the creation and sustenance of organizational resources. The KBV emphasizes seeking, integrating, applying, and transferring (SIAT) knowledge to sustain distinctive resources for CA. In addition to the conventional perspectives of RBV, attention must be paid to Halal aspects of product, price, place, promotion, and people (5Ps), safeguarding them from Haram influences in the business environment and adhering to the *Ilmal, Eyenal*, and *Haqqul* (IEH) certainty of KBV.

Halal marketing researchers, managers, policymakers, and practitioners need to consider RBV, KBV, and HCA from Islamic viewpoints and strategic perspectives. Traditional approaches alone cannot adequately serve the stakeholders of Halal marketing, as HCA constitutes both spiritual and economic resources requiring scholarly attention from a Shariah perspective. Therefore, academics should take the lead in developing lenses of RBV and KBV interconnected with HCA to advance Halal Marketing. It is imperative to utilize scholarly insights to shift mindsets and embrace theoretical frameworks of Islamic marketing rooted in the Quran and authentic Sunnah. By employing Islamic principles as a theoretical foundation, Halal certification can be managed as an economic resource imbued with spiritual significance.

References

Abd Rahman, A., Singhry, H. B., Hanafiah, M. H., & Abdul, M. (2017). Influence of perceived benefits and traceability system on the readiness for Halal Assurance System implementation among food manufacturers. *Food Control*, *73*, 1318–1326. https://doi.org/10.1016/j.foodcont.2016.10.058

Ab Talib, M. S., Ai Chin, T., & Fischer, J. (2017). Linking Halal food certification and business performance. *British Food Journal*, *119*(7), 1606–1618. https://doi.org/10.1108/BFJ-01-2017-0019

Ab Talib, M. S., Abdul Hamid, A. B., & Chin, T. A. (2016). Can *halal* certification influence logistics performance? *Journal of Islamic Marketing*, *7*(4), 461–475. https://doi.org/10.1108/JIMA-02-2015-0015

Ali, S. A., Loussaief, A., & Ahmed, M. (2022). A comparative analysis of employees' and customers' attitude towards Islamic banking. *International Journal of Ethics and Systems*, *38*(2), 209–234. https://doi.org/10.1108/IJOES-03-2021-0053

Azhar, A., & Tu, Y. T. (2021). The investigation of key factors for successful implementation of sustainable halal food supply chain management. *Food Research*, *5*(6), 221–228. https://doi.org/10.26656/fr.2017.5(6).235

Balogun, J., & Jenkins, M. (2003). Re-conceiving Change Management: *European Management Journal*, *21*(2), 247–257. https://doi.org/10.1016/S0263-2373(03)00019-7

Barney, J. B., & Hesterly, W. S. (2020). *Strategic management and competitive advantage: Concepts and cases.* Pearson.

Chiang, H., Han, T., & Chuang, J. (2011). The relationship between high-commitment HRM and knowledge-sharing behavior and its mediators. *International Journal of Manpower*, *32*(5/6), 604–622. https://doi.org/10.1108/01437721111158224

Curado, C., & Bontis, N. (2006). The knowledge-based view of the firm and its theoretical precursor. *International Journal of Learning and Intellectual Capital*, *3*(4), 367. https://doi.org/10.1504/IJLIC.2006.011747

Das, T. K., & Teng, B.-S. (2000). A resource-based theory of strategic alliances. *Journal of Management*, *26*(1), 31–61. https://doi.org/10.1177/014920630002600105

Islam, M. M., Ab Talib, M. S., & Muhamad, N. (2024). Developing theoretical lenses for upstream halal businesses. *Journal of Islamic Marketing*, *15*(1), 192–220. https://doi.org/10.1108/JIMA-05-2022-0156

Islam, M.M. (2023). Institutionalization of Halal Entrepreneurship for a Sustainable Economy. In: Raimi, L., Adekunle, S.M., Shabbir, M.S. (eds) Contemporary Discourse of Halal and Islamic Entrepreneurship. Springer, Singapore. https://doi.org/10.1007/978-981-99-6427-7_5

Islam, M. M., Ab Talib, M. S., & Muhamad, N. (2023). Challenges of Halal Standards and Halal Certification for Islamic Marketing. *Muslim Business and Economic Review*, *2*(1), 104–124. https://doi.org/10.56529/mber.v2i1.156

Islam, M. M. (2022a). Reaching halal and Islamic market segments: tapping marketing opportunities beyond the borders in *Handbook of Research on Ethnic and Intra-cultural Marketing*, Chap. 15, Edward Elgar Publishing, Inc., the USA, 200–212.

Islam, M.M. (2022b). Strategic Perspectives of Islamic Entrepreneurship and Marketing in *Strategic Islamic Marketing*, Chap. 13, Springer: New York, 183–200.

Islam, M.M. (2022c). Evaluating negative attitudes of the students and shoppers towards halal cosmetics products. *Journal of Islamic Marketing*, *13*(3), 565–585. https://doi.org/10.1108/JIMA-03-2020-0067

Islam, M. M. (2021a). Segmenting, targeting and positioning in Islamic marketing. *Journal of Islamic Marketing*, *12*(7), 1385–1404. https://doi.org/10.1108/JIMA-10-2018-0181

Islam, M. M. (2021b). The Satisfaction of Bangladeshi Pilgrims: Service gaps in spiritual tourism based on gender and expenditure. *International Journal of Religious Tourism and Pilgrimage*, 9 (1), 106–117. doi:https://doi.org/10.21427/2hw0-cd28

Karia, N., Abu Hassan Asaari, M. H., Mohamad, N., & Kamaruddin, S. (2015). Assessing Halal logistics competence: An Islamic-based and resource-based view. *2015 International Conference on Industrial Engineering and Operations Management (IEOM)*, 1–6. https://doi.org/10.1109/IEOM.2015.7093744

Latif, I. A., Mohamed, Z., Sharifuddin, J., Abdullah, A. M., & Ismail, M. M. (2014). A Comparative Analysis of Global Halal Certification Requirements. *Journal of Food Products Marketing*, *20*(sup1), 85–101. https://doi.org/10.1080/10454446.2014.921869

Nee, A. Y. H., & Mohamad, Z. Z. (2022). Theories used in Halal logistics studies. In *Halal Logistics and Supply Chain Management* (pp. 45–63). Routledge. https://doi.org/10.4324/9781003223719-6

Szulanski, G. (2000). The Process of Knowledge Transfer: A Diachronic Analysis of Stickiness. *Organizational Behavior and Human Decision Processes*, *82*(1), 9–27. https://doi.org/10.1006/obhd.2000.2884

Wannasupchue, W., Mohamad, S. F., Ishak, F. A. C., & Ungku Zainal Abidin, U. F. (2023). Challenges to obtain halal certification among restaurants in northeast Thailand. *Journal of Islamic Marketing*, *14*(2), 607–621. https://doi.org/10.1108/JIMA-04-2021-0124

Whicker, L. M. (2004). HRM in the Knowledge Economy: Realising the Potential. *Asia Pacific Journal of Human Resources*, *42*(2), 156–165. https://doi.org/10.1177/1038411104045359

Index

https://doi.org/10.1515/9783111575407-016